BUSINESS ECONOMICS IN A RAPIDLY-CHANGING WORLD

BUSINESS CYCLES IN ECONOMICS

TYPES, CHALLENGES AND IMPACTS ON MONETARY POLICIES

Business Economics in a Rapidly-Changing World

Additional books in this series can be found on Nova's website under the Series tab.

Additional e-books in this series can be found on Nova's website under the e-book tab.

BUSINESS ECONOMICS IN A RAPIDLY-CHANGING WORLD

BUSINESS CYCLES IN ECONOMICS

TYPES, CHALLENGES AND IMPACTS ON MONETARY POLICIES

JASON C. HSU
EDITOR

nova publishers
New York

LIBRARY OF CONGRESS CATALOGING-IN-PUBLICATION DATA

Business cycles in economics : types, challenges and impacts on monetary policies / editor, Jason C. Hsu.
pages cm. -- (Business economics in a rapidly-changing world)
Includes index.
ISBN 978-1-63321-322-7 (hardcover)
1. Business cycles. 2. Monetary policy. I. Hsu, Jason C., 1974-
HB3722.B836 2014
338.5'42--dc23
2014026713

Published by Nova Science Publishers, Inc. † New York

CONTENTS

PREFACE

This anthology presents papers that challenge conventional viewpoints and received ideas about business cycles and monetary policy. Some of the selections bring fresh thinking to customary topics, such as business cycle models in perfectly competitive markets, the cyclicality of research and development expenditures, and the effect of uncertainty shocks on consumer spending. Others address concerns that have come to the fore in the aftermath of the global financial crisis—the consequences of quantitative easing, the effectiveness of macro prudential policies, the impact of shadow banking on the fractional-reserve banking system, and correlations in credit default losses, among others. The collection is not meant to be comprehensive (an impossible goal) but rather to bring together noteworthy contributions that might otherwise be submerged in the torrent of contemporary economic writing. The selection criteria were the quality of thinking, clarity of expression and soundness of empirical research on topics of compelling interest to people who are actively engaged in the field of monetary economics.

The book is divided into three major parts. The first part includes essays that examine, at a high level of abstraction, the traditional definition of the business cycle and its political overtones, and that delve into the parts different economic mechanisms might have played in generating post-war business cycles. Those mechanisms include cyclicality in R&D investment and the wealth effect from positive stock market and housing price shocks. Other articles home in on the most recent downturn—the Great Recession—to judge whether traditional business cycle theory is a useful approach to understanding what happened.

The second part contains papers of relevance to researchers in monetary and fiscal policy. The selections included here emphasize the impact of the business cycle on unemployment. The authors explore both the initial negative shock resulting directly from the widening output gap and the effect of the ensuing monetary and fiscal easing policies. Of particular interest is the impact of quantitative easing. This section also examines the other side of rising unemployment during recessions—falling household consumption as families and individuals adapt to their straitened circumstances.

The third part of this book introduces models which incorporate the business cycle as a key component for pricing assets, understanding liquidity in the bond market, and estimating defaults. It also presents other modeling innovations equipping readers to explore potential applications on their own.

The papers chosen for this volume represent a range of approaches to theoretical and applied research. Some of them describe econometric tools and analytical techniques that are adapted to the study of business cycles and monetary policies. Others set forth conceptual frameworks and conduct empirical analyses that offer new insights into macroeconomic fluctuations. Still others adopt a strategy closer to field work, in the form of case studies supported by extensive statistical documentation. In sum, the papers presented here not only tackle topics of pressing interest; they also illustrate the state of the art in the research methodologies employed by monetary economists. Working on this book has been a most rewarding experience, and it is a pleasure, now, to make it available to fellow students of the business cycle.

Jason Hsu, Ph.D.
Founding Partner and Vice Chairman
Research Affiliates, LLC
Newport Beach, California, US

Adjunct Professor in Finance
UCLA Anderson School of Business
Los Angeles, California, US

In: Business Cycles in Economics
Editor: Jason C. Hsu
ISBN: 978-1-63321-322-7

Chapter 1

ON THE COMPETING DEFINITIONS OF ECONOMIC RECESSION—AND THEIR UNFORTUNATE POLITICAL OVERTONES

John F. Gaski*
University of Notre Dame, IN, US

Abstract

The long-standing multi-factor approach to recession definition employed by the U.S. National Bureau of Economic Research in its dating of the business cycle is reviewed and challenged. The concept of the macroeconomic expansion/contraction cycle has long been intended to apply to total output, literally aggregate production or "gross domestic product" (GDP)—which, in the U.S., is reported quarterly by the federal government's Bureau of Economic Analysis. Reflect upon the original dictionary definition of the generic word "recession," e.g., "receding ... industrial activity; ... a giving back."Why must the NBER fixate on insinuating additional nuance or variables? An argument is made in favor of the practical superiority of the common-use alternative of two consecutive down quarters of aggregate output. This mechanical, single-factor approach is endorsed over the high-profile NBER method on objectivity grounds. A likely by-product of the recommended method's application could be less suspicion, or reality, of political influence.

Keywords: business cycle, business cycle history, business cycle measurement, economic cycle, recession scoring

Introduction

Now that it has declaimed from Mount Olympus once again, pinpointing the latest economic turn in the U.S. with artificial precision, the National Bureau of Economic Research might benefit itself and others by cultivating some institutional humility. It has always been a

* E-mail address: jgaski@nd.edu; Address: Department of Marketing, Mendoza College of Business, Notre Dame, IN 46556, US (Corresponding author).

reach for that body to presume to dictate the definition of what, and when, a recession is, on the basis of multiple factors it selects judgmentally. The more modest, straightforward, mechanical definition always has offered the competitive advantage of being *objective*—i.e., at least two consecutive quarters of negative change in national economic output, or "negative growth" in the popular (and professional) vernacular (Blanchard 1997, p. 25). But the NBER's panel of recession "daters" cannot leave well enough alone.

The NBER actually has been arrogating to itself the role of identifying the starting and ending points of U.S. economic expansions and contractions retrospectively since 1929, via its Business Cycle Dating Committee in particular since 1978. In arriving at its Delphic declarations, the BCDC considers several indices including production, employment, real income, and sales.

That is the problem. *Which* criteria, exactly, should be used? And how much weight should be attached to each? This introduces an element of subjectivity, and subjectivity invites personal motives or bias, no matter how pure the committee members intend to be. The NBER even admits, in one of its most basic documents, to an ethereal, personalized interpretation of the concept of recession itself—i.e., "a significant decline in activity ... the way we use the word [recession]" (NBER 2008, p. 4). Moreover, "(t)he Committee does not have a fixed definition of economic activity" (NBER 2010b)! This is scientifically inadmissible. Air-tight definition is essential for clear classification of phenomena, which is the starting point or launch pad for scientific investigation and theoretical advancement (Bunge 1967, p. 75; Caws 1959, pp. 203, 207, 210, 220; Harvey 1969, pp. 326, 334). Without such grounding, the scientific enterprise breaks down before it begins. Needless to say, one would have thought, the *definiendum* itself should not be allowed to be ambiguous. Tell us again, NBER: What is your stylized definition of recession—"the way we use the word," as you put it? Dismal science, indeed.

There must be a better way. In fact, one does suggest itself. Toward conceptual and operational parsimony (worthy values in most sciences other than the present anomalous case, apparently), let us give due respect to the most basic, universal, and now traditional measure of national economic scale: aggregate output (Shiskin 1971; *Business Dictionary* 2010).

The Argument

The concept of the macroeconomic expansion/contraction cycle has long been intended to apply to gross output, literally aggregate production. Reflect upon the original dictionary definition of the generic word "recession," e.g., "receding ... industrial activity; ... a giving back" (*Britannica* 1959, p. 1053).Why must the NBER fixate on insinuating additional nuance or variables? The mechanical, single-factor approach is endorsed over the NBER method, on objectivity grounds, by Mora and Siotis (2005).To be sure, output is not the only meaningful or crucial macroeconomic variable. We can stipulate that the NBER approach therefore can be regarded as more comprehensive than the alternative one-factor, output-based metric. Likewise, so could a measure incorporating total market capitalization of the S&P 500, interest rates, the *Index of Consumer Sentiment*, major league baseball batting averages, or some of the national "happiness" (*qua* utility) measures that are going around (such as Brooks 2008; Kammann, Farry, and Herbison 1984; McDonald 2005).Which to include is ultimately a matter of subjective judgment, and subjectivity is a hazard to be avoided, if possible.

A broader expansion/recession measure possibly even favored by professional consensus—such as the NBER method, in fact—may well have considerable value, perhaps incremental value beyond the alternative "two quarters of negative real output growth" standard. Emphatically, however, the two are not perfect substitutes conceptually. Given the historical importance applied to the output cycle per se, continued attention to that parameter receives a powerful endorsement from history. Similarly, aggregate output remains the universal measure of national economic scale. See the current attention to China's pending overtaking of Japan's world runner-up position in GDP. This also constitutes a contemporary, real-time endorsement of the "two quarter negative change in *output*" (2Q/-) definition of recession.

Yet if a parallel approach such as that taken by the NBER's definition is to be indulged, it should be recognized that it addresses and represents a *different construct* from the traditional "2Q/-" recession interpretation. As such, it should be given a different name. Instead of presuming to date the *business cycle* by arbitrary means, the Dating Committee could at least show deference and modesty by calling its target concept the "national economic health cycle", "periodic economic depth assessment", "multi-factor economic barometer", or something comparable (and preferably more creative).Maybe "augmented recession" or "recession penumbra" would do.

In the interest of equal time, surely the NBER has available a rationale or defense for its multi-faceted subjective interpretation of recession which can be quoted here. In fact, NBER official documents mainly declare the rejection of a GDP basis in favor of the bureau's alternative approach, without detailed justification (NBER 2010a, p.1).If anything, the NBER argues for a two-factor measure, incorporating gross domestic income as a redundant output proxy measure only to offset measurement error.

Of course the NBER method and *2Q/-* are highly convergent historically (Layton and Banerji 2001, pp. 10, 16-17).The exact time-series correspondence metric (which happens to be an R^2 of about .999 in the cited work) is not especially germane, however, because the issue is distortion, disinformation, potential injustice, and derived practical consequences from the inevitable occasions when divergence does occur. That is, the exceptions, which can produce inconsistency and public confusion, could still matter. Layton and Banerji did find between a one- and two-month average discrepancy in estimated recession start/end dates between the two general methods. (Their study presents the U.S. historical comparison, for the 1949-91 period, between NBER and a variant of *2Q/-* scoring results; pp. 16-17.)Yes, a .999 R^2 value does suggest *practical* perfect substitutes and an implication of nit-picking here, but the lingering concerns are conceptual accuracy, truly scientific taxonomy, a wholesome and transparent process, and hazards of residual imprecision. An example of such negative side-effects appears in a following section.

A Corollary Matter: Semantics and Timing

One additional issue is embodied in a particular NBER self-contradiction. Granted, it may be very legitimate and worthwhile to count and report the number of months from peak to trough, and back again, for a national economy. It is hardly fair, though, to apply the term "recession" to the entire peak-trough period—given the NBER's prime rule of *significant* decline in activity.

No matter the ultimate magnitude of any particular economic decline, the initial off-peak period when output (or a composite of multiple factors) is still very near the peak—generally an all-time peak—does not merit the charged and pejorative "recession" label. Likewise with any inclination to terming the first baby steps after bottoming-out as "prosperity" (not that the NBER is guilty of this latter locution. It uses the inert "expansion" instead.) In other words, when only a fraction of a percent off a secular high point in economic vitality, an economy still deserves to be celebrated, not derogated or belittled. (Recall the Carter administration's economic adviser, Alfred Kahn, who resorted to the word "banana" instead of "recession" because of the economic term's sensitivity. There was also the Nixon-Reagan-era economist Herb Stein's satirical euphemism "growth horse" in lieu of the contemporarily trendy "growth recession.") This observation qualifies as more argumentation ammunition favoring the objective definition's two-consecutive-quarters threshold, although the 2Q element itself is subjective.

Surely, someone—perhaps the economics profession collectively—has to have decided at some point that the official temporal delimiter of a recession, even per the output-based alternative definition, is to be two quarters, one quarter, one month, three quarters, or the next full moon. The NBER itself references, vaporously, "a few months" as lower limit (2008; 2010b). This inescapable overlay of subjectivity may very well be tolerable comparatively, though, because it represents only a minute fraction of the mega-compound subjectivity imposed by the NBER recession dating group in its operational definition. The committee's deliberations, after all, require qualitative choices about inclusion and exclusion of criteria and relative weights of each. Oh, to be a fly on the wall to observe the sausage manufacture!

Or is the simple *2Q/-* standard as advocated here a *simplistic* definition? No more simplistic than using GDP as primary measure of the size of a national economy, is it? Narrow focus on a single variable does have consensus precedent for many purposes in economics and other sciences, such as the very analogous *temperature* gist in the present climatology controversy. In federal government reporting, a close analog would be the Census Bureau's primary attention to numerical *population*, despite collecting data on many variables.

Derived Implications

One manifest lesson concerning the danger inherent in the NBER's subjectivity-laden recession "measure" is found in this test question: How many years of economic growth were there in the U.S. during the eight years of George W. Bush's presidency? The answer: nearly seven, give or take a few weeks. That is correct. Except for two isolated quarters of residual Clinton-era contraction starting about the day Mr. Bush took office and a few months at the end of the second term coinciding with the subprime meltdown, the Bush administration was actually one of non-stop economic growth. If the reader did not know that, s/he should ponder why not. Or why did the public never hear about it from the mainstream media? (Based on a conventional Google search, it appears that "never" may be literally true.)

In fact, pity the poor mainstream media consumer. After eight years of relentless "Bush recession" propaganda, that person must have been very confused when recession finally arrived and was declared about the time Bush-43 was leaving office. Severe cognitive dissonance would have been a natural reaction.

Candidly, the NBER is one of the disinformation culprits, although a lesser offender. Based on that body's multi-factor definitional subjectivity alone, the recent Bush Presidency featured only 6 ¼ years of *non*-recession—i.e., excepting the 21 total months from March 2001 to November 2001 and from December 2007 to January 2009.Still a good record for a national administration relative to long-term business cycle history, but not quite as striking a rebuttal to the (apparently) partisan economic disinformation campaign as "seven of eight," is it? Such political overtones have no place in macroeconomic reporting, which is what the NBER recklessly risks and abets via its dating method. The same discrepancy issue would be true of any alternative method to some degree, but because the NBER committee's recession dating approach allows subjectivity, therefore bias and, in turn, *political* bias to potentially infect recession dating decisions (to the extent that committee members have any political beliefs at all—and who does not?), tolerance of that subjectivity, or even the NBER method itself for that matter, is problematic. In general, whenever a difference obtains between an objective and subjective scoring method, the subjective one is the nuisance.

A possible concern for partisans of the other camp is the (2000-)01 "recession"—which never did feature two consecutive quarters of real GDP shrinkage. As the NBER-defined recession arrived with a March 2001 cyclical peak, it can justifiably be claimed that it was born during the Clinton administration which, of course, ended in late January of '01.If the single-factor output recession standard nominated here were used, retrospective finger pointing at the Clinton economic policies as recession blame-worthy loses its basis, because recession never occurred! Use a more objective scoring metric such as *2Q/-*, in other words, and a perceived reason for partisan suspicion dissipates.(Of course, the objective method also absolves the Bush administration of recession culpability as well, in that event.)

More Recession Politics, for Better or Worse

Still on the subject of truth in recession dating, although regarding a different aspect of the 2000-01 U.S. trough, suspicion could also target whether the meager Y2000 third quarter 0.3% reported GDP gain was authentic, in particular *because of* the political implications. Recall that late 2000 was a time when President Bill Clinton, concerned with his legacy and already notorious for public dishonesty and opportunism, was understandably desperate for the economic history books not to tarnish his term in office with the recession stigma. It would be preternatural restraint or ingenuousness for economic observers not to wonder if the Clinton administration might have, let us say, indirectly *influenced* the Bureau of Economic Analysis (the federal office responsible for GDP estimation) to, just this once, commit some rounding error on the upside. To put it delicately, has Mr. Clinton ever exhibited that he is the type who might have pressured someone at BEA, or had one of his people do that? We must regretfully acknowledge that Clinton and other recent American Presidents have done worse, so the question is fair. Suspicion and skepticism may even be heightened because the initial GDP report for that 2000 third quarter was +2.7% before being revised, and then revised again and again, literally, into almost vanishing as the slight fractional growth number cited. For the sake of the BEA's enduring credibility, should not the Y2000 Q3 report be independently audited?

The rest of the story, significantly: In December of 2003, a retroactive revision by the BEA confirmed the "true" Q3 growth rate for Y2000 as -0.5%! The downward revision results in two down GDP quarters out of three, and three out of five between Q3 '00 and Q3 '01, but still not two in a row. Bill Clinton, however (like everyone else in the world), did not know that as of Y2000 Q3. A review of the integrity of that 2000 Q3 *process*, not just the result, is still in order. The BEA frequently performs revisions of its data long after the more contemporaneous reports (and there has even been another for 2000 Q3 done since 2003), but the mysterious historical baggage is salient in this instance. The relative difference between first (2.7%), or even first Y2000 "final" (2.2%) third quarter growth estimate, and the later 0.3% and -0.5% numbers is far beyond the norm of 0.3 percentage points of change for such BEA revisions.

It is totally facile for partisans to resort to the accusation of "cooking the books" whenever an official macroeconomic number is reported that favors an incumbent administration, but this case is just too eerie circumstantially. The magnitude of the post hoc corrections, together with the natural incentive for political intrigue, demands a formal investigation and resolution. (After all, one post-mortem, the 2003 special revision, has only increased the appearance of impropriety). If the Clinton administration indeed fabricated a false quarterly growth report on one politically crucial occasion, history needs to know that. If a final review would exonerate, so much the better.

So the BEA data that are input for the *2Q/-* ideal can cause problems, too, and even political mischief, because they are assembled by humans. But at least the standard is objective.

Ironically, the NBER dating method does implicitly assign President Clinton responsibility for the recession that purportedly arrived in 2001, to the extent that any U.S. President actually *causes* macroeconomic cycle phenomena, again because of the time lag between causes and manifestation. (Disciples of the Keynesian multiplier will tend to indict the Clinton tax-induced surplus as sire and villain, would they not?) The *2Q/-* method excuses both Clinton and G. W. Bush, insofar as the latter could have been blamed at all for a downturn nascent before he took office, or the former for one occurring on a different President's watch.

Simplicity Trumps Politics

To further dramatize the NBER issue, and pitfall, we can now proffer a normative political proposition, of all things, that nearly every reader may be able to agree with: Any organizational functionaries who hold political beliefs opposed to one's (your) own, possibly including the economists of the NBER some may suspect, just cannot seem to keep their politics out of the work they do—because politics is everything to their kind. Correct? No matter your politics, the other side usually seems to politicize everything. Empirically, there is indeed a tendency to perceive those who are opposed politically as overly ideological (Bullers, Reece, and Skinner 2010; Greene 1999, pp. 393-394). If this proposition does not connect personally, let us concede that it would for many. So now can all agree that the subjective NBER recession dating approach is sub-optimal and even dangerous based on the principle that it is best to minimize the opportunity for politics to intrude where it does not belong? The *2Q/-* alternative is at least safer operationally and insulated from suspicion because of its objectivity.

But is it not equivalently subjective to select a single variable, among several candidates, for special focus to embody the concept of economic recession? Actually, it is no more subjective and no less legitimate than studying the time series of any other single economic variable in isolation. Again, aggregate output has long served as the pre-eminent indicant of national economic scale, so it is a most natural proxy when the issue is change in gross economic magnitude.

In other words, we can allow that a different single factor, such as total employment, would offer the core advantage of *2Q/-* as touted here. Yet one surpassing quality remains in favor of output alone as recession-dater: That single indicator is already the universal standard for assessing aggregate economic magnitude. Measuring changes in that variable, so conceptualized, i.e., the cycle, would therefore show fidelity to the conceptual progenitor and practical baseline. Employment, retail sales, or even total number of glass window panes in a nation are worthy of individual focus for many purposes, but they are not used as sole proxies for national economic scale. This difference supports output (2Q/-) as primary recession definer.

Politics, Again, but Neutered

Incidentally, one political implication may be invariate regardless of the dating method used. Whether June '09 (per NBER) or Q3 '09 (objective method) is the latest recession's defined end point, it occurred during the last Bush fiscal year. Therefore, the Obama administration cannot claim to have had any fiscal impact on ending that downturn. To be contrarian, credit G. W. Bush, perhaps!

The elaborative arithmetic of the issue is this: Conservatively accepting Q3 '09 as the end of the recession, i.e., first growth quarter following four negative, the Obama government had spent only about $70 billion of its $800B "stimulus" package by then. That amounts to less than ½ of one percent of Y2009 GDP. The economic growth rate during Q3 '09 was over two percent. So divide by four (to represent one quarter) and then even if all stimulus spending were net increment to aggregate demand or GDP, the total is not enough to account for the positive quarterly growth. That is, the U.S. economy came out of recession on its own in Q3 '09 even without any stimulus assistance. QED. So it is mathematically impossible, per this rough analysis, for Obama policy to be given credit for curing the recession, as its political advocates naturally like to claim.[1]And any future revisions from the BEA will likely change

---

[1] This footnote should not be necessary. "Non-partisan" does not mean that one may only criticize the two major U.S. political parties or ideologies equally. What if the two are not equally wrong on a particular issue? There is no a priori or empirical reason to believe that the two major political parties in the U.S. are always identically right and wrong, or equally good and bad. If that were true, it would be a probabilistic freak. In the same way, for example, a book or article about Richard Nixon's crimes is not ethically obliged to give equal time and space to criticism of Jimmy Carter. (Some answers, such as in the realm of political preference, cannot escape the subjective eye of the beholder, but others, as here, are amenable to objective test and resolution. To illustrate with the substantive subject matter of this treatment: A single factor, output, has long been the instrumental indicant of national economic scale, and the recession construct is literally a derivative of that concept. It is objective fact that the multiple NBER recession-defining variables have not served the same function in macroeconomic metrics.)

the inequality only marginally: Either the Obama stimulus did not cure the recession, or its contribution was miniscule.(This also illustrates how overcoming and improving upon the NBER method could turn the familiar recession blame-game politics inside-out when there really is a divergence between the alternative dating approaches.)

Or, if one claims that the *expectation* of the stimulus impacted recovery in 2009, or prior thereto, a fair balancing claim would be that the anticipation of an Obama election contributed to the recession's occurrence in the first place. Regardless, indefinite speculative contortions such as these or many others in the arsenal of political actors are rather intractable to answer empirically or analytically, and argue for removal of subjectivity wherever possible. Hence, the argument adduced here.

Alternatively, more explicitly, and this time abetting partisans of the other faction by accepting the existence of a Keynesian multiplier, the third quarter Y2009 GDP growth in the U.S., according to the BEA "final" estimate released in December 2009, was 2.2%. Annualized Y2009 GDP itself based on the third quarter estimated level was $14,114.7 billion. Therefore, the approximately $70 billion of stimulus spending as of that time represented 0.496% of contemporaneous GDP. Dividing the Q3 growth rate by four to quarterize, it (0.55%) still exceeds the implied stimulus' economic share. However, it would therefore only require a federal deficit spending multiplier of 1.11 (.55/.496) for the '09 stimulus to deserve exclusive responsibility for ending the recession—if there is a multiplier greater than unity.

If the recession ended during Q2 '09, as it did according to the NBER standard—actually proclamation—then even less of the stimulus had been spent as of then. A lesser growth hurdle would also be required for comparison, but because the NBER's method does not even feature an objective growth score, this approach to the question is inescapably moot. So the ultimate politico-economic answer on the 2009 stimulus effectiveness may not depend upon the recession definition used as much as on the existence and magnitude of the Keynesian multiplier.

Conclusion

The preceding is far from the first time that questions have been raised about the most appropriate operational definition of economic recession (Moore 1967; Shiskin 1974).The underlying taxonomic problem is a weak constitutive definition, one far too nebulous by the norms of behavioral science—especially when the focal entity to be measured consists of observables. This leads inexorably to elastic operationalization. The NBER verges perilously close to the *Alice in Wonderland* method of anti-scientific definition and classification:

Likewise, "partisan" means opposing a political or ideological position only because it is the opposing position, rather than for substantive reasons. The remedial taxonomic strategy proposed in this paper happens to lead to rebuttal of one common assertion of a major political faction—and tends to partly exonerate the opposing side on that focal issue, and the original camp again on a variant of the same. Any suggestion that this result renders all related content partisan is therefore disqualified as inadmissible because it presumes motives—a non-legitimate argumentation mode unless possessing considerable state-of-mind evidence. (Sometimes, of course, political groups and individuals do furnish that evidence via the totality of their conduct.) The author is the one in a position to best know the partisan or non-partisan posture of the argument in this case. Unfortunately, the reader can only judge under uncertainty based upon the full montage of surrounding text and this disclaimer.

"When I use a word, it means just what I choose it to mean" (Gray 1971, p. 163).Compare the quote, actually from Lewis Carroll's Humpty Dumpty character, with the NBER's "the way we use the word" (2008, p. 4; cited previously). Earlier here the NBER/BCDC comfortable subjectivity was termed presumptuous or arrogant. This side-by-side display of definitional misadventures provides grounding for that adverse assessment, regrettably.

It is long overdue for the NBER to receive a detailed classificatory re-appraisal with a serious alternative suggested, such as this ontological and existential challenge. None of this had to happen, though. Had the NBER demonstrated a larger quotient of appreciation for objectivity and parsimony, the definitional detriment outlined here would not have materialized.

Government contra-cyclical monetary and especially fiscal policy is notorious for being mistimed—to the point of being pro-cyclical (Bolton, Santos, and Scheinkman 2009, pp. 598-599; Friedman 1960, p. 87; Samuelson 1967, pp. 340-341; Taylor 2000, pp. 27-28, 35; although results have been better in recent years). Even though recession dating the NBER way is done long after the fact, at best, a refined understanding of past recessions' temporal limits, by a quarter or two, even a month or two, could translate into better understanding of a contemporary or near-term cycle. That, in turn, may induce better policy responses and even the pleasant by-product of lessened political recrimination, so this taxonomic initiative is hardly idle.

Even if the NBER recession dating method came first, as it did, the NBER-BCDC may wish to acknowledge that its subjectivity-saturated measure is bettered by the more objective and suspicion-resistant *2Q/-*. In fact, to avoid being seen as superfluous, a new and proper role for the NBER dating formula—whatever the secret weights are—could be the attempt to date economic turns *within* the quarter identified by the objective BEA-based GDP number. In other words, the NBER could accept and defer to the 2Q-type finding, and then go beyond and add value by dating the cyclical turn more precisely within quarter—very much as it does now but with the addition of an objective constraint. (It is not held here that the BEA GDP growth estimates are perfect, only objective—subject to the one unfortunate question raised earlier.)

Let us continue to frankly expose the NBER's rigidity and inconsistency, and maybe that organization will be shamed into reform. In this matter, reform will merely mean abandonment of the practice of superimposing unnecessary subjectivity on one of the most fundamental definienda of macroeconomics, especially since a less objective scheme is fraught with danger of bias—political or otherwise. Given the potential for divergent real consequences of the two leading definitional approaches, perhaps this fresh look with new arguments can prove to be productive. The author hopes the anti-political subtext of this analytic treatment will also resonate with the scientific audience.

References

Blanchard, Olivier. (1997). *Macroeconomics.* Upper Saddle River, NJ: Prentice-Hall.

Bolton, Patrick, Tano Santos & José A. Scheinkman. (2009). "Market and Public Liquidity," *American Economic Review: Papers & Proceedings*, 99 (No. 2), 594-599.

Britannica World Language Dictionary. (1959). Vol. 2.New York: Funk & Wagnalls Company.

Brooks, Arthur. (2008).*Gross National Happiness.* New York: Basic Books.

Bullers, Susan, Melissa Reece & Christy Skinner. (2010). "Political Ideology and Perceptions of Bias Among University Faculty," *Sociation Today*, 8 (No. 2, Fall/Winter), www.ncsociology.org/sociationtoday/v82/political.htm (accessed January 11, 2011).
Bunge, Mario. (1967). *Scientific Research I: The Search for System.* New York: Springer-Verlag.
Business Dictionary. (2010). www.businessdictionary.com/definition/recession/html (accessed August 9, 2010).
Caws, Peter. (1959). "The Functions of Definition in Science," *Philosophy of Science*, 26 (No. 3, July), 201-228.
Friedman, Milton. (1960). *A Program for Monetary Stability.* New York: Fordham University Press.
Gaski, John F. (2012). "On the Competing Definitions of Recession," *Society*, 49 (No. 2, March-April), 118-121.
Gray, Donald J., ed. (1971). *Lewis Carroll: Alice in Wonderland.* New York: W. W. Norton & Co.
Greene, Steven. (1999). "Understanding Party Identification: A Social Identity Approach," *Political Psychology*, 20 (No. 2), 393-403.
Harvey, David. (1969).*Explanation in Geography.* New York: St. Martin's Press.
Kammann, Richard, Marcelle Farry & Peter Herbison. (1984). "The Analysis and Measurement of Happiness as a Sense of Well-Being," *Social Indicators Research*, 15 (No. 2, August), 91-115.
Layton, Allan P. & Anirvan Banerji. (2001).*What Is a Recession?: A Reprise.* Working paper, School of Economics and Finance, Queensland University of Technology.
McDonald, Ross. (2005). *Rethinking Development. Local Pathways to Global Wellbeing.* Antigonish, Nova Scotia, Canada: St. Francis Xavier University.
Moore, Geoffrey H. (1967). "What Is a Recession?" *The American Statistician*, 21 (No. 4, October), 16-19.
Mora, Ricardo & Georges Siotis. (2005). "External Factors in Emerging Market Recoveries: An Empirical Investigation," *European Economic Review*, 49 (No. 3, April), 683-702.
National Bureau of Economic Research. (2008), *Determination of the December 2007 Peak in Economic Activity.* Cambridge, MA: National Bureau of Economic Research, Inc.
National Bureau of Economic Research. (2010a).*The NBER's Business Cycle Dating Procedure: Frequently Asked Questions.* Cambridge, MA: National Bureau of Economic Research, Inc., http://www.nber.org/cycles/recessions_faq.html (accessed August 25, 2010).
National Bureau of Economic Research. (2010b). *The NBER's Business Cycle Dating Committee.* Cambridge, MA: National Bureau of Economic Research.
Samuelson, Paul A. (1967).*Economics*, 7thed.New York: McGraw-Hill.
Shiskin, Julius. (1971). "Modernizing Business Cycle Concepts," *The American Statistician*, 25 (No. 4, October), 17-19.
Shiskin, Julius. (1974). "The Changing Business Cycle," *The New York Times* (December 1), Sec. 3, p. 12.
Taylor, John B. (2000). "Reassessing Discretionary Fiscal Policy," *The Journal of Economic Perspectives*, 14 (No. 3, Summer), 21-36.

In: Business Cycles in Economics
Editor: Jason C. Hsu
ISBN: 978-1-63321-322-7

Chapter 2

THE FACTOR-SHARES CYCLE AND ITS RELATION TO THE BUSINESS CYCLE

William A. Jackson*
University of York, York, UK

Abstract

The traditional assumption of constant factor shares (Bowley's Law) may be misleading, for factor shares vary in both the short run and the long run. This chapter looks at short-run factor share movements, asking how they relate to the business cycle. Theoretical arguments differ about whether profit and wage shares are procyclical or counter-cyclical, and empirical evidence too yields no neat conclusions. On average, factor share movements roughly offset each other while adhering to a factor-shares cycle, which has similar periodicity to the business cycle but is out of phase with it – the profit share reaches a peak before the top of the cycle and a trough before the bottom of the cycle. Recent experience in developed countries, marked by financialisation, a rising profit share and financially induced recession, has changed the factor-shares cycle. Pressure on the wage share has softened profit squeezes and shifted the cycle towards an underconsumption mode with a procyclical profit share and greater risks of financial instability.

Keywords: Factor shares; business cycles; financialisation; underconsumption; financial instability

Introduction

Factor shares in national income are generally assumed to stay almost constant in the short run and even the long run. The assumption stemmed from empirical research by Arthur Bowley, who studied British income data for the early twentieth century and found that factor shares were remarkably stable (Bowley and Stamp, 1927). Later studies by Paul Douglas using US data confirmed Bowley's findings (Douglas, 1934). Stability of the factor income

* E-mail address: william.jackson@york.ac.uk; Address: Department of Economics and Related Studies, University of York, York YO10 5DD, UK (Corresponding author).

distribution, supposedly true at all times and places, has acquired the status of a statistical law (Bowley's Law) or stylised fact that can inform macroeconomic analysis (Kaldor, 1961). It allows modelling to go ahead without worrying about factor shares, on the grounds that they remain inert and have little effect on how the economy adjusts. Macroeconomics can then be simplified by abstracting from distribution. To do so has never been entirely satisfactory, as factor shares are not fixed and show both short-run and long-run movements. Nor are the movements random or accidental – they are correlated with economic activity and follow recognisable patterns.

Instead of being constant, long-run factor shares change gradually, not always in the same direction. Experience since the late twentieth century divides into two segments. From the 1940s to the 1970s, the wage share in developed countries expanded and the profit share contracted; from the 1980s onwards, the trend reversed as the profit share began to increase (Mohun, 2006; Kristal, 2010). Changes have been slow but well defined and robust enough to cast doubt on any law about factor share constancy. The switch from a falling to a rising profit share was a symptom of changes in the wider economic and political climate – among the key ones were globalisation, the shift towards neoliberalism, higher unemployment, and technological developments (Wolff, 2003; Glyn, 2006; Fichtenbaum, 2009; Hein, 2012, Chapter 2). Long-run trends might seem to have little bearing on short-run analysis under given technology and institutions. They may, nonetheless, have implications for how short-run adjustment takes place and should not be debarred from macroeconomic discussion.

Superimposed on long-run factor share changes are short-run variations that have similar periodicityto business cycles. Potentialshort-run influences on factor shares are multiple, leading to diverse arguments as to why profit and wage shares might be procyclical or counter-cyclical. Empirical evidence and practical experience suggest that factor shares move in a complex fashion, procyclically and counter-cyclically at different stages of the cycle (Nolan, 1987; Sherman, 1990; Buchele and Christiansen, 1993; Jefferson and Pryor, 2010). The movements offset each other, limiting the net changes, but factor shares are far from constant. Rather than being fixed, they follow their own cyclical sequence bound up with the business cycle but out of phase with it. A full understanding of business cycles should incorporate the factor-shares cycle and not presume that factor shares stay constant.

The present chapter assesses cyclical factor shares, considering the causality behind them and how they mesh with the business cycle. Existing theoretical and empirical work portrays a standard factor-shares cycle, in which factor shares vary little in the long run but pass through a regular sequence of short-run movements that roughly cancel each other out. This standard cycle has been unsettled by recent trends towards a rising profit share and financialised economies. As the balance in factor shares has swung towards profits, the profit-squeeze stage of the cycle has diminished to leave a procyclical profit share and counter-cyclical wage share. The revised pattern, tallying with underconsumption theories of the business cycle, increases the likelihood that future economic growth will have to be sustained by expanded credit that runs the risk of renewed financial instability.

Reasons for Short-Run Factor Share Movements

Factor shares, defined at high levels of aggregation, embrace many separate components subject to various causal influences. The wage share comprises wage incomes from a vast range of occupations, all facing their own distinctive circumstances. Experience in one occupation will not necessarily match that elsewhere, so that trends may go in opposite directions. The profit share is usually interpreted to include profits in the classic sense, as returns to industrial capital, along with other property incomes such as interest (returns to financial capital) and rent (returns to land and other resources). As with wages, components of the profit share may face different circumstances and show diverse trends. Any attempt to explain factor share movements must pick out causal influences that dominate at a particular time and determine how aggregate factor shares are moving. Numerous arguments have been put forward about the causality behind factor share movements, though they have never reached a consensus on causes or directions of change. Table 1 lists some examples.

Diminishing returns to labour, a normal assumption in orthodox economic theory, should call forth a procyclical profit share and counter-cyclical wage share. All else being constant, higher employment reduces the marginal product of labour, since workers now operate with lower per capita levels of the other, fixed factors. In competitive labour markets, real wages equal the marginal product of labour and fall as productivity declines. Short-run macroeconomic fluctuations occur with given capital and technology, so diminishing returns would imply a falling wage share and rising profit share as the economy expands. If most industries fit this mould, then the aggregate profit share should be procyclical and the wage share counter-cyclical.

Table 1. Causal influences on cyclical factor shares

Procyclical profit share Counter-cyclical wage share	**Counter-cyclical profit share Procyclical wage share**
Diminishing returns to labour	Bargaining power
Lagged wage adjustments/ Overhead labour costs	Industrial composition of output
Raw materials prices	

Other arguments supporting a procyclical profit share revolve around lagged wage adjustments and overhead labour costs during the business cycle (Hahnel and Sherman, 1982; Sherman, 1990). In an economic upswing, the rise in incomes goes disproportionately into profits rather than wages, for wage payments and employment will not be adjusted immediately. Only in the late upswing can workers respond and improve their share of the rising incomes: the result will be a mainly positive relationship between profit share and national income. A similar argument appeals to the effect of overhead labour costs on the wage share. Many types of work, especially administrative and professional occupations, can be classed as overhead labour that changes slowly with economic activity. When the economy expands, overhead labour remains constant and does not rise in proportion to national income; only in the event of long-run growth will staff be recruited. The static overhead fraction of wage incomes implies a falling wage share and rising profit share. In a downswing the converse applies: overhead labour is retained, and wage incomes fall less quickly than total income, producing a rising wage share and falling profit share. Such arguments are found chiefly in the heterodox economic literature, notably underconsumption theories of the business cycle (Hahnel and Sherman, 1982). With classical savings assumptions (in the manner of Ricardo), profit recipients save proportionately more than wage recipients – a procyclical profit share raises the propensity to save during an upswing and hinders expansion. This may provoke an underconsumption crisis that creates a turning point when profits cannot be realised and investment is discouraged. The process reverses in the downswing as a rising wage share sustains demand, eases the realisation of profits and encourages renewed investment.

A further reason for a procyclical profit share may be raw materials prices, which vary more than wages (Kalecki, 1971, Chapters 5 and 6). When firms increase production, the prices of raw materials rise faster than wages to leave wage costs as a smaller share of the firm's total costs. When firms reduce production, the prices of raw materials fall quickly to leave wage costs as a larger share of the total. Across the whole economy, these trends would yield a counter-cyclical wage share and procyclical profit share. In common with the overhead labour arguments, the reasoning centres on differences in the variability of components of firms' costs. Each firm and industry will have its own unique features, but the same overall pattern would be enough to generate cyclical profit and wage shares.

Arguments for a counter-cyclical profit share have focused on changes in the bargaining power of labour as the economy expands and contracts (Boddy and Crotty, 1975; Goldstein, 1985). During an upswing the fall in unemployment makes labour scarcer and bolsters the workers' position in wage negotiations, enabling them to gain higher money wages and improve the real wage. Their strength should be visible at the aggregate level as a rising wage share in national income and falling profit share. A profit squeeze at the top of the cycle may induce a loss of business confidence and fall in investment sufficient to explain the turning point and provide a theory of the business cycle. Once the downswing has begun, unemployment rises again and the bargaining power of labour dwindles. As real wages prove harder to defend, the wage share in national income will fall and the profit share will rise, until higher profitability restores business confidence and revives investment. The boost to economic activity brings about the lower turning point and upswing of the next cycle.

Another stimulus for counter-cyclical profits may be cyclical changes in the industrial composition of output. Investment is more volatile than consumption and its prominence in national income/output varies cyclically, peaking near the top of the cycle. Changes in output composition are inherent in the cycle and bear upon the factor income distribution whenever industries have different wage shares (Kalecki, 1971, Chapter 6). Any differences are an empirical matter, but it seems likely that investment goods industries will have a higher wage share than others (as Kalecki assumed). If true, then this would raise the aggregate wage share during an upswing because investment goods account for a larger proportion of national income. The trend would be reversed in the downswing as investment goods decline in significance. Hence the profit share could become counter-cyclical merely through the varying composition of output during the cycle, a process distinct from the profit squeeze.

The causal influences in Table 1 give no universal principles about factor share movements. Profit and wage shares could be procyclical or counter-cyclical depending on which causal influences happen to be strongest. Since factor share changes are small in proportionate terms, a possible response would be to assume they stay approximately constant in the short run. This was the argument made by Kalecki, who acknowledged that factor shares are not actually fixed but thought that the various counteracting forces would nullify each other (Kalecki, 1971, Chapter 6). One can therefore find a theoretical justification for assuming factor shares stay constant. It should be possible, all the same, to go further and identify which causal influences on factor shares prevail at certain stages of the business cycle. Even if factor shares are quite invariant and exhibit no simple procyclicity or counter-cyclicity, they may still move cyclically out of phase with other economic variables. The upshot would be a factor-shares cycle that exists in tandem with the business cycle but remains apart from it.

The Standard Factor-Shares Cycle

Empirical evidence on cyclical factor shares and real wages has borne out the theoretical ambiguities, with contrasting and apparently inconsistent results (Brandolini, 1995). At times profit and wage shares seem procyclical and at other times counter-cyclical. Their waywardness might be taken to mean that they are aloof from business cycles – they might be assumed constant on average, despite the variance around the average. Drawing this conclusion would overstate the randomness of the factor shares at each stage of the business cycle. They are not just random but follow their own cyclical path related to the business cycle yet distinct from it. By recognising the cyclical regularities, we can specify a standard factor-shares cycle.

Table 2 shows the usual sequence of factor-share movements, observed over many business cycles and corroborated by empirical studies (Weisskopf, 1979; Hahnel and Sherman, 1982; Buchele and Christiansen, 1993; Van Lear, 1999; Sherman, 2003). As the economy begins an upswing, the profit share rises and the wage share falls (Stage I). The trend persists through much of the upswing until the economy nears the top of the cycle, whereupon the profit share stops rising and a profit squeeze ensues. The late upswing sees a fall in profit share and rise in wage share (Stage II). When the economy starts to contract, the profit share continues to fall and the wage share to rise, a trend that lingers well into the downswing. Economic activity is now declining, so the cyclicity of factor shares has changed again (Stage III). Towards the bottom of the cycle the wage share falters and the profit share recovers, reversing the cyclical trends until the lower turning point (Stage IV). Once the economy embarks on the next upswing, the sequence will be repeated. The timing and duration of the stages varies case by case, but a common pattern can be discerned.

Table 2. Stages in a typical business cycle

Stage	National income	Wage share	Profit share
I (Early upswing)	Rising	Falling	Rising
II (Late upswing)	Rising	Rising	Falling
III (Early downswing)	Falling	Rising	Falling
IV (Late downswing)	Falling	Falling	Rising

What causes this standard factor-shares cycle? A similar outcome can be obtained from Goodwin's growth cycle model and related approaches, which rest on a version of the profit squeeze argument (Goodwin, 1982; Skott, 1989, Chapter 3). In Goodwin's model, the bargaining power of labour is manifested not by the wage share but by its direction of change, such that high employment brings a rising wage share. The model ties the growth rate of employment to the profit share, on the assumption that investment comes from profits and drives economic growth. These two dynamic relationships, combined in a mathematical model, are enough to generate cyclical factor share changes as in Table 2, where the profit and wage shares switch between procyclical and counter-cyclical movements. Goodwin's growth cycle can offer a simple and mathematically elegant way to account for the standard factor-shares cycle, subject to the strong assumptions required by the model.

A wider explanation would appeal to a mixture of the causal factors in Table 1. During the early upswing, when unemployment is still high and the bargaining power of labour is low, the biggest influence on factor shares will be lagged wage adjustments and overhead labour costs, creating a rising profit share. Things change once unemployment falls: workers' bargaining power revives and they can push for higher real wages, which will impose a profit squeeze and falling profit share. During the early downswing, lagged wage adjustment and overhead labour costs initially protect the wage share and let it keep rising. Eventually, higher unemployment erodes the bargaining power of labour and the wage share falls. The logic here is that the standard factor-shares cycle can be explained through cyclical shifts in the balance between causal influences in the two columns of Table 1.

Although the factor-shares cycle and business cycle are connected, they do not reach their upper and lower turning points at the same time – they have similar periodicity but are out of phase. The profit share rises in the early upswing but peaks before the top of the business cycle and then starts to fall, reaching a trough before the bottom of the business cycle. The wage-share cycle is the mirror image of the profit-share cycle. Figure 1 shows the standard factor-shares cycle and how it relates to the business cycle. Over a complete cycle, factor shares alternate twice between procyclical and counter-cyclical movements. Whether the factor-shares cycle precedes or lags the business cycle is arbitrary, given that the profit share attains its maximum before the peak of economic activity, while the wage share attains its maximum after the peak. The profit and wage shares are, by definition, inversely related and add up to unity at all times. As average long-run values for the US case, a figure of a third is sometimes quoted for the profit share and two-thirds for the wage share (Young, 2010). In the lower diagram of Figure 1, factor shares vary around a benchmark of one-third profit, two-thirds wages: these proportions typify the values observed in the US but have no special significance.

When factor shares are plotted against national income, the trends in Figure 1 yield a circular path that can be termed the distributive loop (Jackson, 2012). The loop passes through the four stages of Table 2 and goes in opposite directions for the wage share and profit share, as in Figure 2. From the bottom of the business cycle, national income expands in the early upswing, with the wage share falling and profit share rising (Stage I): the distributive loop goes clockwise for the wage share and anticlockwise for the profit share. By the late upswing the wage share has reached its minimum and starts to rise again, the profit share to fall (Stage II). The rising wage share and falling profit share persist after the top of the business cycle and continue into the early downswing (Stage III). Trends in factor shares are reversed in the late downswing – the wage share falls and the profit share rises (Stage IV). After the lower turning point, the sequence is ready to begin again with Stage I. Limited variation of wage and profit shares, under Bowley's Law, would narrow the gap between maximum and minimum values for factor shares in Figure 2 and compress the distributive loop into a thinner, more vertical oval.

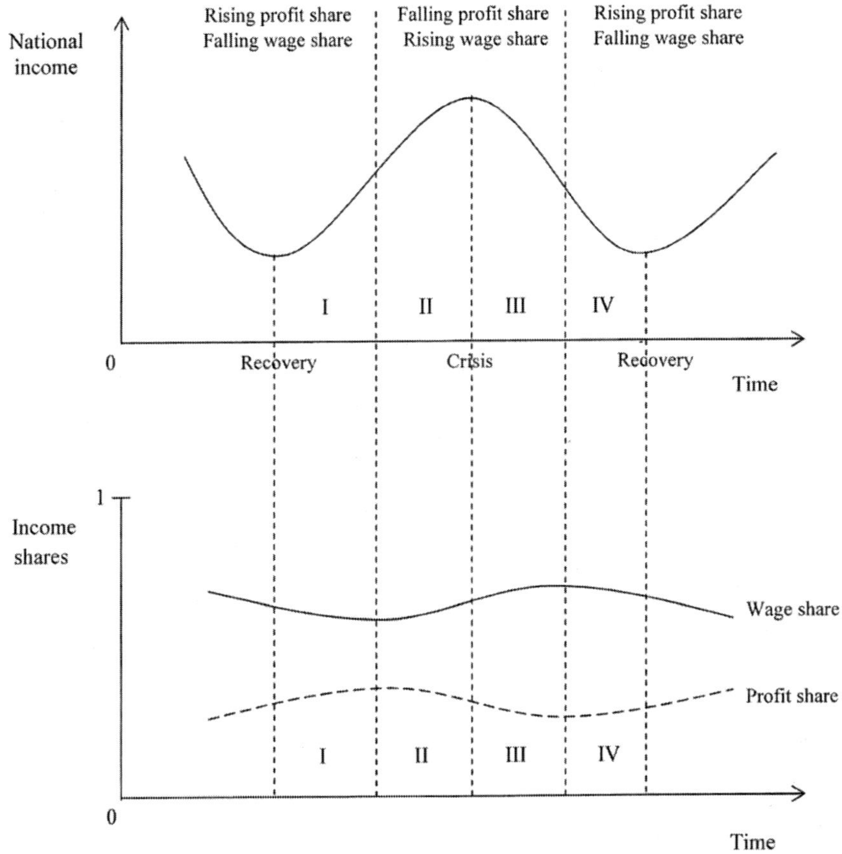

Figure 1. The factor-shares cycle in relation to the business cycle.

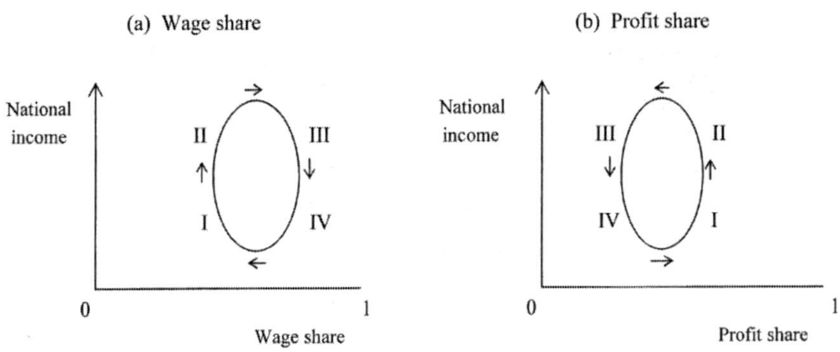

Figure 2. Distributive loops.

Actual factorshare movements will not conform exactly to the standard factor-shares cycle, and each cycle will have its own traits. The periodicity, amplitude and phasing of the cycles in Figure 1 may vary, together with the shape of the distributive loops in Figure 2. Any factor-shares cycle takes place against all the other forces that impinge on the economy in the short run. Also relevant are the longer term forces causing chronic changes in factor shares that coexist with short-run cyclical movements and may have a bearing on them. Especially relevant to the factor-shares cycle are two features of recent economic experience: the financially induced recession and the long-run rise of the profit share. As economies have become financialised, the causality behind business cycles has swayed towards financial issues; as the profit share has flourished, doubts have arisen about profit squeeze theories. The evolving economic environment may alter the factor-shares cycle and how it relates to the business cycle.

Changes in the Factor-Shares Cycle

From the 1980s onwards, the long-run trend in the factor income distribution has been a rising profit share and falling wage share for virtually all developed countries (Duménil and Lévy, 2002; Mohun, 2006; Carter, 2007; Kristal, 2010; Dünhaupt, 2013). Having lasted several decades, this trend must reflect changes in how capitalist economies are structured and how they function. A detailed causal explanation lies beyond the scope of the present chapter, but the rising profit share coincides with the switch towards neoliberalism and financialisation in the late twentieth century (Glyn, 2006; Zalewski and Whalen, 2010; Hein, 2012, Chapter 2). The end of the Keynesian era loosened commitment to activist macroeconomic policies and saw greater tolerance of high unemployment, which became ubiquitous throughout the developed world. Organised labour suffered a loss of bargaining power at all stages of the business cycle (Peters, 2011). Workers could not uphold their real wages, and the wage share in national income started to decline. Reduced bargaining power of labour affects the business cycle because it curtails the profit squeeze near the upper turning point; the forces that evoke a counter-cyclical profit share are weakened. With less of a profit squeeze from capital-labour conflict in manufacturing industry, the role of finance is enhanced. Neoliberalism has been accompanied by financialisation, which has spawned a deregulated financial sector whose transactions and rentier incomes have swollen relative to the size of national economies (Epstein and Jayadev, 2005; Krippner, 2005; Palley, 2008; Van Treeck, 2009; Onaran, Stockhammer and Grafl, 2011). More than just providing services to the rest of the economy, finance has been seen as a source of growth in its own right and a spearhead of innovation. Financial instability was an attendant danger (albeit underestimated), and financial problems have been pivotal to the current recession.

How will the factor-shares cycle react to these changes? The profit share will trend upwards and the wage share downwards, so that cycles no longer occur around the horizontal trends of Figure 1. Lost bargaining power from permanently high unemployment means that workers will find it hard to squeeze profits even at the top of the cycle. Components of the factor-shares cycle that rely on the profit squeeze and its relaxation will have less weight compared with others: Stages I and III will expand and Stages II and IV will contract, as in Figure 3. Forces generating a procyclical profit share will gain at the expense of those generating a counter-cyclical profit share. As a cause of the upper turning point, a profit squeeze becomes less plausible than other explanations (underconsumption, financial fragility) and loses ground as a prime mover of business cycles.

A reduced profit squeeze will change the shape of the distributive loops in Figure 2. Stages II and IV, dependent on the imposition and relaxation of the profit squeeze, will become shorter; Stages I and III will assume more importance and stretch out to cover more of the loops. These stages entail a procyclical profit share and counter-cyclical wage share, so they will impart an upward slant to the profit-share loop and downward slant to the wage-share loop, as in Figure 4. No longer symmetrical, the loops will be distorted into a narrow oval that gets narrower as Stages II and IV shrink further. The pattern of factor share movements comes to resemble the procyclical profit share and counter-cyclical wage share predicted by underconsumption theories of the business cycle. With a chronic rise in the profit share, the average profit and wage shares cannot remain stable and the distributive loop drifts leftward for the wage share and rightward for the profit share. The main stage of profit expansion (Stage I) will exceed the main stage of profit contraction (Stage III) in its length and intensity. Distributive loops will not repeat themselves exactly and will change their shape and position.

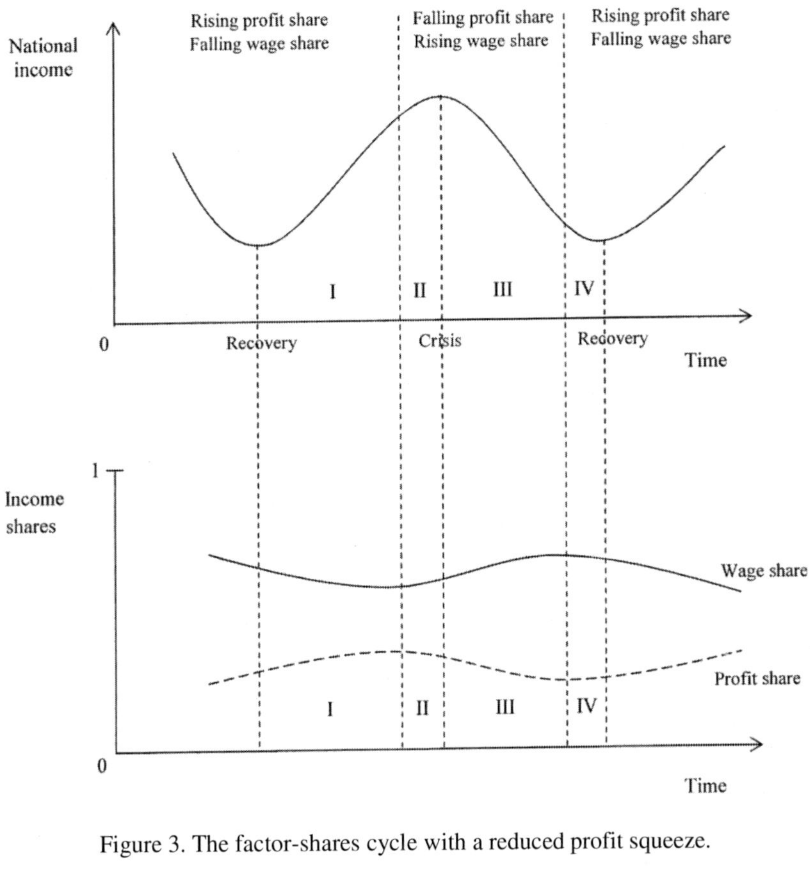

Figure 3. The factor-shares cycle with a reduced profit squeeze.

The slope of the loops in Figure 4 is broadly consistent with evidence on cyclical factor shares. Empirical studies have found that profits are procyclical and wages counter-cyclical during most of the upswing and downswing, confirming that the profit share is on the whole positively correlated with economic activity and the wage share negatively correlated (Sherman, 2003; Schneider, 2011; Hein, 2012, Chapter 2). Any profit squeeze resides just before the peak of the cycle and a profit revival just before the trough – as economies have moved from the Keynesian to the neoliberal era, the scope for a profit squeeze has declined (Boddy, 2009). Shorter stages of profit squeeze and revival will reduce the time lag between the factor-shares cycle and business cycle, as in Figure 3. In practice, one would not envisage well behaved distributive loops that keep the same shape and position for every cycle – other variables are not held constant, and many extraneous influences can upset how the economy adjusts. Studies that trace cyclical factor-share movements do, nevertheless, indicate circular motions along paths reminiscent of those in Figures 2 and 4 (Harvie, 2000; Mohun and Veneziani, 2008; Skott and Zipperer, 2010; Zipperer and Skott, 2010). The circular motions, melded with a procyclical profit share, should engender distributive loops with the slanted shapes of Figure 4. In the same way that each business cycle has distinctive attributes, actual distributive loops will differ in scale and shape. The loops in Figure 4 can only be an outline of what might be expected, rather than an exact trajectory to be followed by every factor-shares cycle.

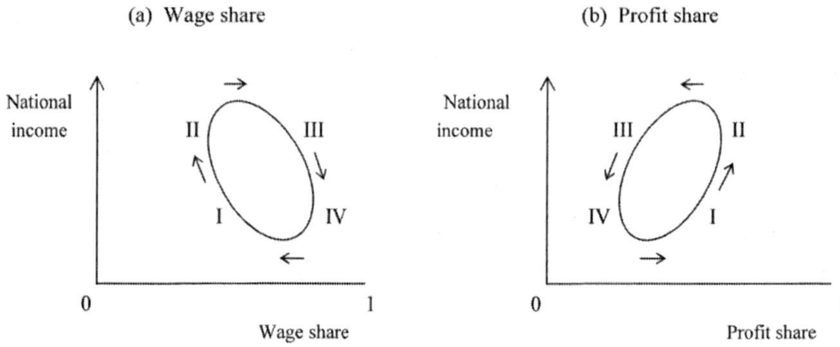

Figure 4. Distributive loops with a reduced profit squeeze.

If the profit squeeze is curtailed, then attention turns towards finance and underconsumption when explaining the turning points of the business cycle. In the most recent cycle, a prolonged credit-fuelled economic boom led to the crisis of 2008 and stagnation since then. This experience matched the train of events foretold by Minsky's financial instability hypothesis: a boom occurs through endogenous money and ever-expanding credit, but finance becomes increasingly insecure until the bubble bursts and economies tumble back into recession (Minsky, 1985, 1995; Papadimitriou and Wray, 1998). The downturn is caused primarily by the collapse of credit and the resulting fall in investment spending that deflates the economy and instigates a slump. Finance thus appears to be the cause of the business cycle, and tighter financial regulation would be the obvious way to curb the cyclical fluctuations.

Procyclical profits are essential to the underconsumption view of business cycles, in which a downturn is prompted by trouble in realising profits, not by a falling profit share. Underconsumption theories may seem distinct from financial ones, but they could be intertwined. The last economic boom, taking place against a backdrop of static real wages, saw aggregate demand sustained by consumer credit despite limited disposable incomes (Sherman, 2011; Palley, 2012, Part I; Taylor, 2012). Normally a rising profit share would slow down expansion by raising the propensity to save, as underconsumption theories would contend, but easy access to credit delayed this dampening effect. The drop in demand, when it finally happened, was triggered by financial crisis, yet the heightened importance of finance was due in part to the long-term decline in the wage share and difficulties in consuming from wage incomes alone. An underconsumption view can merge with a Minsky-style financial analysis to give a more rounded perspective on events. As far as policy is concerned, this hints that financial regulation on its own may not be enough to forestall future crises (Kotz, 2009; Palley, 2010). Important too is a return to rising real wages that permit steady economic growth without unsafe credit to pump up aggregate demand. The goal would be to stop the slide towards a lower wage share and allow workers to maintain their share of national income and benefit from higher real incomes as the economy grows. Plainly in the interests of the average worker, this would have a collective benefit in so far that it would aid the realisation of profits and yield steadier growth with less intense cycles and lower risks of boom and bust.

The rising profit share witnessed in recent years might seem unambiguously to benefit recipients of property incomes, whether derived from ownership of financial assets or industrial capital. With financialisation, however, the chief beneficiaries have been financial and rentier interests, as against manufacturers and nonfinancial corporations (Epstein and Power, 2003; Epstein and Jayadev, 2005; Dünhaupt, 2012). For industrial capital, the deflationary policy stance and slow aggregate demand growth during the neoliberal era has caused stagnation in product markets, which makes it difficult to sell output and realise profits. Financialisation has urged a switch away from long-run growth objectives towards immediate profitability, with shorter planning horizons, higher real interest rates and different management priorities. The plight of industry has been termed the 'neoliberal paradox': nonfinancial corporations face reduced demand and greater product competition that restricts their profits, but at the same time must provide regular short-run profitability in order to satisfy the financial markets and escape the perils of falling stock prices and hostile takeover bids (Crotty, 2005). Even though financialisation has boosted property incomes and the profit share, the dominance of financial and rentier interests has had adverse consequences for the real economy and nonfinancial activities (Dore, 2008; Orhangazi, 2009; Hein, 2011). A revival of the wage share would benefit not only workers but those nonfinancial corporations whose profitability relies on wage-led demand that will persist in the longer term. Improved ability to realise profits would help adjust the distribution of property incomes away from financial capital towards industrial capital. The unbalancing of developed economies has included a shift of factor shares from industrial to financial capital, as well as from labour to capital, and any rebalancing should aim to reverse both these trends.

Conclusion

Factor shares, if they obey Bowley's Law, are supposed to stay constant with only small, negligible divergences from a norm. Yet business cycles cause changes in bargaining power, cost structures and other variables that move factor shares around their (slowly evolving) long-run values. The standard factor-shares cycle sees factor shares varying alongside the business cycle but out of phase with it. We cannot say that the profit share and wage share are procyclical or counter-cyclical: each upswing and downswing of the business cycle is subdivided into stages where factor shares expand and contract. The overall story of near-static factor shares hides a complex sequence of movements that roughly cancel out in every cycle. This applies not only to the business cycle as a whole but to the upswing and downswing viewed separately, as they both include procyclical and counter-cyclical factor share movements for profits and wages. Factor shares do display some stability, though a blanket assumption of constancy gives a false impression. There is no smooth growth path that holds factor shares steady at equilibrium values. Capitalist economies grow through bursts of economic activity, including factor-share variations, which permit long-run progress and benefits shared between profits and wages.

Economic developments since the late twentieth century have challenged the rule of thumb about stable factor shares. From the 1940s to the 1970s, post-war expansion, Keynesian macroeconomic policies, regulated finance and generous welfare measures buttressed the bargaining power of labour relative to capital. Labour raised its share of national income and, within the business cycle, imposed an effective profit squeeze. Today remembered as a golden age of prolonged economic growth, the post-war decades were prone to frequent but mild business cycles. Unemployment remained low by current standards – there were no major recessions or financial crises. On the downside, industrial tensions became widespread by the 1970s and capital-labour conflicts brought high inflation and the pitfall of a deflationary backlash. Big changes in economic and political climate came about from the 1980s onwards. Neoliberalism, deregulation of finance, passive macroeconomic policies and high unemployment reduced the bargaining power of labour and restored that of capital. The trend towards a rising wage share petered out, to be replaced by a rising profit share. Unable to protect real wages, labour was too weak to impose a substantial profit squeeze within the business cycle. Deregulated finance temporarily deferred underconsumption through easy consumer credit and rising property prices in the lengthy boom at the beginning of the twenty-first century. The ultimate outcome was destabilising, for the boom could not persist and ended with the 2008 crisis and ongoing global recession. Recovery, elusive at the moment, would raise the spectre of repeated, severe financial crises if it was linked to another credit-propelled boom.

The changes since the 1980s have disrupted the factor-shares cycle and moved it towards an underconsumption mode based on procyclical profits. With real wages stagnant, expansion is biased towards rising property incomes that generate less expenditure than wage incomes and reduce the chances of sustained growth. Consumer spending can be funded through easier credit (which could become normalised within a reconfigured business cycle), but this would promote financial instability and perennial crises. Despite the learning opportunities offered by the current recession, it still seems likely that any recovery will have to lean heavily on insecure credit. As things stand, the developed economies are locked into Minsky-style problems of unstable finance compounded by underconsumption issues from suppressed real wages. Financial instability has long been a feature of business cycles, but it looms larger through its extension to consumer spending as well as investment.

Prospects for greater stability and smoother growth would improve if the developed economies could regain the standard factor-shares cycle of Figure 1, which would amend the imbalance of bargaining power between capital and labour. Once workers could defend real wages and take a share of income growth, it would become easier for the economy to expand through spending from current incomes rather than consumer credit. Business cycles would not disappear, but they would be shorter and less intense, with lower risk of financial collapse. Financial regulation on its own cannot accomplish these changes, which need coordinated action to raise employment and augment real wages. The message resembles the Post Keynesian arguments to preserve balance between capital and labour in order to lubricate the functioning of the economy. Such arguments are usually made in the context of anti-inflationary measures that seek to combine full employment with low inflation by restraining the bargaining power of labour. Now the problem occurs in reverse: chronic recession and high unemployment have undermined labour's bargaining power and damaged the capacity for revival through real income gains across the population as a whole. Without more equal bargaining power and a return to the standard factor-shares cycle, the next economic expansion is liable to rest upon insecure finance and leave us vulnerable to further crises.

References

Boddy, R. (2009).Cyclical labor shares under Keynesian and neoliberal regimes. In J.P. Goldstein and M.G. Hillard (Eds), *Heterodox Macroeconomics: Keynes, Marx and Globalization* (165-175). London: Routledge.

Boddy, R. &Crotty, J.R. (1975). Class conflict and macro-policy: the political business cycle. *Review of Radical Political Economics*, 7, 1-19.

Bowley, A.L. & Stamp, J. (1927).*The National Income 1924: A Comparative Study of the Income of the United Kingdom in 1911 and 1924.* Oxford: Clarendon Press.

Brandolini, A. (1995). In search of a stylised fact: do real wages exhibit a consistent pattern of cyclical variability? *Journal of Economic Surveys*, 9, 103-163.

Buchele, R. & Christiansen, J. (1993).Industrial relations and relative income shares in the United States. *Industrial Relations*, 32, 49-71.

Carter, S. (2007). Real wage productivity elasticity across advanced economies, 1963-1996. *Journal of Post Keynesian Economics*, 29, 573-600.

Crotty, J. (2005). The neoliberal paradox: the impact of destructive product market competition and 'modern' financial markets on nonfinancial corporation performance in the neoliberal era. In G.A. Epstein (Ed.), *Financialization and the World Economy* (77-110). Cheltenham: Edward Elgar.

Dore, R. (2008). Financialization of the global economy. *Industrial and Corporate Change*, 17, 1097-1112.

Douglas, P.H. (1934). *Theory of Wages.* London: Macmillan.

Duménil, G. &Lévy, D. (2002). The profit rate: where and how much did it fall? Did it recover? (USA 1948-2000).*Review of Radical Political Economics*, 34, 437-461.

Dünhaupt, P. (2012). Financialization and the rentier income share: evidence from the USA and Germany. *International Review of Applied Economics*, 26, 465-487.

Dünhaupt, P. (2013). The effect of financialization on labor's share of income. Working Paper, Institute for International Political Economy Berlin, No. 17/2013.

Epstein, G.A. & Power, D. (2003). Rentier incomes and financial crises: an empirical examination of trends and cycles in some OECD countries. *Canadian Journal of Development Studies*, 24, 229-248.

Epstein, G.A. & Jayadev, A. (2005). The rise of rentier incomes in OECD countries: financialization, central bank policy and labor solidarity. In G.A. Epstein (Ed.), *Financialization and the World Economy* (46-74). Cheltenham: Edward Elgar.

Fichtenbaum, R. (2009). The impact of unions on labor's share of income: a time-series analysis. *Review of Political Economy*, 21, 567-588.

Glyn, A. (2006). *Capitalism Unleashed: Finance, Globalization, and Welfare.* Oxford: Oxford University Press.

Goldstein, J.P. (1985). The cyclical profit squeeze: a Marxian microfoundation. *Review of Radical Political Economics*, 17, 103-128.

Goodwin, R.M. (1982). A growth cycle. In R.M. Goodwin, *Essays in Economic Dynamics* (165-170). Basingstoke: Macmillan.

Hahnel, R. & Sherman, H.J. (1982). Income distribution and the business cycle: three conflicting hypotheses. *Journal of Economic Issues*, 16, 49-73.

Harvie, D. (2000). Testing Goodwin: growth cycles in ten OECD countries. *Cambridge Journal of Economics*, 24, 349-376.

Hein, E. (2011). Distribution, 'financialisation' and the financial and economic crisis – implications for post-crisis economic policies. Working Paper, Institute for International Political Economy Berlin, No. 9/2011.

Hein, E. (2012). *The Macroeconomics of Finance-dominated Capitalism – and its Crisis.* Cheltenham: Edward Elgar.

Jackson, W.A. (2012). Factor shares, business cycles and the distributive loop. *Metroeconomica*, 63, 493-511.

Jefferson, P.N. & Pryor, F.L. (2010). Dynamics of factor income shares in the United States. *Journal of Income Distribution*, *19*, 96-119.

Kaldor, N. (1961). Capital accumulation and economic growth. In F.A. Lutz and D.C. Hague (Eds), *The Theory of Capital* (177-222). London: Macmillan.

Kalecki, M. (1971). *Selected Essays on the Dynamics of the Capitalist Economy.* Cambridge: Cambridge University Press.

Kotz, D.M. (2009). The financial and economic crisis of 2008: a systemic crisis of neoliberal capitalism. *Review of Radical Political Economics*, 41, 305-317.

Krippner, G.R. (2005). The financialization of the American economy. *Socio-Economic Review*, 3, 173-208.

Kristal, T. (2010). Good times, bad times: postwar labor's share of national income in capitalist democracies. *American Sociological Review*, 75, 729-763.

Minsky, H.P. (1985). The financial instability hypothesis: a restatement. In P. Arestis and T. Skouras (Eds), *Post Keynesian Economic Theory* (24-55). Brighton: Wheatsheaf.

Minsky, H.P. (1995). Financial factors in the economics of capitalism. *Journal of Financial Services Research*, 9, 197-208.

Mohun, S. (2006). Distributive shares in the US economy, 1964-2001. *Cambridge Journal of Economics*, 30, 347-370.

Mohun, S. &Veneziani, R. (2008).Goodwin cycles and the US economy, 1948-2004.In P. Flaschel and M. Landesmann (Eds), *Mathematical Economics and the Dynamics of Capitalism: Goodwin's Legacy Continued* (107-130). London: Routledge.

Nolan, B. (1987). Cyclical fluctuations in factor shares and the size distribution of income. *Review of Income and Wealth*, 33, 193-210.

Onaran, Ö.,Stockhammer, E. &Grafl, L. (2011). Financialisation, income distribution and aggregate demand in the USA. *Cambridge Journal of Economics*, 35, 637-661.

Orhangazi, Ö. (2009). Did financialization increase macroeconomic fragility? An analysis of the US nonfinancial corporate sector. In J.P. Goldstein and M.G. Hillard (Eds.), *Heterodox Macroeconomics: Keynes, Marx and Globalization* (127-139). London: Routledge.

Palley, T.I. (2008). Financialisation: what it is and why it matters. In E. Hein, T. Niechoj, H.-P. Spahn and A. Truger (Eds), *Finance-led Capitalism? Macroeconomic Effects of Changes in the Financial Sector* (29-60). Marburg: Metropolis-Verlag.

Palley, T.I. (2010). The limits of Minsky's financial instability hypothesis as an explanation of the crisis. *Monthly Review*, 61 (11), 28-40.

Palley, T.I. (2012). *From Financial Crisis to Stagnation: The Destruction of Shared Prosperity and the Role of Economics.* Cambridge: Cambridge University Press.

Papadimitriou, D.B. & Wray, L.R. (1998). The economic contributions of Hyman Minsky: varieties of capitalism and institutional reform. *Review of Political Economy*, 10, 199-225.

Peters, J. (2011). The rise of finance and the decline of organized labour in the advanced capitalist countries. *New Political Economy*, 16, 73-99.

Schneider, D. (2011). The labor share: a review of theory and evidence. SFB 649 Discussion Paper 2011-069.

Sherman, H.J. (1990). Cyclical behavior of the labor share. *Review of Radical Political Economics*, *22*, 92-112.

Sherman, H.J. (2003). Institutions and the business cycle. *Journal of Economic Issues*, 37, 621-642.

Sherman, H.J. (2011). Portrait of a crisis. *Journal of Economic Issues*, 45, 703-716.

Skott, P. (1989). *Conflict and Effective Demand in Economic Growth.* Cambridge: Cambridge University Press.

Skott, P. & Zipperer, B. (2010). Dynamic patterns of accumulation and income distribution. *Political Economy Quarterly*, 46, 34-53.

Taylor, L. (2012). Growth, cycles, asset prices and finance. *Metroeconomica*, 63, 40-63.

Van Lear, W. (1999).Profitability in business cycle theory and forecasting. *Review of Radical Political Economics*, 31, 46-60.

Van Treeck, T. (2009).The political economy debate on 'financialization' – a macroeconomic perspective. *Review of International Political Economy*, 16, 907-944.

Weisskopf, T.E. (1979). Marxian crisis theory and the rate of profit in the postwar US economy. *Cambridge Journal of Economics*, 3, 341-378.

Wolff, E.N. (2003). What's behind the rise in profitability in the US in the 1980s and 1990s? *Cambridge Journal of Economics*, 27, 479-499.

Young, A.T. (2010). One of the things we know that ain't so: is US labor's share relatively stable? *Journal of Macroeconomics*, 32, 90-102.

Zalewski, D.A. & Whalen, C.H. (2010). Financialization and income inequality, a Post Keynesian Institutionalist analysis. *Journal of Economic Issues*, 44, 757-777.

Zipperer, B. &Skott, P. (2010). Cyclical patterns of employment, utilization and profitability. *Economics Department Working Paper 2010-02*, University of Massachusetts Amherst.

In: Business Cycles in Economics
Editor: Jason C. Hsu
ISBN: 978-1-63321-322-7

Chapter 3

BUSINESS CYCLE MECHANISMS ON MARKETS WITH PERFECT COMPETITION

*Monica Dobrescu**
Academy of Economic Sciences, Bucharest, Romania

Abstract

Current economic research generally acknowledges that the central issues in macroeconomics are essentially the same as those identified by Keynes in the *General Theory of Employment, Interest and Money*. One way or another, economists are addressing the same issues that they did several decades ago: How can we account for the different growth rates and various fluctuations observed in national economies? Which are the economic policies most suitable to solve the issues of growth and cyclical behavior? Both the New Classical School and New Keynesian Economics have made considerable progress within their research paradigms. On the whole, the New Classicals believe that the business cycle can best be understood within the market-clearing model, which postulates that markets are perfectly competitive and they function efficiently; on such markets, prices instantly adjust to equilibrate supply and demand. On the other hand, the New Keynesians take a disequilibrium approach: these economists believe that business fluctuations are due to certain market failures of various sorts. To explain economic fluctuations, New Classical economists focus on monetary disturbances, technology shocks or the intertemporal substitution of leisure. The New Keynesians, on the other hand, investigate the role of nominal and/or real imperfections in the economy and they analyze the business cycle in terms of *monopolistic competition*, *menu costs* or *efficiency wages*.

The present chapter focuses on the market-clearing approach to business cycles, given that the theoretical progress of the New Classical School has indeed been significant and relevant for economic policy during the past decades. We start the analysis with the early New Classical models, which focus on the role of monetary disturbances in generating economic fluctuations. These monetary models somewhat depart from the Walrasian paradigm, by assuming imperfect information regarding prices. We then go on to analyze the apparent similarity with the Austrian business cycle theory, considered by many to have inspired the New Classical monetary models. We find that these models were abandoned in the '80s due to two failures: on the one hand, they could not rigorously explain monetary non-neutrality and they were generally invalidated by empirical evidence, on the other.

* E-mail address: monicam_dobrescu@yahoo.com; Address: Str. Cpt. Pavel Zăgănescu, nr. 1, sector 6, 060206, Bucharest, Romania.

The analysis continues with a more recent direction of research, which attributes cyclical fluctuations to certain real disturbances in the economy. These *real business cycle* theories postulate that fluctuations in the real economic activity are based on shocks primarily in the existing technology. Since these technology fluctuations lead to fluctuations in relative prices, individuals rationally adjust their labour supply and consumption levels, and therefore, the business cycle is the natural efficient response of the economy to the shifts in the existing technology.
On the whole, we conclude that these real business cycle theories have generated a new perspective and novel techniques for modeling the macroeconomic area and constructing economic policy. However, it is not yet very clear to what extent these theories contribute to an effective understanding of the business cycle mechanism or to the formulation of economic policy.

Keywords: market-clearing models, real business cycles, monetary neutrality, New Classical Economics

Introduction

For more than two hundred years, economic science has been divided between two fundamentally different visions on capitalism. The first vision – the classical approach – focuses on the virtues of market economies and investigates the way prices transmit information between producers and consumers to allocate resources efficiently. The second vision – corresponding to the socialist approach – points out the flaws of market economies, particularly those periods of chronic under-utilization of capital and labor. The supporters of the classical view usually approach unemployment as a temporary dysfunction that the usual market mechanisms will eventually correct, when left to operate freely. To the market economy opponents however, not only is this vision unscientific, it is also really dangerous, because it can mislead public authorities into accepting the costs of high unemployment. To a certain extent, Keynes managed to resolve these opposed visions on capitalism. He approached the issue of unemployment explicitly, claiming that state intervention could handle it successfully. And once the unemployment problem was solved, the classical merits of the market economy could be reintroduced and accepted in economic analysis – and that is precisely what Paul Samuelson and the Neoclassical Synthesis did.

There were two main reasons lying behind the departure of Keynesian economics from the classical orthodoxy in the '30s: the first was the persistence of high involuntary unemployment – many individuals were willing to get a job at the existing wages, but could not find employment; the second was the observation that aggregate demand fluctuations were the central source of short-term fluctuations in economic activity: the changes in the level of public expenses, in the monetary and financial markets, or even in economic agents' confidence seemed to have strong effects on production and employment. In this context, the need for a new theory to incorporate these realities became imperative. The economic theory that developed during the next three decades – culminating with the outstanding "neoclassical synthesis" – provided one single explanation to both phenomena: nominal prices adjust slowly to the imbalances between supply and demand. The most important of these slowly-adjusting prices was the price of labor – or the nominal wage – which meant that market imbalances between labor supply and demand could occur, thus generating involuntary unemployment. Moreover, since this rigidity characterized nominal wages, the classical dichotomy – nominal versus real variables – was questioned; as a result, changes in nominal variables – such as money supply – could have large effects on the real variables, such as output and employment. Apart from these differences, the neoclassical synthesis was, in essence, Walrasian in nature. The goods and labor markets were competitive, externalities were absent, and information was perfect. The synthesis reached its peak in the late '60s – early '70s, with the creation of several disequilibrium models: paradoxically, these models integrated perfectly rigid prices within Walrasian-type equilibrium models. The neoclassical synthesis was thus confronted with a contradiction which proved impossible to overcome: how come such a competitive environment is marked by such an important deficiency as price rigidity? Because one of Walras' fundamental postulates is that, within a competitive environment, economic agents are "constrained" to adjust prices when confronted with supply and demand imbalances.

The new vision of the Neoclassical Synthesis was universally accepted as the keystone of mainstream economics at that time, even though it eluded several essential problems related to market failures, such as the causes of the business cycle or the unemployment accompanying the crises. On the other hand, Keynesian economics had created a chaos in the approach of economics, at least at the academic level: microeconomics lectures teaching Smith's invisible hand, the price mechanism and free competition, were followed by macroeconomics lectures explaining market failures and authorities' role in correcting them. In this context, micro and macroeconomics emerged as distinct new disciplines; and within each discipline, microeconomists criticized macroeconomists for the lack of scientific rigour and theoretical foundations, whereas the latter criticized the former for the lack of realism and for the empirical inconsistency of microeconomic theories.

The 1970s saw a distinctive shift in macroeconomic research. The traditional Keynesian research program was concerned with the determination of output and employment and with how to alter and stabilize the time paths of major macroeconomic variables. In the 1970s, this research program was gradually replaced by business cycle theory, that is, the theory of the nature and causes of economic fluctuations. The acceleration of both inflation and unemployment in the late `60s and early `70s led economists to question the Keynesian policy prescription that unemployment could be reduced by accepting a higher dose of inflation. In this context at the end of the `60s, Milton Friedman and Edmund Phelps rejected the validity of the long-run Phillips curve, and claimed that the inflation-unemployment trade-off could only work over the short term: in the long run, agents would realize their purchasing power has diminished and consequently, production and employment would return to their initial levels. The two authors argued, using solid microeconomic foundations that the empirical relationship between inflation and unemployment would collapse if public authorities tried to exploit it. They claimed that the equilibrium of the labour market – characterized by a *natural rate of unemployment* – depended on labour supply and demand, the optimal search time, as well as other microeconomic factors, and not on the average growth of money supply. Subsequent events confirmed Friedman and Phelps' theories: inflation rose without a corresponding decrease in unemployment. The collapse of the Phillips curve, together with Friedman and Phelps' predictions, set the ground for the heavy *critique* of Robert E. Lucas, Jr.[1], who attacked the lack of microeconomic foundations of both the Phillips curve and the

---

[1] Lucas, Robert E., Jr. – *Econometric Policy Evaluation: A Critique*, 1976, J. Money. Econ., Suppl. Series, 1976, I, p.19-46, 62.

complex macroeconometric models used by decision-makers at that time. More specifically, the decisions that determine most macroeconomic variables, such as consumption and investment, depend crucially on expectations regarding the future functioning of the economy. Lucas also pointed out that most policy interventions altered the way individuals formed their expectations about the future, and criticized the existing macro models precisely for ignoring these modifications.

Due to these considerations, the macroeconomic models and the consensual vision on the economy collapsed, causing the apparent neoclassical consensus to break down. This led to a state of turmoil in economic science, which, in part, still goes on today. Essentially, the breakdown was due to two major flaws, one empirical and one theoretical. The empirical flaw was that the mainstream view could not adequately cope with the rising rates of inflation and unemployment experienced during the 70s. The theoretical flaw was that the mainstream view continued to preserve a chasm between macroeconomic practice and microeconomic principles. These theoretical and empirical failures led to a period of confusion and division in economics, which, in part, still continues today. Consequently, much of the economic research of the past 30 years has attempted to reconcile the two fields of study, and to integrate microeconomic principles and macroeconomic analysis.

Current Approaches to Business Cycle Theory

Market-clearing models vs. imperfections. At the theoretical level, the reunification of the two fields could be done either by adapting macroeconomics to microeconomics, or the other way round, by adapting microeconomics to macroeconomics; in this context, two main directions of research emerged: the **New Classical School,** which adopted the former approach to economic science; and the **New Keynesian School**, which followed the latter. New Classical economists try to capture the dynamic aggregate behavior of the economy, starting from the rational, maximizing behavior of economic agents. On the other hand, since the existence of unemployment and business cycles was incompatible with standard microeconomic principles, New Keynesian economics tried to formulate a theory to account for such phenomena.

The development of the New Classical macroeconomics led to a revival of business cycle theory. The New Classical school, also known as the *"market-clearing approach",* tried to account for the existence of cycles in perfectly competitive economies with rational expectations. It emphasized the role of imperfect information, and saw nominal shocks, in the form of monetary misperceptions, as the cause of cycles. The early New Classical contributions posed a challenge to Keynesian economics and stimulated the development of both New Keynesian economics and real business cycle (RBC) theory. On the other hand, New Keynesians have generally accepted the idea of rational expectations, but they emphasize the importance of imperfect competition, costly price adjustment and externalities and consider nominal shocks as the predominant impulse mechanism. In other words, to explain economic fluctuations, the New Classicals focus on monetary disturbances, technological perturbations or the intertemporal substitution of leisure, as deviations from perfect competition and equilibrium; on the other hand, the New Keynesians speak in terms of monopolistic competition, menu costs or efficiency wages, as imperfections that occur in the economy.

Important theoretical progress has been made within these two research paradigms – particularly in what regards business cycle theory – and each of them comprises numerous distinct directions of research. But on the whole, the common feature uniting these directions is that the New Classicals analyze the economy within the Walrasian equilibrium framework, using the so-called *market-clearing* models; whereas the New Keynesians analyze the economy in terms of disequilibrium. On the whole, the New Classicals believe that the business cycle can best be understood as a temporary deviation within the market-clearing model, whereas the New Keynesians believe that business fluctuations are due to certain market failures of various sorts. In other words, the main difference between the two schools lies in the way they analyze the economy: equilibrium vs. disequilibrium approach.

The New Classical School is probably the most interesting recent evolution in the macroeconomic field and, certainly the most exciting, from a theoretical point of view (Friedman, 1983)[2]. This direction of research, as the name itself suggests, uses a mixture of theoretical concepts and specific hypotheses, often accompanied by modern mathematical and econometric tools, in order to promote the market-clearing model, the specific business cycle theories and the inefficiency of monetary policy in a rigorous manner.

The New Classical equilibrium approach has important implications for the business cycle mechanism: these models attempt to explain macroeconomic phenomena starting from the assumption that prices are perfectly flexible; in these models, prices continually adjust to equilibrate supply and demand – or to clear markets – hence the name *"market-clearing"* models. The view that markets always clear is closely related to the idea that private markets function efficiently. Specifically, on cleared markets, it is impossible to improve on any outcomes by matching potential buyers and sellers of goods or potential borrowers and lenders: cleared markets already accomplish all of these mutually beneficial trades.

A central idea introduced by the New Classical School is that a more realistic macroeconomic theory develops when it is founded on the underlying microeconomic principles – meaning that it avoids internal inconsistencies and we obtain a better understanding of the real world. In addition, according to rational expectations, individuals act rationally when making their predictions about the future. This implies that individuals behave rationally in the environment in which they act: they make the most of the information they possess or are willing to acquire, by using it efficiently. In this context, market-clearing reflects the optimizing behaviour of individuals, which is related to the microfoundations of the macroeconomic model. On the one hand, people determine their individual choices of work, consumption and so on, to make themselves as well off as possible. On the other hand, market clearing means that people who participate on the market – and are guided by the pursuit of their own interest – do not waste resources, and therefore achieve efficient outcomes. Recent research has pointed out more profound implications than 40 years ago, when disequilibrium models were prevalent in macroeconomic analysis.

The essential features of New Classical macroeconomics are the (1) adoption of the equilibrium approach to model construction, (2) the acceptance of the natural rate hypothesis, and (3) a belief in the superiority of firm rules of economic policy (McCallum, 1989). Recent Keynesian analyses, stressing the interaction of monopolistic competition with "menu costs", are not incompatible with the New Classical approach, but have not been very successful.

2 Benjamin M. Friedman – *Recent Perspectives in and on Macroeconomics*, NBER Working Paper no.1208, Sept.1983

But even though the New Classical School focuses on the approach of the economy in terms of equilibrium – by constructing well-articulated equilibrium theories – their macroeconomic analysis has been directed primarily towards business fluctuations. By contrast to New Keynesian economists though, the fundamental premises in explaining business fluctuations is that these cannot be attributed to market failures that can be corrected by state intervention. As a consequence, business fluctuations have to reflect monetary or real disturbances, whose economic effects depend on the cost of acquiring information, the cost of adjustment etc. These disturbances were initially investigated by Lucas (1972), who constructed a monetary business cycle model; more recently, the monetary cycle theory gave way to real business cycle theories – which comprise several models, depending on the real disturbance lying at the origin of the business cycle.

At the heart of New Classical Economics lie Friedman and Phelps' predictions regarding the Phillips curve and the inflation – unemployment trade-off: starting from microeconomic arguments, the two economists demonstrated that sustained inflation can have no effect whatsoever, since individuals are concerned with real, rather than nominal variables: once they anticipate sustained inflation, they will adjust their decisions on prices and employment levels accordingly, which means that inflation cannot incur a permanent reduction in unemployment. The New Classical economists built on Friedman and Phelps' predictions about the long-run Phillips curve and they carried on the monetarist tradition in what regards the quantity theory of money; but they departed from Friedman's approach on various issues, such as the short-run Phillips curve. In addition, they were even more radical in pointing out the inefficiency of monetary policy and in rejecting state intervention.

Friedman and Phelps' prediction about the long-run Phillips curve also set the ground for Lucas' *monetary theory of the business cycle* (Lucas Jr., 1972: pp.103-124). Friedman had pointed out that agents' expectations adjust gradually to permanent shifts in inflation; still, this adjustment implied the possibility of a temporarily low unemployment rate, when the economy was stimulated, say, through expansionist monetary policy. In the long run however, monetary expansion would result in higher price levels and unemployment would go back to its original level.

New Classical economists brought up the possibility of *grounding macroeconomics on strong microeconomic principles:* since New Classical models infer macroeconomic implications starting from the maximizing behaviour of individuals, they seemed more rigorous to some economists; on the other hand, several economists rejected these models as irrelevant, because neither the microeconomic behaviour they were based on, nor the macro implications of this behaviour were realistic. In addition, numerous economists rejected the New Classical business cycle theories, based on the market-clearing model, so that the resurrection of Keynesian ideas in the '80s – as the New Keynesian macroeconomics – came as no surprise to economists. The New Keynesian School comprises a multitude of different sub-directions of research, but one common element of these approaches is the assumption of imperfect and incomplete markets and information[3]. Recent research has generated models where economic agents – driven by optimizing behaviour – "choose" to create nominal rigidities. These theoretical evolutions resulted primarily from the observation that small barriers to price adjustment can have significant macroeconomic effects and can generate

[3] Bruce Greenwald, Joseph E. Stiglitz – *Keynesian, New Keynesian and New Classical Economics*, Oxford Economic Papers 39, 1987, p.119-132

considerable non-neutralities. However, the "label" *Keynesian* is very broad today and there are numerous approaches within New Keynesian economics, but the one feature that unites this variety of models is the belief that economic fluctuations reflect some sort of market failure on a grand scale. On the whole, the Keynesian view considers that outcomes are not efficient, notably some mutually advantageous trades do not take place. As a reflection of this market failure, there tends to be chronic unemployment and underproduction, which, most often, have led economists to advocate "corrective" actions by the government.

New Keynesian models can be viewed as attempting to put textbook Keynesian analysis on a firmer microeconomic foundation since Keynes' doctrine was originally centred upon macroeconomics and ignored microeconomic principles almost completely. In this respect, we must note that many New Keynesians have acknowledged the importance of rational expectations, and have started to incorporate them into their analyses. At the same time, this direction of research is the most compatible with the textbook model that combines the IS-LM model with the modern version of the Phillips curve.

The market imperfection that recurs most frequently in Keynesian theories is the failure of prices and/or wages to adjust instantly to equilibrate supply and demand. This is actually the main difference between the New Keynesians and the New Classicals – who assume that prices and wages are perfectly flexible and they adjust continuously so that markets tend towards equilibrium.

An alternative way of classifying business cycle models is through the location of the dominant impulses driving the cycle: do they arise on the demand side or the supply side of the economy? The initial monetary cycles of the New Classical School, as well as the New Keynesian models are driven by demand-side shocks, while real business cycles (RBC) are driven by supply-side shocks. Some writers question the usefulness of this distinction, pointing out that any supply-side innovation causes a change in demand and vice versa. That assertion is correct, but from an analytical point of view, this distinction is extremely relevant: the two types of models emphasize opposite causes of the business cycle, leading to completely different business cycle mechanisms; and this is extremely important for economists' understanding of economic fluctuations, because they must identify and address the real causes of the cycle in order to alleviate its phases.

In conclusion, a major part of macroeconomic research during the past 3 decades has been trying to deal with the problems that triggered this crisis in macroeconomics. Economists have focused upon founding their macro theories on sound microeconomic principles. Unfortunately, the relevance of research to the current economic problems is often neglected and there seems to be a large gap between theoretical progress and economic practice, as economists have failed to incorporate the new contributions into their policies. To many practitioners, the research endeavours appear esoteric, or even useless, and on many occasions research seems indeed futile for practical purposes.

Monetary Business Cycles

Monetary business cycle theories regard monetary mismanagement as the origin of macroeconomic dysfunctions in the intertemporal allocation of resources, leading to economic fluctuations; these theories focus on the relative-price effects – and the corresponding quantity adjustments – of a monetary disturbance, instead of focusing on macroeconomic aggregates, which actually conceal relative-price effects. Early monetary models of the business cycle originated from Austrian economist Ludwig von Mises and were further developed rigorously by Friedrich von Hayek.

Richard Cantillon is often considered to be the first economist who successfully investigated the cyclical nature of the capitalist economy. During his time, the institutions of the modern capitalist economy were fully established and the first major business cycles occurred. According to Cantillon, the main cause of imbalances in the economy was authorities' manipulation of money. The economist showed that money, interest rates, and international trade were all "well regulated" and relatively stable in their natural state. Furthermore, interference by national banks and monetary interventions by government would cause instability and lead to harmful disturbances in the economy. Very importantly, he showed that consumption and production patterns were altered and the economy was ultimately harmed when money and interest were manipulated by government, creating what we now call Cantillon effects. His approach provides both a methodological approach for studying business cycles and a pertinent cause of the business cycle (government intervention) that has subsequently been absorbed and elaborated by David Ricardo and the Currency School, Wicksell, Mises, Hayek, and the modern Austrian School, and, more recently by the New Classical economists.

Monetary models postulate that trade cycles are triggered by the excessive growth of circulating credit, which affects the real economy, leading to unsustainable investments that are corrected during the recession, when credit contraction occurs. Mises (1912) showed that money-induced movements in the interest rate (as identified by Knut Wicksell) have identifiable effects on the capital structure (as conceived by Eugen von Böhm-Bawerk). According to Mises, an artificially low interest rate leads to credit expansion which brings about booming business, since the policy of cheap money makes some unprofitable investment projects appear attractive to entrepreneurs. As credit expands in the economy, prices begin to rise, and entrepreneurs find themselves short of funds to sustain the investment projects they initiated. However, as credit continues to expand, investors find no need to worry, since they borrow more to continue their activities.

Through a policy of easy money, public authorities expose economic agents to the perception of profitable investments and diminishing risk. Consequently, moral hazard triggers more credit growth. While, in the short run, these policies may stimulate economic activity, they determine malinvestment in the economy over the long run. Credit growth lays the premises for over-investment and consumption patterns that are inconsistent with individual time preferences and the availability of specific resources. Hayek's contribution consists in developing the theory that monetary injections can have a systematic effect on the intertemporal behaviour of prices, leading to the so-called *intertemporal discoordination.* The prosperity which precedes a recession is marked by a lowering of the nominal interest rate below its market level, in the absence of monetary expansion. While the interest rate is artificially low during the expansion, firms invest primarily in physical capital. Since the interest rate is so low, the production process can take longer to produce the same amount of real output. Resources are allocated among the different stages of production by entrepreneurs' decisions based on price signals. But because of the distinct temporal dimension of the structure of production, the supplies and demands for resources throughout different production stages react differently to shifts in the rate of interest: the demand for the output of extraction industries, for example, is more interest elastic than the demand for the output of service industries. Interest rate changes will have a systematic effect on the pattern of prices: a fall in the interest rate, for instance, will strengthen the relatively interest-elastic demands drawing resources into the early stages of production.

In the Austrians' monetary cycle, the artificially low rate of interest will determine an unsustainable boom in which excess resources are committed to the early stages of production. The market process triggered by the injection of money is a self-reversing process. More production projects are initiated than can possibly be completed and subsequent resource scarcities turn the artificial boom into a bust. Economic recovery cannot occur unless the "malinvestments" are terminated and resources are reallocated according to actual intertemporal preferences and resource availabilities.

At the same time, however, the lower interest rate means that consumers increase their consumption and decrease saving. The injection of credit in the economy provides more funds both for investment in early-stage, higher-order production, and in later-stage, lower-order production at the same time. The effect of the low interest rate is an economy where final real output takes longer to produce, while consumers are less willing to wait for their needs to be satisfied. This production structure is unsustainable, and eventually will result in the abandonment of many entrepreneurial plans, of much installed capital and of goods in early production stages, and, as well as in high labor unemployment, even if the interest rate is kept low. Both producers' and consumers' entrepreneurial plans are disrupted because they were grounded on a lower interest rate and a longer production structure.

Lucas' Monetary Business Cycle. The New Classical School developed business cycle theory in the context of certain pressing uncertainties in economic policy – as "substitute" of a paradigm whose implications had been decisively falsified by experience. `And the central event that triggered this development was the accelerating inflation associated with rising unemployment. This event was in conflict with traditional Keynesian policy, which claimed that an ascending trend of employment could be maintained indefinitely, by accepting a higher – yet stable – dose of inflation. In this context, the greatest challenge for the New Classical Economics was to explain why money is not neutral in the economy and, particularly, why monetary disturbances play a major role within the business cycle mechanism. This challenge was based on two major, opposite explanations: firstly, empirical evidence seems to confirm – at least to some extent – monetary non-neutrality in modern economies; and secondly, from the equilibrium models incorporating flexible prices – that the New Classicals constructed – we would deduce the implication that money is neutral in the economy. At first, this approach seemed to achieve notable success. At the theoretical level, the real short-term effects of monetary disturbances appeared to be determined by the existence of imperfect information regarding the money supply and the price level. Monetary shocks, which affected the general price level, could be temporarily perceived incorrectly as shifts in the relative prices, and could thus determine adjustments of the real variables – particularly output and employment. These effects gradually disappeared over the long term, but they could persist for a while due to information lags and to the adjustment costs of inputs. On the other hand, anticipated shifts in the money supply – including systematic monetary policies – have no effects on real variables, because they do not lead to confusions regarding information[4]. This approach also seemed plausible at the empirical level: monetary

[4] T.J. Sargent, N. Wallace – *Rational Expectations, the Optimal Monetary Instrument and the Optimal Money Supply Rule*, Journal of Political Economy, 83, April 1975, 241-254

disturbances appeared to be important causes of economic fluctuations, and several statistical data pointed out that particularly unanticipated shifts – namely "monetary surprises" – did have an influence on real economic activity[5]. At the same time, the theory was consistent with the absence of a long-run substantial relationship between real economic activity and the growth rates of money supply and prices, in other words it was inconsistent with the long-run Phillips curve. More detailed subsequent analyses raised a series of doubts on these theoretical achievements. First of all, the information lag observed in the evolution of the money supply and the general price level did not seem to be so important, as the New Classical theory claimed. To the extent that imperfect information about these two variables does exist and is a determining factor within the model, then everything economic agents need to do is get informed adequately, which can be done quite easily. Secondly, the New Classical theory did not produce very fortunate predictions of the monetary effects on interest rates, real wages and consumption. Moreover, the potential relationship – of the Phillips curve type – between monetary surprises and real economic activity disappeared completely during the 8th decade. Finally, the positive correlation between monetary shocks and output appears more obvious in the case of larger monetary aggregates and is weaker in the case of narrower monetary aggregates.

The direct consequence of these aspects is that the New Classicals' line of reasoning is deficient in what regards the importance and role of money within the business cycle. This flaw is not altogether justified, since the empirical arguments showing a correlation between money and real variables also seem a bit exaggerated. In other words, explaining the situations of short-term non-neutrality was a badly chosen priority for the New Classical economists. This is due to the fact that, according to empirical data, most observed correlations between the money supply and real variables in the economy can be attributed to endogenous shifts in the money supply – which are determined, in part, by public authorities' behaviour and, in part, by the functioning of the financial system itself. This shortcoming however, does not question the notable theoretical achievements of New Classical economists. From a methodological point of view, for instance, the New Classicals achieved the most important contributions in the application – within the general equilibrium framework – of modeling to macroeconomic analysis, the use of rational expectations as part of the modeling process, as well as the fundamental change of vision in what regards the evaluation of economic policies. One area where the equilibrium approach turned out to be very successful is the analysis of public authorities' fiscal policies[6]. Part of this research is carried out within the framework of Ricardo's equivalence theorem, which specifies under what terms the substitution of budgetary deficits by additional taxes has no effect whatsoever. Moreover, subsequent research revealed the real effects of public acquisitions and public services, or of other taxes with distorting effects.

Lucas' innovative contribution (1972) addressed a question almost as old as economic science: How do shifts in monetary policy influence inflation, production and unemployment? And even though the answer to this question is still subject to lively debates, there is however, an observation confirmed beyond doubt by empirical evidence: during expansions,

---

[5] Robert Barro – *Unanticipated Money Growth and Economic Activity in the United States*, *Money, Expectations and Business Cycles*, Academic Press, New York, 1981

[6] One of the economists that investigated this matter thoroughly is Robert Barro himself in "*The Neoclassical Approach to Fiscal Policy*", 1989, in Barro, Robert J.(ed) *Modern Business Cycle Theory,* Harvard University Press, 1989

the growth rate of monetary aggregates is above average, whereas in recessions, the growth rate is below average. Lucas' contribution is twofold: at the theoretical level, he formulated and analyzed a specific mechanism in which monetary instability leads to fluctuations in output and inflation rates. Within this mechanism, individuals – who possess limited information – identify monetary perturbations as shifts in relative prices, which leads to aggregate output fluctuations.

Lucas' model relies on the premise that individuals are more informed about the prices of the goods they produce than the price of the goods they purchase. Consequently, they tend to mistake movements in the general price level – which are irrelevant in the model – for movements in the relative prices – which are relevant to economic agents. In the case of unanticipated inflation, individuals infer that the relative prices of the goods they produce are temporarily high, and thus decide to increase output.

Lucas constructs his model within a framework initially developed by Paul Samuelson (Samuelson, 1958: pp.467-482) – where we find two generations of people, young and old, and only one commodity, which cannot be stored. In this stylized model, both current and future generations must find a way to transfer part of each period's output to the old generation. For the purpose of the analysis, Lucas is interested in another instrument that can perform the same function, namely money. In this situation, the old pay the money they possess in exchange for the goods they consume. The young, on the other hand, are willing to sell part of their production, with a view to buying goods from the future generations when they are old. In choosing the amount of output supplied, they will have to anticipate the value of money at the time they are old. And the value of money, in turn, depends on the next generation's decisions and thus, on their anticipations. This means that making rational decisions by the present generation implies anticipating the anticipations of others.

In this economy, the notion of equilibrium implies that the anticipations or forecasts of future prices coincide with the actual prices prevailing over the next period; in other words, equilibrium implies such a price and such a quantity of goods supplied, that the amount of money supplied by the old equals the amount of money that the young wish to possess in the future. The main feature of this market-clearing model is that monetary units have no effect on real variables, in other words, money is neutral.

Other types of monetary injections may or may not be neutral. Suppose, for instance, that the central bank decides to expand the money supply at a constant growth rate and does so by continuously giving the old generation money in a lump sum, that is, independently of the amount of money each of them possesses. Such an injection will naturally have inflationary effects, leading to a constant price increase. Lucas however, is looking for a framework in which a monetary expansion initially creates an increase in economic activity – as empirical evidence points out – but to this aim, the above mechanism is not satisfactory.

On the other hand, there are ways of injecting money which do not alter decisions on real variables, even though they generate continuous inflation. In the above example, if the old receive the money in proportion to the amount of money they possess, money is neutral, because this type of injection preserves the purchasing power that the young will have when they retire.

In order to ground his model on the information mechanism, Lucas assumes that transfers are proportional and therefore neutral at the real level; he constructs a model made up of two islands, each having the same number of old people. The number of the young people is fixed, but they are distributed randomly between the two islands. In addition, money supply is constant. On the island having few young people, prices will be high, since there are few producers, which will signal that they should produce more; conversely, on the island with many young people, prices will be low, which will make them produce less. In this economy, production is above average on one island and below average on the other. In this case, total output on the two islands fluctuates over time in line with the distribution of the young over the islands, but these fluctuations have no connection to the business cycle: one of the main features of business cycles is that all economic sectors have similar evolutions.

If we go on to add monetary perturbations, then an injection of money in the economy incurs a rise in prices. For a young person, this rise can have two possible explanations: (i) prices may be high due to monetary perturbations, in which case the optimal decision is to maintain current production levels or (ii) prices may be high due to the low number of producers, in which case the optimal decision is to increase production. If the producers do not know for sure, then the best decision is a tradeoff between the two extremes, so that production rises on the whole. Therefore, in this economy, prices exceed their average level precisely when production is above average, and when the money supply growth rate is above average. If the extent of the monetary perturbation is known, there are no reasons for confusion about the origin of the price increase and monetary perturbations are neutral. In other words, the model implies a clear distinction between anticipated monetary fluctuations – which are neutral – and unanticipated monetary fluctuations – which do influence real variables; and this is precisely the reason why the information mechanism plays the central role in the model.

Finally, Lucas' business cycle model has, at the same time, an important consequence at the policy level; in essence, this consequence is not new, it was initially formulated by Milton Friedman and it finds confirmation in Lucas' model; thus, starting from the implications of the model, the author argues that the best monetary policy rule is to fix an annual constant growth rate for money supply; this is to be accompanied by a series of rules regarding fiscal measures and public expenditure, but they are necessarily minimal rules. In a way, the best economic policy, in the New Classical view, is the absence of monetary policy.

There are several similarities between Lucas' model and the Austrian business cycle theory – starting with the monetary origin of the cycle – which require a comparative analysis of the two theories; some Austrian economists even argue that Hayek's theory represented the very source of inspiration for the New Classical model. Thus, in both Lucas' (1981) and Barro's (1981) approaches, as well as Mises' and Hayek's models, at the origin of the business cycle lie agents' difficulties in interpreting price signals. The similarity ends here though, since the two research programs are aimed at different goals: Hayek explains the business cycles in terms of the inconsistency of the numerous individual plans of producers; Lucas on the other hand, attempts to make predictions about the behaviour of the representative individual agent throughout the business cycle.

Generally speaking, the business cycle can be described in a manner that corresponds to both theories, but at the same time differentiates them from Keynesian or Marxist theories. The common denominator can be identified in the participants' reactions to a price change, whose origin may be of monetary, real, or combined origin. Even though the Austrians take into consideration the price of credit, whilst the New Classicals analyze the price of goods, the two theories converge to a common point: economic agents are not able to discern easily – that is costlessly – the real from the monetary component in the overall change.

In both theories, the way economic agents will react depends in the origin or cause of the change in prices: if this change reflects a change in economic circumstances, then a corresponding adjustment of real variables is required; if, on the contrary, the price change results from monetary perturbations, then such an adjustment is not only useless, but can also be harmful. However, until they determine the actual nature of price changes, agents will react – at least in part – as if it were real. If the price change has only monetary causes, agents will readjust their activities to their previous level, as soon as they realize the true cause. In this way, both schools admit the existence of significant systematic non-neutrality during the period the economy adjusts to the increased money supply.

One important difference between the two theories relates to the specific pattern of the business cycle mechanism; simply put, according to the New Classical School, agents' initial reaction consists of an increase in output and employment due to the increase in the nominal prices of goods. In the Austrian approach, agents are determined to start an unsustainable amount of investments in response to the artificially lowered interest rate. Once they learn the true nature of the price increase, agents either return to the initial level of employment – in the New Classical vision, or they liquidate the excess malinvestments – according to the Austrian theory.

Moreover, the two theories differ in the specific way they approach the concept of equilibrium. The New Classicals demonstrate that the cyclical evolution of the macroeconomic variables is consistent with the general equilibrium framework all throughout the business cycle. From a methodological point of view, the model complies with the market-clearing hypothesis: in order to be analyzed and interpreted, every phase of the cycle must be represented as a set of equilibrium prices and quantities.

The New Classicals' market-clearing approach is opposed to the Austrian model, which assumes that the business cycle is precisely a form of systematic intertemporal disequilibrium. In the Austrian approach, the very language used to describe the business cycle is that of disequilibrium, and the concept of equilibrium itself is defined against the initial conditions – prior to the expansion phase – and enables the analysis of the disequilibrium induced by cheap credit.

These are the main similarities and differences between the two models. There exists, indeed, a certain resemblance – even in what regards policy implications; however, this does not mean that we can label the Austrian theory as a source of inspiration for the New Classical model: not only do the two models differ in their approach, but, more importantly, in the methodological approach, which clearly distinguishes them.

To conclude, the first New Classical models tried to construct a monetary business cycle and to this goal, they somewhat departed from the Walrasian paradigm, by assuming imperfect information regarding prices. In this context, New Classical models postulate that supply depends upon the deviation of real inflation from its anticipated level, an assumption that Friedman and Phelps used in order to incorporate anticipations in the Phillips curve. Although this type of models generated a lot of interest in the `70s, more recently it has attracted very few supporters for reasons not altogether clear. Its opponents claim that the confusions about the price level cannot be so important as to generate the large shifts in output and employment observed over the business cycle. Moreover, empirical evidence generally infirmed the monetary models, but there is no firm proof to assert the reasons for its decline.

Barro (Barro, 1984: pp.179-182) asserts that this theory based on the rational expectations hypothesis, as well as the empirical research in the field have not offered a clear analysis in what regards either monetary non-neutrality, or business cycles in general. The main shortcomings of this theory arise in the attempt to explain monetary non-neutrality, which is the most important issue in macroeconomics and still triggers lively debates.

Real Business Cycle Theories

Once monetary models were abandoned in the `80's, most New Classical economists undertook several analyses that attribute cyclical fluctuations to certain real disturbances in the economy. These ***real business cycle theories*** (Long, Plosser, 1983; Barro, King, 1984; Prescott 1986) postulate that fluctuations in real economic activity are based on shocks, primarily in the existing technology – to this aim, they rely on the assumption that the rate of technological change is subject to large and random fluctuations. Since these technology fluctuations lead to fluctuations in relative prices, individuals rationally adjust their labor supply and consumption levels. Under these circumstances, the business cycle is nothing but the natural efficient response of the economy to the shifts in the existing production technology.

Just like the early New Classical models, RBC theories view cycles as arising in frictionless, perfectly competitive economies, subject to real shocks. RBC models demonstrate that, even in such environments, cycles can arise through the reactions of optimizing agents to real disturbances, such as random shifts in technology or productivity. Furthermore, such models are capable of accounting for the most important empirical observations displayed by business cycles. Thus, RBC theory has the merit of showing that fluctuations in economic activity are compatible with general equilibrium markets, in which all agents are rational maximizers. Coordination failures, price rigidity, monetary policy or psychological pressure are not in a position to explain business cycles. (Stadler, 1994)

The only forces that can trigger economic fluctuations, according to RBC theory, are those that affect the Walrasian equilibrium, that is, the set of prices and quantities that simultaneously equate supply and demand in all markets. Therefore, in order to understand real business cycle mechanisms, we must investigate the fundamental causes that influence the supply and demand for various goods and services. In principle, fluctuations can be triggered by numerous sorts of macroeconomic disturbances in real business cycle models. These include changes in public expenses, or in the investment tax credit, or even changes in the relative price of oil, for instance. Many of these disturbances are common to New Keynesian economics and to real business cycle models. The difference between the two schools however, lies in the mechanisms through which these disturbances work. Consider the case of a temporary increase in government purchases. Almost all macroeconomists agree that such a change causes an increase in output and employment, and the evidence, mainly from wartime experience, supports this prediction. Yet the explanations of this effect of government purchases differ greatly. Real business cycle theory emphasizes the intertemporal substitution of goods and leisure (Barro, 1987). It begins by pointing out that an increase in government purchases increases the demand for goods. To achieve equilibrium in the goods market, the real interest rate must rise, which reduces consumption and investment. The increase in the real interest rate also causes individuals to reallocate leisure across time. In particular, at a higher real interest rate, working today becomes relatively more attractive than working in the future; today's labor supply therefore increases. This increase in labor supply causes equilibrium levels of employment and output to rise. While Keynesian theory also predicts an increase in the real interest rate in response to a temporary increase in government purchases, the effect of the real interest rate on labor supply does not play a crucial role. Instead, the increase in employment and output is due to a reduction in the amount of labor unemployed or underutilized. In most Keynesian theory, the labor market is often characterized as being in a state of excess supply. In contrast, the Walrasian approach to real business cycle theory does not allow for the possibility of involuntary unemployment. Both real business cycle theory and Keynesian theory thus conclude that increases in government purchases increase output and employment. This example shows that some of the prominent implications of Keynesian models are also derived from intertemporal Walrasian models. Therefore, macroeconomists face a problem of approximate observational equivalence: many observed phenomena are consistent with both the classical and Keynesian paradigms.

In opposition to both the Keynesian models and the initial New Classical models, real business cycle theories subscribe to the classical dichotomy; first of all, they postulate the absolute irrelevance of monetary policy, thus rejecting a principle almost unanimously accepted at the end of the `70s; in addition, real business cycle theories do not assign nominal variables – such as money supply or the price level – any role in explaining fluctuations in real variables. In this manner, real business cycle theories push the Walrasian model further than any previous models.

Real business cycles are focused on technological shocks or other types of supply-side perturbations as central determinants of cyclical behavior and assign an important role to the dynamic elements that influence the pattern of shock propagation. As in all New Classical models, these models incorporate competitive markets and agents driven by optimizing behavior. And even though these theories ignore monetary shocks, the analysis of the propagation patterns of business cycle phases can be successfully applied to both real business cycle models and the initial monetary models. The difference is that in real models, any positive correlation between output and money supply reflect endogenous responses of monetary aggregates.

In what regards the empirical confirmation of these theories, the results are in many respects consistent with the observed patterns of business cycles, according to Robert Barro (1984). For instance, real business cycle theories are able to explain accurately the relative variations of consumption, investment, capital stocks and labor in the economy, and at the same time, to account for the pro-cyclical behavior of these variables. However, they tend to exaggerate the pro-cyclical evolution of productivity, real interest rates and real wages.

The evolution of RBC theory is notable for its emphasis on the microeconomic foundations of macro analysis: this implies that economic fluctuations are the outcome of maximizing decisions made by many individual agents. To obtain aggregates, we need to sum up the decision outcomes of the individual players, and provide a solution that makes those decisions consistent. Generally, RBC models exhibit the following features: i) they adopt a representative agent framework, focusing on a representative firm and household, and in this manner, the models avoid aggregation difficulties; ii) firms and households strive to optimize well-defined objective functions, subject to the resource and technology constraints that they face; iii) the cycle is driven by exogenous shocks to technology that shift production functions up or down. The impact of these shocks on output is amplified by the intertemporal substitution of leisure – a rise in productivity raises the cost of leisure, causing the unemployment rate to decrease; iv) all agents form rational expectations and there is continuous market clearing. Models encompass complete markets and no information asymmetries; v) actual cycles are generated by a propagation mechanism for the effects of shocks. This can take several forms. Firstly, agents generally try to even out consumption over time, so that a rise in output will manifest itself partly as a rise in investment and in the capital stock. Secondly, lags in the investment process can result in a shock today, which affects future investment, and thus, future output. Thirdly, individuals will tend to substitute leisure intertemporally in response to temporary shifts in wages – they will work more when wages are temporarily higher and they will prefer more leisure when wages fall to their initial level. Finally, firms may resort to stocks to meet unexpected changes in demand. If these are exhausted, then, if firms are confronted with rising marginal costs, these inventories will tend to be replenished only gradually, causing output to rise for several periods. The first propagation mechanism is likely to be weak; most RBC models focus on the second and third propagation mechanisms (Fischer, 1988). The intertemporal substitution mechanism is also likely to be weak. Most innovations in technology are regarded as long-lasting or even permanent, raising the real wage permanently. This is unlikely to cause a large labor supply response, because the substitution effect of the higher wage will probably be offset by the income effect. Significant intertemporal substitution is only likely to occur in response to temporary shocks. However, to fit the data, RBC models assume that most technology innovations are highly persistent.

In order to explain recessions in real business cycle theories, we must admit the existence of technological or some other type of shocks on the supply of goods, in both directions, either positive or negative. In this context, critics of these theories claim that technological regress is not possible, a statement which is easily opposable. Apart from technological shocks, other circumstances able to generate negative shocks on output include the cartelization of markets, failure of crops or strikes. The collapse of the financial system in the US during the Great Depression may also be regarded as a negative shock.

The initial versions of real business cycle theories reflect the Pareto optimum and demonstrate that economic fluctuations do not justify state intervention through stabilization policies. Negative shocks and recessions are merely unfortunate or unfavorable events and public authorities cannot do anything to correct the situation.

We have seen that one important strength of RBC theories is their firm grounding on microeconomic principles. Real business cycle models are usually standard intertemporal models of general equilibrium, traditionally used in the analysis of economic growth and adapted only slightly to incorporate random changes in technology.

In a study of real business cycle theories, Mankiw (1989) asserts that a lot of the New Classical initial contributions tried to break down the classical dichotomy, without abandoning the fundamental market-clearing hypothesis (Lucas, 1973). These models – whose central element is the assumption of imperfect information regarding prices – exerted a real fascination in the `80s, but attracted relatively few adepts later on. The main reason identified by Mankiw: it is hard to believe that agents' confusions regarding prices are strong enough to generate the large fluctuations of real variables identified during business cycles.

According to some authors, real business cycle models do not provide an empirically plausible explanation for economic fluctuations, since they rely on unrealistic assumptions; in this context, the reliance on large technological disturbances as the main source of fluctuations and on the intertemporal substitution of leisure to explain changes in employment are seen as fundamental weaknesses. Moreover, to the extent that it trivializes the social cost of observed fluctuations, real business cycle theory is potentially dangerous. The danger is that those who advise policy-makers might attempt to use it to assess the effects of alternative macroeconomic policies or to conclude that macroeconomic policies are unnecessary.

In evaluating the validity of RBC theory, two main questions emerge: How can we account for such large fluctuations in production and employment? and Why do changes in some nominal variables – such as the money supply – seem to be connected to the movements in real variables?

According to real business cycle theory, the only forces triggering fluctuations are those affecting Walrasian equilibrium – namely the set of relative prices and quantities that equate demand and supply on all markets at the same time. Consequently, in order to understand the business cycle mechanism, we must analyze the fundamental factors influencing demand and supply for different categories of goods and services. In real models, fluctuations seem to be generated, in principle, by numerous types of macroeconomic disturbances, but the technological type is the most common.

One of the obvious empirical observations that RBC theory had to account for is that during the economic cycle, consumption and leisure move in opposite directions: when recession starts, consumption decreases and leisure increases, and the other way round, during the expansion phase. The explanation appeared rather problematic for real business cycle theorists: consumption and leisure should – at least in principle – move in the same direction, since both are normal goods. In these circumstances, the New Classicals tried to explain why during recessions, individuals find it rational to increase leisure and at the same time reduce their demand for goods: the price of leisure relative to goods – namely the real wage – decreases during recessions. In this way, an essential implication of real business cycle theories is the pro-cyclical evolution of real wages.

In the event that the production function remained unchanged and at the origin of fluctuations lay demand shocks, then generating the implication of a pro-cyclical wage would pose serious problems. Since employment is low during recessions, we would expect the marginal product of labor and the real wage – to be high; in the situation of a constant production function, decreasing marginal returns of labor would generate a counter-cyclical real wage – as is necessary to explain fluctuations in consumption and leisure.

Under these circumstances, the New Classicals start from the premise that in the rate of technological change there exist substantial fluctuations. During the recession, the available production technology is relatively unfavorable; also the marginal product of labor and, implicitly, the real wage, are low. In response, individuals choose to reduce consumption and increase leisure.

An interesting conclusion of this type of models is that – since economic fluctuations represent a disruption in Walrasian equilibrium – these fluctuations are actually characterized by efficiency. In equilibrium, when technological possibilities and preferences are given, the levels of employment, output and consumption cannot be improved. At the same time, public authorities' attempts to influence allocation processes on private markets – such as employment stabilization policies – are, at best, inefficient, or even harmful, since they obstruct the "invisible hand" mechanism.

Of all the implications of real business cycle theories, the „optimality" of fluctuations is probably the most astonishing: there is no doubt that during a recession, the level of welfare decreases compared to the preceding expansion. Keynesian theories explain the reduction in welfare as a coordination failure: since wages and prices do not adjust instantly to equilibrate supply and demand, some mutually advantageous exchanges do not take place during recessions. By contrast, the real business cycle theories reject this hypothesis, by motivating the decline in welfare through a decline in the technological capacities of the society.

RBC theories' supporters rely on the premise that employment fluctuations are entirely voluntary, in other words, that the economy is at all times positioned on the labor supply curve. However, throughout the business cycle, employment varies substantially, whereas labor supply determinants – the real wage and the real interest rate – fluctuate only slightly. To comply with this observation, real business cycle models bring forward the premise of individuals' inclination towards an intertemporal reallocation of leisure. Under these circumstances, individuals will substantially reduce labor supply in response to small and temporary reductions in the real wage or the real interest rate. This hypothesis however, is not feasible, since empirical evidence documents a low inclination of individuals to substitute leisure in time. If leisure had a high degree of substitutability – as assumed by the real business cycle models – then individuals who anticipate a real wage increase should work less now and more in the future and the other way round when anticipating a real wage decrease. But studies on individual labor supply show that anticipated shifts in the real wage only lead to small shifts in the amount of labor supplied: individuals do not react to anticipated shifts in real wages through a substantial reallocation of leisure in time (Ball, 1985; Altonji, 1986).

Real business cycle theories contrast strongly to the consensual vision of the `60s on a series of assumptions still extremely controversial in our days. First of all, the theory relies on the premise that the economy experiences sudden and large shifts in the existing production technologies. Many such models regard recessions as periods of technological regress, declines in the technological abilities in society. Their opponents[7] argue that the assumption of large shifts in technology – particularly in what regards technological regress – is not plausible; on the contrary, they assert that knowledge accumulation and technological progress usually occur gradually. Secondly, real business cycle theories assume that employment fluctuations reflect shifts in the amount of labor that individuals are willing to supply. Since employment varies considerably, whereas the real wage and the real interest rate vary only slightly, these models require that leisure be highly substitutable in time. This hypothesis is inconsistent with numerous econometric studies of labor supply, which evidence a low elasticity of intertemporal substitution during recessions; moreover, it is also inconsistent with economists' belief that high unemployment during recessions is to a large extent involuntary. Thirdly, real business cycle theory assumes that monetary policy is irrelevant in alleviating economic fluctuations. Prior to its formulation in the early `80s, most economists agreed on the non-neutrality of money; and even though the ability of systematic monetary policy was a controversial issue, it was, at the same time, generally acknowledged that an inadequate monetary policy can destabilize the economy. In this context, real cycle theorists brought up a new challenge, by using the old Keynesian argument that any correlation between money supply and output derive from the fact that money supply is an endogenous factor.

The opponents of the theory have at the same time proved skeptical to the possibility that aggregate real shocks might have such a large amplitude and frequency to trigger and account

[7] Most notably N. Gregory Mankiw and L. Summers.

for economic cycles. In this respect, they posit that concrete examples are limited to the oil shocks and harvest failures, but subsequent empirical research demonstrate that a large dispersion of shifts in preferences and technology can lead to persistent significant effects on aggregate output and employment (Lilien, 1982). On the whole, this research points out that real cycle theories are capable of explaining sudden fluctuations in real economic activity and the tendency of rising unemployment starting with the `70s.

Another important objection to real business cycle theories is that they do not address the link between monetary and real variables appropriately (Barro, 1984). According to Barro, during the `30s, the main empirical association between monetary aggregates and real variables derives not from the shifts in the monetary base, but rather from fluctuations in the volume of financial intermediation, namely the volume of loans and deposits. A reduction in the volume of financial intermediation is not, in essence, different from shocks on the production function, in that it may have adverse real consequences on the economy; therefore, the issue to be solved does not concern the reason why these crises had serious consequences on production and employment; rather, we need to find an explanation for the reason why occasional crises occurred during that period. Even for the post-war period, a lot of empirical data suggest that the link between money and real economic activity reflects fluctuations in the aggregate volume of loans and deposits, and not the monetary base. Under these circumstances, money appears more of an indicator of shifts in the business climate rather than an exogenous factor with major influence on real variables. However, statistical data on the interaction between the monetary base and the real variables suggest certain monetary non-neutrality which requires further explanation. Thus, this type of connection between real and monetary variables is consistent with those rational expectations models focusing on the role of incomplete information on prices and money, and therefore it could be accounted for on this basis. A strong supporter of monetary neutrality, Barro asserts that by judging in such a manner, we could actually solve this puzzle of neutrality: thus, on the one hand, many of the empirical associations between real variables and money do not represent in themselves proofs of monetary non-neutrality and on the other hand, the remaining circumstances considered as examples of monetary non-neutrality can be explained by existing theories.

In approaching the business cycle mechanism, real models usually take into account technological changes at the macroeconomic scale, as if these occurred in a single sector. There are however, theories focusing on the technological shifts occurring in several sectors (Long and Plosser, 1983). All these models rely on an essential premise: even though shocks on different sectors are independent, the outputs of these sectors evolve together throughout the cycle. For instance, a negative shock on a sector will reduce the level of welfare for all individuals, which will incur a demand decrease for all the goods in the economy.

Theoretical research of multi-sector models has revealed a very interesting premise: in order for these models to function, it is essential that the number of independent sectoral shocks be relatively low, and those sectors be subject to large technological fluctuations; if the number of sectors is large and labor is mobile between sectors, the aggregate effect is almost null. Thus, multi-sector models are similar to one-sector models and in addition, experience the same weaknesses: lack of any direct empirical evidence attesting the existence of large technological shifts, as well as lack of feasibility of the strong substitutability of leisure in time.

Finally, another multi-sector approach of the business cycle is the *sectoral shifts theory*, which focuses on the cost of labor adjustment across different sectors of the economy (Lilien,

1982; Black, 1987). Similar to real business cycle theory, the sectoral shifts theory observes the classical dichotomy, by ignoring the role of monetary perturbations; but unlike real business cycle theory, it departs to a certain extent from the Walrasian paradigm, by assuming that when workers move from one sector to another, a certain period of unemployment is inherent, while they are searching for new jobs. According to this theory, recessions are periods in which sectoral shocks are more numerous than usual, and as a consequence, a larger sectoral adjustment is required.

This real business cycle type of models seems more plausible than those based on substantial shocks of aggregate productivity and on intertemporal substitution. In this respect, the assumption that recessions require an inter-sectoral re-allocation drastically seems more realistic than that of recessions being the result of a major technological regress, which renders leisure completely unattractive.

Numerous empirical studies are carried out at present in order to confirm the validity of this theory, but the available data do not seem to support the sectoral shifts theory. To the extent that during recessions we are confronted with voluntary unemployment caused by the transfer of labor to other sectors, we would expect to see high unemployment in some sectors of the economy and excess labor demand in other sectors. But in real economies, fluctuations occur in a completely different manner: the rise in unemployment in some sectors is not accompanied by vacant jobs in others (Katz, 1986). Moreover, even though the sectoral shifts theory asserts that workers move between sectors during recessions, empirical studies point out that their movement is pro-cyclical (Murphy, Topel, 1987). All these empirical findings suggest that a plausible reconciliation between economic realities and the theory of sectoral adjustment is rather unlikely. The supporters of the theory argue that this kind of empirical evidence is not convincing. Since the sectoral adjustment process implies a period of high unemployment and low income, there exists the possibility of a demand decrease in all sectors of the economy. Thus, it is possible to notice high unemployment in some sectors and, at the same time, few available jobs in others, despite the fact that initially, the recession was caused by the necessity of labor re-allocation between sectors. To the extent that we admit the validity of this argument, it becomes unclear how we can distinguish empirically the real business cycle theories – which focus on technological fluctuations at the macroeconomic level – from Keynesian theories – which bring forward fluctuations in aggregate demand.

Conclusion

The recent global crisis has once again questioned economists' ability to explain the business cycle mechanism and to provide policy solutions to economic crises. Considerable theoretical progress has been made within the main research paradigms; on the whole, the New Classical economists analyze the business cycle within the market-clearing model, while the New Keynesians attribute business fluctuations to various market failures and the Austrian economists analyze the cycle in terms of intertemporal disequilibrium. Ever since the onset of the recent crisis, monetary business cycle theories have started to regain their relevance and timeliness in explaining business fluctuations. According to these theories, it is monetary mismanagement that lies at the bottom of macroeconomic dysfunctions in the intertemporal allocation of resources. Recent empirical studies point out that in many

European countries, the current global crisis was also triggered by artificially low interest rates and credit expansion – either investment credit, or consumer credit.

In what regards real business cycle theories, we can conclude that these theories have generated a new perspective and novel techniques for modeling the macroeconomic area and for constructing economic policy. However, it is not yet very clear to what extent these theories contribute to an effective understanding of the business cycle mechanism or to the formulation of economic policy.

Despite considerable progress during the past four decades, business cycle research has had little impact on economic policies to stop recessions. At the theoretical level, monetary business cycles do provide a feasible explanation for the causation of the business cycle; as to the practical implications, monetary theories postulate that the best policy is the absence of economic policy. At the empirical level, we find that statistical data also support monetary business cycle mechanisms. As to economic policy measures, the mainstream view still approaches the discretionary, fine-tuning policy, focused on fiscal activism. Despite the theoretical progress, economists have not substantially changed the way they formulate economic policy. Instead of holding on to outdated policy prescriptions, they should be more innovative in their thinking, address the causes of the business cycle and correlate them with the proposed remedies.

References

Altonji, Joseph G., (1994). Intertemporal Substitution in Labor Supply: Evidence from Micro Data, *Journal of Political Economy*, June, part 2: Hoover Institution Labor Conference (Jun., 1986), S176-S215.

Abraham, K., Katz, L., (1986). Cyclical Unemployment: Sectoral Shifts or Aggregate Disturbances?" *Journal of Political Economy*, 1986, 94 (3), 507 - 522

Ball, L., (1985). *Intertemporal Substitution and Constraints on Labor Supply: Evidence from Panel Data*, manuscript, MIT Press.

Ball, L., Romer, D., (1987). Are Prices Too Sticky?, *Working Paper 2171*, NBER, Febr.

Ball, L., Romer, D., (1990). Real Rigidities and the Non-Neutrality of Money, *Review of Economic Studies*, April, no.57, 183-203.

Barro, R. J., (1976). Rational Expectations and the Role of Monetary Policy, *Journal of Monetary Economics*, vol. 2(1), 1-32.

Barro, R. J., Rush, M., (1980). Unanticipated Money Growth and Economic Activity, NBER Chapters, in: *Rational Expectations and Economic Policy,* National Bureau of Economic Research, Inc., 23-73.

Barro, R. J., (1984). Rational Expectations and Macroeconomics in 1984, *AEA Papers and Proceedings*, vol.74, nr.2, May, 179-182.

Barro, R. J., (1987). *Macroeconomics*, John Wesley & Sons, New York.

Barro, R. J., (1989). New Classicals and New Keynesians, or the Good Guys and the Bad Guys, *Swiss Journal of Economics and Statistics (SJES),* Swiss Society of Economics and Statistics (SSES), 125 (III), 263-273.

Barro, R. J.(ed) (1989). *Modern Business Cycle Theory,* Harvard University Press,

Beaud, M., Dostaler, G., (2000).*Gândirea economică de după Keynes*, Ed. Eurosong& Book, Bucureşti.

Black, F. (1987). *Business cycles and equilibrium*. New York: Basil Blackwell

Blanchard, O. J., (1982). Price Desynchronization and Price Level Inertia, *NBER Working Paper no.900*, June, 3-24.

Blanchard, O. J., (2000). What Do We Know About Macroeconomics that Fisher and Wicksell Did Not?, *The Quarterly Journal of Economics,* Vol. 115, No. 4, Nov., 1375-1409.

Dobrescu, M., (2004). New foundations for Economic Policy, *Oeconomica*, Romanian Economic Society, 4, 103-144.

Dobrescu, M., (2006). *Tendinţe, curente şi şcoli de gândire în ştiinţa economic actuală*, Bucharest, Ed.ASE.

Dobrescu E. M., Dobrescu (Tarţa), M.,Nuţu L., (2007). Some considerations on the NAIRU hypothesis, *Economy, Society, Civilization*, ASE Publishing House, Bucharest.

Dobrescu, M., Paicu, C. (2012). New approaches to business cycle theory in current economic science, *Theoretical and Applied Economics,* No. 7 / 2012 (572), 147 – 160.

Dobrescu, M., (2012). The New Keynesian Approach to Business Cycle Theory: Nominal and Real Rigidities, *International Journal of Economic Practices and Theories*, Vol. 2, No. 1, 13-22.

Friedman, B. M., (1983). Recent Perspectives in and on Macroeconomics, *NBER Working Paper* no.1208, Sept.

Friedman, M., (1968). The Role of Monetary Policy, *American Economic Review*, no. 58, 1 – 17.

Friedman, M., (1973). Perspectives on Inflation, *Newsweek*, 24 June.

Friedman, M., (1977). Nobel Lecture: Inflation and Unemployment, *Journal of Political Economy*, vol.85, no.3, 451-472.

Greenwald, B., Stiglitz, J. E., (1987). Keynesian, New Keynesian and New Classical Economics, *Oxford Economic Papers* 39, 119-132.

Kydland, F., Prescott, E., (1977). Rules Rather than Discretion: The Inconsistency of Optimal Plans, *Journal of Political Economy,* June, 85, 777-93.

Hall, R. E. (1989). A Framework for Studying Monetary Non-Neutrality, *NBER Working Paper* no. 3145, Oct.

Lilien, D. M., (1982).Sectoral Shifts and Cyclical Unemployment, *Journal of Political Economy*, no.90 (4), 1982, 777 – 793.

Long, J. B., Jr., Plosser, Ch. L., (1983). Real Business Cycles, *Journal of Political Economy*, Febr., vol. 91, 39-69.

Lucas, R. E.,Jr. (1972). Expectations and the Neutrality of Money, *Journal of Economic Theory*. no.4, 103-124.

Lucas, R. E.,Jr. (1973). Some International Evidence on the Output-Inflation Trade-off. *American Economic Review*, 63(3), 326-334.

Lucas, R. E., Jr. (1976). Econometric Policy Evaluation: A Critique, *J. Money. Econ., Suppl. Series*, I, 19-46, 62.

Lucas, R. E, Jr., (1980). Methods and Problems in Business Cycle Theory. *Journal of Money, Credit and Banking*, Blackwell Publishing, 12(4), 696-715.

Lucas, Robert Jr. (1986). Principles of fiscal and monetary policy, *Journal of Monetary Economics*, 17(1), 117-134.

Lucas, R. E., Jr. (1996). Nobel Lecture: Monetary Neutrality. *Journal of Political Economy*, vol.104, no4, 661-682.

Mankiw, N. G., (1988). Recent Developments in Macroeconomics: A Very Quick Refresher Course, *Journal of Money, Credit and Banking*, Aug, Part.2, 436 – 449.

Mankiw, N. G., (1989). Real Business Cycles: A New Keyensian Perspective, *Journal of Economic Perspectives*, vol.3, no.3, 79-90.

Mankiw, N.G., (1990). A Quick Refresher Course in Macroeconomics, *Journal of Economic Literature*, 28, 1645-1660.

Murphy, K., Topel, R., (1987). The Evolution of Unemployment in the United States 1968-1985, *NBER Macroeconomics Annual*, 2, p.11-58.

Muth, J. F. (1961). Rational Expectations and the Theory of Price Movements, *Econometrica*, Vol. 29, No. 3. (Jul., 1961), 315-335.

O'Driscoll, G. P., Shenoy S. R., (1976). *Inflation, Recession, and Stagflation. The Foundations of Modern Austrian Economics*. Edwin G. Dolan, ed., Kansas City: Sheed and Ward, 185–211

Phelps, E. S., (1968). Money-Wage Dynamics and Labor Market Equilibrium, *Journal of Political Economy*, 1968, no.76, 678 – 711.

Phelps, E. S., (1970). *The New Microeconomics in Employment and Inflation Theory,* New York, Norton.

Reynolds, M. O., (2010). The Poverty of Modern Macroeconomic Theory and Power of Austrian Business Cycle Theory, *Quarterly Journal of Austrian Economics,* 13 (3), 11-41.

Samuelson, P., (1958). An Exact Consumption-Loan Model of Interest with or without the Contrivance of Money, *Journal of Political Economy*, December, no. 66 (6), 467-482.

Sargent, Th. J., Wallace, N. (1975). "Rational" Expectations, the Optimal Monetary Instrument, and the Optimal Money Supply Rule, *The Journal of Political Economy*, Vol. 83, No. 2. (Apr.), pp. 241-254.

Stadler, G. W., (1994). Real Business Cycles, *Journal of Economics Literature* Vol. XXXII, December 1994, 1750-1783

In: Business Cycles in Economics
Editor: Jason C. Hsu

ISBN: 978-1-63321-322-7

Chapter 4

TECHNOLOGY AND BUSINESS CYCLES IN THE US (1957-2006): A SCHUMPETERIAN APPROACH

Konstantinos N. Konstantakis and Panayotis G. Michaelides*
National Technical University of Athens, Athens, Greece

Abstract

The purpose of this chapter is to deal with questions of instability and economic crisis, deriving theoretical arguments from Schumpeter's works and presenting relevant empirical evidence for the case of the US economy for the time period 1957-2011 which includes the recent recession.

More precisely, we make an attempt to interpret the economic fluctuations in the US economy and find causal relationships between the crucial variables such as Technology, dictated by Schumpeterian theory.

In this context, a number of relevant techniques have been used, such as de-trending, cointegration analysis, white noise tests, periodograms, cross-correlations and Granger causality tests. Our findings seem to give credit to certain aspects of the Schumpeterian theory of economic crises.

The paper contributes to the literature in the sense that it introduces a relevant methodological framework building on Schumpeterian crisis theory. The results are discussed in a broader context, related to the US economy, as a whole.

Keywords: Business Cycles, technology, US, Schumpeter

Introduction

In this paper, we are dealing with questions of instability and economic crises, deriving arguments from Schumpeterian theory and presenting relevant empirical evidence for the case of the US economy in the time period 1957-2006, based on relevant quantitative techniques.

* E-mail address: pmichael@central.ntua.gr; Tel: 302107721624; Fax: +302107721618; Address: Laboratory of Theoretical and Applied Economics, School of Applied Mathematics and Physics, National Technical University of Athens, Greece, Heroon Polytechneiou 9, 157.80, Zografou Campus (Corresponding author: Panayotis G. Michaelides. Assistant Professor of *Economics*).

In the Schumpeterian tradition a crisis is the by-product of innovative activity which can create long waves that are caused by the clustering of innovations. Schumpeter conceptualized business cycles as disturbances in the equilibrium and a return to a new equilibrium point which gives the process a cyclical character. The paper investigates how technological change affects indicators of economic activity, such as Rand D expenses and output in the US economy for the period 1958-2006. The "business cycle component" is regarded as the movement in the time series that exhibits periodicity within a certain range of time duration. This approach is based on Burns and Mitchell (1946) and the National Bureau of Economic Research (NBER) arguing that business cycles are characterized by the "turning point" which indicates, roughly speaking, the beginning of an expansionary period at the end of a recession. Another popular approach regards business cycles as fluctuations around a trend, the so-called "deviation cycles".

Previous Literature

Schumpeter defined economic development as "such changes in economic life as are not forced upon it from without but arise by its own initiative, from within" (Schumpeter 1912, 63). It was a phenomenon foreign to what might be observed in the circular flow or in the tendency towards equilibrium (*ibid*, 64).

It involved spontaneous and discontinuous change in the channels of flow, disturbance of equilibrium, which forever altered and displaced the equilibrium state previously existing.

According to Schumpeter, economic development is accompanied by growth; however quantitative growth does not constitute development *per se*.

In practice, economic systems do not achieve equilibrium. They just move into "neighborhoods of equilibrium [...] in which the system approaches a state which would, if reached, fulfill equilibrium conditions" (Schumpeter 1936, 45). In fact, in his *Business Cycles* Schumpeter (1939, 106) emphasized that major innovations are introduced around the neighborhood of equilibrium given that conditions are ideal.

For Schumpeter economic development is the result of innovation, i.e., "the outstanding fact in the economic history of capitalist society" (Schumpeter 1939, 61). For him, innovation is the leading force in what he calls "evolution". Economic evolution is however discontinuous because of a discontinuity in the introduction of major innovations into the economic system.[1]

"[The] historic and irreversible changes in the way of doing things we call "innovation" and we define: innovations are changes in production functions which cannot be decomposed into infinitesimal steps. [...] *The kind of wave-like movement, which we call the business cycle, is incident to industrial change and would be impossible in an economic world displaying nothing except unchanging repetition of the productive and consumptive process*" (Schumpeter 1935, 4; emphasis added).

Schumpeter conceptualized fluctuations as disturbances in the equilibrium and a return to a new equilibrium point which gives the process its cyclical character. All economic systems have an esoteric tendency towards equilibrium and move toward these "neighborhoods" after

[1] However, Schumpeter's concept of innovation was different than what is generally assumed because he stressed that innovation per se is not a force in economic development. Rather, the real force in economic development is the consequences of these innovations (Schumpeter 1928).

the disruptions have exhausted themselves. The most important characteristic of these "neighbour-hoods" is that conditions are stable (Schumpeter 1912, 214).

Technological change expresses various kinds of knowledge that can make it possible to produce (i) a qualitatively superior output (or even a completely new output) or (ii) a greater volume of output (Rosenberg 1982, p.3). The majority of studies and essays on technological change regard it only as a cost reducing-phenomenon, which introduces new processes that reduce the total cost while the product remains unchangeable. However, following the same author (Rosenberg 1982, p. 4), "to ignore product innovation and qualitative improvements in products is to ignore what may very well have been the most important long-term contribution of technical progress to human welfare".

After World War II, as we know, the recognition of the crucial role of technological change in economic growth has its roots in the work of Abramovitz (1956) and Solow (1957), who were probably the first to quantify the contribution of technological progress in the growth of the US economy. The authors found that only a portion of the growth in the American output was the result of an increase in capital and labor, while a large part of it remained unexplained, the so-called, "residual". In that context, Solow (1956, 1957) suggested using an exogenous factor, called "technological change".

The econometric studies by Denison (1962a, 1962b, 1967), and Denison and Chung (1976), estimated that the components of the residual were the advances in knowledge and the role of economies of scale. However, these studies did not manage to come to realistic conclusions, and after some other studies had been conducted by Griliches (1957), Parker and Klein (1966), Parker (1967) leading to similar results, the assumption of the exogenous nature of technological change was serious questioned.

A new series of articles by Johansen (1959), Solow (1960) and Nelson (1964), treated technological change as endogenous, embodied in new techno-logical goods. Improvements to these articles came through the works of Kaldor and Mirlees (1962), and Arrow (1962) and were extended by Uzawa (1965), Phelps (1966), Shell (1967), and Gomulka (1970, 1971).

As far the literature relating technological progress and innovation at the firm level is concerned, the seminal studies trying to test empirically this relation, were those of Horowitz (1963), Hamberg (1964), Mansfield (1964), Scherer (1965a,b), Comanor (1967), Philips (1971), Malecki (1980), Link (1980), Meisel and Lin (1983), Scherer (1984) and others.

Relatively recently, some new efforts by Romer (1986), Lucas (1988) and Scott (1989) who treat technology as "internal' to the firm, have taken place. Accordingly, the articles by Romer (1990), Grossman and Helpman (1991), Aghion and Howitt (1992) argue that firms buy their innovations from the technological sector. On the other hand, a series of studies outside the neo-classical view made an effort to explain the differences in economic growth among nations. These approaches follow Gerschenkron (1962), Ohkawa and Rosovsky (1973) and suggest that new institutions should be developed in order to enable nations to increase their growth potential and reduce the great inequality observed among nations (Abramovitz 1986, 1994, Nelson 1993 and Lundvall 1992).

In this work, we deal with questions of causality in business cycle theory deriving theoretical arguments from Schumpeter's work who conceptualized business cycles as disturbances in the equilibrium due to the introduction of technological changes and a return to a new equilibrium point. The adjustment of the economic system after the introduction of innovations cannot take place smoothly and fluctuations rise.

Methodology

The main purpose of this section is to test the Schumpeterian business cycles theory using modern econometric techniques. In specific, we provide a framework under which the investigation of business cycles is examined in the context developed by Joseph Schumpeter.

Stationarity Test

According to Schumpeterian tradition, business cycles are perceived as deviations from an equilibrium point towards a new one. In order to identify this deviation we first need to know whether the data at hand are stationary or not. First, we examine the stationarity characteristics of each time series. If the results suggest that a time series is not stationary then de-trending is highly recommended. As we know, there are several ways to test for the existence of a unit root. In this paper, we use the popular Augmented Dickey-Fuller (ADF) methodology (Dickey and Fuller, 1979). The ADF test is based on the following regression:

$$\Delta Y_t = \alpha + bt + \rho Y_{t-1} + \sum_{i=1}^{m} \gamma_t \Delta Y_{t-1} + \varepsilon_\tau$$

where Δ is the first difference operator, t the time and ε the error term:

(a) if $b \neq 0$ and $-1<\rho<0$ implies a trend stationary model;
(b) if $b=0$ and $-1<\rho<0$ implies an ARMA Box/Jenkins class of models;
(c) if $b= 0$ and $\rho= 0$ implies a difference stationary model where Y variable is integrated of degree one I(1). If we assume that the cyclical component is stationary, the secular component has a unit root and Y follows a random walk process, i.e., it revolves around the zero value in a random way (Heyman and Sobel, 2004, p. 263); furthermore, if $a \neq 0$ Y follows a random walk process with a drift.

The trend is important for the propagation of shocks (Nelson and Plosser, 1982). De-trending is highly recommended and the estimated residuals constitute the de-trended data series.

Filtering

. In this paper, we use the Hodrick - Prescott (HP) filter because of its widespread acceptance in the literature (see, for instance, Montoya and de Haan (2008), Danthine and Girardin (1989), Danthine and Donaldson (1993), Blackburn and Ravn (1992), Backus and Kehoe (1992), Dimelis et al. (1992), Fiorito and Kollintzas (1994), Christodoulakis et al. 1998, Dickerson et al. 1998)[2], especially in extracting the business cycles component.

[2]Of course, HP filtering has some shortcomings, as well. See Harvey and Jaeger (1993), King and Rebelo (1993), Cogley and Nason (1995) and Billmeier (2004).

The robustness of the HP de-trending method is confirmed, among others, by Artis and Zhang (1997) and Dickerson et al. (1998). The parameter used for annual data is equal to λ=100 (Hodrick and Prescott, 1997; Kydland and Prescott, 1990).

The trend is obtained by minimizing the fluctuations of the actual data around it, i.e., by minimizing the following function:

$$\Sigma[\text{In } y\,(t) - \text{In } y^*\,(\text{t})]2 - \lambda\Sigma\,[[\text{In } y^*\,(t+1) - \text{In } y^*\,(t)] - [\text{In } y^*\,(t) - \text{In } y^*\,(t-1)]]^2$$

where y* is the long-term trend of the variable y and the coefficient λ>0 deter-mines the smoothness of the long-term trend.

White Noise Test

Testing for white noise in our stationary time series is the next step of our econometric methodology. The significance of white noise testing lies in the fact that if our de-trended i.e., business cycle data proved to be white noise then the argument that the data follow certain patterns - that could be attributed to a number of factors such as technology in the Schumpeterian theory - is invalid. In fact, if the data is white noise then our time series could be described as a random walk process. On the other hand, if the null hypothesis of white noise for our data is rejected then our time series is not a random walk and follows some distinctive pattern, possibly affected by technology in a Schumepetrian spirit.

In technical terms, white noise is a data generating process where auto-correlation is zero between lagged versions of the signal (except when the lag is zero). White noise does not permit any temporal dependence and so its auto-covariance function is trivially equal to zero for the various lags. The sample autocorrelation function measures how a time series is correlated with its own past history. In order to test for autocorrelation (AC), we use the Ljung and Box (1978) test (Q-Stat) which practically tests the null hypothesis of white noise for a maximum lag length k. The alternative hypothesis is that at least one of these ACs is non-zero, so that the series is not white noise. The sample AC function measures how a time series is correlated with its own past history; in order to test for AC we use the Ljung and Box (1978) test (Q-Stat) which practically tests the null hypothesis of white noise for a maximum lag length k:

$$Q = n(n+2)\sum_{j-1}^{h}\frac{\hat{p}_j^2}{n-1}$$

where n is the sample size, $\hat{p}_j$ the sample AC at lag j, and h the number of lags being tested; for significance level a, the critical region for rejection of the hypothesis of randomness is $Q > \chi^2_{1-a,h}$ is the a-quantile of the chi-squared distribution with h degrees of freedom; the alternative hypothesis is that at least one of these ACs is non-zero, so that the series is not white noise. In case the null hypothesis is rejected, then the underlying time series is not white noise and can be considered a cycle.In case we are dealing with a trending time series, then we study and test not the raw series but its deviations from trend, i.e., the residuals from which sample ACs can be computed. As we know, white noise does not permit any temporal dependence and so its auto-covariance function is trivially equal to zero for the various lags. The sample AC function measures how a time series is correlated with its own past history. Its graphical illustration is the correlogram.

Spectral Analysis

Schumpeter conceptualized business cycles as disturbances in the equilibrium and a return to a new equilibrium point which gives the process a periodic character. Thus, from an econometric perspective we are about to examine the periodical pattern in the data. If periodicity is not present in our analysis then any Schumpeterian argument could not possibly have any valid ground. In this context, we investigate the periodicities of business cycles assuming that the actual fluctuations of the data are chiefly of a periodic character. The length of the period in an economic series may, in general, be variable. Therefore, we understand by the term "period" the average length of the cycles and the periodogram can assist in finding these average lengths. Our work is consistent with Metz (2010) and Baubeau (2008) who argue that, in the presence of regular cycles in the time series, spectral analysis is appropriate for testing for cycles. Using the standard notation, a periodogram is a graph of the spectral density function of a time series as a function in the frequency domain. The function has the following form:

$$f(\omega) = (1/\pi)\sum_{k=-\infty}^{\infty} \gamma_k e^{-ik\omega} = (1/\pi)\gamma_0 + (2/\pi)\sum_{k=1}^{\infty} \gamma_k \cos(\omega k)$$

The dynamics of the above Fourier transformation is that it first standardizes the amplitude of the density by the sample variance of the time series, and then plots the logarithm of that standardized density. Peaks in the periodogram represent the cyclical behavior (frequencies) in the data.

Cointegration and Causality Test

Next, we conduct bivariate causality tests between technology as expressed through Rand D and real output GDP, in the original variables.

Meanwhile, the use of causality tests is very extensive because they relate variables and find predictive powers among them. Causality tests have been extensively used to count the effects of technology. There is a plethora of studies trying to link Rand D expenditures with variables such as national output, trade, productivity, profitability, etc. (Salim and Bloch, 2007; Verbeek and Debackere, 2006; Thirtle et al., 2002).

The concept of causality, introduced by Granger (1969), has been widely used in *Economics*. In general, we say that a variable X causes another variable Y if past changes in X help to explain current change in Y with past changes in Y. The concept of causality, introduced by Granger (1969), has been widely used in economics.

In general, we say that a variable X causes another variable Y if past changes in X help to explain current change in Y with past changes in Y. Of course, the general autoregressive model is appropriate for testing Granger causality only if the variables are not cointegrated. As is well known, cointegration implies that two or more variables have a long-run equilibrium relationship. Granger (1986) and Engle and Granger (1987) suggested a test based on cointegration and error-correction models. If cointegration is not detected, the autoregressive model is estimated. Alternately the Johansen (1988) Cointegration test could be used to test the same aspects.

The empirical investigation of (Granger) causality is based on the following general autoregressive model:

$$\Delta Y_t = a_0 + \sum_{i=1}^{m} a_{1i} \Delta Y_{t-1} + \sum_{i=0}^{n} a_{2i} \Delta X_{t-i} + \varepsilon_t$$

where Δ is the first difference operator, ΔY and ΔX the stationary time series and ε_t the white noise error term with zero mean and constant variance; the null hypothesis that X does not Granger cause Y is rejected if the coefficient a_{2i} is statistically significant.

Various lag lengths are tested. In order to identify the optimal lag length, we use the Akaike information criterion (AIC) and the final prediction error (FPE) criteria (Thornton and Batten, 1985; Gutierrez et al., 2007; Hsiao, 1981; Ahking and Miller, 1985; Khim and Liew, 2004; Hacker and Hatemi-J, 2008).

Empirical Results and Discussion

At this point, a major problem in examining technological change and one that makes it difficult to define or characterize it is that it can take many different forms (Rosenberg, 1982). In that sense, there is no generally accepted measure of technological change and all measures are imperfect. As a result, we use the most popular measure in order to quantify technological change, i.e., RandD expenditures given that it is widely argued that there is convincing evidence that cumulative RandD is an important determinant of technology. Meanwhile, the use of causality tests is very extensive because they relate variables and find predictive powers among them. Causality tests have been extensively used to count the effects of technology. There is a plethora of studies trying to link RandD expenditures with variables such as national output, trade, productivity, profitability, etc. (Salim and Bloch, 2007; Verbeek and Debackere, 2006; Thirtle et al., 2002).

We make use of data for the US economy for the period 1957-2006 just before the first signs of the US and global economic recession made their appearance, referring to the fourteen main industrial sectors of the economy. In terms of the variables employed: (R) is the total RandD obligations and authority, (Y) is the gross- domestic product. All observations are in billions of dollars in 1957 prices. The data regarding RandD come from the National Scientific Foundation of US and those regarding Y from the National Bureau of Economic Activity. The econometric analysis was conducted using the natural logarithm of the aggregate variables.

To begin with, the stationarity properties of the various macroeconomic variables were checked. All macroeconomic variables in levels are non-stationary, see Table 1. The next step was to extract the business cycle component using HP filtering, and the results show that the cycles are stationary as expected (Table 2). The graphs of the cyclical components are shown in Figures 3, 4. The results of the Ljung and Box test, tables 3, 4, indicate a rejection of the null hypothesis of white noise for all the de-trended variables under investigation.

In other words, the existence of cyclical regularities is a valid hypothesis from a statistical viewpoint for the US economy. The periodograms reveal the periodicities of the cycles and are shown in Figures 1 and 2.

The real output and RandD seem to follow the same pattern since they both experience a short term cycle (3-5 years) with no mid or long term cycle due to the smoothness of the US economy, over the period investigated.

Table 1.Original variables

ADF-test Original variables		
Variable	**p-value**	**stationarity**
Output	0.87	No
R and D expenses	0.89	No

Table 2. HP variables

ADF-test business cycle variables		
Variable	**p-value**	**stationarity**
Output	0	Yes
RandD expenses	0	Yes

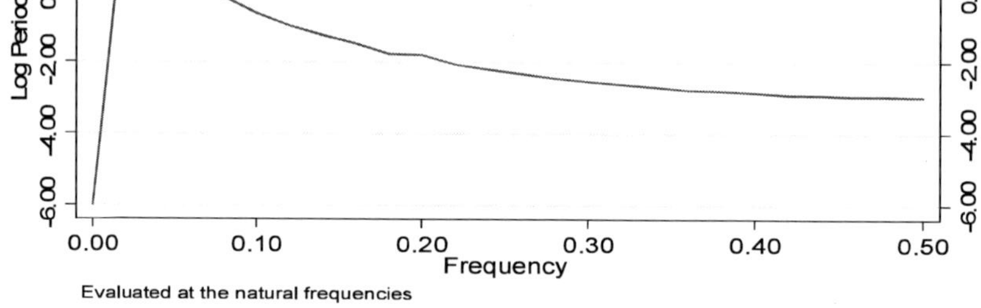

Figure 1. Periodogram of Y.

The spectral content of the cyclical component of RandD also exhibits a short cycle (2-5 years) with the appearance of another long-term cycle (20-25 years).

Also, the results of the analysis based on the correlation coefficient between RandD and output for various leads and lags, are shown in Table 5. In this way, we assess the co-movements between the cyclical components of real output and RandD by the magnitude of the correlation coefficient, and find that technological change is transmitted to the output, relatively quickly.

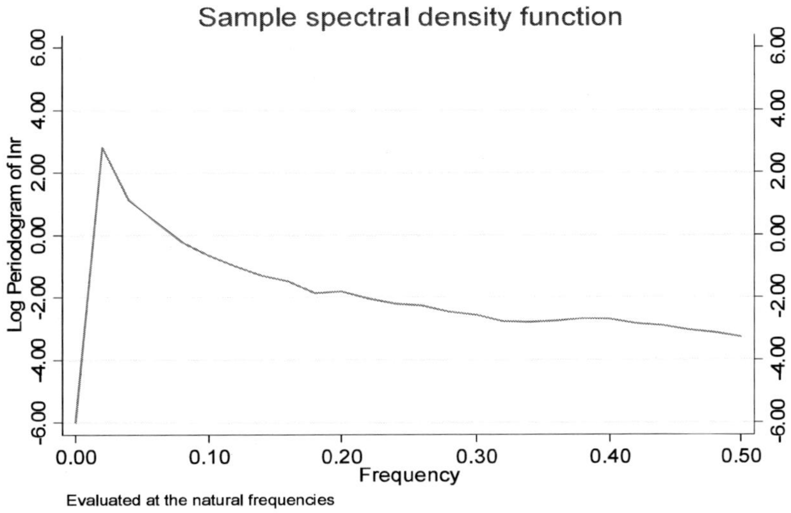

Figure 2. Periodogram of R.

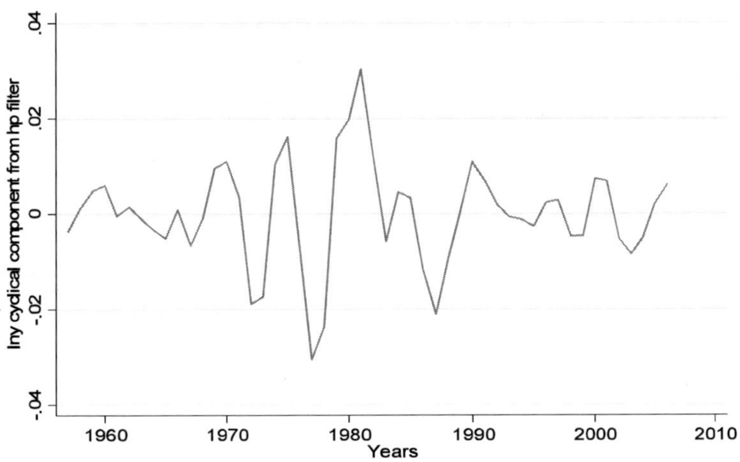

Figure 3. Plot of Y.

Next, since the original variables were found to be I(1), we check for the existence of a cointegrating relationship between them. The results of the Johansen co-integration, show that the variables are co-integrated implying the existence of a long-run relationship between Aggregate Output and R and D expenses. In specific Coefficient denotes the speed of adjustments towards equilibrium. Values of close to zero imply slow convergence.

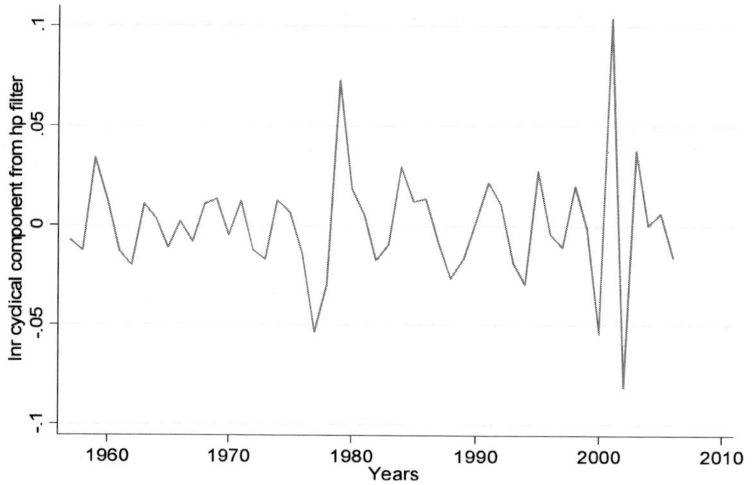

Figure 4. Plot of R.

Table 3. White Noise test for Y cycle

Aggregate Output				
Lags (i)	**AC**	**PAC**	**Q**	**Prob>Q**
1	0.45	0.45	10.76	0
2	-0.31	-0.65	15.99	0
3	-0.51	0.03	30.17	0
4	-0.16	0.01	31.65	0
5	0.14	-0.13	32.85	0
6	-0.01	-0.35	32.85	0
7	-0.29	-0.22	38.21	0
8	-0.27	-0.15	42.76	0
9	0.09	-0.06	43.23	0
10	0.36	-0.06	21.86	0

Table 4. White Noise test for R cycle

RandD expenses				
Lags (i)	**AC**	**PAC**	**Q**	**Prob>Q**
1	-0.38	-0.38	7.57	0.01
2	-0.03	-0.21	7.63	0.02
4	-0.01	-0.29	8.83	0.07
5	0.11	-0.14	9.49	0.09
6	0.15	0.27	10.91	0.09
7	-0.15	-0.23	12.04	0.08
8	-0.07	-0.06	12.72	0.12
9	-0.09	-0.41	13.28	0.14
10	0.04	-0.34	13.45	0.19

Table 5. Correlation

Lags (i)	Coefficient
-10	0.23
-9	0.01
-8	-0.22
-7	-0.26
-6	-0.06
-5	0.29
-4	0.17
-3	-0.16
-2	-0.28
-1	0.03
0	0.39
1	0.18
2	-0.04
3	-0.2
4	-0.18
5	0.12
6	0.06
7	-0.13
8	-0.21
9	-0.04
10	0.22

A larger value suggests faster convergence in cases of short-run deviations from equilibrium. Coefficient denotes the long run relationships among the variables. The results presented in table 6 indicate a low convergence rate, a=0.01, between the variables aggregate output and RandD expenses, whereas the large values of b, b=39.46, suggest that there is a strong long run relationship between the two variables.

Furthermore, for every model under investigation the Granger causality for the original variables, test was conducted using the appropriate error correction term, and the optimal lag length was selected according to Hsiao's (1981) methodology, as extended by Ahking and Miller (1985) according to which the lag length should be chosen in accordance with Akaike's Final Prediction Error (FPE) criterion.

The results of the Granger causality tests show a straightforward causality between RandD and Real Output. See Table 7.

We note that the fluctuations of Aggregate Output tend to be consistent with the US total economy. Analytically, we observe a collapse of output following the first oil crisis. Between 1963 and 1972, there is a clear upward pattern in the output that was stopped by the "oil crisis", the effect of which is evident in the de-trended time series. Furthermore the cyclical component follows the same pattern in 1979-1982 and 1990-1991. The 1990s began with a shallow recession (Basu et al. 2001) and, according to the Economic Report of the President (1994), the speed of recovery was very slow.

Furthermore, between 1991 and 1997 – the so-called "new economy" period – a sharp increase of output took place. Also, productivity growth in the sector coincided with an exceptionally good performance of the US economy (Mankiw 2001). According to Norrbin and Schlagenhauf (1990), differences exist with respect to the magnitude of the fluctuations because of aggregate (national) shocks, industry group specific shocks and idiosyncratic factors.

According to Basu et al. (2001) the 1990s experienced a boom in business investment of unprecedented size and duration. The 1970s was a decade characterized by an investment boom (just like the 1990s) but less prolonged that was due to investment in information technology (IT) equipment (computers plus communications equipment). Our findings are fully consistent with the aforementioned patterns. Finally, a clear decreasing pattern is evident after 2001, which may be related to the IT technology bubble and the terrorist attacks of 2001. The downward trend could be an early indicator of the then forthcoming US crisis. Regarding RandD expenditures the "oil crisis" caused the contraction of RandD expenditures until 1983. The tax-cut policy introduced by the Reagan government pushed profitability upwards and gave motives for investment.

Table 6. Alpha and Beta between Aggregate Output and R and D expenses

	Alpha (a)	Beta (b)	ab'
Y and R and D	0.01	39.46	3.95

Table 7. Bivariate Granger causality

Hypothesis	Lags by FPE	Obs	F-statistic	p-value
Y *does not Granger cause* R and D expenses	5	45	0.77	0.58
RandD expenses *does not Granger cause* Y	5	45	4.25	0

The increase in the US RandD expenditures might be related to this policy. The fact that RandD seems not to follow the downward fall of the aggregate output could be attributed to the fact that RandD seems to follow the move of aggregate output with a lag.

Conclusion

In this paper, we built on Schumpeterian insights to examine economic instability for the case of the US economy for the period (1958-2006). As we know, the interpretation of Schumpeter's analysis, regarding the crisis, is that it is the by-product of long waves which are caused by innovations. Schumpeter conceptualized business cycle as disturbances in the equilibrium and a return to a new equilibrium point which gives the process its cyclical character. We assessed the co-movements between the cyclical components of each time series observed and our reference series by the magnitude of the correlation coefficient, and found that technological change is transmitted in the economy relatively quickly. In the next step, we conducted bivariate (Granger) causality tests between real output and technological change.

As regards technological change, there is a clear relationship between RandD as a driver of aggregate output. Our empirical findings give credit to certain aspects of the Schumpeterian theory of economic crises. An interesting finding is that most economic time series exhibit, roughly speaking, a similar pattern characterized by periodicities exhibiting a short-term cycle and a mid-term cycle.

Given that technology is crucial for productivity and economic growth, our estimates are important. In this context, our investigation has direct relevance for policy issues for the US economy.

For instance, in case the US economy would need to augment its output it could choose to increase the Rand D expenses. We believe that the results of this study could also be utilized for the feedback of the policy formulation procedure. We hope that that our research could help inspire further theoretical and empirical research on economic fluctuations. No doubt, future and more extended research on the subject would be of great interest.

Appendix

Tables 1, 2- Augmented Dickey Fuller Test (Raw and HP detrended Variables)
Figures 1, 2-Periodograms of Aggregate Output (Y) and RandD expenses (R)
Figures 3, 4-Plots of HP detrended Aggregate Output (Y) and Rand D expenses (R)
Tables 3, 4- White noise test Aggregate Output (Y) and RandD expenses (R)
Table 5 -Correlation coefficients between Aggregate Output (Y) and RandD expenses (R)
Table 6 – Error Correction Model estimates
Table 7 - Bivariate Granger causality

References

Abrahamson, M. (1978), *Functionalism*, Englewood Cliffs N.J: Prentice –Hall.

Abramovitz, M. (1986), Catching up, Forging Ahead, and Falling Behind, *Journal of Economic History*, 46(2), June σσ.386-406.

Abramovitz, M. (1956), Resource and Output Trends in the United States since 1980, *American Economic Review*, 46(2), May, pp. 5-23.

Abramovitz, M. (1994), Catch-Up and Convergence in the Postwar Growth Boom and After, In: *Convergence of Productivity: Cross-Country Studies and Historical Evidence*, ed. W. Baumol, R. Nelson and E. Wolff, Oxford: Oxford University Press. 86-125.

Agresti, A-M. and Mojon, B. (2001), Some stylized facts on the euro area business cycle, ECB Working Paper No. 95.

Backus, D.K. and Kehoe, P.J. (1992), International evidence on the historical properties on business cycles, *American Economic Review*, Vol. 82 No. 4, pp. 864-88.

Baubeau, P. and Cazelles, B. (2008), French economic cycles: a wavelet analysis of French retrospective GNP series, *Cliometrica, Journal of Historical Economics and Econometric History*, vol. 3(3), pp. 2.75-300.

Baxter, M. and King, R.G. (1999), Measuring business cycles: approximate band-pass filters for economic time series, *Review of Economic and Statistics*, Vol. 81 No. 4, pp. 575-93.

Benati, L. (2001), *Band-pass filtering cointegration and business cycle analysis*, Working Paper No. 142, Bank of England, London.

Bhuyan, S. and Lopez, R. (1998), Oligopoly power and allocative efficiency in US food and tobacco industries, *Journal of Agricultural Economics*, Vol. 49 No. 3, pp. 434-42.

Blackburn, K. and Ravn, M. (1992), Business cycles in the United Kingdom: facts and frictions, *Economica*, Vol. 59, pp. 382-401.

Burns, A.F. and Mitchell, W.C. (1946), *Measuring Business Cycles*, National Bureau of Economic Research, New York, NY.

Canova, F. (1998), Detrending and business cycle facts, *Journal of Monetary Economics*, Vol. 41, pp. 475-512.

Comanor, W. S (1967), Market Structure, Product Differentiation and Industrial Research, *Quarterly Journal of Economics,* 81.

Danthine, J.P. and Girardin, M. (1989), Business cycles in Switzerland. A comparative study, *European Economic Review*, Vol. 33, pp. 31-50.

Darné, O. and A. Charles, (2011), Large shocks in US macroeconomic time series: 1860-1988, *Cliometrica, Journal of Historical Economics and Econometric History*, vol. 5(1), pp. 79-100.

Degner H. (2010), Do technological booms matter? New evidence on the relationship between firm size and innovativeness", *Cliometrica, Journal of Historical Economics and Econometric History*, vol. 5(2), pp. 121-144.

Denison, E. and Chung, W. (1976), *How Japan's economy grew so fast: The sources of postwar expansion*, Washington D.C Brookings Institution.

Denison, E. (1962a),United States Economic Growth, *Journal of Business*, August.

Denison, E. (1962b),*The Sources of Economic Growth in the US and the Alternatives before Us*, Committee for economic Development, New York.

Denison, E. (1967), *Why Growth Rates Differ*, Washington D.C.: The Brookings Institution.

Denison, E. (1985), *Trends in American Economic Growth, 1929-1982*, Washington, D.C.: The Brookings Institution.

Dickey, D.A. and Fuller, W.A. (1979), Distribution of the estimates for autoregressive time series with a unit root, *Journal of the American Statistical Association*, Vol. 74, pp. 427-31.

Dobson, P., Waterson, M. and Davies, S. (2003), The patterns and implications of increasing concentration in European food retailing, *Journal of Agricultural Economics*, Vol. 54 No. 1, pp. 111-25.

Dosi, G. (1988), Sources, Procedures and Microeconomic Effects of Innovation, *Journal of Economic Literature*, XXVI, September, σσ. 1120-1171.

Faere, R., Grosskopf, S. and Margaritis, D. (2005), US productivity in agriculture and RandD, paper presented at NZESG Meetings at Universi-ty of Canterbury, Christchurch, New Zealand.

Field, J. A. (2007), The origins of US total factor productivity growth in the golden age, *Cliometrica, Journal of Historical Economics and Econo-metric History*, vol. 1(1), pp. 63-90.

Fine, B. (1998), *The Political Economy of Diet, Health and Food Policy*, Routledge, London.

Fiorito, R. and Kollintzas, T. (1994), Stylized facts of business cycles in the G7 from a real business cycle perspective, *European Economic Review*, Vol. 38, pp. 235-69.

Gerschencron, A. (1962), *Economic backwardness in historical perspective*, Cambridge, MA: Belknap Press.

Gomulka, S. (1970), Extensions of the Golden Rule of Research of Phelps, *Review of Economic Studies*, 37(1), January, σσ. 73-93.

Gomulka, S. (1971), *Inventive Activity, Diffusion, and the stages of Economic Growth*, Aarhus Institute of Economics.

Goodwin, B. and Brester, G. (1995), Structural change in factor demand relationships in the US food and kindred products industry, *American Journal of Agricultural Economics*, Vol. 77, pp. 69-79.

Granger, C.W.J. (1969), Investigating causal relations by econometric models and cross-spectral methods, *Econometrica*, Vol. 37, July, pp. 424-38.

Griliches, (1957), Hybrid Corn: An Exploration in the Economics of Techno-logical Change, *Econometrica*, October.

Grossman, G. and Helpman, E. (1991), *Innovation and growth in the global economy*, Cambridge, MA: MIT Press.

Gualerzi, D. and Edward Nelly (2011), The crisis, long term depression and new markets'', *International Journal of Management Concepts and Philosophy*, Vol. 5, No. 3.

Hall, A. (1963), *The Historical Relations of Science and Technology*, London.

Hobsbawn, E. (1968), *Industry and Empire*, Harmondsworth, England: Penguin Books.

Hodrick, R.J. and Prescott, E.C. (1997), Post-war US business cycles: an empirical investigation, *Journal of Money, Credit, and Banking*, Vol. 29, pp. 1-16.

Hsiao, C. (1981), Autoregressive modelling of Canadian money income data, *Journal of the American Statistical Association*, Vol. 74, pp. 85-106.

Johansen, L. (1959), Substitution versus Fixed Production Coefficients in the Theory of Economic Growth: a Synthesis, *Econometrica*, 27(2), April, σσ. 157-76.

Johansen, S. (1988), Statistical analysis of cointegation vectors, *Journal of Economic Dynamics and Control*, Vol. 12, pp. 231-54.

Kaldor, Nicholas and Mirlees, James A. (1962), A new Model of Economic Growth, *Review of Economic Studies*, 29(3), June, σσ.174-92.

Khim, V. and Liew, S. (2004), Which lag length selection criteria should we employ?, *Economics Bulletin*, Vol. 3 No. 33, pp. 1-9.

Kydland, F.E. and Prescott, E.C. (1990), Business cycles: real facts and a monetary myth, *Federal Reserve Bank of Minneapolis Quarterly Review*, Vol. 14, pp. 3-18.

Lio, M. and Hu, J. (2009), "Governance and agricultural production efficiency: a cross-country aggregate frontier analysis", *Journal of Agricultural Economics,* Vol. 60 No. 1, pp. 40-61.

Ljung, G. and Box, G.E.P. (1978), On a measure of lack of fit in time series models, *Biometrika*, Vol. 65, pp. 297-303.

Lundvall, B. (1992), *National systems of innovation: Towards a theory of innovation and interactive learning*, London: Pinter.

MacDonald, R. and Kearney, C. (1987), On the specification of Granger causality tests using the cointegration methodology, *Economics Letters*, Vol. 25, pp. 149-53.

Malecki, E. J. (1980), Firm Size, Location and Industrial RandD: A Disaggregated Analysis, *Review of Business and Economic Research*, 16, 29-42.

Marx, K. (1867), *Capital*, Modern Library, New York.

Marx, K. (1867), *Capital*, Vol. I, London: Penguin Classics [1990].

Marx, K. and Engels, F. (1848), *The Communist Manifesto*, όπως ανατυπώθηκε στο Marx, K. and F. Engels, *Selected Works*, Foreign Languages Publishing House.

Massmann, M. and Mitchell, J. (2004), "Reconsidering the evidence: are Euro-zone business cycles converging?", *Journal of Business Cycle Measure-ment and Analysis*, Vol. 1, pp. 275-307.

Meisel, J.B. and Lin, S.A. Y. (1983), The impact of market structure on the firm's allocation of resources to research and development, *Quarterly Review of Economics and Business*, 23, σσ.28-43.

Metz, R. (2010a) Filter-design and model-based analysis of trends and cycles in the presence of outliers and structural breaks, Cliometrica, *Journal of Historical Economics and Econometric History*, vol. 4(1), pp. 53–71.

Metz, R. (2010b), Do Kondratieff waves exist? How time series techniques can help to solve the problem, *Cliometrica, Journal of Historical Economics and Econometric History*, vol.5(3), pp.205-238.

Mills, C.T. (2008), Modelling trends and cycles in economic time series: historical perspective and future developments", *Cliometrica, Journal of Historical Economics and Econometric History*, vol. 3(2), pp. 221-224.

Nason, M. James and Shaun P. Vahey, (2012), UK World War I and interwar data for business cycle and growth analysis, *Cliometrica, Journal of Historical Economics and Econometric History*, vol. 6(2), pp. 115-142.

Nelson, R. (1964), Aggregate Production Functions and Medium- Range Growth Projections, *American Economic Review*, 54(5), September, σσ. 575-606.

Nelson, C.R. and Plosser, C.I. (1982), Trends and random walks in macroeconomics time series: some evidence and implications, *Journal of Monetary Economics*, Vol. 10, pp. 139-67.

Nelson, R. (1987), *Understanding Technical Change as an Evolutionary Process*, Amsterdam, North Holland.

Nelson, R. (1993), *National Innovation Systems: A Comparative Analysis*, Oxford University Press.

Ohkawa, K. and Rosovsky, H. (1973), *Japanese economic growth*, Stanford: Stanford University Press.

Parker, W. (1967),Sources of Agricultural Productivity in the 19th Century, *Journal of Farm Economics*, December.

Pensieroso L. (2011), Real business cycle models of the Great Depression, *Cliometrica, Journal of Historical Economics and Econometric History*, vol. 5(2), pp. 101-119.

Phelps, E. (1966), Models of Technical Progress and the Golden Rule of Research, *Review of Economic Studies*, 33(2), April, 133-145.

Philips, L. (1971), Effects of Industrial Concentration: *A cross- section analysis for the Common Market*, Amsterdam, North Holland.

Rosenberg, N. (1982), *Inside the Black Box: Technology and Economics*, Cambridge University Press, New York, NY.

Rudin, W. (1976), *Principles of Mathematical Analysis*, McGraw-Hill Inter-national Edition, New York, NY.

Salim, R. and Bloch, H. (2007), Business expenditures on RandD and trade performances in Australia: is there a link?, *Applied Economics*, Vol. 41, pp. 1-11.

Scherer, F. (1984), *Innovation and Growth: Schumpeterian Perspectives*, Cambridge, Mass., MIT Press.

Schumpeter, J. A. [1912] 1934, 1951, 1961. *The Theory of Economic Development*. Cambridge: Harvard University Press.

Schumpeter, J. A. 1950. *Capitalism, Socialism and Democracy*. New York: Harper and Row[1942].

Schumpeter, J. A. 1964. *Business Cycles*. New York: McGraw-Hill[1939].

Scott, M. F. (1989), *A New View of Economic Growth*, New York and Oxford: Oxford University Press [1998].

Serra, T., Goodwin, B. and Feathertone, M. (2005), Agricultural policy reform and off-farm labor decisions, *Journal of Agricultural Economics*, Vol. 56 No. 2, pp. 271-85.

Shell, K. (1967), A Model of Inventive Activity and Capital Accumulation, In: K. Shell (ed.), *Essays on the theory of optimal growth*, Cambridge MA: MIT Press, σσ. 67-85.

Solow, R. (1956), A Contribution to the Theory of Economic Growth, *Quarterly Journal of Economics*, LXX, σσ. 65-94.

Solow, R. (1957), Technical Change and the Aggregate Production Function, *Review of Economics and Statistics*, 39(3), August, 312-320.

Solow, R. (1960), Investment and Technical Progress, In: K. Arrow, S. Kablin and P. Suppes (eds), *Mathematical methods in the social sciences*, Stan-ford: Stanford U. Press, σσ. 89-104.

Stock, M. and Watson, M. (1999), Business cycles fluctuations in US macro-economic time series, In: Taylor, J.B. and Woodford, M. (Eds), *Handbook of Macroeconomics, Ch. 1*.

Subervie, J. (2008), The variable response of agricultural supply to world price instability in developing countries, *Journal of Agricultural Economics*, Vol. 59 No. 1, pp. 72-92.

Thirtle, C., Lin, L., Holding, J., Jenkins, L., and Piesse, J. (2004), Explaining the decline in UK agricultural productivity growth, *Journal of Agricultural Economics*, Vol. 55, No. 2, pp. 343-66.

Thirtle, C., Schimmelpfennig, D. and Townsend, R. (2002), Induced innovation in United States, 1880–1990: time series tests and error correction model, *American Journal of Agricultural Economics*, Vol. 84 No. 3, pp. 598-614.

Thornton, D.L. and Batten, D.S. (1985), Lag-length selection and tests of Granger causality between money and income, *Journal of Money Credit and Banking*, Vol. 17, pp. 164-78.

Tiffin, R., Traill, W.B. and Mortimer, S. (2006), Food choice in an inter-disciplinary context, *Journal of Agricultural Economics*, Vol. 57 No. 2, pp. 213-20.

Uzawa, H. (1965), Optimum Technical Change in an Aggregative Model of Economic Growth, *International Economic Review*, 6(1), January, σσ.18-31.

Verbeek, A. and Debackere, K. (2006), Patent evolution in relation to public/private RandD investment and corporate profitability: evidence from the United States, *Scientometrics*, Vol. 35 No. 6, pp. 601-15. Vol. 66 No. 2, pp. 279-94.

Wang, S.S., Stiegert, K. and Rogers, R. (2006), Structural change in the US food manufacturing industry, paper presented at American Agricultural Economics Association Annual Meeting, Long Beach, CA, July 23-26.

Woodrow W. Clark and Xing Li (2004), 'Social capitalism: an economic paradigm for the transfer and commercialisation of technology', *International Journal of Technology Transfer and Commercialisation*, Vol. 3, No. 1.

Wynne, M. and Koo, J. (2000), Business cycles under monetary union: a comparison of the EU and US, *Economica,* Vol. 67, pp. 347-74.

In: Business Cycles in Economics
Editor: Jason C. Hsu

ISBN: 978-1-63321-322-7

Chapter 5

COEFFICIENT CRITERION FOR SHIL'NIKOV CHAOS: APPLICATION TO A SIMPLE INVESTMENT MODEL

***Eiji Tsuzuki*[1,*], *Shunsuke Shinagawa*[2] and *Tomohiro Inoue*[2]**
[1]Faculty of Economics, Chiba Keizai University, Chiba, Japan
[2]Faculty of Political Science and Economics,
Waseda University, Tokyo, Japan

Abstract

This chapter (a) represents one of the conditions of the Shil'nikov theorem in terms of the coefficients of a characteristic equation, and (b) demonstrates the existence of chaos by applying the theorem to a simple investment model. To demonstrate the existence of chaos, we adopt a numerical method of combining a condition of the Shil'nikov theorem with Kopell and Howard's theorem. Consistently with our intuition, it is confirmed that the more active the firm's expectations about investment, the more complex the economic behavior.

JEL Classification: E22, E32

Keywords: adjustment costs of investment, chaos, homoclinic orbit, Hopf bifurcation, period doubling bifurcation

1. Introduction

Applied scientists benefit from translating mathematical theorems into conditions described by the coefficients of a characteristic equation of a system because such alterations facilitate the application of theorems to the relevant model.

For example, Asada (1995) represents the conditions for a Hopf bifurcation in a three-dimensional system of differential equations by the coefficients of its characteristic equation and briefly shows the existence of cycles in a macroeconomic model. Asada and Yoshida

*E-mail address: tsuzukie5@gmail.com (Corresponding author)

(2003) represent conditions for a Hopf bifurcation in a four-dimensional system of differential equations by the coefficients of its characteristic equation.[1]

In this chapter, we represent one of the conditions of Shil'nikov's (1965) theorem by the coefficients of a characteristic equation. This chapter's alteration of a condition of the Shil'nikov theorem also benefits scientists who are searching for chaos originating in a homoclinic orbit in three-dimensional systems of differential equations.

As an approach to determine the existence of chaos, we adopt a numerical method of combining a condition of the Shil'nikov theorem with Kopell and Howard's (1975) theorem. In this chapter, we propose a simple investment model and demonstrate the existence of chaos by applying these theorems to the model.

Let us consider a comprehensive view of the theory of investment.[2] The neoclassical theory of investment proposed by Jorgenson (1963) is one of the classic theories of investment, which holds that investment serves to bridge the gap between the optimal capital stock and the actual capital stock. This theory implicitly assumes the existence of adjustment costs of investment because it allows the actual level of capital stock to differ from its optimal level. If no adjustment costs exist, the gap between the optimal and actual capital stocks should be instantaneously resolved and the two are identical.

Lucas (1967), Gould (1968), and Uzawa (1969) attempt to derive an investment function from a firm's optimization problem, in which the existence of adjustment costs is explicitly considered. These studies apply the adjustment cost approach.[3]

Independent of these studies, Tobin (1969) proposes an investment theory called the q theory, which defines q as "the market value of a firm divided by the replacement costs of capital stock held by a firm," now called the average q. Although Tobin explains firms' investment behavior using this indicator, the actual volume of investment is determined from the theoretical perspective by the marginal q, defined as "the marginal increment of the market value of a firm divided by the marginal replacement costs of capital stock held by a firm." If the marginal q is greater than 1, the firm invests. The average q is observable from the actual information; however, the marginal q is not.

Yoshikawa (1980) and Hayashi (1982) demonstrate that the investment function derived from the adjustment cost approach is equivalent to that from the q theory. Therefore, we can interpret the adjustment cost approach as a theory providing a microeconomic foundation with the q theory. They also propose the conditions for the average q to be consistent with the marginal q.[4] Accordingly, researchers can theoretically use the average q instead of the marginal q in the estimation of an investment function.

Furthermore, Asako and Kuninori (1989) demonstrate that the q theory can be considered as the general theory, which includes the neoclassical investment theory as a special

[1]A necessary condition for a Hopf bifurcation is that a matrix associated with the vector fields linearized around the fixed point should have pure imaginary eigenvalues and the real factors of the other eigenvalues should be nonzero. Asada (1995) and Asada and Yoshida (2003) represent these conditions by the coefficients of a characteristic equation.

[2]For development of the theory of investment, see Caballero (1999), Hayashi (2000), and Bond and Van Reenen (2007). Our survey is based on Asada (1997) Chap.7 and Asako et al. (2013).

[3]Developing these studies further, Lucas and Prescott (1971), Mussa (1977), Nickell (1978), and Abel (1980) derive an investment function by considering a dynamic optimization problem with adjustment costs.

[4]The conditions are as follows: (a) production function and adjustment cost function are linearly homogeneous and (b) the goods market is perfectly competitive.

case. Thus, the q theory, completed in the early 1980s, has been regarded as a comprehensive theory of investment.

In the derivation of an investment function, Christiano et al. (2005) assume that firms incur adjustment costs in proportion to the variation in the level of investment and not to the level of investment itself. According to Eberly et al. (2012), this type of investment function has a precise description for large companies. In this chapter, we incorporate the assumption considered by Christiano et al. (2005) to the Eisner–Strotz model, which is a variant of the neoclassical theory of investment, and derive an investment function describing variations in the level of investment.

This paper proceeds as follows. Section 2 presents the Shil'nikov (1965) theorem and represents one of the conditions of the theorem by the coefficients of a characteristic equation. Section 3 proposes a simple investment model. Section 4 applies a condition of the Shil'nikov theorem and Kopell and Howard (1975) theorem to the model proposed in Section 3 and demonstrates the existence of a homoclinic orbit and chaos.[5] Section 5 concludes.

2. Shil'nikov Theorem

Shil'nikov's (1965) theorem presents the sufficient conditions for the existence of chaos.[6]

Theorem 1. (Shil'nikov, 1965) *Assume that vector fields of a three-dimensional system of differential equations S have the fixed point X^* that satisfies the following conditions:*

(i) The eigenvalues evaluated at X^* are given by $\alpha \pm i\beta$ ($\beta \neq 0$) and γ, and $|\alpha| < |\gamma|$.
(ii) A homoclinic orbit Γ to X^* exists.

The perturbed system S has a homoclinic orbit Γ' located near Γ and the Poincaré map of Γ' has countable horseshoes.

Coefficient Representation of Condition (i)

The characteristic equation of the matrix associated with vector fields of S linearized around the fixed point can be written as follows:

$$\Delta(\lambda) \equiv \lambda^3 + a_1\lambda^2 + a_2\lambda + a_3 = 0. \tag{1}$$

Lemma 1. *Necessary and sufficient conditions for the characteristic equation $\Delta(\lambda) = 0$ to have roots $\alpha \pm \beta i$ and γ ($\alpha \lesseqgtr 0$, $\beta \neq 0$, and $\gamma \gtreqless 0$), and to hold $\alpha + \gamma \gtreqless 0$ are as*

[5]There are few applications of the Shil'nikov theorem to economics. As an example, we can cite Sportelli (2000).

[6]For details of the Shil'nikov (1965) theorem, see Guckenheimer and Holmes (1983) Sect. 6.5.

follows:

$$27a_3^2 + 4a_2^3 + 4a_1^3 a_3 - a_1^2 a_2^2 - 18a_1 a_2 a_3 > 0, \tag{2}$$

$$a_3 \lesseqgtr 0, \tag{3}$$

$$a_1 a_2 - a_3 \gtreqless 0, \tag{4}$$

$$2a_1^3 + a_1 a_2 + a_3 \lesseqgtr 0, \tag{5}$$

where the multiple signs are in the same sequence.

Proof. See Appendix A.1.

Conditions for Assuring the Existence of a Homoclinic Orbit (Condition ii)

We present the Kopell and Howard (1975) theorem that provides conditions for assuring the existence of a homoclinic orbit.

Theorem 2. (Kopell and Howard, 1975; Theorem 7.1 and Corollary 7.1) : *Let $\dot{X} = F_{\mu,\nu}(X)$ be a two-parameter family of ordinary differential equations on $\mathbb{R}^n$, F smooth in all its arguments, such that $F_{\mu,\nu}(\mathbf{0}) = \mathbf{0}$. Using a Taylor expansion, $\dot{X} = F_{\mu,\nu}(X)$ can be written as follows:*

$$\dot{X} = (A + \mu A_1 + \nu A_2)X + Q(X, X) + R_1(X, \mu, \nu),$$

where A, A_1, A_2 are $n \times n$ matrices, the vector $Q(X, X)$ contains terms quadratic in x_i and is independent of (μ, ν), and $R_1(X, \mu, \nu) = o(\mu x_i, \nu x_i, x_i x_j)$. Also assume the following:

1. *$dF_{0,0}(\mathbf{0})$ has a double-zero eigenvalue corresponding to a single eigenvector e.*
2. *The mapping $(\mu, \nu) \rightarrow (\det dF_{\mu,\nu}(\mathbf{0}), \sigma(dF_{\mu,\nu}(\mathbf{0})))$ has a nonzero Jacobian at $(\mu, \nu) = (0, 0)$, where $\sigma(dF_{\mu,\nu}(\mathbf{0}))$ is the sum of the principal minors of $dF_{\mu,\nu}(\mathbf{0})$.*
3. *$[dF_{0,0}(\mathbf{0})Q(e, e)]$ has rank n.*

Then there is a curve $f(\mu, \nu) = 0$ such that if $f(\mu_0, \nu_0) = 0$, $\dot{X} = F_{\mu_0,\nu_0}(X)$ has a homoclinic orbit. This one-parameter family of homoclinic orbits (in X, μ, ν space) is on the boundary of a two-parameter family of periodic solutions. For all sufficiently small values of $|\nu|$, $|\mu|$, if $\dot{X} = F_{\mu,\nu}(X)$ has neither a homoclinic orbit nor a periodic solution, there is a unique trajectory joining the critical (fixed) points (i.e., a saddle connection).

3. Investment Model

Consider a simple investment model represented by the following three-dimensional system of differential equations:

$$\begin{aligned} &(i) \quad \dot{K} = I - \delta K, \\ &(ii) \quad \dot{I} = a[b(K^e - K) - I] + c, \\ &(iii) \quad \dot{K}^e = nK(\bar{K} - K) - qK + [e^{j(I - I^*)} - 1], \end{aligned} \tag{6}$$

where K is the capital stock, I is the volume of investment, K^e is the capital stock that firms subjectively regard as desired, and a, b, δ, n, q, j, and $\bar{K}$ are positive constants.[7] I^* is the steady-state value of the volume of investment I.

Eq. (i) in (6) implies that capital stock increases by investment and decreases by depreciation. δ denotes the rate of capital depreciation; therefore, we assume that $0 < \delta < 1$.

Eq. (ii) in (6) describes the investment behavior of firms. Jorgenson (1963) proposed a model in which investment is made to bridge the gap between the targeted volume of capital and the actual volume of capital, which is now called the elastic accelerator model. Therefore, Eq. (ii) is regarded as an anomaly of the Jorgenson's approach. In Appendix A.2, we derive Eq. (ii) from a dynamic optimization problem of investment, which is a variant of the Eisner–Strotz model.[8]

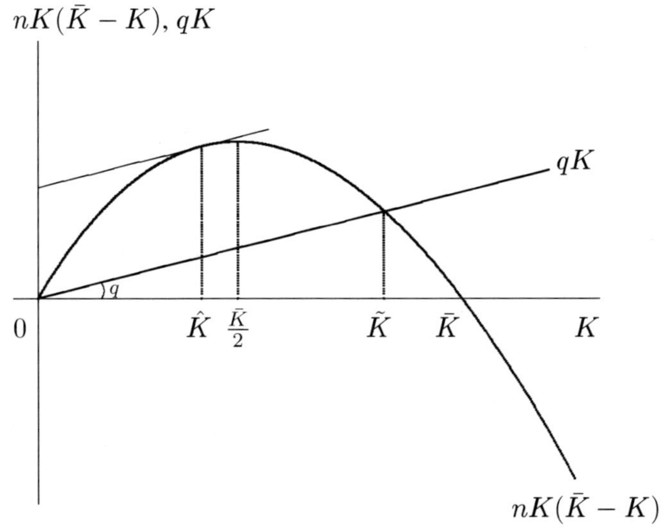

Figure 1. Logistic function.

The first term of the right-hand side of Eq. (iii) in (6), $nK(\bar{K} - K)$, implies that changes in the desirable volume of capital follow a logistic function (Fig. 1). However, a firm's expectation formations are assumed to be asymmetric; a bear always exists. The effect of asymmetry is represented by the second term $-qK$: the larger the actual volume of capital, the more bear the expectation formations. q denotes the degree of bear expectation. Therefore, if the value of q increases, the maximum point of $\dot{K}^e$ (given by $\hat{K}$) moves to the left.

$\tilde{K}$ is a crucial value for firm expectation formation. If $K < \tilde{K}$, firms regard the actual volume of capital as too little and optimistically form the expectation: K^e increases. On the condition that $K > \hat{K}$, where $\hat{K}$ corresponds to the maximum value of $\dot{K}^e$, firms become conservative in the expectation formation ($\dot{K}^e$ decreases). In contrast, if $K > \tilde{K}$, firms

[7] Basically, this dynamic system has a similar structure to that studied by Coullet et al. (1979) and Arneodo et al. (1982). They demonstrate that this type of dynamic system can generate chaotic dynamics under particular parameter sets. As another application of this type of system to economics, we can cite the inventory cycle model proposed by Lorenz (1993) Chap.5.

[8] See Chiang (1992) Sect. 5.2 for details of the Eisner–Strotz model.

negatively form the expectation, fearing surplus capital: K^e decreases. The third term, $e^{j(I-I^*)} - 1$, implies that firms consider the trend growth of investment.

The steady-state values of System (6) are given by $(K^*, I^*, K^{e*}) = (0, 0, -c/ab)$ and $(\tilde{K}, \delta\tilde{K}, [a(b+\delta)\tilde{K} - c]/ab)$. The steady state $(0, 0, -c/ab)$ has economically no significance as $K^* = 0$. Therefore, we consider the only steady state $(\tilde{K}, \delta\tilde{K}, [a(b+\delta)\tilde{K}-c]/ab)$.

4. Chaos

We demonstrate that chaotic dynamics exist in System (6). The procedure is as follows. First, we show the existence of a homoclinic orbit by applying Theorem 2. Next, we set parameters at plausible values and numerically examine whether the conditions of Lemma 1. hold around the steady state $(\tilde{K}, \delta\tilde{K}, [a(b+\delta)\tilde{K} - c]/ab)$.

Applying Theorem 2.

Consider the three-dimensional System of differential equations in (6). To make the fixed point the origin, we translate the variables as follows:

$$x_1 = K - K^*, \quad x_2 = I - I^*, \quad x_3 = K^e - K^{e*}.$$

Then System (6) can be rewritten as follows:

$$\begin{aligned} \dot{x}_1 &= x_2 - \delta x_1, \\ \dot{x}_2 &= a[b(x_3 - x_1) - x_2], \\ \dot{x}_3 &= nx_1(\bar{K} - 2K^* - x_1) + nK^*(\bar{K} - K^*) - q(x_1 + K^*) + e^{jx_2} - 1, \end{aligned} \tag{7}$$

where we posit $(\mu, \nu) = (n - (q - j\delta)/(\bar{K} - 2K^*), j - 1 - \delta/b)$ and $\bar{K} \neq 2K^*$.

Denoting that $X = [x_1, x_2, x_3]'$, we can write System (7) as follows:

$$\dot{X} = F_{\mu,\nu}(X) = (F1(X, \mu, \nu), F2(X, \mu, \nu), F3(X, \mu, \nu)).$$

F is smooth and $F_{\mu,\nu}(\mathbf{0}) = \mathbf{0}$. Therefore, the presuppositions of Theorem 2. are satisfied.

We can formulate the following proposition.

Proposition 1. *In System (7), if* $\bar{R} \equiv -\frac{q-\delta(1+\delta/b)}{\bar{K}-2K^*} + \frac{1}{2}(1 + \frac{\delta}{b})^2\delta^2 \neq 0$, *a homoclinic orbit exists for certain sets of* n *and* j.

Proof. See Appendix A.3.

Numerical Analysis

To confirm the existence of chaos through computational simulation, we set parameter values as shown in Table 1.[9]

[9] Fig. 1 demonstrates that $\tilde{K}$ satisfies $nK(\bar{K} - K) = qK$. Solving this equation for K, we obtain $\tilde{K} = \bar{K} - q/n$.

Table 1. Parameter values

a	b	$\bar{K}$	q	j	δ
0.4	2.5	2	1.2	0.4	0.01

Regarding n, which represents the adjustment speed of the expected capital requirement, as a bifurcation parameter, we explore the region satisfying all conditions of Eqs. (2)–(5). Inequation (2) holds for all values of $n > 0$ per Table 1. In addition, $a_3 \gtrless 0$ for $n \gtrless 0.602$, $a_1 a_2 - a_3 \lesseqgtr 0$ for $n \gtrless n_h \simeq 0.726$, and $2a_1^3 + a_1 a_2 + a_3 \gtrless 0$ for $n \gtrless 0.409$, where the multiple signs are in the same sequence.[10]

Thus, for $n < 0.409$ or $n > n_h$, all equations of (2)–(5) are satisfied, and chaos can exist. Incidentally, n_h is the value satisfying the conditions of the Hopf bifurcation theorem presented in Appendix A.4.[11]

Fig. 2 depicts the result of a numerical calculation when $n = 0.755$, and demonstrates the existence of a cycle.[12] In this case, a cycle is stable, and the bifurcation is supercritical.

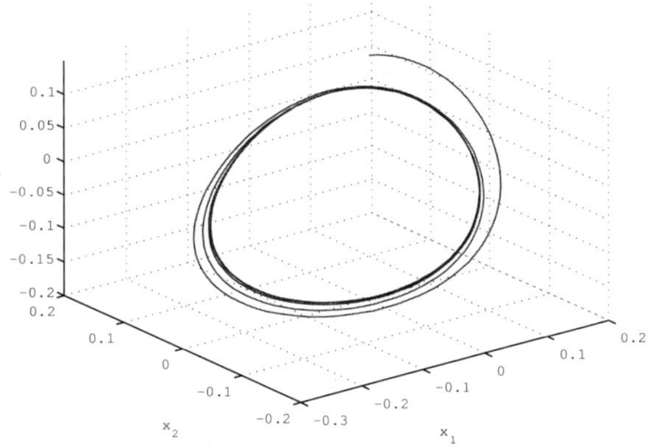

Figure 2. Stable cycle.

With the increase in the value of n, period doubling bifurcations occur; a two-period cycle and a four-period cycle emerges. Figs. 3 and 4 show the results of numerical calculations in cases where $n = 0.809$ and $n = 0.8204$, respectively.

At $n = 0.8261$, chaos emerges. Fig. 5 depicts the result of a numerical calculation when $n = 0.839$. The maximum Lyapunov exponent in this case is given by roughly $0.054 > 0$. The dynamics of Lyapunov exponents are shown in Fig. 6.[13]

Thus, the dynamics of solutions of System (7) are summarized in Table 2.

[10]The value of n at which the signs of the left-hand side of Eqs. (3)–(5) change is unique because they are linear functions of n.

[11]One-parameter family of homoclinic orbits is on the boundary of a two-parameter family of periodic solutions (Theorem 2.); therefore, we can infer that a homoclinic orbit and chaos exist in the region of $n > n_h$.

[12]The initial values of (x_1, x_2, x_3) are taken as $(x_1, x_2, x_3) = (0.1, 0.1, 0.1)$.

[13]This figure is generated by a Matlab code presented by Wolf et al. (1985).

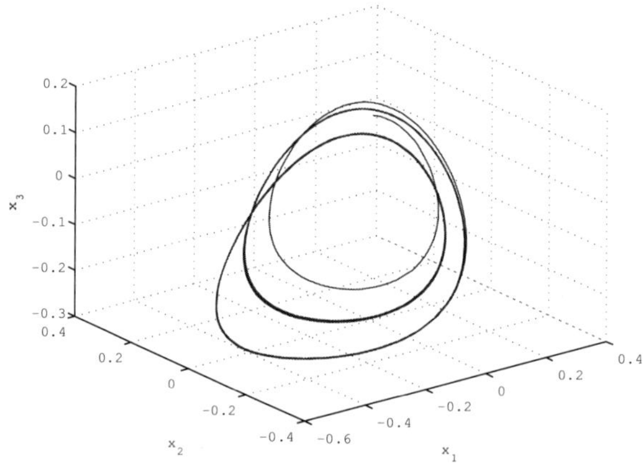

Figure 3. Two-period cycle.

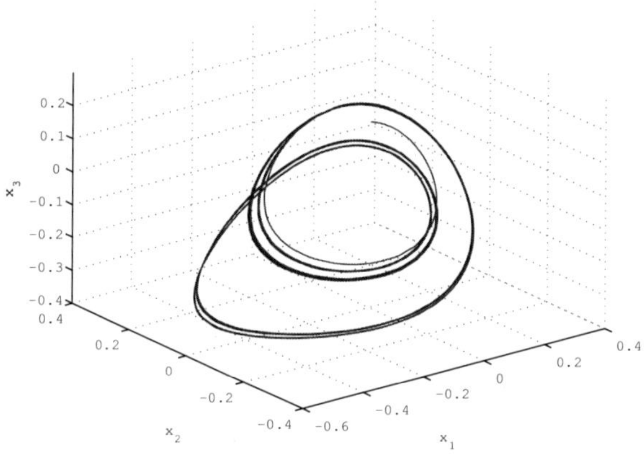

Figure 4. Four-period cycle.

Table 2. Dynamics of solutions of System (7)

Values of n	
$n \in (0, n_h)$	Stable spiral
$n = n_h \simeq 0.726$	Hopf bifurcation
$n \in (n_h, 0.787)$	Unstable spiral & stable cycle
$n = n_d \simeq 0.787$	Period doubling bifurcation
$n \in (n_d, 0.811)$	Two-period cycle
$n \in (0.811, 0.821)$	Four-period cycle
$\vdots$	
$n \in (0.826, 0.850)$	Chaos

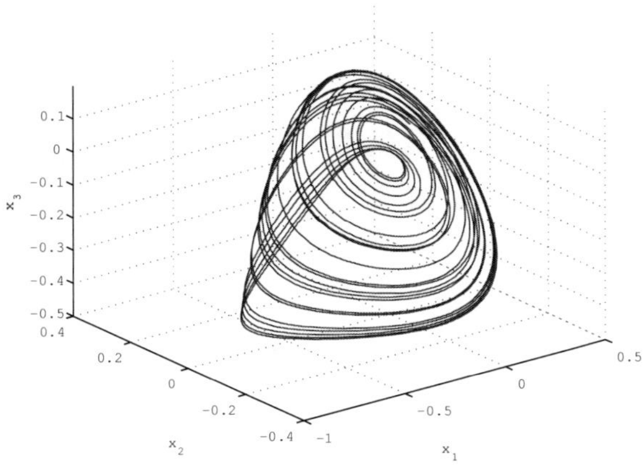

Figure 5. Chaos.

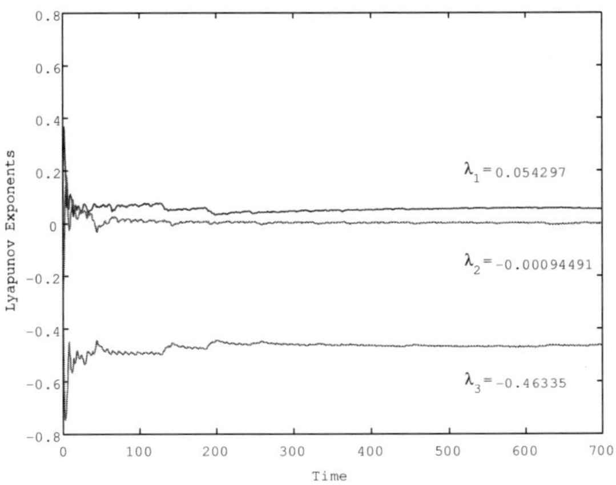

Figure 6. Dynamics of Lyapunov exponents.

Fig. 7 describes how the values of n_h (Hopf bifurcation) and n_d (period doubling bifurcation) changes when j increases, where j is on the vertical axis and n is on the horizontal axis.

It should be noted that the Shil'nikov theorem provides only a sufficient condition for the existence of chaos; therefore, the theorem's not being satisfied does not mean the absence of chaos.

5. Conclusion

In this chapter, we represented one of the conditions of Shil'nikov's (1965) theorem by the coefficients of a characteristic equation, and demonstrated the existence of chaos by applying the theorem to a simple investment model.

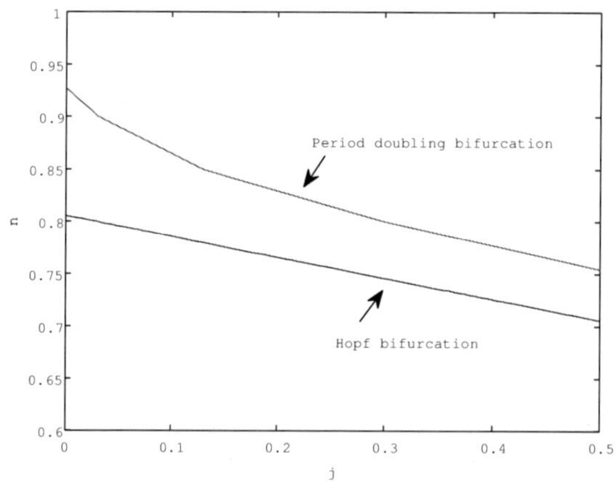

Figure 7. Changes in n_h and n_d.

According to numerical calculations, period doubling bifurcations occur at certain sets of parameter values, and chaos eventually emerges. Specifically, noting firms' adjustment speed of capital requirement (represented by n) and the degree of consideration of the trend growth (represented by j), a stable spiral point changes to a periodic orbit, resulting in chaos as these values increase. This behavior suggests that the more active the firm's expectation formations, the more complex their economic behavior. This is consistent with our intuition.

The method developed here for numerically determining the existence of chaos by combining Lemma 1. (Condition i of the Shil'nikov theorem) with Theorem 2. (Kopell and Howard's theorem) would be generally applicable to a three-dimensional system of differential equations.

A. Appendix

A.1. Proof of Lemma 1.

Eq. (2) is the sufficient condition for the characteristic equation $\Delta(\lambda) = 0$ to have a pair of complex roots. This condition has been obtained previously by Takagi (1965) and Asada et al. (1998).[14]

Let the characteristic roots of Eq. (1) be as follows:

$$\lambda_1 = \alpha + i\beta,$$
$$\lambda_2 = \alpha - i\beta,$$
$$\lambda_3 = \gamma.$$

[14] See Takagi (1965) p.114 and the Appendix of Asada et al. (1998).

Then we can write

$$\begin{aligned}\Delta(\lambda) &= (\lambda-\lambda_1)(\lambda-\lambda_2)(\lambda-\lambda_3),\\ &= [\lambda-(\alpha+i\beta)][(\lambda-(\alpha-i\beta)](\lambda-\gamma),\\ &= \lambda^3-(2\alpha+\gamma)\lambda^2+(\alpha^2+\beta^2+2\alpha\gamma)\lambda-(\alpha^2+\beta^2)\gamma,\\ &\equiv \lambda^3+a_1\lambda^2+a_2\lambda+a_3. \end{aligned} \tag{A.1}$$

Therefore, we obtain

$$a_1 = -(2\alpha+\gamma), \tag{A.2}$$

$$a_2 = \alpha^2+\beta^2+2\alpha\gamma, \tag{A.3}$$

$$a_3 = -(\alpha^2+\beta^2)\gamma, \tag{A.4}$$

and

$$a_1a_2-a_3 = -2\alpha[(\alpha+\gamma)^2+\beta^2]. \tag{A.5}$$

Therefore, $\gamma \gtrless 0$ if and only if $a_3 \lessgtr 0$. In addition, $\alpha \lessgtr 0$ if and only if $a_1a_2-a_3 \gtrless 0$.

Finally, we demonstrate that Eq. (5) is the necessary and sufficient condition for $\alpha+\gamma \gtrless 0$ under the assumptions that $\alpha \lessgtr 0$ and $\gamma \gtrless 0$. First, we prove that the necessary and sufficient condition for $\alpha+\gamma>0$ is given by $2a_1^3+a_1a_2+a_3<0$ when $\alpha<0$ and $\gamma>0$.

(Necessity) Suppose $\gamma > -\alpha$. Then we obtain $\gamma > a_1$ from Eq. (A.2). Because $d\Delta(\gamma)/d\lambda > 0$ (see Fig. 8),[15] $\Delta(\lambda) > 0$ for all values of $\lambda > \gamma$ and $\Delta(\lambda) < 0$ for all values of $\lambda < \gamma$. Therefore, the following relationship holds:

$$0 = \Delta(\gamma) > \Delta(a_1) = 2a_1^3+a_1a_2+a_3.$$

(Sufficiency) On the contrary, we assume that $\gamma \le -\alpha$. Then we obtain $\gamma \le a_1$. Therefore,

$$0 = \Delta(\gamma) \le \Delta(a_1) = 2a_1^3+a_1a_2+a_3.$$

The proof that the necessary and sufficient condition for $\alpha+\gamma<0$ is given by $2a_1^3+a_1a_2+a_3>0$ when $\alpha>0$ and $\gamma<0$ is completed by inverting the signs of the inequalities in the preceding proof.

Remark 1. *The extremal values of Eq. (A.1) are calculated as follows:*

$$\Delta'(\lambda) = 3\lambda^2+2a_1\lambda+a_2 = 0,$$

$\therefore$

$$\begin{aligned}\hat{\lambda} &= \frac{-a_1+\sqrt{a_1^2-3a_2}}{3} = \frac{(2\alpha+\gamma)+\sqrt{(\alpha-\gamma)^2-3\beta^2}}{3},\\ \hat{\hat{\lambda}} &= \frac{-a_1-\sqrt{a_1^2-3a_2}}{3} = \frac{(2\alpha+\gamma)-\sqrt{(\alpha-\gamma)^2-3\beta^2}}{3}.\end{aligned}$$

[15] If two extremal values exist, they are definitely located on the left of γ (see Remark 1). However, the following two facts are sufficient to prove this Lemma: there is one real root (that is, the curve crosses the x-axis once), which is assumed, and the coefficient of the cubic term of the characteristic equation is positive. Notably, this lemma holds even if no extremal value exists.

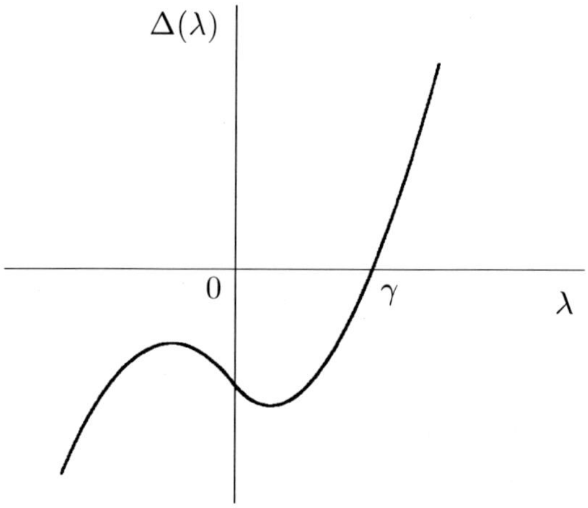

Figure 8. $\Delta(\gamma)$.

For these roots to be real, $(\alpha - \gamma)^2/3 > \beta^2$ *must hold. That is, the absolute value of* β *must be sufficiently small. In what follows, we consider cases wherein real roots exist.*

Incidentally, we obtain

$$\begin{aligned}\hat{\lambda} &= \frac{(2\alpha+\gamma)+\sqrt{(\gamma-\alpha)^2-3\beta^2}}{3} \\ &< \frac{(2\alpha+\gamma)+\sqrt{(\gamma-\alpha)^2-3\beta^2+3\beta^2}}{3} = \frac{\alpha+2\gamma}{3},\end{aligned}$$

and

$$\begin{aligned}\hat{\hat{\lambda}} &= \frac{(2\alpha+\gamma)-\sqrt{(\gamma-\alpha)^2-3\beta^2}}{3} \\ &> \frac{(2\alpha+\gamma)-\sqrt{(\gamma-\alpha)^2-3\beta^2+3\beta^2}}{3} = \alpha.\end{aligned}$$

Because $\alpha < 0$*, the following relationship holds:*

$$\alpha < \hat{\hat{\lambda}} < \hat{\lambda} < \frac{\alpha}{3} + \frac{2}{3}\gamma < \gamma.$$

Therefore, two extremal values of $\Delta(\lambda)$ *(if they exist) are located left of* γ.[16]

[16]Depending on the sign of a_2, the curve $\Delta(\gamma)$ can slope either upward or downward at $\lambda = 0$.

A.2. Optimal Investment Problem

Eq. (ii) in (6) is derived from the following optimization problem:

$$\begin{aligned} &\max \quad P = \int_0^\infty -[G(I,v) + H(\dot{I})]e^{-\rho t}dt, \\ &\text{subject to} \quad I(0) = I_0 \text{ (given)}. \end{aligned} \tag{A.6}$$

This is a cost minimization problem. $G(I,v)$ is the investment cost function, $H(\dot{I})$ is the adjustment cost function, and $\rho > 0$ is the discount rate. In addition, $v = I^e - I$; G includes the costs incurred when the actual volume of investment I diverges from the targeted volume of investment I^e. The existence of these costs can be explained as follows: firms must sign an employment contract with workers whose scale is proportional to the volume of the targeted investment, and so, if the actual volume of investment differs from the targeted volume, they must pay a penalty.

We also assume that the function $G(I,v)$ is convex with respect to $I > 0$ and has an extremum for $I > 0$. Moreover, the function $H(\dot{I})$ satisfies $H_{\dot{I}} > 0$ and $H_{\dot{I}\dot{I}} > 0$. To solve this problem, a firm is assumed to regard I^e as a given constant.

In what follows, we specify the functional forms of G and H as the quadric:

$$\begin{aligned} G &= I + \eta(I^e - I) + [I + \phi(I^e - I)]^2, \\ &= (1-\phi)^2 I^2 + [1 - \eta + 2\phi(1-\phi)I^e]I + \eta I^e + \phi^2 I^{e2}, \\ H &= \psi \dot{I}^2 + \omega \dot{I}, \end{aligned}$$

where $\eta, \phi, \psi, \omega > 0$. For G to have an extremum for $I > 0$, $(1-\eta)+2\phi(1-\phi)I^e < 0$ must hold. To assure this condition, we assume that $\eta > 1$, $\phi < 1$, and $|1-\eta| > 2\phi(1-\phi)I^e$.

The Euler equation of Eq. (A.6) is given by the following equation:

$$\ddot{I} - \rho\dot{I} - \frac{(1-\phi)^2}{\psi}I + \frac{\rho\omega + 1 - \eta + 2\phi(1-\phi)I^e}{2\psi} = 0.$$

The general solution of this differential equation is given by the following equation:

$$\begin{aligned} I(t) &= A_1 e^{r_1 t} + A_2 e^{r_2 t} + \bar{I}, \\ r_1, r_2 &= \frac{1}{2}\left(\rho \pm \sqrt{\rho^2 + \frac{4(1-\phi)^2}{\psi}}\right), \\ \bar{I} &= \frac{\rho\omega + 1 - \eta + 2\phi(1-\phi)I^e}{2(1-\phi)^2}, \end{aligned}$$

where the eigenvalues r_1 and r_2 are positive and negative numbers. We posit that $r_1 > 0$ and $r_2 < 0$.

For the solutions to converge, $A_1 = 0$ must hold. Then we obtain $A_2 = I_0 - \bar{I}$. Therefore,

$$I(t) = (I_0 - \bar{I})e^{r_2 t} + \bar{I}. \tag{A.7}$$

Differentiating this equation with respect to time t, we obtain the following:

$$\dot{I}(t) = r_2(I_0 - \bar{I})e^{r_2 t}.$$

Substituting Eq. (A.7) into this equation, we obtain the following:

$$\begin{aligned}\dot{I} &= -r_2(\bar{I} - I)\\ &= -r_2\left(\frac{\phi}{1-\phi}I^e - I\right) - r_2\frac{\rho\omega + 1 - \eta}{2(1-\phi)^2}.\end{aligned}$$

Defining that $a = -r_2$, $b = \phi/(1-\phi)$, $c = -r_2\frac{\rho\omega+1-\eta}{2(1-\phi)^2}$, and $I^e = K^e - K$, we obtain Eq. (ii) in (6). To ensure that the steady-state value of K^e is positive, we assume that $c < 0$: $\rho\omega + 1 < \eta$.

A.3. Applying Theorem 2. to the System of Differential Equations (7)

Condition 1. The Jacobian matrix of F is given by the following:

$$dF_{\mu,\nu}(X) = \boldsymbol{J} = \begin{bmatrix} -\delta & 1 & 0 \\ -ab & -a & ab \\ n(\bar{K} - 2K^* - 2x_1) - q & je^{jx_2} & 0 \end{bmatrix}.$$

Evaluating $\boldsymbol{J}$ at $X = \mathbf{0}$, we obtain the following:

$$dF_{\mu,\nu}(\mathbf{0}) = \boldsymbol{J}^* = \begin{bmatrix} -\delta & 1 & 0 \\ -ab & -a & ab \\ n(\bar{K} - 2K^*) - q & j & 0 \end{bmatrix}.$$

The characteristic equation of $\boldsymbol{J}$ evaluated at $X = \mathbf{0}$ is written as follows:

$$\begin{aligned}\Delta(\lambda) &= \det(\boldsymbol{J}^* - \lambda\boldsymbol{I}),\\ &= \det\begin{bmatrix} -\delta - \lambda & 1 & 0 \\ -ab & -a - \lambda & ab \\ n(\bar{K} - 2K^*) - q & j & -\lambda \end{bmatrix},\\ &= \lambda^3 + (a+\delta)\lambda^2 + a(b + \delta - bj)\lambda - abn(\bar{K} - 2K^*) + abq - abj\delta.\end{aligned}$$

Because $n = [q - \delta(1 + \delta/b)]/(\bar{K} - 2K^*)$ and $j = 1 + \delta/b$ at $(\mu, \nu) = (0, 0)$, we obtain

$$dF_{0,0}(\mathbf{0}) = J^*_{0,0} = \begin{bmatrix} -\delta & 1 & 0 \\ -ab & -a & ab \\ -\delta(1 + \delta/b) & 1 + \delta/b & 0 \end{bmatrix}.$$

Then the characteristic equation is rewritten as follows:

$$\Delta_{0,0}(\lambda) = \lambda^3 + (a+\delta)\lambda^2 = \lambda^2(\lambda + a + \delta),$$

which has double-zero eigenvalue and one nonzero eigenvalue of $-(a + \delta)$. Therefore, Condition 1 is satisfied.

The eigenvector associated with zero eigenvalue $e = [e_1, e_2, e_3]'$ satisfies

$$dF_{0,0}(\mathbf{0})e = 0e,$$

$$\begin{bmatrix} -\delta e_1 + e_2 \\ -abe_1 - ae_2 + abe_3 \\ -\delta(1 + \delta/b)e_1 + (1 + \delta/b)e_2 \end{bmatrix} = \begin{bmatrix} 0 \\ 0 \\ 0 \end{bmatrix},$$

and therefore

$$e = m \begin{bmatrix} 1 \\ \delta \\ 1+\delta/b \end{bmatrix},$$

where m is an arbitrary constant.

Condition 2.

$$\begin{aligned} \det dF_{\mu,\nu}(\mathbf{0}) &= abn(\bar{K} - 2K^*) - abq + abj\delta \\ &= ab\mu(\bar{K} - 2K^*). \end{aligned}$$

Therefore, the Jacobian matrix of the map $(\mu, \nu) \to (\det dF_{\mu,\nu}(\mathbf{0}), \sigma(dF_{\mu,\nu}(\mathbf{0})))$ is given by

$$\begin{bmatrix} ab(\bar{K} - 2K^*) & 0 \\ \sigma_\mu & \sigma_\nu \end{bmatrix}.$$

Evaluating this matrix at $(\mu, \nu) = (0, 0)$, we obtain the following:

$$\begin{bmatrix} ab(\bar{K} - 2K^*) & 0 \\ \sigma_\mu(dF_{0,0}(\mathbf{0})) & \sigma_\nu(dF_{0,0}(\mathbf{0})) \end{bmatrix}.$$

This is a nonzero matrix, and so Condition 2 is satisfied. There is no need to calculate σ because it is only necessary to confirm that the preceding matrix is nonzero.

Condition 3. The Hessian matrix of $F1$ is given by

$$\boldsymbol{H}_1 = \frac{d^2F1}{dX^2} = \begin{bmatrix} 0 & 0 & 0 \\ 0 & 0 & 0 \\ 0 & 0 & 0 \end{bmatrix},$$

the Hessian matrix of $F2$ is given by

$$\boldsymbol{H}_2 = \frac{d^2F2}{dX^2} = \begin{bmatrix} 0 & 0 & 0 \\ 0 & 0 & 0 \\ 0 & 0 & 0 \end{bmatrix},$$

and the Hessian matrix of $F3$ is given by

$$\boldsymbol{H}_3 = \frac{d^2F3}{dX^2} = \begin{bmatrix} -2n & 0 & 0 \\ 0 & j^2e^{jx_2} & 0 \\ 0 & 0 & 0 \end{bmatrix}.$$

Evaluating these matrices at $(X, \mu, \nu) = (\mathbf{0}, 0, 0)$, we obtain the following:

$$\boldsymbol{H}_1 = \mathbf{0}, \quad \boldsymbol{H}_2 = \mathbf{0}, \quad \boldsymbol{H}_3 = \begin{bmatrix} -\frac{2[q-\delta(1+\delta/b)]}{\bar{K}-2K^*} & 0 & 0 \\ 0 & (1+\delta/b)^2 & 0 \\ 0 & 0 & 0 \end{bmatrix}.$$

Using these expressions, we obtain

$$Q(X,X)=\begin{bmatrix}\frac{1}{2}X'H_1X\\ \frac{1}{2}X'H_2X\\ \frac{1}{2}X'H_3X\end{bmatrix}=\begin{bmatrix}0\\ 0\\ -\frac{q-\delta(1+\delta/b)}{\bar{K}-2K^*}x_1^2+\frac{1}{2}(1+\frac{\delta}{b})^2x_2^2\end{bmatrix}.$$

Substitute the eigenvector $e=[1,\delta,1+\delta/b]'$ into X to obtain

$$Q(e,e)=\begin{bmatrix}0\\ 0\\ \bar{R}\end{bmatrix},$$

where $\bar{R}\equiv-\frac{q-\delta(1+\delta/b)}{\bar{K}-2K^*}+\frac{1}{2}(1+\frac{\delta}{b})^2\delta^2$.

Therefore,

$$[dF_{0,0}(\mathbf{0})Q(e,e)]=\begin{bmatrix}-\delta & 1 & 0 & 0\\ -ab & -a & ab & 0\\ -\delta(1+\delta/b) & 1+\delta/b & 0 & \bar{R}\end{bmatrix}.$$

The rank of this matrix is 3 as long as $\bar{R}\neq0$. Therefore, if $\bar{R}\neq0$, Condition 3 is satisfied.

A.4. Hopf Bifurcation Theorem

Asada (1995) proposes the Hopf bifurcation theorem for a three-dimensional system of differential equations represented by the coefficients of a characteristic equation.

Theorem 3. (Asada, 1995) *There are periodic solutions that bifurcate from the fixed point X^* if the characteristic equation $\Delta(\lambda;\mu)=\lambda^3+a_1\lambda^2+a_2\lambda+a_3=0$ satisfies the following conditions at $\mu=\mu_1$:*

(i) $a_1\neq0,\ a_2>0,\ \Delta_1\equiv a_1a_2-a_3=0,$

(ii) $\frac{d\Delta_1}{d\mu}\neq0.$

References

[1] Abel, A. B. (1980). "Empirical Investment Equations: An Integrative Framework," *Carnegie-Rochester Conference Series on Public Policy*, 12, North-Holland, 39–91.

[2] Arnéodo, A., P. Coullet, and C. Tresser (1982). "Oscillations with Chaotic Behavior: An Illustration of a Theorem by Shil'nikov," *Journal of Statistical Physics* 27, 171–182.

[3] Asada, T. (1995). "Kaldorian Dynamics in an Open Economy," *Journal of Economics*, 62, 239–269.

[4] Asada, T. (1997). *Macrodynamics of Growth and Cycles* Nihon Keizai Hyouronsya (in Japanese).

[5] Asada, T. (2004). "Price Flexibility and Instability in a Macrodynamic Model with a Debt Effect," *Journal of International Economic Studies*, 32, 19–38.

[6] Asada, T. (2012). "Modeling Financial Instability," *Intervention: European Journal of Economics and Economic Policies*, 9, 215–232.

[7] Asada, T., W. Semmler and A. J. Novak (1998). "Endogenous Growth and the Balanced Growth Equilibrium," *Research in Economics*, 52, 189–202.

[8] Asada, T. and H. Yoshida (2003). "Coefficient Criterion for Four-Dimensional Hopf Bifurcations: A Complete Mathematical Characterization and Applications to Economic Dynamics," *Chaos, Solitons & Fractals* 18, 525–536.

[9] Asako, K. and M. Kuninori (1989). "Theory of Capital Investment and Empirical Research in Japan," in H. Uzawa ed., *Japanese Economy: History of Accumulation and Growth*, University of Tokyo Press, 151–182 (in Japanese).

[10] Asako, K., K. Tonogi, and J. Nakamura (2013). "Development of Research in Capital Investment and Multiple q," *Discussion Paper Series A*, No. 584, Institute of Economic Research, Hitotsubashi University, Japan (in Japanese).

[11] Bond, S. and J. Van Reenen (2007). "Microeconometric Models of Investment and Employment," *Handbook of Econometrics*, 6, 4417–4498.

[12] Caballero, R. J. (1999). "Aggregate Investment," *Handbook of Macroeconomics*, 1, 813–862.

[13] Chiang, A. C. (1992). *Elements of Dynamic Optimization*, McGraw-Hill.

[14] Christiano, L. J., M. Eichenbaum, and C. L. Evans (2005). "Nominal Rigidities and the Dynamic Effects of a Shock to Monetary Policy," *Journal of Political Economy* 113, 1–45.

[15] Coullet, P., C. Tresser, and A. Arnéodo (1979). "Transition to Stochasticity for a Class of Forced Oscillators," *Physics Letters A*, 72, 268–270.

[16] Eberly, J. C., S. Rebelo, and N. Vincent (2012). "What Explains the Lagged-Investment Effect?" *Journal of Monetary Economics*, 59, 370–380.

[17] Gandolfo, G. (2010). *Economic Dynamics*, Fourth Edition, Springer-Verlag.

[18] Gould, J. P. (1968). "Adjustment Costs in the Theory of Investment of the Firm," *Review of Economic Studies*, 35, 47–55.

[19] Guckenheimer, J. and P. Holmes (1983). *Nonlinear Oscillations, Dynamical Systems, and Bifurcation of Vector Fields*, Springer-Verlag.

[20] Hayashi, F. (1982). "Tobin's Marginal q and Average q: A Neoclassical Interpretation" *Econometrica: Journal of the Econometric Society*, 213–224.

[21] Hayashi, F. (2000). *"The Cost of Capital, Q, and the Theory of Investment Demand"*, Lau, ed., 55–84.

[22] Jorgenson, D. W. (1963). "Capital Theory and Investment Behavior," *American Economic Review*, 53, 247–259.

[23] Kopell, N. and L. N. Howard (1975). "Bifurcations and Trajectories Joining Critical Points," *Advances in Mathematics*, 18, 306–358.

[24] Lorenz, H. (1993). *Nonlinear Dynamical Economics and Chaotic Motion*, Second, Revised and Enlarged Edition, Springer-Verlag.

[25] Lucas Jr, R. E. (1967). "Adjustment Costs and the Theory of Supply," *Journal of Political Economy*, 75, 321–334.

[26] Lucas Jr, R. E. and E. Prescott (1971). "Investment under Uncertainty", *Econometrica: Journal of the Econometric Society*, 659–681.

[27] Mussa, M. (1977). "External and Internal Adjustment Costs and the Theory of Aggregate and Firm Investment," *Economica*, 44, 163–178.

[28] Nickell, S. J. (1978). *The Investment Decisions of Firms*, Cambridge: Nisbet.

[29] Shil'nikov, L. P. (1965). "A Case of the Existence of a Countable Number of Periodic Motions," *Doklady Matemacheskii SSSR*, 6, 163–166.

[30] Sportelli, M. C. (2000). "Dynamic Complexity in a Keynesian Growth Cycle Model Involving Harrod's Instability," *Journal of Economics*, 71, 167–198.

[31] Takagi, T. (1965). *Lectures on the Theory of Algebra*, Tokyo: Kyoritsu Shuppan (in Japanese).

[32] Tobin, J. (1969). "A General Equilibrium Approach to Monetary Theory," *Journal of Money, Credit and Banking*, 1, 15–29.

[33] Uzawa, H. (1969). "Time Preference and the Penrose Effect in a Two-Class Model of Economic Growth," *Journal of Political Economy*, 77, 628–652.

[34] Wolf, A., J. B. Swift, H. L. Swinney, and J. A. Vastano (1985). "Determining Lyapunov Exponents from a Time Series," *Physica D: Nonlinear Phenomena*, 16, 285–317.

[35] Yoshikawa, H. (1980). "On the "q" Theory of Investment," *American Economic Review*, 70, 739–743.

In: Business Cycles in Economics
Editor: Jason C. Hsu

ISBN: 978-1-63321-322-7

Chapter 6

MONETARY POLICY REGIMES AND THE STOCK MARKET

Marcelle Chauvet* and Chuanlei Sun†
University of California, Riverside, CA, US

Abstract

This paper studies the relationship between monetary policy and the stock market across business cycle recessions and expansions. A nonlinear two-state Markov switching model is used to obtain regimes in interest rate cycles and in stock market cycles. The model identifies tight and loose monetary policy phases, and bear and bull stock market regimes. Turning points for each cycle are established and their lead-lag relationship is examined and contrasted with NBER recessions. We also examine the linear predictive relationship between interest rates and stock returns. The results indicate that there are strong linkages among interest rate cycles, stock market cycles, and business cycles. We find that, generally, the stock market enters a bear market phase at around the same time as monetary policy enters a tight phase, which is associated with the onset of economic recessions. We also find that future stock returns are substantially impacted by information on monetary policy regimes (i.e. loose or tight). On the other hand, interest rates are most influenced by future inflation and recessions rather than by changes in the stock market.

Keywords: Business Cycle, Interest Rates, Markov Switching, Turning Points, Forecast

JEL Classification Code: C32, E32, E44

1. Introduction

The stock market experiences recurrent fluctuations, which are linked through different channels to changes in economic activity and in monetary policy. Understanding these fluctuations is a primary concern for businesses and investors and, consequently, for policy

---

* E-mail address: chauvet@ucr.edu; Tel: (951) 827-1587; Fax: (951) 827-5685.
† E-mail address: csun007@ucr.edu.

makers, since they reflect private economic agents' expectations. Financial market participants use all available data to infer monetary policy actions as well as the state of the business cycle, seeking to take positions that maximize their profits. As new economic data are released, information is promptly included in market participants' expectations regarding future economic activity. Over the course of the month, as agents trade assets based on their perceptions of the state of the economy and monetary policy actions, stock market prices reflect these expectations.

Accordingly, there is a large literature showing evidence of systematic movements in excess stock returns associated with estimates of the underlying state of the business cycle. On the other hand, monetary policy is also closely associated with the phases of the business cycle. As the economic activity booms, monetary authorities tend to increase interest rates to ease possible inflation pressures. Conversely, monetary policy becomes loose in anticipation of economic weakness with the goal of minimizing or avoiding an economic contraction. Thus, stock market fluctuations might be linked to monetary policy not only through the direct effect of interest rates on stock prices, but also through expectations as changes in monetary policy regimes signal future economic recessions or expansions. Thus, stock market, monetary policy, and the business cycle might be connected, to some extent, through expectations about changes in future economic activity.

The goal of this paper is to study the relationship among monetary policy phases, stock market phases, and the U.S. business cycle. First, a nonlinear two-state Markov switching model is used to obtain different regimes in interest rate cycles and in stock market cycles Based on the model estimates, the beginning and end of each cycle phase (turning points) are established and analyzed. Next, we examine the lead-lag relationship of monetary policy phases, stock market cycles, and economic NBER expansions and recessions.[1]

Many papers focus on the relationship between the stock market cycle and the business cycle. This paper builds on the work of Chauvet (1999), Chauvet and Potter (2000, 2001), and Chauvet and Senyuz (2009). Chauvet (1999) proposes dynamic factor models with Markov switching to represent business cycle phases and stock market states, and to examine their linkages. The paper finds that the business cycle factor moves very closely to NBER recessions, while changes in the stock market factor is a leading indicator of future recessions. Chauvet and Potter (2000, 2001) construct a coincident indicator of excess stock return based on financial variables using a nonlinear dynamic factor model. The model identifies bear and bull market phases. During bear markets, mean stock return is negative and its volatility is high, while during bull markets, stock returns are high and positive, and stock volatility is low. The paper finds that all bear markets are associated with future NBER recessions. Chauvet and Potter (2000) construct leading indicators of the stock market and finds that information about future recessions is the most important predictor of changes in the stock market. Chauvet and Potter (2001) study the relationship between risk and mean stock return of small, medium and large firms. They find that small firms are more sensitivity to bear markets and recessions. Moreover, volatility for all firms is significantly related to average return, but the sign of the relationship changes across business cycle phases: risk-return is negative at the beginning of recessions when the conditional mean decreases in anticipation to the economic downturn and the conditional volatility rises. This relationship reverses towards

[1] The National Bureau of Economic Research (NBER) has been dating U.S. recessions for the last 60 years. The dates are widely regarded as being the 'official' beginning and end of recessions. The NBER recession dates are obtained from http://www.nber.org/cycles/ cyclesmain.html.

the end of recession when the conditional expected return increase in anticipation to the onset of expansions, but the conditional volatility is still high due to the uncertainty surrounding economic turning points. Thus, the paper concludes that the risk-return relationship is strongly influenced by the phases of the business cycle.

Chauvet and Senyuz (2009) propose a dynamic bi-factor model with Markov switching model to study the relationship between the yield curve and the business cycle. The paper finds that the resulting yield curve factor is a strong predictor of business cycle phases, and has the best accuracy compared to several alternative models, displaying no false or missed turning point.

This paper extends the previous literature by investigating the relationship among monetary policy, the stock market, and the economy. In particular, it models and predicts the links among these sectors using Markov switching models, as proposed by Hamilton (1989), which are widely used to capture turning points of financial and macroeconomic variables. This paper follows the approach in Chauvet (1999), Chauvet and Potter (2000, 2001) and Chauvet and Senyuz (2009) using nonlinear models to characterize phases of the stock market and the business cycle. We extend this approach by further modeling monetary policy phases and studying the nonlinear (turning points) as well as the linear predictive relationship between stock returns and monetary policy regimes.

The results indicate that there is a strong relationship between interest rate cycles and stock market cycles, and those with economic expansions and recessions. In particular, we find that loose monetary policy phases start, on average, about one quarter before the beginning of NBER recessions, while interest rates start to increase, on average, about five quarters after the end of NBER recessions. On the other hand, all bear market phases begin before or at the same time as the onset of NBER recessions, with an average lead of three quarters. Bear markets also end before or at the same time as the end of NBER recessions (average lead of two quarters), with the exception of the last two recessions (in 2001 and in 2007-2009).

Thus, the results imply that stock market return and interest rates are leading indicators of business cycles. Further, we find a strong relationship between stock market and monetary policy phases. Since both the stock market and monetary policy react to future economic activity, their changes reflect expectations of transitions in future business cycle phases. Thus, changes in monetary policy affect the stock market, and changes in the stock market impact monetary policy, as they signal perceptions and uncertainty of private agents regarding future economic activity.

In particular, we find that during a small window loose monetary policy regimes are associated with negative stock returns, as both occur during economic recessions. However, as the economy moves towards a recovery, interest rates are still low, while stock returns rebound. Thus, towards the end of recessions and low monetary policy phases, stock returns become positive, anticipating the beginning of the economic recovery.

We construct several linear models to examine the predictive relationship between interest rates and stock returns. We find that the most important drivers of future interest rates are inflation and the prospect of recessions. Stock market returns play a minor role in predicting interest rates. On the other hand, future stock market return is largely impacted by changes in interest rate phases and by inflation. In particular, tight monetary policy is associated with negative future stock returns. This paper is structured as follows. Section 2 presents the Markov switching model. Section 3 discusses the empirical characterization of stock market and monetary policy regimes. Section 4 examines the relationship between stock market and interest rates through turning point analysis, as well as through out-of-sample linear forecasting using linear models. Section 5 concludes.

2. Econometric Model

We use the univariate Markov switching model based on Hamilton (1989). Let y_t be a time series representing the interest rate or the stock market price, which has two components: a Markov trend term n_t, and a stationary $\tilde{z}_t$. The model can be written as:

$$\tilde{y}_t = n_t + \tilde{z}_t \tag{1}$$

The Markov trend is:

$$n_t = \alpha_1 S_t + \alpha_0 (1\text{-}S_t) + n_{t\text{-}1},\ S_t = 0 \text{ or } 1 \tag{2}$$

The stationary component $\tilde{z}_t$ follows the ARIMA (p,1,0) process:

$$\tilde{z}_t - \tilde{z}_{t-1} = \phi_1(\tilde{z}_{t-1} - \tilde{z}_{t-2}) + \phi_2(\tilde{z}_{t-2} - \tilde{z}_{t-3}) + \cdots + \phi_p(\tilde{z}_{t-p} - \tilde{z}_{t-p-1}) + \varepsilon_t \tag{3}$$

where $\varepsilon_t \sim \text{i.i.d.} N(0, \sigma^2_{\varepsilon_t})$, and ε_t and n_{t+h} are independent for all *h*. Taking the first difference of (1), we obtain:

$$y_t = \alpha_1 S_t + \alpha_0 (1\text{-}S_t) + z_t \tag{4}$$

where, $y_t \equiv \tilde{y}_t\text{-}\tilde{y}_{t\text{-}1}$, $z_t \equiv \tilde{z}_t\text{-}\tilde{z}_{t\text{-}1}$ and $z_t = \phi_1 z_{t\text{-}1} + \phi_2 z_{t\text{-}2} + \cdots + \phi_p z_{t\text{-}p} + \varepsilon_t$.

This framework can be used to model the phases of interest rates and of stock returns. In particular, we can write:

$$y^i_t = \alpha^i_1 S^i_t + \alpha^i_0 (1\text{-}S^i_t) + \phi^i(L) y^i_{t\text{-}1} + \varepsilon^i_{S_t} \tag{5}$$

where $\varepsilon^i_{S_t} \sim \text{i.i.d.} N(0, \sigma^2_{\varepsilon^i_{S_t}})$, y^i_t = observable variables, and *i* = interest rate or S&P 500 returns. *L* is the lag operator and $\phi(L)$ is the lag polynomial.

S_t is the unobserved Markov state that takes the value of zero, representing low mean phases or the value of one, representing high mean phases. Anticipating the empirical results, $S_t = 0$ represents phases of low mean and high variance for stock returns, while $S_t = 1$ represents phases of high mean and low variance of stock returns. In the case of interest rates, state zero represents phases of low mean and low variance in monetary policy regime, and state one characterizes phases of high mean and high variance in monetary policy. The transition probabilities are:

$$Prob[S_t = 1|S_{t-1} = 1] = p_{11}$$

$$Prob[S_t = 0|S_{t-1} = 1] = 1 - p_{11}$$

$$Prob[S_t = 0|S_{t-1} = 0] = p_{00}$$

$$Prob[S_t = 1|S_{t-1} = 0] = 1 - p_{00}$$

3.3. Empirical Results

Data

Interest rates are represented by the Federal Funds Rate, which is obtained from the Board of Governors of the Federal Reserve System, and stock market return is obtained as 100 times the log first difference of the S&P 500 Index from the Standard and Poor. Inflation rate is defined as the 100 times the log first difference of the consumer price index (CPI for all urban consumers: all items less food), which is obtained from the Bureau of Labor Statistics. The data are analyzed in quarterly frequency from 1957Q2 to 2011Q4. The sample is determined by the availability of the data.

3.1. Characterization of Stock Market Phases and Monetary Policy Regimes

The goal of this paper is to analyze interest rate cycles and stock market cycles, and their potential linkages. Figure 1 plots interest rate and stock market return, and the NBER recession dates are represented in the shaded areas.[2] Interest rate usually decreases around NBER recessions and increases during economic expansions.

The Federal Reserve generally pursues loose monetary policy by lowering interest rates to spur economic activity during recessions, and pursues tight monetary policy (by raising interest rates) to curb inflationary pressures during expansions. Thus, changes in the Federal Funds Rate are correlated with NBER recessions. On the other hand, stock returns generally decreases before NBER recessions, anticipating weak economic activity and earnings, and increase in the middle of recessions, anticipating their end. Thus, stock returns are also highly correlated with NBER recessions.

We model monetary policy and stock market using two-state Markov switching models to capture tight and loose monetary policy regimes, as well as bear and bull stock market phases, respectively, and the results are presented below.

Interest Rates Cycles

Table 1 shows the maximum likelihood estimates of the univariate Markov Switching model applied to detrended interest rates. The model identifies two Markov regimes: state

[2] In this figure the S&P 500 stock return is smoothed using the H-P filter, for visualization purpose.

one, which is associated with a positive and significant mean (0.43) and high variance (19.12), and state zero with a negative and significant mean (-0.51) and low variance (1.35). The transition probability estimates indicate that the duration of the high mean interest rate state is longer (0.957, which implies an average duration of 23 quarters) than the duration of the low mean state (0.939, with an average duration of 16.4 quarters).[3]

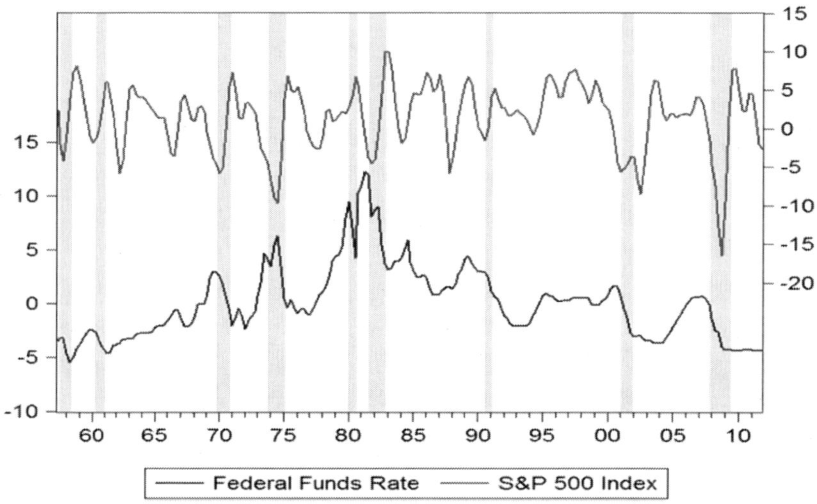

Figure 1. Interest Rate, S&P 500 Stock Return, and NBER Recessions (shaded area).

Table 1. Maximum Likelihood Estimates - Interest Rate Model

Parameters Estimates	
α_1	0.434(0.423)
α_0	-0.506(0.197)
σ_1^2	19.125(2.596)
σ_0^2	1.353(0.290)
p_{11}	0.957(0.020)
p_{00}	0.939(0.025)
Log L	-328.765

Note: the results are for detrended interest rates.

Figure 2 plots the smoothed probabilities of low interest rate state (loose monetary phase).

As it can be observed, the probabilities generally increase to values close to one towards the end of economic expansions or at the beginning of recessions, and decrease to values close to zero at or a couple of quarters after the end of recessions. Thus, loose monetary policy phases are associated with economic recessions.

3 The average phase duration is: $\sum_{k=1}^{\infty} kp^{k-1}(1-p) = \frac{1}{1-p}$.

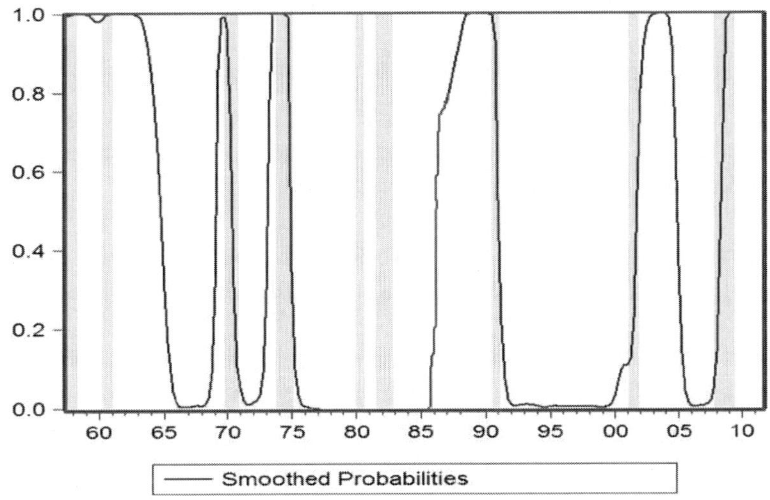

Figure 2. Smoothed Probabilities of the Low Mean Interest Rate State and NBER Recessions (Shaded Area).

We adopt the criterion widely used in the literature to date turning points, based on the smoothed probabilities. State zero starts when the smoothed probabilities of low mean are greater than or equal to 50%, $P(S_t = 0|I_T) \geq 0.5$, and ends when they reach values below 50% $P(S_t = 0|I_T) < 0.5$. Table 4 compares turning points of interest rate cycles and business cycles using this criterion. Changes in interest rates are associated with most NBER recessions.

Generally, monetary policy enters a loose regime with a median of two quarters before the beginning of recessions.[4] Loose monetary regimes end at about the same time as recessions, with the exception of the 1961 and 2001 recessions. In those cases, interest rates remained low for almost three years after these recessions ended. Although data do not allow a full analysis of the most recent recession in 2007-2009, in this case interest rate also remained in the low regime many years after this recession peak in June 2009 to stimulate the economy in face of the slow recovery that followed this contraction.[5]

On the other hand, the analysis indicates that monetary policy remained tight before, during, and after the 1980 and 1981-1982 recessions. This was the period of the Great Inflation, in which the Federal Reserve pursued contractionary monetary policy to curb inflation. In addition, the Fed changed its operating procedures during the period between 1979 and 1982, targeting reserves (McCallum 1989). During this time, interest rates increased substantially, reaching two digits. The probabilities of monetary policy regime captures this phase.

In particular, the smoothed probabilities of low interest rates did not increase during this period even though it was characterized by a severe contraction in economic activity. In summary, we find that the interest rate usually enters a loose regime before the onset of recessions, and it starts to rise a couple of quarters after recessions end.

[4] Unavailability of data precludes full analysis of the first two recessions in the sample.
[5] At the time this paper was written in May 2014 interest rates were still in the low regime.

Stock Market Cycles

Table 2 shows the maximum likelihood estimates of the univariate Markov Switching model fitted to stock returns. The model identifies bull market phases (state 1), which are associated with positive mean return and low variance, and bear market phases (state 0), with negative mean return and high variance. The probability of staying in the bear market phase is a lot lower (p_{00} = 0.801) than the probability of staying in bull market phases (p_{11} = 0.907).

The average duration of bear markets is five quarters, while the average duration of bull markets is eleven quarters. Similar results are also found in Chauvet (1999) and Chauvet and Potter (2000).

Figure 3 plots the smoothed probabilities of bear market phases and NBER recessions (shaded areas). The association of low stock return phases with recessions is striking. The probabilities generally increase to values around one a couple of quarters before recessions, and fall to values around zero before recessions end.

Table 2. Maximum Likelihood Estimates - Stock Return Model

Parameters Estimates	
α_1	3.684(0.264)
α_0	-3.299(0.605)
σ_1^2	5.232(0.795)
σ_0^2	11.543(2.177)
p_{11}	0.907(0.027)
p_{00}	0.801(0.052)
$\text{Log}\,L$	-368.484

Note: The numbers in parentheses are asymptotic standard errors.

Table 3. NBER Recessions, Low Interest Rate Cycles, and Low Stock Returns

Cycles	NBER Recessions	Interest Rate Cycles	Stock Market Cycles
	1957Q3-1958Q2	1957Q2-1964Q3	1957Q3-1958Q1
	1960Q2-1961Q1		1959Q4-1960Q2
	-		1962Q1-1962Q3
	-	-	1966Q1-1966Q4
	1969Q4-1970Q4	1969Q2-1970Q2	1969Q1-1970Q3
	1973Q4-1975Q1	1973Q2-1974Q4	1973Q1-1974Q4
	1980Q1-1980Q3	-	1976Q4-1978Q1
	1981Q3-1982Q4	-	1981Q2-1982Q2
	-	-	1984Q1-1984Q2
	-	1985Q2-1991Q1	1987Q3-1988Q2
	1990Q3-1991Q1		1990Q2-1990Q3
	2001Q1-2001Q4	2001Q4-2004Q4	2000Q3-2003Q1
	2007Q4-2009Q2	2008Q3-	2007Q4-2009Q1
	-	-	2011Q3-
Total	9	6	14

Note: Interest rate turning points are chosen by the criterion: $P(S_t = 0|I_T) \geq 0.5$.

The probabilities of bear markets remain close to zero during economic expansions. Note that all recessions were preceded by bear market phases, with the exception of the 1980 recession. Notice that there were times in which the probability of bear market increased but no economic recession followed in the U.S.

This can be more formally studied in Table 3, which dates each of the bear market phases based on the smoothed probabilities.

Between 1957Q2 and 2011Q4 there were 14 bear market phases and 9 recessions defined by the NBER. All nine NBER recessions were preceded by bear markets (Tables 3 and 5). During this period, bear markets did not miss any business cycle peaks or troughs. Thus, the stock market is a leading indicator of the beginning and end of recessions.

Table 4. Turning Points of Interest Rate Cycles, Stock Market Cycles and NBER Business Cycle

Peaks (9 peaks)	Interest Rate Cycles	Stock Market Cycles
1957Q3	NA	0
1960Q2	-	+2
1969Q4	+2	+3
1973Q4	+2	+3
1980Q1	+7	+13
1981Q3	-	+1
1990Q3	+17	+1
2001Q1	-3	+2
2007Q4	-3	0
Mean	3.7	2.8
Median	2.0	2.0
Standard Deviation	7.5	4.0
Troughs (9 troughs)	**Interest Rate Cycles**	**Stock Market Cycles**
1958Q2	-	+1
1961Q1	-14	+3
1970Q4	+2	+1
1975Q1	+1	+1
1980Q3	-	+10
1982Q4	-	+2
1991Q1	0	+2
2001Q4	-12	-5
2009Q2	NA	+1
Mean	-4.6	1.8
Median	0	1.0
Standard Deviation	7.7	3.8

Note: + indicates leads, – indicates lags, and 0 means contemporaneous.

On the other hand, some bear markets were not associated with future recessions (5 out of 14 peaks and 4 out of 13 troughs). In this sense, these can be considered as false future signals of business cycle turning points. These bear market phases occurred in 1962, 1966, 1984, and in 1987. Interestingly, with the exception of 1987, these events were associated with the economic slowdown in Europe and in the U.S. in 1961-1965, and in 1984-1986 (Vanous 1982, Chauvet 1999). Although these low economic growth phases did not turn into more severe recessions, they negatively impacted the stock market. On the other hand, the 1987 bear market was associated with the stock market crash this year, known as the 'Black Monday' in October 1987. These four false signals from stock market cycles are similar to the ones obtained in Chauvet (1999).

Table 4 shows the lead-lag relationship between stock market phases and business cycle phases. As it can be observed, each one of the recession peaks (beginning) coincided or was preceded by a bear market peak. The 1957 recession and the 2007-2009 recession started at the same time as bear markets. For all other recessions, stock returns entered a low growth phase around 2 or 3 quarters *before* the beginning of recessions.[6]

Stock market phases also anticipate the end of economic recessions. As seen in the bottom panel of Table 4, bear market troughs anticipate the end of recessions with an average lead of 2 quarters. Thus, the stock market can also be used as a leading indicator of economic troughs. The only time in which a bear market did not anticipate a recession trough was for the 2001:Q1-2001:Q4 recession. The slow recovery that followed this recession in 2002-2003 curbed expectations and kept stock returns at lower levels until mid 2003, at which point economic growth became more robust.

Summing up, the analysis indicate that stock market return is a leading indicator of business cycles.

Table 5. Turning Point Evaluation of Interest Rate Cycles and Stock Market Cycles

Peaks (9 peaks)	**Interest Rates Cycles**	**Stock Market Cycles**
Correct Turning Point	5	9
Missed Turning Point	3	0
False Turning Point	-	5
Total Turning Point Error	3	5
Troughs (9 troughs)	**Interest Rates Cycles**	**Stock Market Cycles**
Correct Turning Point	5	9
Missed Turning Point	3	0
False Turning Point	-	4
Total Turning Point Error	3	4

Note: Total turning point error equals the sum of missed and false turning points.

[6] The longest lead was for the 1980 recession in which stock market returns fell 13 quarters earlier. This decrease in returns in 1978-1979 is associated with a mild but persistent decrease in economic growth during this period that later turned into a recession in 1980.

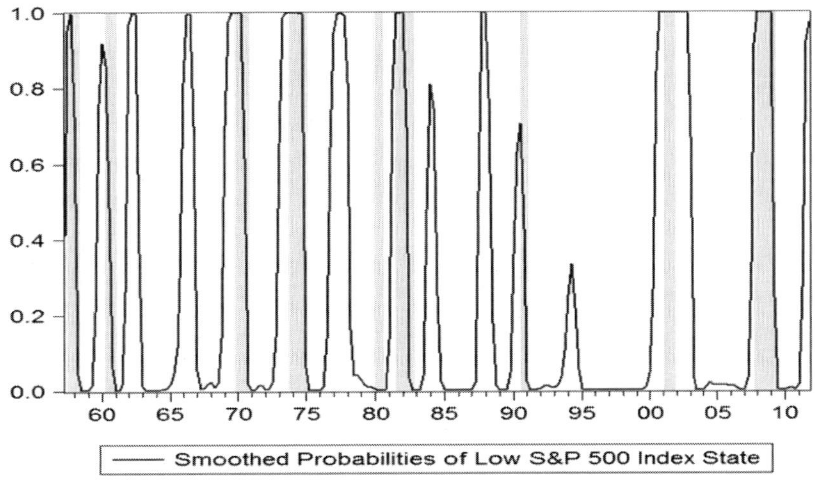

Figure 3. Smoothed Probabilities of the Bear Markets and the NBER Recessions (Shaded Area).

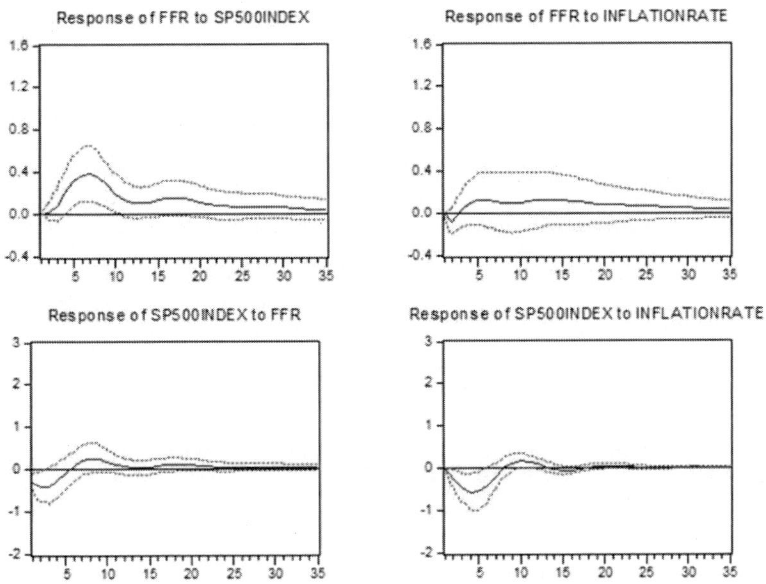

Figure 4. Impulse Response Functions of Interest Rate and Stock Returns to Inflation Rate[7].

4. Relationship between Stock Market Cycles and Monetary Policy Regimes

The analysis indicates a strong association between stock market phases and business cycles, and monetary policy regimes and business cycles. Since both the stock market and monetary policy react to future economic activity, their changes capture expectations of transitions in future business cycle phases. Thus, changes in monetary policy may affect the

[7] The responses are within 2 standard error bands.

stock market, and changes in the stock market may influence monetary policy, as both signal perceptions and uncertainty of regarding future economic activity.

In this section, we study the relationship between stock market fluctuations and monetary policy regimes. As a start point, Figure 4 shows the impulse response functions from a vector autoregressive model (VAR) including stock returns, interest rates, and inflation.[8]

The impact of an inflation shock on interest rate is positive and gradual, reaching a peak (0.122) at quarter 5, while the effect of an inflation shock on stock returns is larger and negative, reaching a peak (-0.592) at quarter 4, but decaying quickly. Further, a monetary policy shock has a negative effect on stock returns, reaching a peak at quarter 2 (-0.419), and lasting for about one year. On the other hand, a shock to stock return has a long-term positive impact on interest rates, reaching a peak (0.383) at quarter 7.

4.1. Turning Point Evaluation

This section evaluates turning points, following the approaches in Chauvet (1999) and Chauvet and Senyuz (2009). First, we define a naive benchmark forecast (MSE_1) as:

$$MSE_1 = \frac{2}{T} \sum_{t=1}^{T} \{X_t - \mu_X\}^2 \tag{6}$$

where X_t is the NBER dummy that takes the value of one during recessions and zero during expansions, and μ_X represents the mean of X_t. Second, the Quadratic Probability Score (denoted as MSE_2) is used to compare the prediction accuracy or the calibration of leads and lags of interest rate cycles and stock market cycles with NBER expansions and recessions. The MSE_2 ranges from zero to two, with a perfect prediction taking the value of zero:[9]

$$MSE_2 = QPS = \frac{2}{T} \sum_{t=1}^{T} \left\{p_{t-k} - X_t\right\}^2, \tag{7}$$

where p_{t-k} are the smoothed probabilities of high interest rate state or the smoothed probabilities of bear markets at the *k* lead or lag, which are obtained from the univariate Markov switching model.

Third, as in Chauvet and Senyuz (2009) we use the skill score and its decomposition as introduced by Murphy (1988) in order to examine the prediction accuracy of stock market phases and interest rate phases to NBER recessions, compared to the benchmark prediction. Murphy's basic skill score (MSE_3) is defined as:

$$MSE_3 = 1 - (MSE_2/MSE_1) \tag{8}$$

Perfect prediction is attained when the MSE_3 equals to one, while the prediction accuracy is not as good as the benchmark model when MSE_3 is negative.

[8] The impulse response functions are based on the VAR(2) from 1957Q2 to 2011Q4. The lag is chosen based on the AIC (Akaike 1973) and the BIC (Schwarz 1978).

[9] See Brier and Allen (1951) and Diebold and Rudebusch (1991), who popularized the Quadratic Probability Score metric.

The upper part of Table 6 reports the leading relationship between low interest rate (smoothed probabilities of low interest rates) and recessions, and bear markets (smoothed probabilities of low stock return) and recessions using the benchmark forecast MSE_1, the MSE_2, and the Murphy's skill score MSE_3 at 0-8 quarters ahead.

The MSE_2 for low interest rates increases with the forecast horizon. Thus, loose monetary policy best predicts recession at one-quarter horizon with its lowest $MSE_2 = 0.795$, while the skill score at the one-quarter forecast is negative, indicating that the benchmark model has a stronger association with recessions.

On the other hand, bear markets best predict recessions at the two-quarter horizon, which has the lowest MSE_2, (0.308) and a skill score close to zero (-0.004). On the other hand, the skill score metric indicates that the best recession prediction by bear markets is at the one-quarter horizon. This is the only horizon at which the skill score is positive among all forecast horizons (0.006), thus providing more accurate prediction than the benchmark model. Similarly to the forecast performance of low interest rate phases, the MSE_2 for bear markets increases with the forecast horizon.

Table 6. Turning Point Prediction Analysis: Quadratic Probability Score (MSE_2) and the Murphy's Skill Score (MSE_3)

Forecast Horizon (Quarter)	Benchmark Forecast	Interest Rate Model		Stock Market Model	
	MSE_1	MSE_2	MSE_3	MSE_2	MSE_3
0	0.3100	0.8105	-1.6145	0.4026	-0.2987
+1	0.3111	0.7949	-1.5551	0.3093	0.0058
+2	0.3065	0.8120	-1.6493	0.3076	-0.0036
+3	0.3018	0.8562	-1.8370	0.3914	-0.2969
+4	0.2970	0.9079	-2.0569	0.5157	-0.7364
+5	0.2921	0.9573	-2.2773	0.6322	-1.1643
+6	0.2932	0.9940	-2.3902	0.7401	-1.5242
+7	0.2942	1.0315	-2.5061	0.8185	-1.7821
+8	0.2953	1.0600	-2.5896	0.8445	-1.8598
-1	0.3111	0.8228	-1.6448	0.5208	-0.6741
-2	0.3122	0.8381	-1.6845	0.6209	-0.9888
-3	0.3133	0.8497	-1.7121	0.6829	-1.1797
-4	0.3144	0.8589	-1.7319	0.6975	-1.2185
-5	0.3155	0.8714	-1.7620	0.6907	-1.1892
-6	0.3166	0.8724	-1.7555	0.6787	-1.1437
-7	0.3177	0.8684	-1.7334	0.6741	-1.1218
-8	0.3189	0.8621	-1.7034	0.6908	-1.1662

Notes: + indicates leads, – indicates lags, and 0 means contemporaneous.

We conclude that the best in-sample recession forecasts occur at the very short-term (one or two quarters) for both loose monetary policy and bear markets. In addition, we find that bear markets have a substantially higher accuracy and resolution in predicting recessions compared to loose monetary policy phases.

The bottom part of Table 6 reports the mean square error metrics at 1-8 quarters lags. We note that for both bear markets and low interest rate phases, the best recession forecast performance is at the lowest lag of one quarter. However, for both indicators, the lowest overall mean square errors are for the one-quarter lead.

That is, bear markets and interest rates are leading indicators of recessions.

As in Lahiri and Wang (2006) and Chauvet and Senyuz (2009), we use as a metric the following decomposition of the skill score (MSE_3), as proposed by Murphy (1988):

$$MSE_4 = \rho^2_{X_t,p_{t-k}} - \left[\rho_{X_t,p_{t-k}} - (\sigma_p/\sigma_X)\right]^2 - [(\mu_p - \mu_X)/\sigma_X]^2 \quad (9)$$

where $\rho_{X_t,p_{t-k}}$ is the correlation coefficient between X_t and p_{t-k}. σ_X and σ_p and μ_X and μ_p are the standard deviations and means of X_t and the p_{t-k}, respectively. The skill score is, thus, equal to the square correlation between NBER recessions (X_t) and the smoothed probabilities (p_{t-k}) of low interest rate phases or bear markets (first term) minus the penalty for non-accurate prediction (second term), and the average mismatch between the prediction and the actual event (third term).

The Murphy's decomposition of the skill score (MSE_4) for leads 0-8 quarters are shown in the upper part of Table 7. This metric confirms previous results that the best recession prediction from both low interest rate phases and bear markets is also at one-quarter horizon. The decomposition allows analysis of the terms that contribute for the prediction accuracy across different horizons. We note that an increase in interest rate forecast horizons decreases the squared correlation with recessions (first term) and increases the penalty for the non-accurate prediction (second term), which results in a smaller skill score (higher negative values). With respect to bear markets, the decomposition shows that the best recession prediction is due to the large squared correlation and the small miscalibration at short-term forecast horizons. Note that the prediction accuracy of bear markets is a lot higher than that of interest rates at any horizon.

Table 7 also reports the MSE_4 for lags 1-8. We find similar results to the ones obtained using the quadratic probability score and the Murphy's decomposition of the skill score. Lower interest rates are related to NBER recessions at lags as well, reflecting the fact that sometimes interest rates fall only after recession peaks. However, the best overall average performance of low interest rates is at the one-quarter *ahead* horizon. The decomposition indicates that this is due mostly to the higher accuracy as measured by the second term of the MSE_4. On the other hand, bear markets display better prediction as measured by the quadratic probability score and skill score within one-year lead horizon than within one-year lag horizon.

Regarding bear market, the decomposition shows that its better prediction performance at short *leads* is due to a higher correlation with NBER recessions (first term of MSE_4), as well as higher accuracy as measured by the second term of MSE_4.

Following Chauvet and Senyuz (2009), we not only focus on accuracy but also study forecast discrimination.

Table 7. Turning Point Prediction Analysis - Murphy's Decomposition of the Skill Score (MSE_4)

	Forecast Horizon (Quarter)	Total Score (MSE_4)	$\rho^2_{X_t,p_{t-k}}$	$[\rho_{X_t,p_{t-k}} - (\sigma_p/\sigma_X)]^2$	$[(\mu_p - \mu_X)/\sigma_X]^2$
Interest Rate Model	0	-1.6107	0.0631	0.8220	0.8517
	+1	**-1.5514**	0.0719	0.7881	0.8352
	+2	-1.6455	0.0591	0.8491	0.8556
	+3	-1.8331	0.0323	0.9884	0.8770
	+4	-2.0528	0.0109	1.1643	0.8994
	+5	-2.2731	0.0010	1.3510	0.9231
	+6	-2.3864	0.0007	1.4822	0.9049
	+7	-2.5015	0.0072	1.6218	0.8868
	+8	-2.5853	0.0169	1.7333	0.8688
	-1	-1.6411	0.0527	0.8583	0.8355
	-2	-1.6808	0.0415	0.9032	0.8191
	-3	-1.7087	0.0335	0.9394	0.8028
	-4	-1.7285	0.0275	0.9694	0.7865
	-5	-1.7585	0.0207	1.0089	0.7704
	-6	-1.7518	0.0190	1.0166	0.7543
	-7	-1.7296	0.0193	1.0107	0.7383
	-8	-1.7002	0.0205	0.9983	0.7223
Stock Market Model	0	-0.2982	0.1765	0.3843	0.0905
	+1	0.0061	0.3146	0.2242	0.0843
	+2	-0.0032	0.3134	0.2297	0.0869
	+3	-0.2966	0.1835	0.3858	0.0943
	+4	-0.7359	0.0535	0.6852	0.1042
	+5	-1.1639	0.0019	1.0507	0.1151
	+6	-1.5240	0.0156	1.4239	0.1157
	+7	-1.7814	0.0606	1.7257	0.1163
	+8	-1.8591	0.0804	1.8225	0.1170
	-1	-0.6736	0.0571	0.6426	0.0881
	-2	-0.9885	0.0064	0.9127	0.0821
	-3	-1.1796	0.0005	1.1040	0.0760
	-4	-1.2183	0.0020	1.1485	0.0718
	-5	-1.1889	0.0009	1.1178	0.0720
	-6	-1.1433	0.0001	1.0709	0.0724
	-7	-1.1213	0.000001	1.0485	0.0728
	-8	-1.1662	0.0005	1.0934	0.0733

Notes: + indicates leads, – indicates lags, and 0 means contemporaneous.

Table 8. Turning Point Prediction Analysis: Yates' Decomposition (MSE_5)

	Forecast Horizon (Quarter)	MSE_5	$\sigma^2_{X_t}$	$\Delta\sigma^2_{p_{t-k}}$	$\sigma^2_{p_{t-k,min}}$	$2\sigma_{p_{t-k},X_t}2\sigma_{p_{t-k},X_t}$	$2\sigma_{p_{t-k},X_t}$
Interest Rate Model	0	0.4069	0.1557	0.1956	0.0132	0.1326	0.0901
	+1	0.3991	0.1563	0.1953	0.0135	0.1305	0.0964
	+2	0.4077	0.1540	0.1953	0.0135	0.1317	0.0868
	+3	0.4298	0.1516	0.1953	0.0136	0.1329	0.0636
	+4	0.4556	0.1492	0.1952	0.0136	0.1342	0.0366
	+5	0.4803	0.1467	0.1952	0.0137	0.1354	0.0108
	+6	0.4987	0.1473	0.1949	0.0140	0.1333	-0.0092
	+7	0.5174	0.1478	0.1946	0.0143	0.1311	-0.0296
	+8	0.5317	0.1484	0.1942	0.0147	0.1289	-0.0456
	-1	0.4131	0.1563	0.1954	0.0135	0.1306	0.0826
	-2	0.4207	0.1568	0.1958	0.0131	0.1284	0.0734
	-3	0.4266	0.1574	0.1963	0.0126	0.1263	0.0661
	-4	0.4312	0.1579	0.1968	0.0122	0.1242	0.0599
	-5	0.4374	0.1585	0.1973	0.0117	0.1221	0.0521
	-6	0.4379	0.1590	0.1970	0.0120	0.1200	0.0501
	-7	0.4359	0.1596	0.1967	0.0123	0.1178	0.0505
	-8	0.4328	0.1602	0.1964	0.0126	0.1157	0.0521

Table 8. Continued

	Forecast Horizon (Quarter)	MSE_5	$\sigma^2_{X_t}$	$\Delta\sigma^2_{p_{t-k}}$	$\sigma^2_{p_{t-k,min}}$	$2\sigma_{p_{t-k},X_t}2\sigma_{p_{t-k},X_t}$	$2\sigma_{p_{t-k},X_t}$
	0	0.2028	0.1557	0.1387	0.0297	0.0141	0.1355
	+1	0.1561	0.1563	0.1368	0.0304	0.0132	0.1805
	+2	0.1553	0.1540	0.1357	0.0305	0.0134	0.1783
	+3	0.1972	0.1516	0.1369	0.0301	0.0143	0.1357
	+4	0.2593	0.1492	0.1379	0.0295	0.0156	0.0728
	+5	0.3176	0.1467	0.1389	0.0288	0.0169	0.0138
	+6	0.3715	0.1473	0.1393	0.0287	0.0170	-0.0392
Stock Market Model	+7	0.4108	0.1478	0.1397	0.0287	0.0172	-0.0773
	+8	0.4238	0.1484	0.1401	0.0286	0.0174	-0.0893
	-1	0.2619	0.1563	0.1392	0.0300	0.0138	0.0773
	-2	0.3119	0.1568	0.1389	0.0291	0.0129	0.0258
	-3	0.3430	0.1574	0.1385	0.0281	0.0120	-0.0070
	-4	0.3503	0.1579	0.1386	0.0279	0.0113	-0.0145
	-5	0.3469	0.1585	0.1368	0.0302	0.0114	-0.0100
	-6	0.3409	0.1590	0.1372	0.0301	0.0115	-0.0030
	-7	0.3386	0.1596	0.1377	0.0300	0.0116	0.0003
	-8	0.3470	0.1602	0.1381	0.0300	0.0117	-0.0070

Notes: + indicates leads, – indicates lags, and 0 means contemporaneous.

In particular, we next use a measure of resolution that discriminates the occurrence of events with high probabilities from those with low probabilities, given by the Yates' Decomposition (1982):

$$MSE_5 = \sigma^2_{X_t} + \Delta\sigma^2_{p_{t-k}} + \sigma^2_{p_{t-k,\min}} + (\mu_p - \mu_X)^2 - 2\sigma_{p_{t-k},X_t} \quad (10)$$

where $\sigma^2_{p_{t-k,\min}} = (\mu_{p|X=1} - \mu_{p|X=0})^2\sigma^2_{X_t}$ and $\Delta\sigma^2_{p_{t-k}} = \sigma^2_{p_{t-k}}$-$\sigma^2_{p_{t-k,\min}}$. $\sigma^2_{X_t}$ and $\sigma^2_{p_{t-k}}$ are the variance of X_t and p_{t-k}, respectively. σ_{p_{t-k},X_t} is the covariance of X_t and p_{t-k}. $\mu_{p|X=1}$ and $\mu_{p|X=0}$ are the mean of p_{t-k} conditional on $X_t = 1$ if the NBER recession occurs or $X_t = 0$ otherwise, respectively. The first term refers to the benchmark. The $\Delta\sigma^2_{p_{t-k}}$ represents the extra variability of the forecast. The $\sigma^2_{p_{t-k,\min}}$ is the conditional minimum forecast variance, which represents the discrimination and has two opposite performance roles. A decrease in $\sigma^2_{p_{t-k,\min}}$ decreases the MSE, but the lowest $\sigma^2_{p_{t-k,\min}}$is obtained only when there is no correlation between the forecast and the actual event. The term $(\mu_p - \mu_X)^2$ represents the mismatch between the prediction and the actual event, and the σ_{p_{t-k},X_t} is the covariance between the prediction and the actual event.

Table 8 shows turning point prediction analysis for interest rates and stock returns using Yates' decomposition. This measure further confirms previous results. We find that recession predictions from loose monetary policy phases achieve the lowest MSE_5 at one-quarter forecast horizon, and the values at other horizon - leads or lags – do not vary much. On the other hand, recession predictions from bear markets yield better performance at the one and two-quarter forecast horizons compared to all other horizons, and these predictions outperform those from interest rates.

4.2. In-Sample and Out-of-Sample Linear Prediction

In this section, we examine the ability of several models to predict interest rates and stock returns. In particular, we investigate the predictive ability of interest rate and monetary policy phases to stock returns, and the forecast ability of stock returns and bear markets to interest rate.

We test an array of variables, and find that the best specifications are composed of different combinations of interest rates, smoothed probabilities of low interest rates, stock returns, smoothed probabilities of bear markets, inflation, and NBER recession dummies. Table 9 lists the top twenty-four models. The first twelve models predict the Federal Funds Rate and the second twelve models predict the S&P 500 stock returns. The models are first estimated in sample from 1957Q2 to 1997Q4. Recursive out-of-sample forecasts are then constructed from 1998Q1 to 2011Q4. In order to compare the forecasting performance of the different specifications, we use as loss functions the Root Mean Squared Error ($RMSE$) and Theil's Inequality Coefficient ($Theil's\ U$) (Theil, 1962, 1966):

$$\text{RMSE} = \sqrt{\frac{1}{K}\sum_{t=T+1}^{T+K}(\hat{Y}_t\text{-}Y_t)^2} \quad (11)$$

$$\text{Theil's U} = \frac{\sqrt{\frac{1}{K}\sum_{t=T+1}^{T+K}(\hat{Y}_t - Y_t)^2}}{\sqrt{\frac{1}{K}\sum_{t=T+1}^{T+K}\hat{Y}_t^2} + \sqrt{\frac{1}{K}\sum_{t=T+1}^{T+K}Y_t^2}} \tag{12}$$

where $\hat{Y}_t$ is the forecast value, Y_t is the actual value, *T* is the number of observations in the estimation, and *K* is the number of observations in the forecast sample.

Table 9. Linear Prediction Models

Model 1:

$$FFR_t = c_1 + \beta_{11}FFR_{t-1} + \beta_{12}FFR_{t-2} + \beta_{13}FFR_{t-3} + \beta_{14}FFR_{t-4} + u_{1t}$$

Model 2:

$$FFR_t = c_2 + \beta_{21}FFR_{t-1} + \beta_{22}FFR_{t-2} + \beta_{23}FFR_{t-3} + \beta_{24}FFR_{t-4} + \rho_{21}inflation\ rate_{t-1} + \rho_{22}inflation\ rate_{t-2} + u_{2t}$$

Model 3:

$$FFR_t = c_3 + \beta_{31}FFR_{t-1} + \beta_{32}FFR_{t-2} + \beta_{33}FFR_{t-3} + \beta_{34}FFR_{t-4} + \gamma_{31}NBER_{t-1} + \gamma_{32}NBER_{t-2} + \gamma_{33}NBER_{t-3} + \gamma_{34}NBER_{t-4} + u_{3t}$$

Model 4:

$$FFR_t = c_4 + \beta_{41}FFR_{t-1} + \beta_{42}FFR_{t-2} + \beta_{43}FFR_{t-3} + \beta_{44}FFR_{t-4} + \alpha_{41}\Delta S\&P_{t-1} + \alpha_{42}\Delta S\&P_{t-2} + u_{4t}$$

Model 5:

$$FFR_t = c_5 + \beta_{51}FFR_{t-1} + \beta_{52}FFR_{t-2} + \beta_{53}FFR_{t-3} + \beta_{54}FFR_{t-4} + \rho_{51}inflation\ rate_{t-1} + \rho_{52}inflation\ rate_{t-2} + \gamma_{51}NBER_{t-1} + \gamma_{52}NBER_{t-2} + \gamma_{53}NBER_{t-3} + \gamma_{54}NBER_{t-4} + u_{5t}$$

Model 6:

$$FFR_t = c_6 + \beta_{61}FFR_{t-1} + \beta_{62}FFR_{t-2} + \beta_{63}FFR_{t-3} + \beta_{64}FFR_{t-4} + \gamma_{61}NBER_{t-1} + \gamma_{62}NBER_{t-2} + \gamma_{63}NBER_{t-3} + \gamma_{64}NBER_{t-4} + \alpha_{61}\Delta S\&P_{t-1} + \alpha_{62}\Delta S\&P_{t-2} + u_{6t}$$

Model 7:

$$FFR_t = c_7 + \beta_{71}FFR_{t-1} + \beta_{72}FFR_{t-2} + \beta_{73}FFR_{t-3} + \beta_{74}FFR_{t-4} + \rho_{71}inflation\ rate_{t-1} + \rho_{72}inflation\ rate_{t-2} + \alpha_{71}\Delta S\&P_{t-1} + \alpha_{72}\Delta S\&P_{t-2} + u_{7t}$$

Table 9. Continued

Model 8:

$$FFR_t = c_8 + \beta_{81}FFR_{t-1} + \beta_{82}FFR_{t-2} + \beta_{83}FFR_{t-3}\beta_{84}FFR_{t-4} + \rho_{81}inflation\,rate_{t-1} + \rho_{82}inflation\,rate_{t-2} + \gamma_{81}NBER_{t-1} + \gamma_{82}NBER_{t-2} + \gamma_{83}NBER_{t-3} + \gamma_{84}NBER_{t-4} + \alpha_{81}\Delta S\&P_{t-1} + \alpha_{82}\Delta S\&P_{t-2} + u_{8t}$$

Model 9:

$$FFR_t = c_9 + \beta_{91}FFR_{t-1} + \beta_{92}FFR_{t-2} + \beta_{93}FFR_{t-3} + \beta_{94}FFR_{t-4} + \varphi_{91}S\&P\_prob_{t-1} + \varphi_{92}S\&P\_prob_{t-2} + u_{9t}$$

Model 10:

$$FFR_t = c_{10} + \beta_{101}FFR_{t-1} + \beta_{102}FFR_{t-2} + \beta_{103}FFR_{t-3} + \beta_{104}FFR_{t-4} + \rho_{101}inflation\,rate_{t-1} + \rho_{102}inflation\,rate_{t-2} + \varphi_{101}S\&P\_prob_{t-1} + \varphi_{102}S\&P\_prob_{t-2} + u_{10t}$$

Model 11:

$$FFR_t = c_{11} + \beta_{111}FFR_{t-1} + \beta_{112}FFR_{t-2} + \beta_{113}FFR_{t-3} + \beta_{114}FFR_{t-4} + \gamma_{111}NBER_{t-1} + \gamma_{112}NBER_{t-2} + \gamma_{113}NBER_{t-3} + \gamma_{114}NBER_{t-4} + \varphi_{111}S\&P\_prob_{t-1} + \varphi_{112}S\&P\_prob_{t-2} + u_{11t}$$

Model 12:

$$FFR_t = c_{12} + \beta_{121}FFR_{t-1} + \beta_{122}FFR_{t-2} + \beta_{123}FFR_{t-3} + \beta_{124}FFR_{t-4} + \rho_{121}inflation\,rate_{t-1} + \rho_{122}inflation\,rate_{t-2} + \gamma_{121}NBER_{t-1} + \gamma_{122}NBER_{t-2} + \gamma_{123}NBER_{t-3} + \gamma_{124}NBER_{t-4} + \varphi_{121}S\&P\_prob_{t-1} + \varphi_{122}S\&P\_prob_{t-2} + u_{12t}$$

Model 13:

$$\Delta S\&P_t = c_{13} + \alpha_{131}\Delta S\&P_{t-1} + \alpha_{132}\Delta S\&P_{t-2} + \alpha_{133}\Delta S\&P_{t-3} + \alpha_{134}\Delta S\&P_{t-4} + u_{13t}$$

Model 14:

$$\Delta S\&P_t = c_{14} + \alpha_{141}\Delta S\&P_{t-1} + \alpha_{142}\Delta S\&P_{t-2} + \alpha_{143}\Delta S\&P_{t-3} + \alpha_{144}\Delta S\&P_{t-4} + \rho_{141}inflation\,rate_{t-1} + \rho_{142}inflation\,rate_{t-2} + \rho_{143}inflation\,rate_{t-3} + \rho_{144}inflation\,rate_{t-4} + u_{14t}$$

Model 15: $\Delta S\&P_t = c_{15} + \alpha_{151}\Delta S\&P_{t-1} + \alpha_{152}\Delta S\&P_{t-2} + \alpha_{153}\Delta S\&P_{t-3} + \alpha_{154}\Delta S\&P_{t-4} + \gamma_{151}NBER_{t-1} + u_{15t}$

Table 9. Continued

Model 16:

$$\Delta S\&P_t = c_{16} + \alpha_{161}\Delta S\&P_{t-1} + \alpha_{162}\Delta S\&P_{t-2} + \alpha_{163}\Delta S\&P_{t-3} + \alpha_{164}\Delta S\&P_{t-4} + \beta_{161}FFR_{t-1} + \beta_{162}FFR_{t-2} + \beta_{163}FFR_{t-3} + \beta_{164}FFR_{t-4} + u_{16t}$$

Model 17:

$$\Delta S\&P_t = c_{17} + \alpha_{171}\Delta S\&P_{t-1} + \alpha_{172}\Delta S\&P_{t-2} + \alpha_{173}\Delta S\&P_{t-3} + \alpha_{174}\Delta S\&P_{t-4} + \rho_{171} inflation\ rate_{t-1} + \rho_{172} inflation\ rate_{t-2} + \rho_{173} inflation\ rate_{t-3} + \rho_{174} inflation\ rate_{t-4} + \gamma_{171}NBER_{t-1} + u_{17t}$$

Model 18:

$$\Delta S\&P_t = c_{18} + \alpha_{181}\Delta S\&P_{t-1} + \alpha_{182}\Delta S\&P_{t-2} + \alpha_{183}\Delta S\&P_{t-3} + \alpha_{184}\Delta S\&P_{t-4} + \rho_{181} inflation\ rate_{t-1} + \rho_{182} inflation\ rate_{t-2} + \rho_{183} inflation\ rate_{t-3} + \rho_{184} inflation\ rate_{t-4} + \beta_{181}FFR_{t-1} + \beta_{182}FFR_{t-2} + \beta_{183}FFR_{t-3} + \beta_{184}FFR_{t-4} + u_{18t}$$

Model 19:

$$\Delta S\&P_t = c_{19} + \alpha_{191}\Delta S\&P_{t-1} + \alpha_{192}\Delta S\&P_{t-2} + \alpha_{193}\Delta S\&P_{t-3} + \alpha_{194}\Delta S\&P_{t-4} + \gamma_{191}NBER_{t-1} + \beta_{191}FFR_{t-1} + \beta_{192}FFR_{t-2} + \beta_{193}FFR_{t-3} + \beta_{194}FFR_{t-4} + u_{19t}$$

Model 20:

$$\Delta S\&P_t = c_{20} + \alpha_{201}\Delta S\&P_{t-1} + \alpha_{202}\Delta S\&P_{t-2} + \alpha_{203}\Delta S\&P_{t-3} + \alpha_{204}\Delta S\&P_{t-4} + \rho_{201} inflation\ rate_{t-1} + \rho_{202} inflation\ rate_{t-2} + \rho_{203} inflation\ rate_{t-3} + \rho_{204} inflation\ rate_{t-4} + \gamma_{201}NBER_{t-1} + \beta_{201}FFR_{t-1} + \beta_{202}FFR_{t-2} + \beta_{203}FFR_{t-3} + \beta_{204}FFR_{t-4} + u_{20t}$$

Model 21:

$$\Delta S\&P_t = c_{21} + \alpha_{211}\Delta S\&P_{t-1} + \alpha_{212}\Delta S\&P_{t-2} + \alpha_{213}\Delta S\&P_{t-3} + \alpha_{214}\Delta S\&P_{t-4} + \phi_{211}FFR\_prob_{t-1} + \phi_{212}FFR\_prob_{t-2} + \phi_{213}FFR\_prob_{t-3} + \phi_{214}FFR\_prob_{t-4} + u_{21t}$$

Table 9. Continued

Model 22:

$$\Delta S\&P_t = c_{22} + \alpha_{221}\Delta S\&P_{t-1} + \alpha_{222}\Delta S\&P_{t-2} + \alpha_{223}\Delta S\&P_{t-3} + \alpha_{224}\Delta S\&P_{t-4} + \rho_{221} inflation\ rate_{t-1} + \rho_{222} inflation\ rate_{t-2} + \rho_{223} inflation\ rate_{t-3} + \rho_{224} inflation\ rate_{t-4} + \phi_{221} FFR\_prob_{t-1} + \phi_{222} FFR\_prob_{t-2} + \phi_{223} FFR\_prob_{t-3} + \phi_{224} FFR\_prob_{t-4} + u_{22t}$$

Model 23:

$$\Delta S\&P_t = c_{23} + \alpha_{231}\Delta S\&P_{t-1} + \alpha_{232}\Delta S\&P_{t-2} + \alpha_{233}\Delta S\&P_{t-3} + \alpha_{234}\Delta S\&P_{t-4} + \gamma_{231} NBER_{t-1} + \phi_{231} FFR\_prob_{t-1} + \phi_{232} FFR\_prob_{t-2} + \phi_{233} FFR\_prob_{t-3} + \phi_{234} FFR\_prob_{t-4} + u_{23t}$$

Model 24:

$$\Delta S\&P_t = c_{24} + \alpha_{241}\Delta S\&P_{t-1} + \alpha_{242}\Delta S\&P_{t-2} + \alpha_{243}\Delta S\&P_{t-3} + \alpha_{244}\Delta S\&P_{t-4} + \rho_{241} inflation\ rate_{t-1} + \rho_{242} inflation\ rate_{t-2} + \rho_{243} inflation\ rate_{t-3} + \rho_{244} inflation\ rate_{t-4} + \gamma_{241} NBER_{t-1} + \phi_{241} FFR\_prob_{t-1} + \phi_{242} FFR\_prob_{t-2} + \phi_{243} FFR\_prob_{t-3} + \phi_{244} FFR\_prob_{t-4} + u_{24t}$$

Interest Rates

Table 10 reports the out-of-sample forecasting performance for interest rate at the 1-8 quarter ahead. The best predictive models for interest rates are Models 5, 8, and 12.

Model 8 uses lags of interest rates, stock return, inflation, and NBER recessions; Model 5 contains the same series, except for stock return; and Model 12 uses the probabilities of bear markets instead of stock returns. Model 8 has the best performance for predicting interest rate at any quarter except for $h = 1$, while Model 5 shows the best performance at $h = 1$. However, the difference in forecasts at this horizon is not statistically significant using Diebold and Mariano's (DM 1995) test. The lowest RMSE overall is attained by Model 8 at five-quarter ahead (1.76).

We find that inflation and NBER recessions are more important than stock returns in predicting interest rates. The Federal Reserve generally pursues contractionary monetary policy to curb inflation, which tend to increase towards the middle and end of economic expansions. On the other hand, the Fed tends to decrease interest rates when economic activity starts to weaken, as in the beginning of recessions.

Table 10. Out-of-Sample Forecasting Performance - Interest Rate Model (In-Sample: 1957Q2-1997Q4; Out-of-Sample: 1998Q1-2011Q4)

	h=1											
	Model 1	**Model 2**	**Model 3**	**Model 4**	**Model 5**	**Model 6**	**Model 7**	**Model 8**	**Model 9**	**Model 10**	**Model 11**	**Model 12**
RMSE	4.3628	3.3720	4.1171	3.7116	1.9524	4.0307	2.5556	1.9703	4.1250	3.0176	4.1223	2.0891
THEIL	0.4302	0.3707	0.3910	0.3763	0.2283	0.3847	0.2934	0.2291	0.4075	0.3346	0.3932	0.2423
	h=2											
	Model 1	**Model 2**	**Model 3**	**Model 4**	**Model 5**	**Model 6**	**Model 7**	**Model 8**	**Model 9**	**Model 10**	**Model 11**	**Model 12**
RMSE	4.2973	3.3305	3.9501	3.5646	1.9118	3.7965	2.4674	1.8886	4.0115	2.9413	3.9590	2.0320
THEIL	0.4237	0.3644	0.3792	0.3655	0.2227	0.3693	0.2841	0.2202	0.3980	0.3255	0.3814	0.2349
	h=3											
	Model 1	**Model 2**	**Model 3**	**Model 4**	**Model 5**	**Model 6**	**Model 7**	**Model 8**	**Model 9**	**Model 10**	**Model 11**	**Model 12**
RMSE	4.2274	3.2936	3.7912	3.4442	1.8790	3.6206	2.4005	1.8367	3.9059	2.8803	3.8099	1.9936
THEIL	0.4168	0.3597	0.3676	0.3557	0.2183	0.3566	0.2770	0.2143	0.3890	0.3187	0.3704	0.2299
	h=4											
	Model 1	**Model 2**	**Model 3**	**Model 4**	**Model 5**	**Model 6**	**Model 7**	**Model 8**	**Model 9**	**Model 10**	**Model 11**	**Model 12**
RMSE	4.1623	3.2698	3.6741	3.3433	1.8951	3.4724	2.3763	1.8393	3.8160	2.8512	3.6997	2.0057
THEIL	0.4097	0.3535	0.3582	0.3468	0.2176	0.3454	0.2721	0.2128	0.3804	0.3126	0.3613	0.2286

Table 10. Continued

	h=5											
	Model 1	**Model 2**	**Model 3**	**Model 4**	**Model 5**	**Model 6**	**Model 7**	**Model 8**	**Model 9**	**Model 10**	**Model 11**	**Model 12**
RMSE	4.0024	3.2277	3.1716	3.1096	1.8208	2.9979	2.3266	1.7613	3.5924	2.7851	3.2552	1.9266
THEIL	0.4012	0.3509	0.3254	0.3323	0.2116	0.3140	0.2689	0.2067	0.3671	0.3079	0.3327	0.2221
	h=6											
	Model 1	**Model 2**	**Model 3**	**Model 4**	**Model 5**	**Model 6**	**Model 7**	**Model 8**	**Model 9**	**Model 10**	**Model 11**	**Model 12**
RMSE	3.9320	3.1918	3.0323	3.0540	1.8217	2.9193	2.3074	1.7713	3.5010	2.7494	3.1203	1.9234
THEIL	0.3935	0.3448	0.3140	0.3252	0.2105	0.3064	0.2643	0.2061	0.3583	0.3023	0.3217	0.2205
	h=7											
	Model 1	**Model 2**	**Model 3**	**Model 4**	**Model 5**	**Model 6**	**Model 7**	**Model 8**	**Model 9**	**Model 10**	**Model 11**	**Model 12**
RMSE	3.8311	3.1409	2.8632	2.9659	1.8185	2.8315	2.2812	1.7795	3.3777	2.7002	2.9641	1.9171
THEIL	0.3848	0.3385	0.3005	0.3167	0.2094	0.2984	0.2598	0.2056	0.3482	0.2964	0.3093	0.2190
	h=8											
	Model 1	**Model 2**	**Model 3**	**Model 4**	**Model 5**	**Model 6**	**Model 7**	**Model 8**	**Model 9**	**Model 10**	**Model 11**	**Model 12**
RMSE	3.8008	3.1117	2.9800	2.9467	1.8778	2.8896	2.2914	1.8224	3.3534	2.6916	3.0563	1.9784
THEIL	0.3775	0.3301	0.3059	0.3118	0.2118	0.3000	0.2569	0.2071	0.3419	0.2907	0.3126	0.2215

Table 11. Out-of-Sample Forecasting Performance: Stock Returns (In-Sample: 1957Q2-1997Q4; Out-of-Sample Forecast: 1998Q1-2011Q4)

	h=1											
	Model 13	**Model 14**	**Model 15**	**Model 16**	**Model 17**	**Model 18**	**Model 19**	**Model 20**	**Model 21**	**Model 22**	**Model 23**	**Model 24**
RMSE	5.3933	5.2751	5.4808	5.6542	5.4469	5.4954	5.6585	5.5210	5.3003	5.0828	5.3360	5.1908
THEIL	0.7698	0.7220	0.7813	0.7988	0.7357	0.7670	0.7990	0.7682	0.7433	0.7134	0.7498	0.7274
	h=2											
	Model 13	**Model 14**	**Model 15**	**Model 16**	**Model 17**	**Model 18**	**Model 19**	**Model 20**	**Model 21**	**Model 22**	**Model 23**	**Model 24**
RMSE	5.3695	5.2663	5.4581	5.6334	5.4415	5.4883	5.6377	5.5143	5.2678	5.0552	5.3038	5.1654
THEIL	0.7381	0.6977	0.7488	0.7680	0.7118	0.7400	0.7682	0.7412	0.7145	0.6874	0.7205	0.7011
	h=3											
	Model 13	**Model 14**	**Model 15**	**Model 16**	**Model 17**	**Model 18**	**Model 19**	**Model 20**	**Model 21**	**Model 22**	**Model 23**	**Model 24**
RMSE	5.4024	5.2907	5.4935	5.6724	5.4706	5.5238	5.6768	5.5504	5.2869	5.0618	5.3238	5.1749
THEIL	0.7412	0.6978	0.7522	0.7707	0.7123	0.7416	0.7709	0.7430	0.7138	0.6844	0.7200	0.6985
	h=4											
	Model 13	**Model 14**	**Model 15**	**Model 16**	**Model 17**	**Model 18**	**Model 19**	**Model 20**	**Model 21**	**Model 22**	**Model 23**	**Model 24**
RMSE	5.4282	5.3264	5.5213	5.7090	5.5105	5.5677	5.7135	5.5946	5.3012	5.0808	5.3394	5.1978
THEIL	0.7387	0.6978	0.7496	0.7686	0.7123	0.7414	0.7689	0.7428	0.7114	0.6845	0.7176	0.6987

Table 11. Continued

	h=5											
	Model 13	**Model 14**	**Model 15**	**Model 16**	**Model 17**	**Model 18**	**Model 19**	**Model 20**	**Model 21**	**Model 22**	**Model 23**	**Model 24**
RMSE	5.3256	5.2502	5.4188	5.6330	5.4387	5.5021	5.6375	5.5293	5.2051	4.9972	5.2444	5.1190
THEIL	0.6934	0.6616	0.7033	0.7239	0.6765	0.7006	0.7241	0.7021	0.6730	0.6488	0.6787	0.6626
	h=6											
	Model 13	**Model 14**	**Model 15**	**Model 16**	**Model 17**	**Model 18**	**Model 19**	**Model 20**	**Model 21**	**Model 22**	**Model 23**	**Model 24**
RMSE	5.3553	5.2638	5.4468	5.6648	5.4518	5.5212	5.6693	5.5483	5.2415	5.0237	5.2807	5.1451
THEIL	0.6856	0.6503	0.6947	0.7164	0.6651	0.6909	0.7167	0.6924	0.6671	0.6376	0.6723	0.6509
	h=7											
	Model 13	**Model 14**	**Model 15**	**Model 16**	**Model 17**	**Model 18**	**Model 19**	**Model 20**	**Model 21**	**Model 22**	**Model 23**	**Model 24**
RMSE	5.4398	5.3251	5.5316	5.7403	5.5125	5.5839	5.7448	5.6110	5.3170	5.0924	5.3568	5.2129
THEIL	0.6985	0.6582	0.7073	0.7280	0.6727	0.7000	0.7282	0.7014	0.6785	0.6454	0.6836	0.6586
	h=8											
	Model 13	**Model 14**	**Model 15**	**Model 16**	**Model 17**	**Model 18**	**Model 19**	**Model 20**	**Model 21**	**Model 22**	**Model 23**	**Model 24**
RMSE	5.4480	5.3223	5.5414	5.7687	5.5143	5.6021	5.7733	5.6295	5.3124	5.0842	5.3537	5.2084
THEIL	0.6922	0.6507	0.7010	0.7233	0.6656	0.6941	0.7235	0.6956	0.6719	0.6377	0.6770	0.6510

Stock Returns

Table 11 shows the out-of-sample forecasting results for stock returns. The best specifications are Models 14, 21, 22, and 24. Model 14 includes lags of stock return and inflation, Model 22 includes additionally interest rates, and Model 24 has the same variables as Model 22 with the addition of the probabilities of low interest rates. These three models display their best predictive ability five-quarter ahead. The lowest RMSE is attained for Model 14 at h=5 (RMSE=4.997), followed by Model 24 and Model 22. At the shorter horizon of one quarter, the best performing specification is Model 22 but, again, the difference in forecast with Model 14 is not statistically significant using DM test.

Thus, we find that the best indicators of future stock returns are inflation and the probabilities of low interest rates. In fact, we find that information on the state of monetary policy phase is more important in predicting stock returns than changes in interest rates themselves.

Conclusion

The stock market undergoes recurrent fluctuations, which are linked through different channels to changes in economy activity. On the other hand, monetary policy has a strong relationship with the business cycle and, as a consequence, with the stock market. This paper models stock market cycles, and their relationship with interest rate phases and business cycles. A nonlinear two-state Markov switching model is used to characterize and analyze the different regimes in each sector. Turning points for each cycle are established and the analysis of their lead-lag relationships is examined, as well as their linear predictive ability.

The results indicate that there are strong connections between monetary policy phases, stock market cycles, and business cycles. In particular, we find that the loose monetary policy regime leads recessions with a median of two quarters, while it only ends, on average, about four or five quarters after recessions end. On the other hand, bear markets starts about three quarters before the onset of recessions, and end about two quarters before the beginning of expansions, anticipating the economic recovery.

Moreover, several linear models are constructed to examine the prediction power of interest rate to stock returns and vice versa. We find that inflation and NBER recessions are more important than stock returns in predicting changes in interest rates. This is consistent with monetary policy pursued by the Federal Reserve, which is generally contractionary to curb inflation, which tends to increase towards the middle and end of economic expansions. On the other hand, the Federal Reserve tends to decrease interest rates when economic activity starts to weaken. Further, we find that the best indicators of future stock returns are inflation and the probabilities of loose monetary policy. Accordingly, information on the state of monetary policy phase is even more important in predicting stock returns than linear projections of changes in interest rates.

References

Akaike, Hirotugu (1973), "Information Theory and an Extension of the Maximum Likelihood Principle." In B.N. Petrov and F. Csaki, Eds., Second International Symposium on Information Theory, Akademiai Kiado, (Budapest, Hungary), 267-281.

Alam, Mahmudul, and Uddin, Gazi Salah (2009), "Relationship between Interest Rate and Stock Price: Empirical Evidence from Developed and Developing Countries." *International Journal of Business and Management,* 4, 3, 43-51.

Avouyi-Dovi, Sanvi, and Matheron, Julien (2003), "Interactions between Business Cycles, Stock Market Cycles and Interest Rates: the Stylised Facts." *Financial Stability Review*, 3, 80-99.

Barro, Robert J., and Ursúa, José F. (2009), "Stock-Market Crashes and Depressions." National Bureau of Economic Research. Working Paper 14760.

Brier, G. W., and Allen, R. A (1951), "Verification of Weather Forecasts." In: T. F. Malone (ed.) Compendium of Meteorology; American Meteorology. Soc. 841-848.

Chauvet, Marcelle (1999), "Stock Market Fluctuations and the Business Cycle." *Journal of Economic and Social Measurement*, 25, 3, 235-258.

Chauvet, Marcelle (1998), "An Econometric Characterization of Business Cycle Dynamics with Factor Structure and Regime Switching." *International Economic Review*, 39, 4, 969-996.

Chauvet, Marcelle and Potter, Simon (2000), "Coincident and Leading Indicators of the Stock Market." *Journal of Empirical Finance*, 7, 1, 87-111.

Chauvet, Marcelle and Potter, Simon (2001), "Nonlinear Risk." *Macroeconomic Dynamics,* 5, 4, 621-646.

Chauvet, Marcelle and Piger, Jeremy M. (2003), "Identifying Business Cycle Turning Points in Real Time." Review, The Federal Reserve Bank of St. Louis, issue March, 47-61.

Chauvet, Marcelle and Senyuz, Zeynep (2009), "A Joint Dynamic Bi-Factor Model of the Yield Curve and the Economy as a Predictor of Business Cycles." University Library of Munich, Germany, series MPRA Paper 15076.

Diebold, Francis X. and Mariano, Roberto S. (1995), "Comparing Predictive Accuracy." *Journal of Business and Economic Statistics*, 13, 253-265.

Estrella, Arturo and Mishkin, Frederic S. (1996), "Predicting U.S. Recessions: Financial Variables as Leading Indicators." Federal Reserve Bank of New York, Research Paper 9609.

Hamilton, James D. (1989), "A New Approach to the Economic Analysis of Nonstationary Time Series and the Business Cycle." *Econometrica*, 57, 2, 357-384.

Harvey, Campbell R. (1989), "Forecasts of Economic Growth from the Bond and Stock Markets." *Financial Analysts Journal*. September-October, 38-45.

King, Robert G., and Watson, Mark W. (1996), "Money, Prices, Interest Rates and the Business Cycle." *The Review of Economics and Statistics*, MIT Press, 78(1), 35-53.

Lahiri, Kajal and Wang, J. George (2006), "Evaluating Probability Forecasts: Calibration Isn't Everything." http://economics.ucr.edu/seminars/spring06/econometrics/KajalLahiri_3_4-12-2006.pdf.

McCallum, Bennett T. (1989), "Monetary Economics: Theory and Policy." Macmillan, Business and Economics.

Murphy, Allan H. (1988), "Skill Scores Based on the Mean Square Error and Their Relationships to the Correlation Coefficient." *Monthly Weather Review,* 116, 2417-2424.

Pesaran, M. Hashem and Timmermann, Allan (1995), "Predictability of Stock Returns: Robustness and Economic Significance." *The Journal of Finance,* L, 4, 1201-1228.

Schwarz, Gideon (1978), "Estimating the Dimension of a Model." *The Annals of Statistics*, 6, 2, 461-464.

Theil, H. (1962), "Economic Forecasting and Policy." 2nd ed., North-Holland.

Theil, H. (1966), "Applied Economic Forecasting." North-Holland.

Vanous, Jan (1982), "East European Economic Slowdown." Problems of Communism. July, 1-19.

Yates, J. Frank (1982), "External Correspondence: Decompositions of the Mean Probability Score." *Organizational Behavior and Human Performance,* 30, 132-156.

Zhou, Chunsheng (1996), "Stock Market Fluctuations and the Term Structure." *Board of Governors of the Federal Reserve System, Finance and Economics Discussion Series*, 96-3.

In: Business Cycles in Economics
Editor: Jason C. Hsu

ISBN: 978-1-63321-322-7

Chapter 7

AN AUSTRIAN SCHOOL EXPLANATION OF THE GLOBAL FINANCIAL CRISIS

Fu Lai Tony Yu[*]
Department of Economics and Finance,
Hong Kong Shue Yan University, Hong Kong

Abstract

This chapter applies the Austrian theory of business cycle to interpret the Global Financial Crisis in 2008. Using the notion that "all economic problems are coordination problems, arising out of unexpected change", this study will argue that the Global Financial Crisis occurs due primarily to investment errors made under uncertainty. In coordination and knowledge perspectives, economic errors mean mismatches of plans in the market. If a producer's plans do not match with market participants' plans, then, coordination fails. If production plans fail to match, people will adjust their expectations and revise their plans subsequently. In the market process, under structural uncertainty, mismatches of plans and plan revisions are normal practices in everyday business life and will not lead to global financial chaos. What causes global financial disaster is systemic or clusters of errors in both real and monetary sectors. In other words, all people commit economic errors at the same time and such errors have cumulated over a period of time. Eventually, economic corrections have to be made one day. Financial bubbles burst implies that clusters of errors need to be corrected. This chapter will explore the factors that cause the delay of plan revisions, thus, forming clusters of errors. These factors, largely institutional, include labor unions, financial intermediaries practice, government bailout plan and most importantly, the central bank's interest rates policy. Moreover, mismatches in production plans (primary errors) induce a chain of mal-investments in the real estate and stock markets (secondary errors), leading to widespread economic crisis. This chapter will use General Motors in the United States as an illustration of a primary source of economic error, and subprime crisis, as an illustration of secondary source of economic errors. Using this coordination framework, this chapter suggests that governments should not shield off economic corrections in their economies. Instead, they should help firms make economic adjustment to the unexpected change as soon as possible, thus, starting new 'healthy' investments. Accordingly, the economy can move out of the general economic recession.

[*] E-mail address: flyu@hksyu.edu; Address: Department of Economics and Finance, Hong Kong Shue Yan University, North Point, Hong Kong (Corresponding author).

Keywords: Global Financial Crisis 2008, Austrian theory of business cycle; economic errors; General Motors; Subprime Crisis

Introduction: Financial Crisis as Economic Errors

> "If you shut the door to all economic errors in a room, corrections will be shut out."
> Inspired by and modified from *Rabindranath Tagore*[1]

In explaining financial crises and economic downturns, Austrian scholars, such as Mises (1949; 1953), Hayek (1933; 1939) and Rothbard (1963; 1969), focus on errors made by the participants in the market. Their aim is to explain the recurrence of the phenomenon that we call crisis. Garrison (1989:3) states that "the Austrian theory [of business cycle] is not primarily about depressions; it is about artificial booms and about the market process that brings them to an end". Hulsmann (1998) claims that the Austrian theory of business cycle is a theory of error cycles. He explains not only the occurrence of error but the recurrence of a cluster of errors as well (Hulsmann 1998:1; Gunning 1985:233). As Rothbard (1969:25) puts it, "a theory of depression must account for the mammoth cluster of errors which appears swiftly and suddenly at a moment of economic crisis, and lingers through the depression period until recovery". It is worthwhile to emphasis that the global financial crisis is not the result of a single error, but a cluster of errors accumulated overtime. Hence, it is necessary to define an economic error and explain the causes of the cluster of errors.

What Is an Economic Error?

In mainstream neoclassical economics, an error is the result of inefficient or suboptimum resource usage. The concept of Paretian Optimality is used to determine if resource allocation is efficient or not. For this, a production or consumption decision is compared to the competitive market which assumes perfect knowledge. Since, in reality, people live in imperfect knowledge, Austrian economists would query whether inefficiency or welfare loss in the neoclassical paradigm can be regarded as an economic error. Kirzner (1979:62) rightly argues that there is no theory of error in the neoclassical paradigm. For Leibenstein (1966), the inadequacy of motivation and of effort is the major source of X-inefficiency, resulting in the failure of achieving, given the level of inputs, the highest possible technical level of outputs. Stigler (1976) argues that inadequacy of motivation does not indicate an error. If a person is not sufficiently motivated to work harder, this may reflect his or her preference for leisure. Similarly, if an organization has not succeeded in enhancing motivation, this may reflect the choice of technology, which in turn implies information cost and knowledge problems. Hence, these technical errors originating in human's ignorance cannot be regarded as economic errors. This chapter takes the Hayekian perspective on error.

[1] Modify from the poem by the Indian poet Rabindranath *Tagore:* "if you shut the door to all errors, truth will be shut out".

Economic Error in the Hayekian Perspective

Hayek regards all economic problems as coordination problems. Successful coordination of economic activities means the compatibility of plans among market participants. If my plan matches your plan on the trading day, then both of us will be happy with the result and gain from exchange. Profit indicates the matching of plans. People bet on their judgments under uncertainty. Correct judgment yields profit to producers (Knight 1921). Producers form expectations or plans by experience. If they find that their current plan works, then they will continue to use the same method to reap profits. Wrong judgment will bring a loss to producers. Business loss means mismatch of plans.

In the Hayekian system, errors are associated with knowledge problems. Human ignorance leads to the mismatch of plans, coordination failure and disequilibrium in the economy (Hayek 1937; see also O'Driscoll and Rizzo 1985:85-89). If producers find that they have made a wrong judgment and committed an error, leading to financial loss, they will revise their plans or reformulate expectations. Accordingly, these producers will reshuffle resources or reorganize the capital structure. One of the resources in production is labor. Hence, labors need to be directed into other uses. If labors cannot handle new work, they have to be laid off. Errors cause catallactic (speculative) unemployment (Gunning 1985).

Matching of Plans: The Case of General Motors (GM)

General Motors (GM), the world's largest automotive manufacturer, was founded by William Durant in 1902. At that time, Durant correctly anticipated that cars would replace horse-drawn carriages in the future. With entrepreneurial spirit, Durant brought GM to its peak by producing cars and trucks that American consumers loved. In 1909, GM sold 25,000 vehicles. The first Cadillac was a landmark of success, and the brand became a metaphor for top-quality goods.[2] In 1921, GM accounted for 12 percent of the American vehicle market. During the financial boom in the 1920's, GM became one of the three auto giants (alongside with Ford and Chrysler) in the United States. After Alfred Sloan took control of GM, the plant produced cars that captured the imaginations of American people. In other words, Sloan's cars 'matched' the expectations of customers. GM produced some classic cars such as Buick Y-Job (1938), Buick Roadmaster (1948), Chevy Corvette (1953), Chevy Impala (1959), Pontiac GTO (1965), and Chevy Camaro (1967).[3] GM also pioneered in styling, accounting, engineering, customer research and annual model changes. Each automotive division in the United States was targeted to specific market segment. Despite some shared components, each product range distinguished itself with unique styling and technology that fitted consumers' wants.[4]GM also successfully introduced important mechanical breakthroughs, including automatic transmissions, power steering, power brakes and fuel-injected engines. In early 1960s, GM controlled over 50 percent of domestic automotive

[2] http://www.newser.com/article/d98gu6bg1/gm-angles-for-bankruptcy-protection-tailfins-corvettes-and-v-8s-in-its-wake.html; accessed on June 23, 2009.

[3] http://www.freep.com/article/20090531/BUSINESS01/905310459/; accessed on June 17, 2009.

[4] http://www.latimes.com/news/la-fi-gm-history1-2009jun01,0,1220928.column?track=ntothtml; accessed on June 22, 2009.

market and set the standards for the world's manufacturing industry[5]. In 1985, GM reached its peak, producing 1,168,982 vehicles. In short, GM's success lied in its ability to match consumers' tastes.

Gm's Economic Errors: Inability to Reach Consumers' Expectations

When GM expanded and became successful, it started to lose its impulse and inspiration to meet consumers' expectations. While the world rapidly changed, GM kept on producing expensive, oil-consuming and boring vehicles. A fundamental mistake GM made was to underestimate the effect of high oil prices. While the company continued to produce oil-consuming models, its Japanese rivals launched fuel-efficient vehicles. The second mistake was that when GM focused on upgrading sports utility vehicles, its competitors expanded their market share in the normal car segment. Third, GM invested on the products that consumers did not want. It paid US$2 billion to buy out Italian Fiat Company.[6] Fourth, GM's models could not catch up with young customers' tastes. As baby boomers aged, GM's image looked even older. Lacking small cars that appealed to young buyers, the average age of its customers rose sharply. In 2003, the average age of Oldsmobile's owners was 50 years old. GM tackled this problem with a promotion campaign that its product was "not your father's Oldsmobile." However, the campaign failed. Sales began to fall and GM was unable to make a profit with the aging brand. Similarly, in 2008, the average age of Buick sedan's buyers was 66 years old, and marketing campaigns could do little to change the situation. When gasoline prices went up to US$4 per gallon, it was too late for GM to produce more fuel-efficient cars. Los Angeles Times concluded, "[GM] treated its customers poorly; it built boring and awful cars that alienated generations of buyers; it built binge-drinking dinosaurs and murdered the electric car".[7] GM finally collapsed. During the first 6 months of 2008, GM lost US$18.8 billion[8]. Between October 2007 and October 2008, GM sales in the United States dropped 45 percent. The business loss indicates that GM manufactured vehicles that did not catch up with customers' expectations.

Revision of Plans and Errors Correction

Austrian economists regard business contraction as a correction of previous errors. As a matter of fact, given uncertainty, business errors are unavoidable. Having poor sales performance, producers need to make change. If they do not, they are doomed to fail. Revision of plans and economic correction are common in everyday business life. A chain of adjustments will follow once a big firm revises its plans. Banks which lend to this firm will call back loan, and perhaps may eventually force to write off their accounts. Components suppliers to this firm also need to readjust their plans. However, the components suppliers do not know if their business with this big firm is right or not. For them, if the deal makes profit,

[5] http://www.rediff.com/money/2006/jan/27spec4.htm; accessed on June 17, 2009.
[6]http://www.rediff.com/money/2006/jan/27spec4.htm; accessed March 18, 2013.
[7] See note 2.
[8] http://en.wikipedia.org/wiki/General_Motors; accessed on June 22, 2009.

then the plan is right. Otherwise, components suppliers realize they err too. Profit or loss shows whether the deal/plan is right or wrong. If the production plan is found to be wrong, it has to be revised. Each day, millions of correction activities occur. In the case of GM, revisions of production plans came too late. In 2009, GM's errors corrections included making call on small car plants, cutting off workers' benefits, winding down medium-duty trucks, reshaping its product lines.[9] On Tuesday, December 23, 2008, the Janesville, Wisconsin plant, and the Moraine, Ohio plant closed permanently. On April 24, 2009, GM announced that it scrapped the Pontiac brand in an effort to invest more money into other profitable brands.[10]

Revisions of plans or correcting errors are essential for a firm to revive and live on. Preventing entrepreneurs to correct errors would raise the cost of readjustment in the future. The only way of not correcting errors today is to delay errors on later days. This will bring higher costs to the producers if adjustments are made in the future. Usually, a rational human agent will not delay the adjustment for too long. The longer it delays, the higher the costs it will be. In the Chinese way of saying, "it is better to bear slighter pain today than endure long deep wound in the future".

Behavior of Private Banks and Error Elimination

Bank is a private enterprise whose objective is to earn profit. Its profit comes from loans with interest. The interest rate reflects the total subjective time preference in the community and is determined by the market. It is always 'right' in the market. Without government intervention, a bank normally tries to make the largest profit subject to risk. It always wants to lend out money at interest rate as low as possible so to appeal customers. However, if the loan rate is too low, the bank may not earn profits. If a business fails, the bank which lends money to this business will not want the business to close down immediately. Instead, it will try to arrange the business a debt relief plan. Business owners need to revise the production plan by reshuffling resources. In other words, the debt relief plan is a kind of economic correction. This is not necessarily a bad move if the business can revive. Revival means error made earlier is corrected. However, given fixed rigid capital structure, if this is impossible, the producer will call upon bankruptcy. Bank will have to write off. This write-off is also required and normal. Overall, given that other loans are profitable, a conservative bank can still survive. Aggressive banks will be more likely to experience a loss if they make risky loan. If both the business and bank fail, of course, this may involve a large numbers of investors and customers. All parties involved have to revise their investment and consumption portfolios. Such revisions are required no matter how painful it is and how extensive the effect it will bring to the community.

Cluster of Errors Due to Delay of Revisionof Plans

People make investment and try to produce goods which match consumers' tastes. Many producers succeed and earn economic profit. Many others fail due to the incapability of

---

[9] See note 3.

[10] http://en.wikipedia.org/wiki/General_Motors; accessed June 18, 2009.

reading the market or anticipating customers' wants. Each day, failing enterprises make adjustments by reshuffling their capital structure or closing down and starting another business again. Clusters of errors will not occur in the whole economy. The major problem is why all people in the economy make systematic errors at the same time. Moreover, we want to explain why such errors are prolonged. The clusters of errors result in severe depression and mass unemployment. It will be argued below that the clusters of errors emerge due to the delays of plan revisions encouraged by the central bank, government and other institutional factors such as trade and labor unions.

Delay in Adjustments: Government Bailout, Labor Union and Central Bank

Hulsmann (1998:9) contends that the cluster of errors is largely the result of the institutional arrangement. He asks, "how is it conceivable that an institution is erroneous irrespective of all other conditions of action?" A research program suggested by Hulsmann is to identify institutional factors which incubate the clusters of errors.

Heavy-handed government intervention into the management of companies, including banks and auto makers, often delay recovery. Rothbard (1962:1001) reminds us that "governmental interference with the depression process can only prolong it, thus making things worse from almost everyone's point of view. Since the depression process is the recovery process, any halting or slowing down of the process impedes the advent of recovery. The depression readjustments must work themselves out before recovery can be complete. The more these readjustments are delayed, the longer the depression will have to last, and the longer complete recovery is postponed."

Correction is the only way to eliminate errors. This chapter suggests that allowing those failing businesses to close down is not necessarily unreasonable. On the contrary, artificial rescues by the government only deepen the errors and delay the pain later. What government can do is to devise a solid system of rule of law to speed up the corrections and reduce transaction costs in readjustment. Government's rescue plans often impede economic correction and hence are harmful to the economy.

The bailout: For generations, General Motors fulfilled America's dreams with the automobile, producing cars that defined the owners' social and economic status. It reflected the industrial era of the United States. As a commentary describes, "GM was more than just the world's largest and most admired corporation; it was the final vindication of the American Way, the perfected and even divinely inspired example of democratic capitalism"[11] In 1953, GM's President, Charles Wilson, said "what was good for the country was good for GM, and vice versa".[12] We can imagine why the Americans were extremely reluctant to see GM collapse. In December 19, 2008, President George W. Bush approved a bailout plan and gave General Motors and Chrysler US$13.4 billion financed from the "Troubled Assets Relief Program (TARP)" funds, as well as US$4 billion to be withdrawn later.

[11] See note 4.

[12] See note 5.

On June 1, 2009, the U.S. bankruptcy judge approved GM's use of a total of US$33.3 billion in financing, with the US$15 billion available for use over the following three weeks. Such bailout impeded the carmakers' intentions to correct their production plans. In other words, auto and policy makers simply sweep dirt under the carpet as a result of the bailout.

Labor unions: Labor union is another factor which helps prolong the period of depression. As mentioned, if the company makes errors in its production plan, then it should correct the errors by reshuffling resources, including labor. Some workers may be sacked or retrenched. However, labor unions use their power to prevent sacking or retrenching of labor. They postpone the recovery indefinitely and make unemployment massive and persistent (Garrison 1966:33). Mises (1931/2006:166) rightly points out that "this adjusting process is severely disturbed ... by the interference of labor unions whose effectiveness evolved under the protection and with the assistance of governmental power".

The central bank as a major source of clusters of errors: For the Austrian economists in general, and Hulsmann in particular, government is a major institution responsible for clusters of errors. In the Austrian view, entrepreneurs are prone to make errors. However, the central bank's credit expansion policy causes a cluster of errors and hence massive unemployment at a particular period of time (Gunning 1985:243).

Austrian theorists argue that economic depression originates in the divergence between the market and the natural rates of interest[13] as a result of the credit expansion of the central bank (Gunning 1985).[14] Strictly speaking, there is no way to know the level of natural rate of interest. Government officials at the central bank normally determine the market interest rate by trial and error, based on their past experiences and social consensus. Usually, the central bank will set a low interest rate to boost the economy so asto get more popularity. This causes a mismatch of expectations of market participants and coordination failures (Hayek 1937).

Assume that due to political reason, the government pursues credit expansion policy by increasing the cash reserves of all commercial banks. Most managers of commercial banks are unlikely aware of a possible economic recession in the future and they take on the advantage of credit expansion. Some bankers who are able to anticipate the ultimate consequences of easy money based on their historical experience may not be eager to participate in a money-induced boom (Garrison 1989:12). However, just like government officials, most bankers in the market often use rule of thumbs to handle uncertainty because it is the most economical and usually effective means of doing things. However, rules can also lead to systematic 'errors' (Vihanto 1999:17). Moreover, a serious general recession is in fact so rare in the market that even bankers themselves have never experienced before. Even if some bankers have experienced a recession, they will be at risk of losing the memory as times

[13]The terms "natural rate of interest", given by Knut K. Wicksell, occurs when the economy is at equilibrium or full employment where investment and saving plans match. Hayek (1933, 1939) adopts this concept in his business cycle theory and assumes the economy at the beginning is at the full employment where market and natural rates of interest are equal. This view has been severely challenged.

[14]There are two positions within the Austrian camp regarding the credit expansion. According to Mises (1949; 1953), the central bank has committed an error by setting a 'wrong' level of interest rate. However, Hayek thinks that it is not an extravagant lending but routine banking practice that is at the heart of the business cycle (Barry 1979:163). Fluctuations are inevitable in the fractional reserve system. A cycle can be initiated even without the change in market rate. If the natural rate of interest rises, then issuing the same credit as before will lower the market rate below the natural rate and bring about an expansion of production not warranted by the level of voluntary saving (see also Block and Garschina 1996).

goes by. When the economy is prosperous, it is difficult for bankers to recall the recession. They just assume everything going alright as it is. Sometimes, bankers even deliberately ignore the possibility of downturn (Vihanto 1999:18). In Vihanto's (1999: 21-22) words,

> The banker seeks the best choice for his purposes in a type of decision situations by trying different alternatives and making inferences from the feedback information. For example, the banker may learn through the trial and error process that after the economy has been stabilized he makes larger profits by making his decisions as if another recession would never come again. He knows perfectly well that his assumption will not be true in the long run. However, the less he has cause for thinking of a recession in the meantime, the more likely the simply forgets how he should proceed once the signs of a recession are again within sight, and the closer he is in his ignorance to those green colleagues just taking their first steps in the profession. The process of experience falling into oblivion is still further intensified by the deliberate choice of the banker to follow a rule...[15]

As a result, entrepreneurs are induced by the central bank's lower interest rate to expand their businesses. Hence, 'malinvestment' occurs in the sense that in the economy, there are not enough savings to buy all the producers' goods. Firms have over-invested in capital goods and under-invested in consumers' goods (O'Driscoll2009:178).

Secondary Errors: Real Estate Boom and Subprime Crisis

In our illustration, due to low interest rates set by the Federal Reserve Bank and the U.S. government intervention polices, auto and other manufacturing industries which should be closed down will manage a profit and even expand their businesses. This effect will transmit to the real estate and stock markets. Share prices in the Wall Street will rise because the public perceives an optimistic future on the firms. People who earn their living through dividends and wages in these seemingly good performance firms will make investment in stock market or buy houses. In this way, not only primary errors made by production firms have not been corrected, but the wrong signal spreads to the real estate and stock markets, resulting in pseudo prosperity in both markets. The real estate market was further fueled by the four major U.S. Government policies in the housing sector concurrently(White 2008; Yeager 2009; Ravier and Lewin2012). First, the Federal Housing Administration (FHA) financed first-time homeownership buyers with modest incomes too easily. Its minimum down payment requirement is just 3.5 percent, compared with 5 percent to 20 percent from conventional, non-government sources. By 2004, the most popular FHA products required only 3 percent. The U.S. Congress even attempted to reduce it to zero percent. It resulted in a drastic increase in home purchases and subsequently, the default rate in mortgage payments.

The second problem in the housing policy is the Community Reinvestment Act(CRA) which over-encouraged lending to low-income applicants. Banks would be punished if they did not comply with the CRA's provisions. As a result, banks distributed millions of dollars in mortgages to low-income buyers in housing, previously ineligible for credit.

[15]In this sense, the banker who is ill suited to be performed as a routine can often survive in recession (Vihanto 1999:18).

Thirdly, in 1993, private banks received legal challenges from the Department of Housing and Urban Development (HUD) on the mortgage standards. To avoid pressures and legal problems, banks felt the need to relax the income requirements to customers in housing market.

Fourthly, the U.S. Congress pressured Fannie Mae and Freddie Mac to increase the purchase of mortgages. By 1996, the HUD required that Fannie Mae and Freddie Mac to fulfill some mortgage requirements in the form of “special affordable” loans, which was typically granted to borrowers with the income less than 60 percent of their area’s median income. Between 2000 and 2005, Fannie and Freddie funded hundreds billions of dollars’ worth of loans, of which many of them were subprime and adjustable-rate loans made to borrowers who bought houses with less than 10 percent down payment (Roberts 2008).White (2008:6) concludes that “the hyper-expansion of Fannie Mae and Freddie Mac was made possible by their implicit backing from the U.S. Treasury”. To finance the rapid growth, Fannie Mae and Freddie Mac borrowed large sums of money from the financial market. Investors were happy to lend money to the two government-sponsored companies, with relatively low interest rates because of the implicit government guarantee. When investors faced financial collapse and became more conservative, the Treasury explicitly endorsed the debts of Fannie Mae and Freddie Mac (Ravier and Lewin 2012: 54-56).

The Fed’s easy-credit policy, combined with government’s encouragement for riskier mortgage lending, inflated the housing bubble (Cardarelli et al. 2008:19). IMF researchers found that “the unusually low level of interest rates in the United States between 2001 and 2003 contributed somewhat to the elevated rate of expansion in the housing market, in terms of both housing investment and the run-up in house prices up to mid-2005” (IMF 2008:121; see also White 2009:19). Moreover, “the increase in house prices and residential investment in the United States over the past six years would have been much more contained had short-term interest rates remained unchanged” (IMF 2008:123). From the 4th quarter of 2002 to the 4th quarter of 2006, “real house prices rose by an additional 31.6 percent, an annual rate of 7.1 percent. This boosted even more construction, with housing starts eventually peaking at 2,070,000 in 2005, more than 50 percent above the rate in the pre-bubble years” (Baker 2009:22).

As house prices soared, the financial industry adopted more sophisticated financial instruments to support the real estate growth. Subprime mortgage loans were issued to people with poor credit history. Homebuyers who obtained subprime mortgages were typically people with irregular employment records or who had defaulted on some loans in the past. The interest rates on subprime loans ranged from two to four percentage points higher than the interest rate available at the time on prime loans given to people with good credit history. In addition to subprime loans, there was also a boom in the “Alt-A” mortgage which is loans to homebuyers who either had a mixed credit record or who provided incomplete documentation of income and assets (Baker 2009:24).

The subprime and Alt-A mortgages together comprised more than 40 percent of the loans issued at the peak of the bubble. With the drastic increase in high-risk loans, policy makers and investors should sense that there was a serious problem in the housing market. In the subprime market, the number of the subprime loan had more than doubled from 2002 to 2004, even as the labor market remained weak and wages lagged behind inflation. The increase in subprime loans over these years was an unambiguous warning signal to the housing market. Unfortunately, policy makers celebrated the record rates of homeownership (Baker 2009:24).

Wrong Incentives Escalating the Crisis

The surge in high-risk loans was made possible by wrong incentives in the real estate and housing markets. First of all, there was a wrong incentive in the real estate appraisal process. Commercial appraisers operate as independent contractors. They are hired by banks to assess a mortgage. In previous years, banks would have valued an honest appraisal. However, during the housing boom, banks wanted to make sure that the appraisal would be high enough to justify the mortgage. Appraisers realized that if they gave an honest appraisal that was too low, they would not be hired by the banks again. Therefore, appraisers had a strong incentive to take an upper-side bias in their appraisals (Baker 2009:77).

Another wrong incentive lies in the securitization process in the financial market. In the secondary market, mortgage issuers had an incentive to approve mortgages even though they knew that the borrower would be unable to meet the terms of the mortgage. The issuers generally faced little risk once the mortgage was sold in the secondary market, so they had the incentive to issue mortgages as many as possible. They just wanted to ensure that the mortgages meet the minimum requirement to be sold in the secondary market (ibid, 77).

Banks also made their money on the fees associated with the securitization process, not on holding the mortgage banked securities (MBS). This meant that the securitizers also had the incentive to maximize the volume with little regard to the actual quality of the loans. The ability of the banks to sell their MBS depended on their ability to secure good credit rating for their bonds. This process was facilitated by issuing new and more complex financial instruments such as "collaterized debt obligations (CDOs)".These new instruments which included mixes of mortgage backed securities along with other assets usually received high rating from the credit agencies, and hence allowing high-risk mortgages (ibid, 77).

Bubble Burst and Its Domino Effect

This chapter argues that errors in American manufacturing industries (such as GM) were not corrected but sustained. These errors were transmitted to property and stock markets. With loose housing loan policies and Fed's quantitative easing strategy, bubble was built up and inflated. It is important to know when and on what conditions the bubble will burst. Admittedly, it takes a long time for manufacturing and real estate firms to discover the errors. In the auto industries, GM competed with Japanese cars. In the global market, GM cars did not sell what consumers want to buy. Such errors were not obvious at the beginning but it finally emerged to the surface as the stockpile of unsold GM cars built up. However, with the labor union, bailout package and low interest rate policies, GM was able to hang on with some capital restructuring. Still, GM was unable to compete in the global market. Eventually, it called for bankruptcy. As Zahringer (2012:317-318) summarizes, "as credit expansion slows or stops, market data begins to return to more realistic levels. This reveals entrepreneurial error committed in the past—projects that once appeared profitable are not. Firms undertaking these projects cut back and retrench or in some cases go bankrupt. Banks that financed those projects must write off some or all of the debt. Workers on the failed enterprises are unemployed".

As manufacturing firms closed down, housing and shares prices declined accordingly. In the housing mortgage market, the bubble burst took downturn after the housing prices peaked in the middle of 2006. This led to rapid rises in default rates, especially in the subprime market. Many subprime homeowners were the most vulnerable groups in the economy. They had little choice but to default on their mortgage. It is worth noting that many of the subprime loans in 2006 and 2007 were not purchase mortgages but rather mortgages used to refinance homes. Subprime lenders often deceptively sold mortgages to low-income homeowners to finance their big purchases such as cars or home remodeling. As a result, families suddenly faced the loss of their home. Sapir (2008: 38) describes the situation as follows:

> Defaults increased steadily from early 2007 onwards, reaching 16% of the outstanding subprime loans by October 200719. By late January 2008, 24% of subprime mortgages were delinquent or in foreclosure. By late September 2007 nearly 4% of all mortgages were delinquent or in foreclosure, meaning that for non-subprime compartments the average rate of delinquency was 2% against the traditional 0.5% rate. By late January 2008 the figure was 7.3% of all mortgaged loans, and 3.7% for all non-subprime compartments or seven times higher than the traditional rate. During 2007, nearly 1.3 million U.S. housing properties were subject to foreclosure, an increase of 79% over 2006.

Murphy (2011) concludes that "Greenspan's Fed didn't actually eliminate the need for a recession, but instead postponed the crisis and made it fester". DeSoto (2009) further claims that Ben Bernanke, the successor of Alan Greenspan, did not correct the primary and secondary errors. Rather, he deepened the errors. In DeSoto's own words, "instead of a crisis that looks like a V, deep and fast (which is what the free market would have produced), monetary and government intervention unnecessarily produced a recession much longer and more painful."

Conclusion

This chapter applies the Austrian theory of business cycle to interpret the Financial Crisis in 2007-8. In explaining the financial crisis, most scholars (for example, see Zelmanovitz 2011) focus largely on the problems in the real estate and financial markets in the United States. They blame on the wrong monetary policies set by the Federal Reserve Bank. In their views, the problems in subprime mortgages and financial institutions are largely responsible for the general recession in 2008. While it is true that the real estate and housing markets contained many problems, analyses focusing mainly on the financial and housing markets tell only part of the story. This chapter starts with the explanation of the formation of primary errors in the industrial sector (real sector), then extend the understanding to secondary errors in the real estate and financial markets (monetary sector). In other words, real sector and money sector are interrelated.

Using General Motors and subprime mortgage loans as illustration, this study has argued that the financial crisis occurs due primarily to investment errors made under uncertainty. Economic errors mean mismatches of plans in the market. If investors' plans do not match with other producers' or consumers' plans, then, coordination fails. If production plans fail to match consumers' tastes, producers will adjust their expectations and revise their plans subsequently. In the market process, mismatches of plans and plan revisions are normal practice in everyday business life and will not lead to global financial chaos. What causes financial disaster is systemic or clusters of errors, both in financial investment or production plans. Clusters of errors form when all people make economic errors at the same time and such errors have cumulated over a period of time. This chapter has explored the factors that cause the delay of economic revision plans, thus, leading to the formation of clusters of errors. These factors, largely institutional, include labor unions, financial intermediaries practices, government bailout plans and most importantly, the central bank's monetary policy. This chapter suggests that governments should not shield off economic corrections by lowering interest rates artificially or bailout package. Instead, they should help firms make economic adjustment as quickly as possible, so that firms can start new and 'healthy' investments and the economy moves out of the general recession.

Acknowledgment

I am very grateful to Diana S. Kwan for proof-reading this article.

References

Baker, Dean. (2009). "The Housing Bubble and the Financial Crisis" in *Crash - Why it Happened and what to do about it*, Edited by Edward Fullbrook, *Real-world Economics Review*, volume 1, 21-29.

Barry, Norman. (1979).*Hayek's Social and Economic Philosophy*, London: MacMillan.

Block, Walter &Garschina, Kenneth M. (1996). "Hayek, Business Cycles and Fractional Reserve Banking: Continuing the De-Homogenisation Process", *The Review of Austrian Economics*, 9 (1), 77-94,

Cardarelli, Roberto, Igan, Deniz & Rebucci, Alessandro.(2008). "The Changing Housing Cycle and the Implications for Monetary Policy," *World Economic Outlook*, 103–133, International Monetary Fund, April.

De Soto, Jesús Huerta. (2009). *Money, Bank Credit, and Economic Cycles*, 2nd edition, Auburn, AL: Ludwig von Mises Institute.

Garrison, Roger W. ed. (1966).*The Austrian Theory of the Trade Cycle and other Essays*, Auburn, AL: The Mises Institute.

Garrison, Roger W. (1989). "The Austrian Theory of the Business Cycle in the Light of Modern Macroeconomics" *The Review of Austrian Economics*, 3(1), 3-29.

Gunning, Patrick. (1985). "Causes of Unemployment: The Austrian Perspective", *History of Political Economy*, 17(2), 223-244.

Hayek, Friedrich A. (1933/1966). *Monetary Theory and the Trade Cycle*, New York: Augustus M. Kelly.

Hayek Friedrich A. (1937)."Economics and Knowledge", *Economica*, no.4, 33-54.Reprinted in *Individualism and Economic Order*, Chicago: University of Chicago Press, 1948.

Hayek, Friedrich A. (1939). *Profits, Interest and Investment -- and Other Essays on the Theory of Industrial Fluctuations*. London: Routledge & Kegan Paul.

Hulsmann, Jorg G. (1998). "Toward a General Theory of Error Cycles", *Quarterly Journal of Austrian Economics*, 1(4), 1-23.

IMF. (2008). *World Economic Outlook: Housing and Business Cycle*, April, Washington DC: IMF.

Kirzner, I.M. (1979). "Economics and Error" in *Perception, Opportunity, and Profit*, Chicago: University of Chicago Press, 120-136.

Knight, Frank H. (1921). *Risk, Uncertainty, and Profit*. New York: Houghton Mifflin.

Leibenstein, H. (1966). "Allocative Efficiency Vs. X-Efficiency" *American Economic Review*, 56(June), 392-415.

Mises, Ludwig von. (1931/2006).*The Causes of the Economic Crisis*, Auburn, AL: Ludwig von Mises Institute.

Mises, Ludwigvon. (1949). *Human Action*, 3rd edition, Chicago: Contemporary Books.

Mises, Ludwig von. (1953). *The Theory of Money and Credit*, New haven: The Liberty Press.

Murphy, Robert. (2011, August 8). "Why is the Stock Market Plunging?" Auburn: AL: The Mises Institute; http://mises.org/daily/5531/Why-Is-the-Stock-Market- Plunging; retrieved on 21 March 2013.

O'Driscoll, G.P. Jr. (2009). "Money and the Present Crisis," *Cato Journal*, 29(1), 167–186.

O'Driscoll, G.P. Jr. & Rizzo, M. (1985).*The Economics of Time and Ignorance*, Oxford: Blackwell.

Roberts, Russell. (2008). "How Government Stoked the Mania: Housing Prices Would Never have Risen So High without Multiple Washington Mistakes," *Wall Street Journal*, October 3.

Ravier, Adrian &Lewin, Peter. (2012). "The Subprime Crisis" *The Quarterly Journal of Austrian Economics*, 15(1/Spring): 45-72.

Rothbard, Murray N. (1962/1993). *Man, Economy and State*, Auburn, AL: Ludwig von Mises Institute.

Rothbard, Murray N. (1963). *America's Great Depression*, Kansas City: Sheed Andrews and McMeel, Inc.

Rothbard, Murray N. (1969). "Economic Depressions: Their Cause and Cure", reprinted in Richard Ebeling (eds) (1983), *The Austrian Theory of the Trade Cycle and Other Essays*, Auburn: The Ludwig von Mises Institute, 21-34.

Sapir, Jacques. (2008). "Global Finance in Crisis: A Provisional Account of the 'Subprime' Crisis and How We Got into it" Edited by Edward Fullbrook, *Real-world Economics Review*, volume 1, 30-49.

Stigler, G.J. (1976). "The Existence of X-Efficiency", *American Economic Review*, 66(March), 213-217.

Vihanto, Martti. (1999). "Extending Austrian Economics Toward Psychology: Rules in Loan Decisions", A paper presented in the workshop "Austrian Economics and the Theory of the Firm" at Copenhagen Business School, 16-17 August.

White, L.H. (2008). "How Did We Get into This Financial Mess?" *Cato Briefing Paper*, No. 108, November18.

White, L.H. (2009). "Federal Reserve Policy and the Housing Bubble," *Cato Journal*, 29(1), 115–125.

Yeager, Leland B. (2009). "The Contagious Crisis," *Liberty*, 23, No. 7, Liberty Fund.

Zahringer, Kenneth. (2012). "Monetary Disequilibrium Theory and Business Cycles: An Austrian Critique" *The Quarterly Journal of Austrian Economics*, 15 (3/Fall), 304-330.

Zelmanovitz, Leonidas. (2011). "The Austrian Business Cycle Theory and the Recent Financial Crisis", *Criterio Libre*, 9(15), 23-58, July –December.

In: Business Cycles in Economics
Editor: Jason C. Hsu
ISBN: 978-1-63321-322-7

Chapter 8

THE STOCK MARKET AND BUSINESS CYCLE FORECASTING: THE WEALTH EFFECT OF THE STOCK MARKET AND THE HOUSING MARKET

William Wei-Choun Yu[1]
Economist, Anderson Forecast, Anderson School of Management,
University of California, Los Angeles, CA, US

Abstract

This chapter provides four findings. First, the stock market fluctuations can predict recession but their forecasts are far from a guarantee. Many of the substantial declines are false alarms. Second, there is no strong evidence of wealth effect on consumer spending from stock market swings while there is significant evidence of wealth effect from housing price movement. Evidence suggests that a 10 percent decrease in housing wealth will decrease consumption by at least 0.5 percent. Third, if an investor can predict the recession 18 months ahead, one might be able to reduce the downside risk of stock markets. When the direction of housing market is clear, through its wealth effect, the prediction of business cycle will be more accurate. Finally, an asset bubble accompanied with a credit bubble could foretell a more substantial stock market decline when the bubble bursts.

Introduction

During the aftermath of the Great Recession, the stock market tumble in mid-2011 caused people to fear another imminent recession. A similar panic occurred in the midst of the declining stock market of mid-2010. Why would such an unrest concerning a possible recession arise every time the stock market slumps? If one believes that stock markets operate efficiently and correctly, the stock prices represent the valuation of future profitability of

[1] E-mail address: william.yu@anderson.ucla.edu; Tel: 310-825-7805; 110 Address: Anderson Forecast, Anderson School of Management, University of California, Westwood Plaza, C-506, Los Angeles, CA 90095.

companies. Since a company's profits directly relates to the economy as a whole, it would follow that the stock market index could also signal the future economy growth and volatility of a nation. Thus, we are worried because the declining stock market prices of today foretell ill economy prospects. We will examine whether if the stock market is a valid predictor of a recession in the following section.

Furthermore, the stock market prices, when seen as representations of the wealth of shareholders, could affect the consumption decisions of a stockowner in addition to consumers' incomes and interest rates. Rather than simply predicting, here the stock market decline could be causing or amplifying a recession. Why? Because the stock market's fluctuation could materialize, translating into the ups and downs of asset values on a household's balance sheet. For example, when investors look at their elevated asset values, they feel more comfortable and secure, so they increase their spending. This confidence in turn helps the real economy prosper. This is called the *wealth effect.* Yet, sometimes the stock market fluctuation might aggravate and destabilize the business cycle. For instance, when the stock market initially rallies to reflect the fundamental resilience of the economy, consumers who feel wealthier due to their increased stock assets will consume more. And higher consumption will lead to higher profits of companies, which leads to even higher stock prices, which then leads to an even higher spending spree, and the cycle continues. This is the asset bubble. And if the ballooned consumption is financed by credit, the asset bubble is accompanied by a credit or debt bubble.

These bubbles, by definition, will not be able to sustain themselves indefinitely. When the bubble bursts, we see the opposite of a vicious cycle. The stock market slump impairs households' wealth, leading to reduced consumption, leading to low profits of companies, leading to further declining stock market prices, etc. For the sake of stabilizing the business cycle, too much wealth effects from an asset boom and bust is undesirable. Hence it is important to understand how much influence the wealth effect has. The troubling fact is that it is not clear if the stock market fluctuation is simply revealing the economy fundamentals and risk or if it will induce further unwanted wealth effect or both. And it is extremely difficult to disentangle the true causality and its magnitude given that all of these economic variables are interrelated and reinforced over time. [1]

Meanwhile, housing is the biggest asset for a homeowner. When the housing prices increase, homeowners might increase their consumption due to higher home equity, and vice versa. How much does the housing price change affect consumer spending? We will discuss the wealth effect of the housing market and its comparison with the wealth effect of the stock market in the following sections.

How Well Has the Stock Market Predicted Recession?

First, let's examine the record of predictability of a stock market slump for recession in US history regardless of the possible wealth effect. Figure 1 shows the monthly real stock market prices from 1871 to December 2013. [2] The shaded periods represent the official recessions dated by the National Bureau of Economic Research (NBER). [3] Within this sample, there are 29 recessions. Prior to World War II, we had 18 recessions, most of which were prolonged, while 11 shorter recessions occurred in the post-war period.

For simplicity, we use 10% and 20% as the threshold in our analysis. The first step we take is to define a reference month. If the stock market decline has ever accumulated to more than 10%over the past six months, the first month to reach this standard will be the reference month. Second, if we see that the reference month is within the recession or that there is a recession coming within the following 12 months, we document that this stock decline incidence successfully predicted a recession.

If the 10% decline is not followed by a recession in the following 12 months, we categorize it as a false alarm. The third possibility is that there is a recession without stock market 10% decline in the preceding 12 months (or within the recession period).

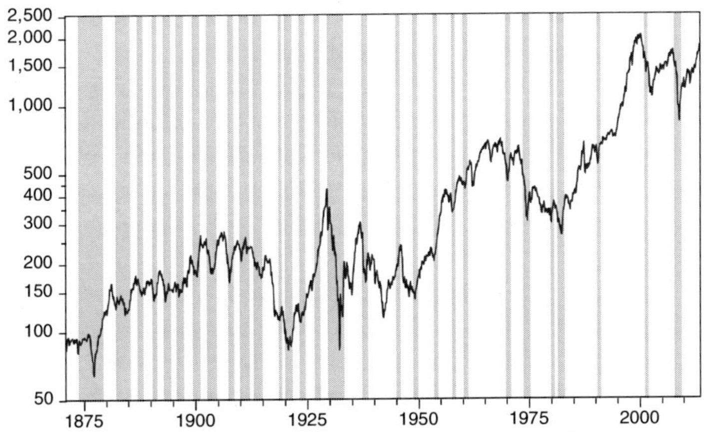

Note: Shaded periods are recessions; the price is presented in the logarithm scale.
Sources: NBER; Robert Shiller online stock market data.

Figure 1. The Monthly Real Stock Market Price from 1871 to 2013.

Table 1. The Recession Predictability of 10%Stock Market Accumulated Decline over the Previous Six Months

	Years of the stock market decline of 10% and/or the beginning year of each recession	total
Correctly predicts the recession	1873, 1882, 1987, 1890, 1893, 1895, 1899, 1902, 1907, 1910, 1913, 1918, 1920, 1923, 1929, 1937, 1948, 1953, 1957, 1969, 1973, 1980, 1981, 1990, 2001, 2007	26
False alarm (no recession following)	1934, 1935, 1939, 1940, 1941, 1942, 1946, 1962, 1966, 1971, 1975, 1978, 1984, 1987, 1998, 2002, 2010, 2011	18
A recession comes without stock market 10% decline	1926, 1945, and 1960	3

As shown in Table 1, out of 29 recessions, the stock market decline predicted 26! Only three recessions came without stock market warnings. This looks like a very good predictor. However, the stock market also made 18 *false warnings*. That said, 40% of the substantial stock market declines are false warnings. While we will rarely see a recession without due warning from the stock market, a decline might simply be the boy who cried wolf. The empirical evidence here echoes the famous joke made by the late economist Paul Samuelson: "Wall Street indexes predicted nine out of the last five recessions."

Table 2. The Recession Predictability of 20% Stock Market Accumulated Decline over the Previous Six Months

	Years of the stock market decline of 10% and/or the beginning year of each recession	total
Correctly predicts the recession	1873, 1890, 1893, 1902, 1907, 1918, 1920, 1929, 1937, 1969, 1973, 2001, 2007	13
False alarm (no recession following)	1934, 1940, 1942, 1946, 1962, 1987, 2002	7
A recession comes without stock market 20% decline	1882, 1887, 1895, 1899, 1910, 1913, 1923, 1926, 1945, 1948, 1953, 1957, 1960, 1980, 1981, 1990	16

In addition, before the Great Depression, we did not have a good measurement of the U.S. economy. Therefore, it is possible that NBER determined those pre-Great Depression recessions partly based on recorded stock market prices. Thus it is not surprising that the stock market is an excellent predictor of recessions prior the 1930s while it made more false alarms after the 1930s.On the other hand, what can we learn from the fact there are only three recessions without precedent 10% stock market declines in the previous six months? It implies that if one can predict the recession 12 months to 18 months ahead, he or she might be able to reduce the downside risk of stock prices.

As shown in Table 2, if we change the threshold from 10% to 20% stock market price decline, we make fewer false alarms: only 7 times (decrease from 18 times). However, this deeper standard of stock market slump will cost us to miss more recessions: 16 times (increase from 3 times). So there is a trade-off between different forecast errors by choosing different thresholds. The larger the decline in the stock market that we see, the higher the chance of a coming recession.

In short, the stock market index is not a perfect barometer of the whole economy. It could be used as a predictor of recession but not a reliable one. To better predict a recession, one should not look at stock market prices alone.

Weath Effects of the Stock Market and the Housing Market

Now let's discuss the wealth effects of stock market prices and housing market prices. Figure 2 presents the real personal consumption expenditures (PCE) year-over-year monthly growth (on the right axis scale), real S&P 500 stock price (deflated by PCE price index; left scale; adjusted to 100 in January 2000), and real S&P/Case-Shiller composite home prices of 20 cities (deflated by PCE price index; left scale; adjusted to 100 in January 2000). From Figure 2, we can see an apparent correlation between consumer spending and stock prices as well as housing prices. In 2001 and 2002, while stock prices dropped 20%, consumption growth decreased from 6% to 2%. From 2003 to 2005, while the stock market rebounded with the run-away housing market, consumption growth increased from about 2% to 3%. The housing market collapse in 2006 and the following stock market crash in 2008 were accompanied by a consumption plummet from 3% to -3%. The revived stock market and stabilizing housing market in 2010 were both associated with resurging consumption growth.

However, from Figure 2, we do not know whether it is the stock and housing wealth change that causes consumption change or if it is the other way around. It is difficult to disentangle the true wealth effect. Again, for example, when we see co-movement between housing price and consumption growth, it could be one of two opposite causality scenarios.

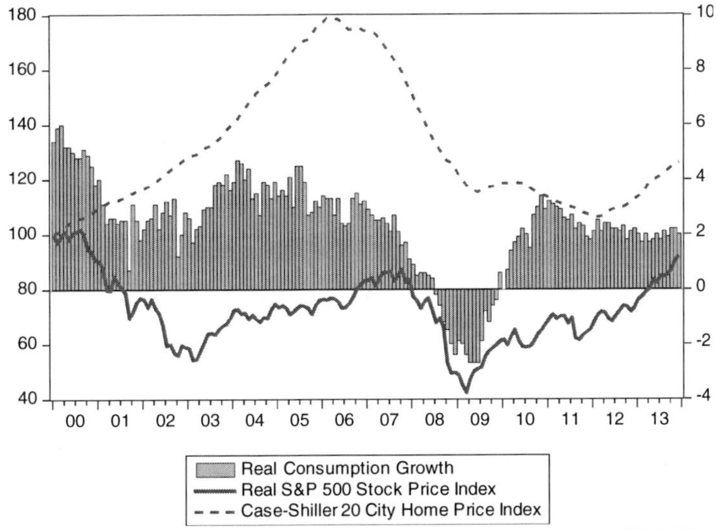

Sources: Bureau of Economic Analysis; S&P/Case-Shiller composite home prices; S&P500 stock index.

Figure 2. The Monthly Real Consumption Growth, Real Stock Price, and Real Home Price from 2000 to 2013.

First, it could be that housing wealth decline reduces the consumer's spending, which is the wealth effect. Second, it could be that weak consumer spending reflects the weak economy and miserable job market and therefore discourages the demand for homes. To get a better estimate of the wealth effects of the stock market and the housing market, Case, Quigley, and Shiller (2005) [4] use two panels of the international and US states data and various regression methods to get robust results. By and large, Case et al. find at best weak evidence of a stock market wealth effect. However, they do find robust and significant wealth effect of the housing market on consumption for various regression settings. For the US state data [5], they suggest that, on average, *a 10 percent increase in housing wealth will increase consumption by 0.5 percent.* Can this estimate explain the national economy in the US?

Figure 3 presents the average annual growth rates of real GDP and consumption in the periods of the 1970s, 1980s, 1990s, 2000-2006, and 2007-2013. From the 1970s to 1990s, we observe that annual GDP growth rates are slightly above 3% and consumption growth rates are hovering by 0.2% more than the GDP growths for those three decades. However, during the run-up of the housing boom in the 2000-2006 period, the gap between consumption and GDP growths widens to 0.59%. Why? Increased US current account deficit might explain this in part. The main driver of higher overspent-consumption growth could come from the housing wealth effect.

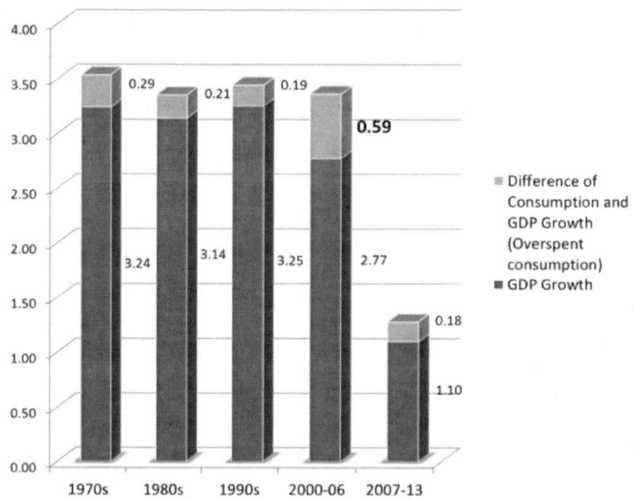

Source: Bureau of Economic Analysis.

Figure 3. The Annual Growth Rates of GDP and Overspent Consumption (%).

According to Figure 2, if we assume that housing wealth increased 10% annually from 2000 to 2006, consumers will have increased their spending by 0.5% every year because of the wealth effect compared to otherwise. The housing bubble could be the main culprit of abnormal over-spending for the period of 2000 to 2006. In the aftermath of the housing bubble for the period of 2007 to 2013, we see the overspent consumption growth reduce back to 0.18% on average.

So why do we see a larger wealth effect of the housing market than that of the stock market (if any)? There are three possible reasons.

(1) *Ownership:* There is an ownership difference between stocks and homes. According to the latest Survey of Consumer Finances (SCF) by the Federal Reserve Board, in 2010, 67.3% of families had a home while only 49.9% of families held stocks (directly and indirectly). The gap between ownerships of stocks and homes is persistent. Therefore, because of this higher percentage of homeownership, it is straightforward to predict that the wealth effect on consumption is larger in housing than in stocks.

(2) *Value of Assets:* The ownership gap does not explain the whole story. Let's take a closer look at the assets. According to the SCF, a family's nonfinancial assets' value is twice the financial assets' value as shown in Table 4. Among nonfinancial assets, primary residence (home) is the largest asset. For instance in 2010, home as a share of total assets was 29.4% while stock as a share of total assets only counted as 5.3%. Nevertheless, there were stock components in the pooled investment funds (5.7%, excluding money market mutual fund) and retirement accounts (14.4%). If we include other residential property, we will get an even bigger share of housing wealth value compared with stock wealth. In 2010, the home and other residential property amounted to 36.4% of a family's total assets.

Table 3. Family Ownerships for Stocks and Homes

Percentage (%)	1989	1992	1995	1998	2001	2004	2007	2010
Stockholdership	31.8	36.9	40.5	48.9	52.3	50.3	53.2	49.9
Homeownership	63.9	63.9	64.7	66.2	67.7	69.1	68.6	67.3

Source: Survey of Consumer Finances 2010.

Table 4.Values of Financial Assets and Nonfinancial Assets of Families

Percentage	1989	1992	1995	1998	2001	2004	2007	2010
Financial Assets	30.5	31.6	36.8	40.7	42.2	35.8	34.0	37.9
Stocks	4.6	5.2	5.7	9.2	9.1	6.3	6.1	5.3
Pooled investment funds	1.6	2.4	4.7	5.0	5.1	5.2	5.4	5.7
Retirement accounts	6.6	8.2	10.4	11.3	12.2	11.6	11.9	14.4
Nonfinancial Assets	69.5	68.4	63.2	59.3	57.8	64.2	66.0	62.1
Primary residence / Homes	32.0	32.1	30.0	27.9	27.1	32.3	31.7	29.4
Other residential property	5.7	5.8	5.1	5.0	4.7	6.4	7.1	7.0

Source: Survey of Consumer Finances 2010.

(3) *Transitory vs Permanent Movement* Economic theory and evidence (e.g. see Lettau and Ludvigson, 2004 [6]) suggest that transitory change of wealth will have smaller impact on consumption than the permanent change of wealth. From Figure 2, it is clear to see that the dynamics of stock prices and housing prices are very different due to the difference in their asset nature and transaction cost. Stock prices are more volatile and harder to predict. Consumers might doubt if the movement is permanent or not; therefore the wealth effect could be limited. In contrast, housing prices are moving more persistently and are easier to predict, so its wealth effect should be more significant.

Table 5. Median Values of Assets, Debt, Net Worth and Income of Family

Median Value, thousands of 2010 dollar	1989	1992	1995	1998	2001	2004	2007	2010
Asset								
Stocks	13.5	12.1	12.7	24	24.5	17.3	17.8	20
Pooled investment funds	21.9	24.3	28.3	33	42.9	47.2	58.7	80
Retirement accounts	18.6	21.2	24.1	32	36	40.5	47.1	44
Homes	118.1	121.3	126.1	133.4	150.7	184.1	209.5	170
Other residential property	84.3	75.8	70.8	86.7	98	115.1	157.2	120
Debt								
Homes	54	66	72.2	82.7	85.8	109.3	112.1	109
Other residential property	43.9	37.9	42.5	54.7	49	100.1	104.8	97
Installment loans	8.4	7	8.6	11.7	11.9	13.5	13.6	12.7
Net Worth	79.4	75.4	81.9	95.6	106.3	107.1	126.8	77
Income	44	40.4	43.5	44.6	49.1	49.6	49.6	45.7

Source: Survey of Consumer Finances 2010.

Table 6. Mean Values of Assets, Debt, Net Worth and Income of Family

Mean Value, thousands of 2010 dollar	1989	1992	1995	1998	2001	2004	2007	2010
Asset								
Stocks	101.7	101.3	133.2	212	235.5	183.9	231.3	203.3
Pooled investment funds	84	76.4	133.2	134.7	161.3	210.9	323.8	386.6
Retirement accounts	64.2	67.4	81.1	101.7	128.5	141.6	154.7	170.9
Homes	179.2	166.5	163	185	222	284.1	317	260.9
Other residential property	154.5	151	154.1	175.3	228.8	314.9	370.3	288.8
Debt								
Homes	76.6	88.2	91.5	103.6	112.6	142.6	156	154.1
Other residential property	65.5	86.5	85.2	94.9	89.7	197.4	186.3	178.1
Installment loans	14.9	11.8	13.4	19	18.3	21.6	22.2	23.5
Net Worth	319.4	283.6	301.9	378.3	487.2	516.8	583.5	494.9
Income	69.2	60.7	63.3	70.8	84.7	81.3	88.2	78.3

Source: Survey of Consumer Finances 2010.

Table 5 presents the median values of assets, debts, net worth, and income for all families in the US. From 1989 to 2001, we can see stock value increasing from $13,500 to $24,500 and then decreasing to $20,000 in 2010. Meanwhile, home median value increased from $118,100 in 1989 to $170,000 in 2010. Again, for a median family, home asset is larger than stock asset and increased more in absolute value over the past two decades. In contrast, the mean values of assets for all families shown in Table 6 reveal something different. All the mean values in Table 6 are higher than those in Table 5, which demonstrates that rich families are disproportionately holding more assets, especially in stocks because their extremely high values will pull up the average number of asset values. From 1989 to 2010, the mean stock value increased from $101,700 to $203,300. And during this same period, the mean home value increased from $179,200 to $260,900. Combining Tables 5 and 6, we could say that rich families have a relatively larger share of wealth in stock than middle-class families although their housing wealth is still larger than their stock wealth. Therefore, here we again see why the wealth effect of the housing market is more influential than that of the stock market.

The most recent research on wealth effects in the US confirms that there exists a wealth effect of housing on consumption. To name a few:

(1) Bostic, Gabriel, and Painter (2009) [7] use the matched household data from the SCF and Consumer Expenditure Survey (CES) from 1989 to 2001. Overall, they find a significantly large housing wealth effect and a smaller financial wealth effect. They suggest that, among homeowners, *a 10 percent increase in housing wealth will increase consumption by 0.6 percent.* And they report that a 10 percent increase in financial wealth will increase consumption by only 0.2 percent.

(2) Carroll, Otsuka, and Slacalek (2011) [8] analyze the immediate and eventual wealth effects on consumption from 1960 to 2007. They suggest that a $1 increase in housing wealth will result in an immediate (next quarter) 2 cents increase of consumer spending, with a final eventual increase around 9 cents. And they suggest a smaller wealth effect from financial wealth: immediate effect of 2 cents and eventual effect of 4 cents.

All in all, the lesson we can learn is that we ought to pay more attention to the housing cycle than to the stock fluctuations because the housing wealth effect is more significant and destabilizing. It is worth noting that despite the weak evidence of stock market wealth effect on aggregate consumption, one should expect much larger stock wealth effect on luxury spending. This is because, as shown in Tables 5 and 6, most of the stockownership is concentrated in the wealthy (see Poterba, 2000 [9]).

Leverage and Deveverage

As the housing bubble and bust evolves, we see an associated household debt cycle as shown in Figure 4. Figure 4 presents the household annual borrowing in billions of dollars, which tells us the total amount of borrowing during the housing bubble and the aftermath of the crash. American families decreased their total household borrowing to $233 billion and 263 billion in 2009 and 2010, respectively. These declining debts mainly come from home mortgage debt reduction. Figure 5 presents the total US household debt as a percentage of GDP. The ratio starts accelerating in 2001 at 74%, shooting up to 97% in 2007, and gradually declining to 79% in 2013. The ongoing deleveraging process helps explain the anemic consumer spending after the Great Recession. In retrospect, we suggest that an asset bubble accompanied with a credit bubble will see more adjustment when the bubbles burst. For instance, the Internet bubble in the 1990s is simply an asset bubble. The stock market decline of the bubble burst is only half of its previous bubble gain as shown in Figure 1. While the asset bubbles in the 1920s and the 2000s came with sizable credit bubbles, their stock market declines after the burst washed out their bubble gains.

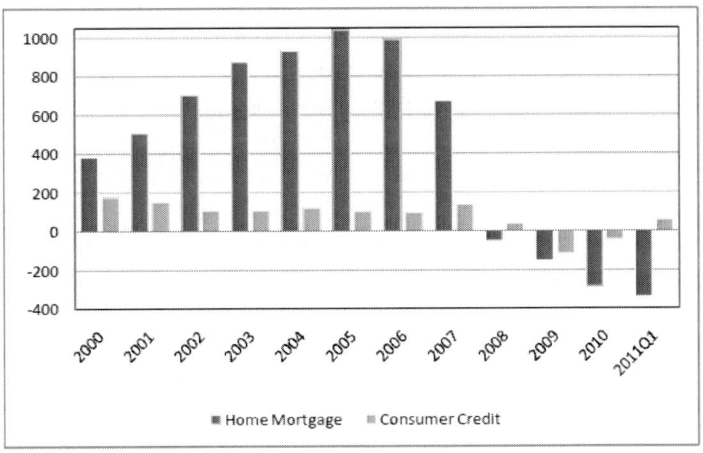

Source: Federal Reserve Board (FRB) Flow of Funds Account.

Figure 4. US Household Credit Market Borrowing, Billion Dollars.

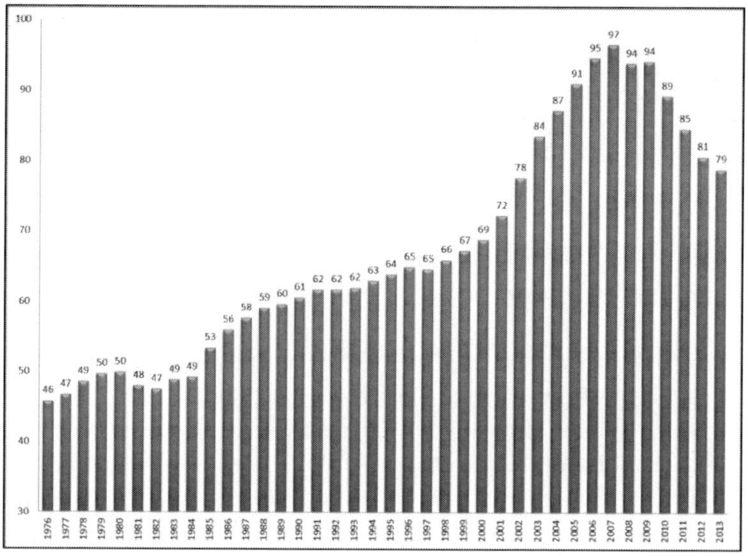

Sources: FRB Flow of Funds Account; Bureau of Economic Analysis.

Figure 5. Outstanding Debt of US Households As a Percentage of GDP.

Conclusion

In summary, the take-away points from this chapter are as follows. First, stock market fluctuations can predict recession but their forecasts are far from a guarantee. 40% of the substantial declines are false alarms. Second, there is no strong evidence of wealth effect on consumer spending from stock market swings while there is significant evidence of wealth effect from housing market movement. Evidence suggests that a 10 percent increase (decrease) in housing wealth will increase (decrease) consumption by at least 0.5 percent.

Third, the relationship among the stock market, the housing market, the credit market, and the business cycle is complex and time varying. For medium-term investors, they are more interested in predicting stock market movement than the business cycle. If one can predict the recession 12 months to 18 months ahead, he or she might be able to reduce the downside risk of stock markets. Furthermore, this chapter suggests that the housing market price movement will have the wealth effect to the economy. And we also know that housing prices are mostly persistent and predictable to some degree. Combining these, we might have a better picture of the future economy and therefore stock markets when the direction of the housing market is clearer.

Finally, an asset bubble accompanied with a credit bubble could foretell a more substantial stock market decline when the bubbles burst.

References

[1] Economists are aware of the difficulty of finding true economic causality by using statistical and econometrics tools. For example, see the renowned work by Ed Leamer (1983): "Let's Take the Con Out of Econometrics," *American Economic Review*, 73(1), 31-43.

[2] The real stock price is adjusted based on the 2013 Consumer Price Index as 100.

[3] The recessions start at the peak of a business cycle, end at the trough, and are determined by NBER (National Bureau of Economic Research)'s Business Cycle Dating Committee.

[4] Case, K., J. Quigley, and R. Shiller, 2005. "Comparing Wealth Effects: The Stock Market Versus the Housing Market," *Advances in Macroeconomics,* 5(1): 1–34.

[5] The data is the quarterly data across 50 states and Washington, DC from 1982 through 1999.

[6] Lettau, M., and S. Ludvigson, 2004. "Understanding Trend and Cycle in Asset Values: Reevaluating the Wealth Effect on Consumption," *American Economic Review*, 94(1), 276-299.

[7] Bostic, R., S. Gabriel, and Painter, 2009."Housing Wealth, Financial Wealth, and Consumption: New Evidence from Micro Data," *Regional Science and Urban Economics,* 39, 79-89.

[8] Carroll, C., M. Otsuka, and J. Slacalek, 2011. "How Large Are Housing and Financial Wealth Effects? A New Approach," *Journal of Money, Credit, and Banking*, 43(1), 55-79.

[9] Poterba, J., 2000. "Stock Market Wealth and Consumption," *Journal of Economic Perspectives*, 14(2), 99-118.

In: Business Cycles in Economics
Editor: Jason C. Hsu

ISBN: 978-1-63321-322-7

Chapter 9

ASYMMETRIC EFFECTS OF QUANTITATIVE EASING: EVIDENCE FOR THE US UNEMPLOYMENT RATE

Georgios Karras*
University of Illinois at Chicago, IL, US

Abstract

The literature has shown that "conventional" monetary policy has asymmetric effects: monetary tightening contracts the economy more than monetary easing expands it. This chapter asks whether the asymmetry continues to hold when monetary policy takes "unconventional" forms, such as the Quantitative Easing expansions that have taken place since the financial crisis of 2008. Using US quarterly data from the 1950-2011 period, monetary base shocks and their effects on the unemployment rate are estimated. The chapter's findings strongly support asymmetric effects: with or without the Quantitative Easing period, monetary base contractions are shown to have larger unemployment effects than monetary base expansions (the effects of which are often statistically insignificant). This characterizes both permanent and temporary (four-year) shocks to the monetary base.

Keywords: Monetary Policy, asymmetric effects, business cycles, unemployment

Introduction

The financial crisis of 2008 and the recession of 2007-2009 have been accompanied in the US, as well as other economies, by a substantial increase in unemployment, as well as an unprecedented expansion of the monetary base. The latter is clearly illustrated in Figure 1 which plots quarterly observations for the US monetary base from 1950:Q1 to 2011:Q4. It is apparent that for most of this period, in particular until the third quarter of 2008, the monetary base is growing relatively smoothly. This is dramatically changed in the fourth quarter of

* E-mail address: gkarras@uic.edu; Address: Department of Economics, University of Illinois at Chicago, 601 S. Morgan St., Chicago, IL 60607-7121, US (Corresponding author, Professor of Economics).
I wish to thank participants at the 2012 Athenian Policy Forum Conference in Chalkidiki, Greece for helpful comments and suggestions. Errors and omissions remain mine.

2008, however, after which the monetary base is increasing at an explosive rate. By the fourth quarter of 2011, the monetary base has grown to $2.7 trillion, or more than three times its magnitude in the third quarter of 2008 ($872 billion)

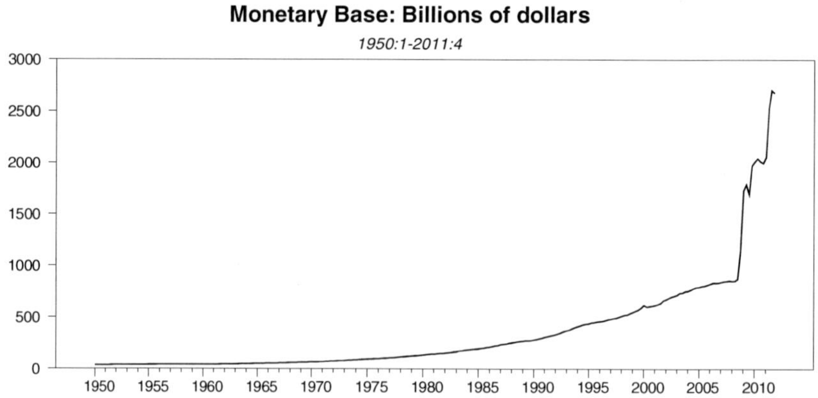

Figure 1.

The monetary base is therefore increased by a factor of 3 in just three years. Figure 2 plots the ratio of the monetary base to nominal Gross Domestic Product, effectively comparing over this time period the expansion of the monetary base with that of economic activity, as captured by GDP. For most of the pre-2008 period, the monetary base is increasing at a slower pace than nominal GDP, so the ratio gradually declines from 0.12 in 1950:Q1 to 0.06 in 2008:Q3 – though the minimum value of 0.05 is achieved in 1980. Again, what stands out is the sharp spike in the ratio beginning with 2008:Q4, raising its value to 0.17 by the end of 2011.

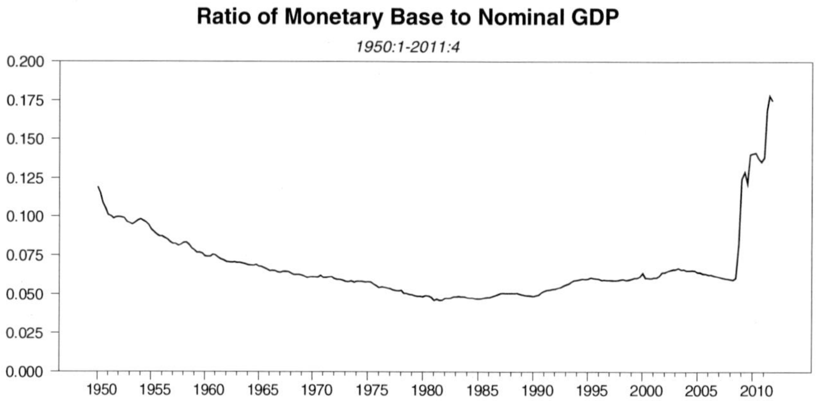

Figure 2.

What has been the effect of this unparalleled monetary expansion on economic activity, in general, and the unemployment rate, in particular? A generally held view is that, by providing ample liquidity, this vigorous policy of Quantitative Easing helped prevent a repeat of the mistakes made during the Great Depression, and thus averted a deepening of the 2007-2009 recession.[1]

As a result of this policy, existing theoretical models have been modified and new ones have been developed to study the effects of such Quantitative Easing policies.[2] It is now commonplace to distinguish between "conventional" monetary policies (that include changes in a short-term interest rate, such as the federal funds rate) and "unconventional" policies (that include Quantitative Easing).

Unconventional policies are usually, though not exclusively, considered at the "zero lower bound": situations when the short term interest rate has been pushed down virtually to zero. A large literature has examined various mechanisms that are thought to determine the efficacy of unconventional monetary options: liquidity effects, inflationary expectations, the credit channel, signaling (commitment) effects, and portfolio effects.[3]

Independent of this, a large number of studies have also been investigating whether the effects of monetary policy are asymmetric.[4] In this context, asymmetry usually refers to a situation in which monetary expansions have smaller effects than monetary contractions (*sign* asymmetry), or large monetary shocks have smaller real effects than smaller monetary shocks (*size* asymmetry), though additional types of asymmetry have also been considered.[5] As t is well known, theoretically, such asymmetries can be generated by (i) a convex aggregate supply, (ii) models that emphasize credit mechanisms, (iii) models with menu costs, or (iv) monetary authorities that respond differently to expansions than to downturns.

These asymmetries have been tested mostly in environments of conventional monetary policies. To assess the potency of policies like Quantitative Easing, it is necessary to know whether such asymmetric effects also govern the effects of unconventional monetary policies.[6] This is the subject of the present chapter.

The chapter investigates the effects of shocks to the monetary base on the US unemployment rate. First, quarterly data are used to identify positive and negative shocks to the monetary base over the period 1950-2011. Then the effects of these shocks on the unemployment rate are estimated.

The chapter's findings strongly support the existence of asymmetric affects, both with and without Quantitative Easing: monetary base contractions have larger effects on unemployment than monetary base expansions (the effects of which are often statistically insignificant). In addition, sign asymmetry characterizes both permanent and temporary (four-year) shocks to the monetary base.

The rest of the chapter is organized as follows. Section 2 outlines the chapter's empirical methodology and discusses the data. Section 3 presents the empirical results. Section 4 summarizes and concludes.

---

[1] See for example Bordo and Landon-Lane (2010) and Gagnon, Raskin, Remache, and Sack (2011).

[2] See for example Curdia and Woodford (2011).

[3] For interesting discussions, see Blinder (2010), Cecchetti and Disyatat (2010), and Nelson (2011). For the experience of economies other than the US, see Anderson, Gascon, and Liu (2010), and Kapetanios, Mumtaz, Stevens, and Theodoridis (2012) .

[4] See Cover (1992), Karras (1996a, 1996b).

[5] This literature is vast. See Florio (2004) for a recent survey. Recent contributions that show some of the variety of monetary asymmetries that have been considered are Sensier, Osborn, and Ocal (2002), Ravn and Sola (2004), Bruinshoofd and Candelon (2005), and Lo and Piger (2005).

[6] Indeed it could be argued that knowing he extent of such asymmetries is even more important in the case of policies that double or triple the monetary base in a few years.

Empirical Methodology and Data

The Estimated Model

The empirical methodology implements a straightforward modification of the approach of Cover (1992), and Karras (1996a, 1996b), and thus will be described briefly.

The estimated system consists of two equations, the first of which describes the money supply process:

$$\Delta m_t = \alpha_0 + \sum_{i=1}^{M} \alpha_i^m \Delta m_{t-i} + \sum_{i=1}^{N} \alpha_i^y \Delta y_{t-i} + e_t^m , \tag{1}$$

where m is the log of the monetary base, y is the log of real GDP, the α 's are coefficients, and e^m is the monetary base shock. Define the positive monetary base shock as

$$e_t^+ = \max(e_t^m, 0) ,$$

and the negative money-supply shock as

$$e_t^- = \min(e_t^m, 0) .$$

Letting o denote the log of the price of oil (a proxy for supply-side shocks), the second equation is:

$$u_t = \beta_0 + \sum_{i=1}^{P} \beta_i^u u_{t-i} + \sum_{i=0}^{Q} \beta_i^o \Delta o_{t-i} + \sum_{i=0}^{R} \left(\beta_i^+ e_{t-i}^+ + \beta_i^- e_{t-i}^- \right) + e_t^u , \tag{2}$$

where u stands for the unemployment rate, the β s are coefficients to be estimated, and e^u is an error term. If $\beta_i^+ = \beta_i^-$, $\forall i$, the effects of money-supply shocks are symmetric. Using (for now) the sum of these coefficients as a simple metric of effectiveness,[7] the "traditional" kind of asymmetry requires $\left| \sum_i \beta_i^- \right| > \left| \sum_i \beta_i^+ \right| \geq 0$, so that monetary contractions have larger effects than monetary expansions.[8]

The system of equations (1) and (2) can be estimated with the 2-step OLS procedure used by Barro (1977, 1978), or by the nonlinear least squares method used by Mishkin (1982,

[7] Alternative metrics include joint statistical significance, as well as the implied impulse response coefficients. All of these are examined formally in the next section.

[8] Note that the estimated β s are expected to be negative: monetary expansions should reduce the unemployment rate, and vice versa. A special case, "pushing on a string", would obtain if $\left| \sum_i \beta_i^- \right| > \left| \sum_i \beta_i^+ \right| = 0$.

1983), or by a system-wide multivariate maximum likelihood (ML) technique. The empirical section will focus mostly on the ML results, so the approach is illustrated here briefly.

The log-likelihood function for the two-equation system, for example, is specified as

$$L(\alpha, \beta, \Sigma) = -.5 \ln|\Sigma| - .5(e'\Sigma^{-1}e),$$

where $\boldsymbol{\alpha}$ and $\boldsymbol{\beta}$ are the parameter vectors of equations (1) and (2), $\boldsymbol{\Sigma} = \begin{bmatrix} \sigma_{11} & \sigma_{12} \\ \sigma_{12} & \sigma_{22} \end{bmatrix}$ is the covariance matrix of the error vectors $\boldsymbol{e}^m$ and $\boldsymbol{e}^u$, and $\boldsymbol{e}' = ((\boldsymbol{e}^m)', (\boldsymbol{e}^u)')$. Initial values are obtained from the 2-step OLS regressions and the function is maximized with the BFGS method (a modification of the Davidon-Fletcher-Powell algorithm).

The Data

All data are quarterly and obtained from the Federal Reserve Economic Data (FRED) database of the Federal Reserve Bank of St. Louis. Real GDP is used to construct the variable *y*, the monetary base is used for *m*, the civilian unemployment rate for *u*, and the West Texas Intermediate spot oil price for *o*.

Four (partially overlapping) time periods will be considered. The two Full Periods start in 1950:Q1, while the two Volcker Periods start in 1979:Q3. In addition, there are two Long Periods that end in 2011:Q4, and thus include the Quantitative Easing expansions; and two Short Periods that end in 2008:Q3, before Quantitative Easing.[9] Summing up, the four time periods are: Full/Long: 1950:Q1 - 2011:Q4, Full/Short: 1950:Q1 - 2008:Q3, Volcker/Long: 1979:Q3 - 2011:Q4, and Volcker/Short: 1979:Q3 - 2008:Q3.

Empirical Results and Discussion

This section estimates the system of equations (1) and (2) for the four time periods defined above.

Table 1 reports the estimated sums of the β^+ and β^- coefficients in equation (2) under the assumption of eight lagged terms of the monetary base shocks in equation (2): $R = 8$.[10] As expected, all estimated money terms are negative. Note, however, that the β^- coefficients are jointly statistically significant (i.e., the null hypothesis $\beta_i^- = 0$, $\forall i$ can be rejected) in

[9] A long list of studies have addressed the question of significant differences in US monetary policy between the pre- and post-Volcker periods, usually in the context of the Taylor rule and the Taylor Principle. See Coibion and Gorodnichenko (2011) for a recent example. The Short/Long split is adopted to allow for structural differences due to Quantitative Easing. We also explored with other period divisions, including the Great Moderation, but without getting significant results.

[10] Various other lag lengths were also tried, but did not alter the basic results.

all four samples, while the β^+ coefficients are jointly statistically significant (i.e., $\beta_i^+ = 0$, $\forall i$ can be rejected) only for the Volcker samples.

Moreover, the sums of positive coefficients, $\sum_i \beta_i^+$, are small and statistically insignificant (except for the Volcker/Long sample). On the contrary, the sums of negative coefficients, $\sum_i \beta_i^-$, are considerably larger and (except for the Full/Long sample) statistically significant. In addition, the null hypothesis $\beta_i^+ = \beta_i^-$, $\forall i$, (the null of symmetry) can be rejected for all four samples, implying that the differences between the β^+ and β^- coefficients are statistically significant.

These findings suggest that the effects of monetary base shocks on the unemployment rate are indeed asymmetric and, in particular, that negative shocks have a much bigger effect on unemployment than positive ones. Put differently, monetary base contractions raise the unemployment rate much more than monetary base expansions reduce it.

Figures 3, 4, 5, and 6 will visualize these results and clarify the implied dynamics, plotting the responses of the unemployment rate and the monetary base itself to various types of monetary base shocks.

Figure 3 reports these responses to a permanent (long-run) increase in the monetary base. The shock has been defined in such a way that its long-run effect has been normalized to be a 1% increase in the monetary base. As the left-hand side of Figure 3 shows, this is achieved rather quickly in the Long period, but is more gradual and therefore takes substantially more time in the Short period.

Table 1. Sign Asymmetric Effects on Unemployment: Monetary Base Systems

	Full		Volcker	
	50:1-08:3	50:1-11:4	79:3-08:3	79:3-11:4
$\sum_i \beta_i^+$	–0.085	–0.023	–0.015	–0.055**
	(0.158)	(0.069)	(0.096)	(0.015)
$\sum_i \beta_i^-$	–0.255*	–0.065	–0.234**	–0.182**
	(0.126)	(0.040)	(0.086)	(0.033)
χ^2 *Tests*				
$\beta_i^+ = \beta_i^-$, $\forall i$	24.04**	50.94**	54.26**	110.5**
$\beta_i^+ = 0$, $\forall i$	7.43	12.08	24.63**	68.5**
$\beta_i^- = 0$, $\forall i$	30.53*	111.1**	31.55**	110.0**

Notes: Joint ML estimation (2-stage OLS used for starting values). Estimated standard errors in parentheses; Lag lengths: $M = N = P = Q = 4$, $R = 8$. **: significant at 1%, *:significant at 5%.

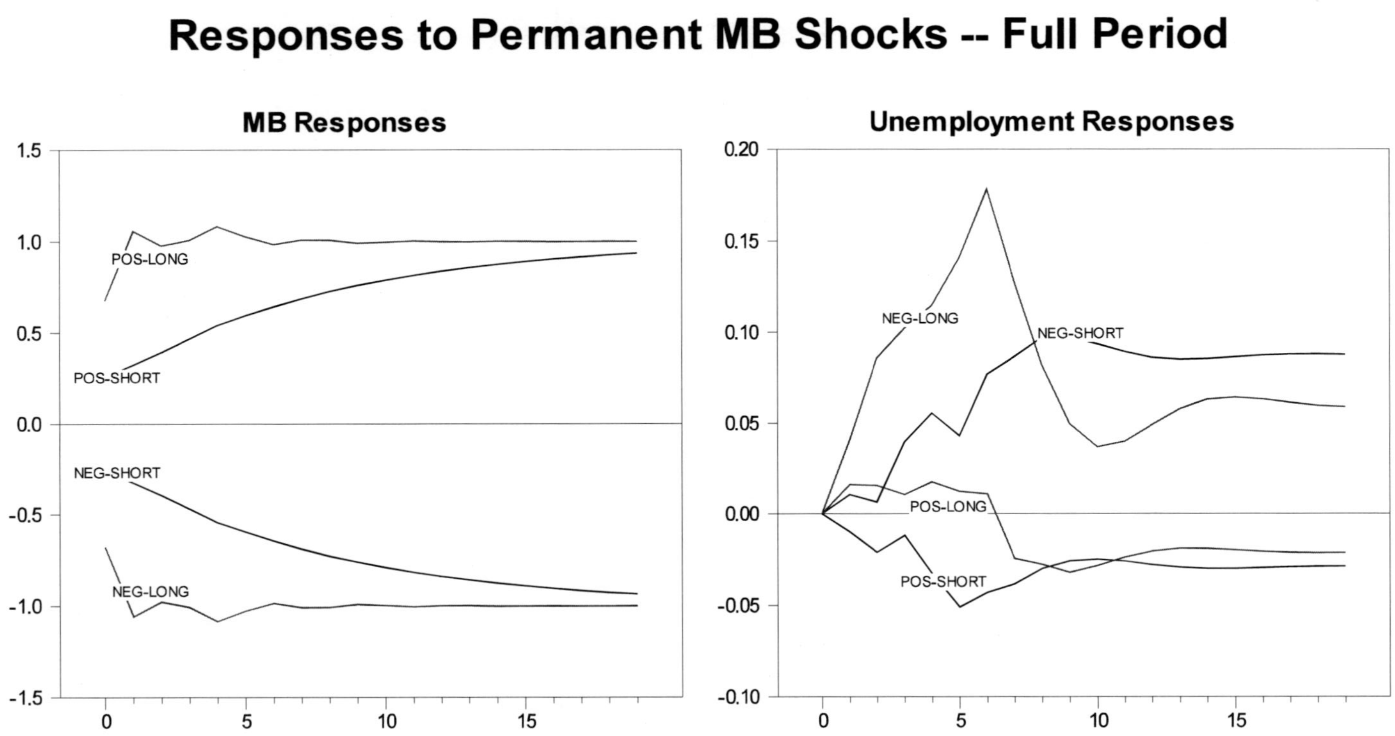

Figure 3. Responses to Positive (POS) and Negative (NEG) Monetary Base (MB) Shocks.

Responses to Permanent MB Shocks -- Volcker Period

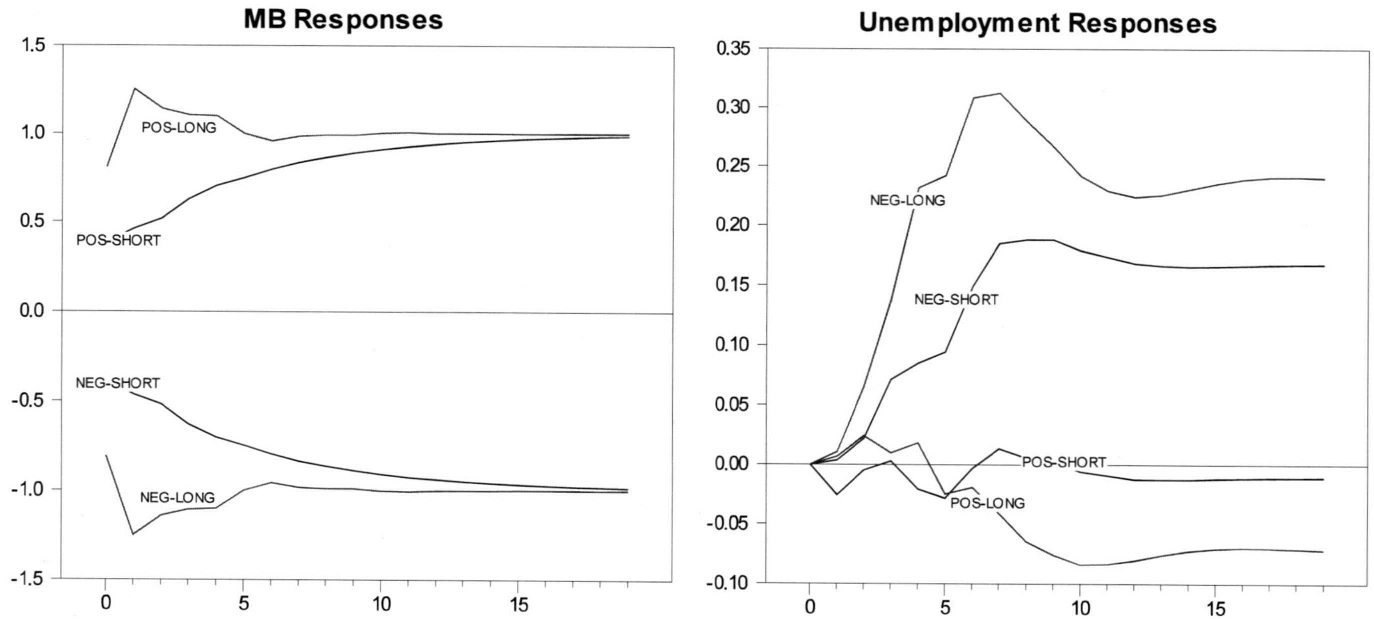

Figure 4. Responses to Positive (POS) and Negative (NEG) Monetary Base (MB) Shocks.

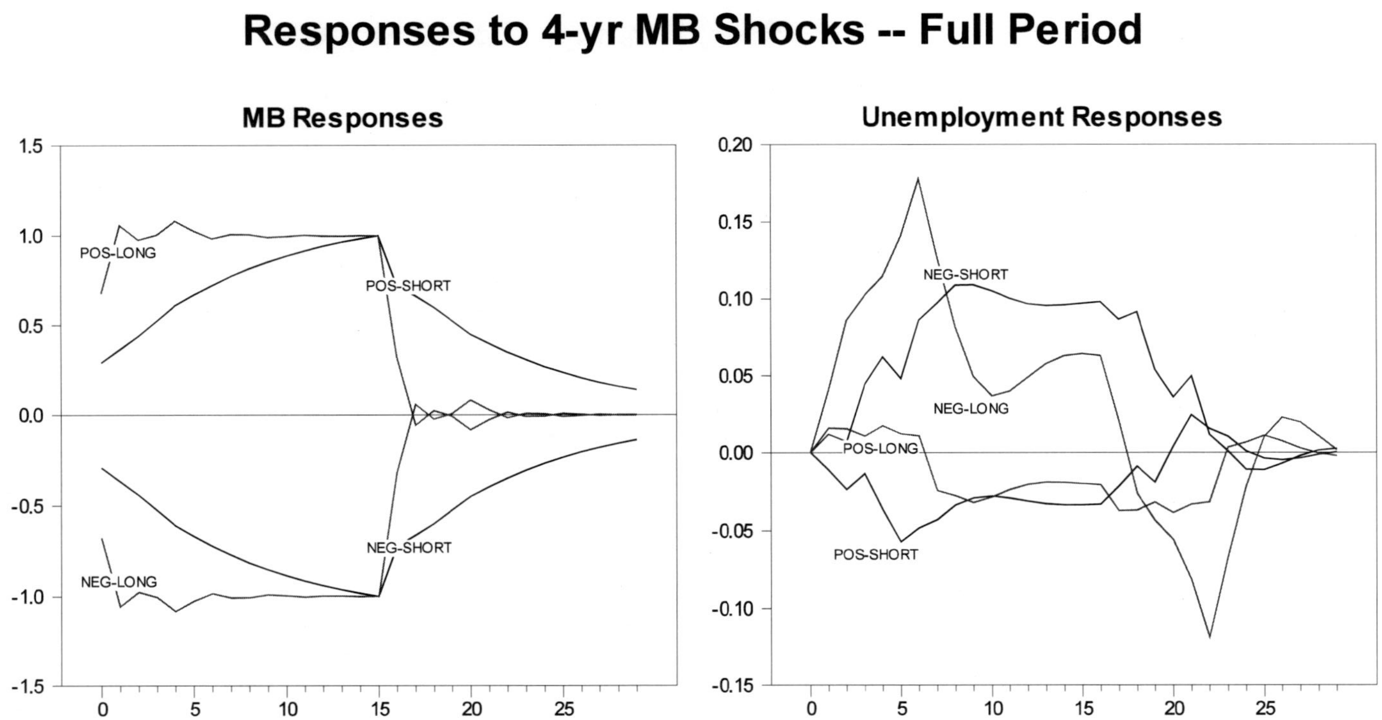

Figure 5. Responses to Positive (POS) and Negative (NEG) Monetary Base (MB) Shocks.

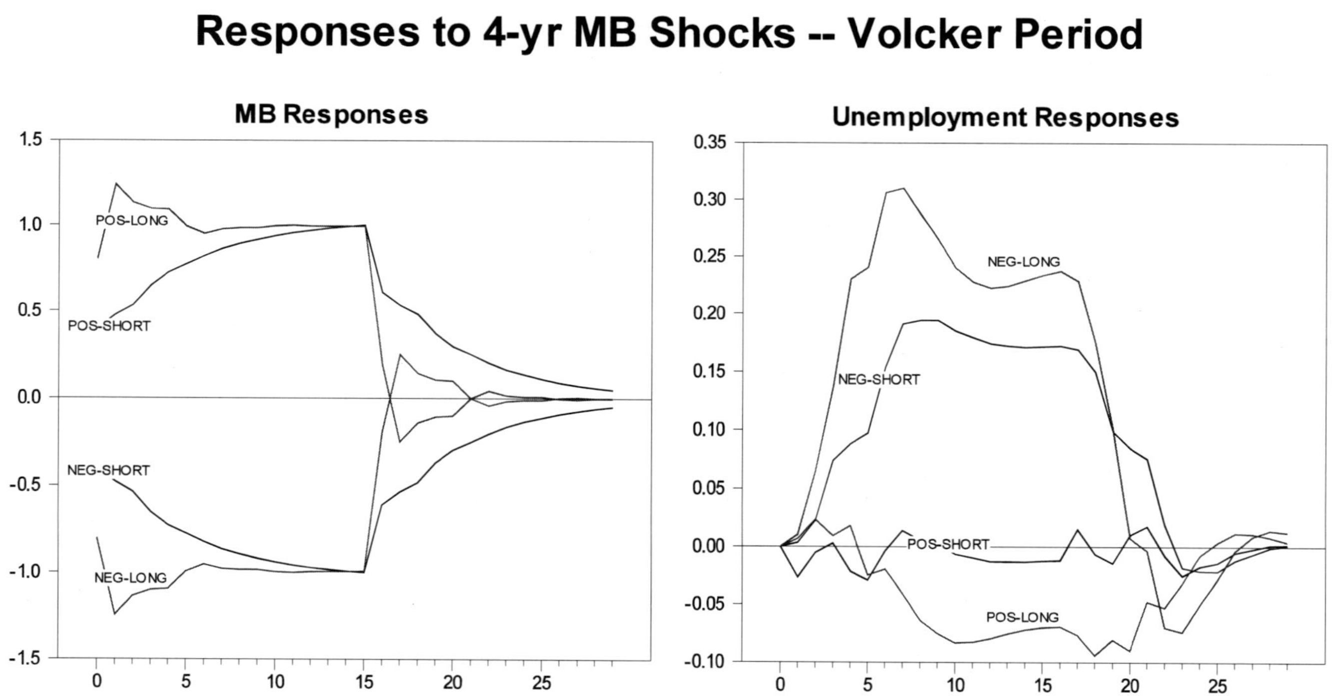

Figure 6. Responses to Positive (POS) and Negative (NEG) Monetary Base (MB) Shocks.

The right-hand side graph of Figure 3 shows the unemployment responses to both negative and positive shocks. As expected, positive monetary base shocks reduce the unemployment rate, while negative shocks raise it. Consistent with the findings of Table 1, however, these effects are clearly asymmetric: negative monetary base shocks have much larger effects on unemployment than positive shocks[1]. Interestingly, this holds both for the Long and Short samples, which implies that the asymmetry is present regardless of whether the Quantitative Easing expansions are included in the sample. Using the point estimates, a 1% permanent increase in the monetary base is followed by a long-run decrease in the unemployment rate by 0.03%, while a 1% permanent decrease in the monetary base results in a long-run increase in the unemployment rate of 0.6% (Long sample) to 0.9% (Short sample).

Figure 4 repeats the same exercise for the Volcker period. The general pattern of these responses is unaffected, though there is an important difference: the unemployment effects of monetary base shocks are considerably larger. This is consistent with a view of greater potency for monetary policy in the Volcker period.

The asymmetry result however is entirely robust in Figure 4: negative monetary base shocks continue to generate bigger output responses than positive shocks in the Volcker period – and this is robust for both the Long and Short time periods, indicating again that it holds with or without the post 2008:Q3 period. Using again the point estimates, a 1% permanent increase in the monetary base has long-run unemployment effect of virtually zero (Short sample) to –0.08% (Long sample), while a 1% permanent decrease in the monetary base has long-run output effect of 0.17% (Short sample) to 0.24% (Long sample).

Figures 3 and 4 assume shocks that produce permanent changes (increases or decreases) in the level of the monetary base. It is, however, unclear whether this is what the Fed intends for the Quantitative Easing that started in 2008:Q3 – and in fact there is evidence that the Fed's exit strategy will involve (at least some) unwinding of this expansion. It is therefore interesting to consider shocks that would change (increase or decrease) the monetary base temporarily, as this may be a more realistic experiment.

Figures 5 and 6 consider such temporary shocks that are constructed to change the monetary base for four years, achieve a peak change of 1%, and die out in the long-run. We call these "4-yr" monetary base shocks. The left-hand side of Figure 5 traces the effects on the monetary base itself for both versions of the Full period. A comparison of those with the corresponding plots of Figure 3 makes apparent the temporary nature of the "4-yr" shocks: they increase or decrease the monetary base for four years by a maximum of 1%, but the change dies out in the long run.

The right-hand side of Figure 5 shows the unemployment responses to these "4-yr" temporary shocks for the Full period. Just like before, positive monetary base shocks reduce unemployment, while negative shocks raise it. The main difference, of course, is that now the effects on the unemployment rate are temporary: the shocks cause a deviation of unemployment from its mean, but this disappears in the long run. This is of course as expected, given the temporary nature of the monetary base expansion.

Once more, however, these effects are clearly asymmetric: negative monetary base shocks have much larger effects on unemployment than positive shocks (the effects of which are statistically insignificant) and this holds both for the Long and Short samples. Using the

[1] In addition, the unemployment responses to negative monetary base shocks are statistically significantly different from zero, while the responses to positive shocks are not.

point estimates, a 1% four-year increase in the monetary base achieves a peak reduction in the unemployment rate by 0.06% (Long sample) to 0.05% (Short sample), while a 1% four-year decrease in the monetary base results in a peak increase in the unemployment rate by 0.11% (Short sample) to 0.18% (Long sample).

Figure 6 repeats the exercise of the 4-yr monetary base shocks for the Volcker period. Again, the general pattern of these responses is very similar, including the evidence of greater potency for the monetary policy in the Volcker period.

The asymmetry result is again robust: negative monetary base shocks generate bigger unemployment responses than positive shocks – even though the output effects are temporary in both cases – and this holds for both the Long and Short time periods. Using the point estimates, a 1% four-year increase in the monetary base has peak unemployment effect of –0.02% (Short sample) to –0.10% (Long sample), while a 1% four-year decrease in the monetary base has a peak unemployment effect of 0.20% (Short sample) to 0.30% (Long sample).

Summing up the results so far, the evidence shows that monetary base shocks have asymmetric effects on unemployment. Depending on the model, the effects of negative monetary base shocks are found to be several times larger than those of positive shocks.

Conclusion

This chapter has investigated two types of asymmetric effects of monetary base shocks on the US unemployment rate. Quarterly data from 1950-2011 have been used to identify monetary base shocks and their effects for various periods, some of which include the Quantitative Easing episodes since 2008:Q4. The chapter's empirical findings support the following conclusions:

(i) There is clear evidence of asymmetric effects: monetary base contractions are shown to have larger effects on the unemployment rate than monetary base expansions (the effects of which are often statistically insignificant).
(ii) This asymmetry characterizes both permanent and temporary (modeled here as four-year) shocks to the monetary base.
(iii) The results are robust to whether the Quantitative Easing period is included in the sample or not, and to whether the model is estimated for the Full period or the Volcker period.

References

Anderson, Richard G., Charles S. Gascon, and Yang Liu. "Doubling your Monetary Base and Surviving: Some International Experience." Federal Reserve Bank of St. Louis *Review*, November/December 2010, 481-506.

Barro, Robert J. "Unanticipated Money Growth and Unemployment in the United States." *American Economic Review*, 67, 1977, 101-115.

Barro, Robert J. "Unanticipated Money, Output, and the Price Level in the United States." *Journal of Political Economy*, 86, 1978, 549-580.

Blinder, Alan S. "Quantitative Easing: Entrance and Exit Strategies." Federal Reserve Bank of St. Louis *Review*, November/December 2010, 465-480.

Bordo, Michael D. and John Landon-Lane. "The Lessons from the Banking Panics in the United States in the 1930s for the Financial Crisis of 2007-2008." *NBER Working Paper* No. 16365, September 2010.

Bruinshoofd, Allard and Bertrand Candelon. "Nonlinear Monetary Policy in Europe: Fact or Myth?" *Economics Letters*, 86, 2005, 399-403.

Cecchetti, Stephen G. and Piti Disyatat. "Central Bank Tools and Liquidity Shortages." Federal Reserve Bank of New York *Economic Policy Review*, August 2010, 29-42.

Coibion, Olivier and Yuriy Gorodnichenko. "Monetary Policy, Trend Inflation, and the Great Moderation: An Alternative Interpretation." *American Economic Review*, 101, 2011, 341-370.

Cover, James Peery. "Asymmetric Effects of Positive and Negative Money-Supply Shocks." *Quarterly Journal of Economics*, CVII, 1992, 1261-1282.

Curdia, Vasco and Michael Woodford. "The Central-Bank Balance Sheet as an Instrument of Monetary Policy." *Journal of Monetary Economics*, 58, 2011, 54-79.

Florio, Anna. "The Asymmetric Effects of Monetary Policy." *Journal of Economic Surveys*, 18, 2004, 409-426.

Gagnon, Joseph, Matthew Raskin, Julie Remache, and Brian Sack. "The Financial Market Effects of the Federal Reserve's Large-Scale Asset Purchases." *International Journal of Central Banking*, 7, 2011, 3-43.

Kapetanios, George, Haroon Mumtaz, Ibrahim Stevens, and Konstantinos Theodoridis. "Assessing the Economy-Wide Effects of Quantitative Easing." Bank of England Working Paper No. 443, January 2012.

Karras, Georgios. "Are the Output Effects of Monetary Policy Asymmetric? Evidence from a Sample of European Countries." *Oxford Bulletin of Economics and Statistics*, 58, 1996a, 267-278.

Karras, Georgios. "Why Are the Effects of Money-Supply Shocks Asymmetric? Convex Aggregate Supply or 'Pushing on a String'?" *Journal of Macroeconomics*, 18, 1996b, 605-619.

Lo, Ming Chien and Jeremy Piger. "Is the Response of Output to Monetary Policy Asymmetric? Evidence from a Regime-Switching Coefficients Model." *Journal of Money, Credit, and Banking*, 37, 2005, 865-886.

Mishkin, Frederic S. "Does Anticipated Policy Matter? An Econometric Investigation." *Journal of Political Economy*, 90, 1982, 22-51.

Mishkin, Frederic S. *A Rational Expectations Approach to Macroeconometrics*, University of Chicago Press, 1983.

Nelson, Edward. "Friedman's Monetary Economics in Practice." Federal Reserve Board, 2011.

Ravn, Morten O. and Martin Sola. "Asymmetric Effects of Monetary Policy in the United States." Federal Reserve Bank of St. Louis *Review*, Sep/Oct 2004, 41-60.

Sensier, Marianne, Denise R. Osborn and Nadir Ocal. "Asymmetric Interest Rate Effects for the UK Real Economy." *Oxford Bulletin of Economics and Statistics*, 64, 2002, 315-339.

In: Business Cycles in Economics
Editor: Jason C. Hsu

ISBN: 978-1-63321-322-7

Chapter 10

ADJUSTMENT IN THE MARKET FOR SKILLS IN AUSTRALIA OVER THE BUSINESS CYCLE

Michael Corliss [*] ***and Phil Lewis***
Centre for Labour Market Research, University of Canberra,
Canberra, Australia

Abstract

Australia is in unique position to investigate the effects of the business cycle on the market for skilled labour. While experiencing a full cycle, Australia has also enjoyed two decades of positive economic growth, from the recession in the early 1990s to the economic boom of 2006. While the 1990s recession focused attention on the unemployment problem, the boom concentrated attention on skill shortages in Australia and their role in preventing the economy from reaching its full potential level of output and putting pressure on inflation. Forces other than economic growth and the business cycle, such as structural change and technological change, have also had considerable influence increasing the demand for skilled labour over recent times. Here we examine the extent to which the market for skilled labour has adjusted to changed economic conditions. This includes changes in the supply and demand of skilled labour, and the role of earnings and rates of return to tertiary education and training. This analysis has policy relevance with respect to skilled migration, inequality, education and training as well as contributing to knowledge of the labour market impacts of the business cycle.

Keywords: Business cycle, skills, rate of return

Introduction

In the last decade and a half, Australia has gone through a considerable change in economic activity, starting in 1991 with a recession and ending in 2006 with a boom before the Global Financial Crisis (GFC). Evidence of the business cycle is given in Figure 1, which shows the unemployment rate for the period.

[*] E-mail address: michael.corliss@canberra.edu.au (Corresponding author).

The unemployment rate is a good indicator of the level of economic activity taking place at any given time, as any increase in economic activity will result in an increase in employment and any decrease in economic activity results in a loss of jobs and an increase in unemployment (Lewis et al. 2010). Figure 1 shows the unemployment rate for December 1991 at 10.3 per cent (recession), 1996 at 8.5 per cent (recovery), 2001 at 6.6 per cent (expansion) and 2006 at 4.6 per cent unemployment (boom).

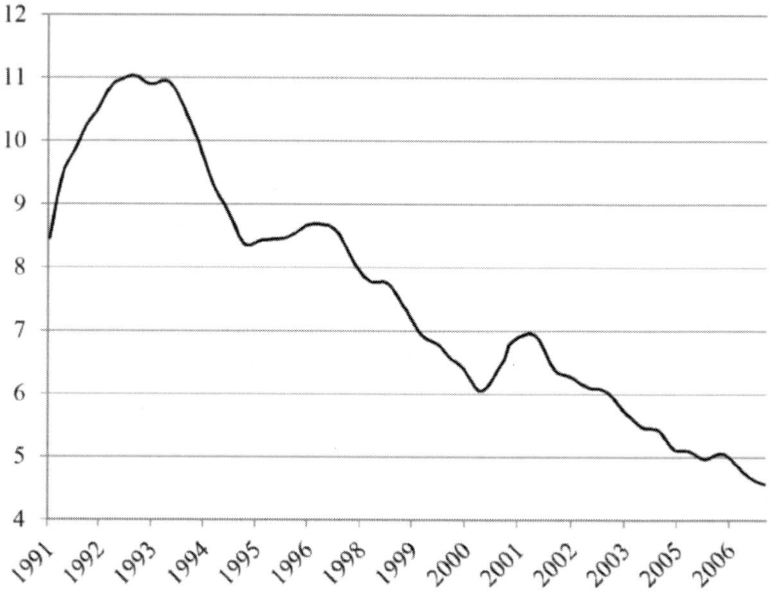

Source: Australian Bureau of Statistics (2007), Labour force Australia, cat. no. 6202.0, Canberra.

Figure 1. Unemployment Rate, 1991 to 2006, (%).

The business cycle affects the labour market in terms of wages and unemployment. At the bottom of the cycle, business cycle effects are concentrated on the unskilled, increasing unemployment and the competition for jobs. Lewis (2006) suggests the effects of a recession are disproportionally larger for unskilled workers compared with the skilled and thus likely to influence the relative income between unskilled and skilled labour. At the top of the cycle, as the pool of unskilled labour has dried up and the business cycle effects put pressure on wages to rise. If all other effects were held constant, it would be expected that the private rate of return to a degree or trades training would be greatest during an economic downturn because the unemployment rate of the unskilled would increase relative to university educated or qualified tradespersons and relative wages of the unskilled would fall. Also, the returns to a degree would diminish at the top end of the business cycle as unemployment decreased and the relative wages of the unskilled increased.

This story is complicated, however, by the long-term structural change that has taken place in the Australian labour market, changing the demand for skills. In 1975, services accounted for just over 50 per cent of all jobs, but by 2010 the service sector accounted for over 70 per cent of all jobs (ABS 2010). By contrast, manufacturing's share of total employment almost halved over the same period, to about 8.5 per cent in 2011. There were similar reductions in the relative shares of jobs in the 'industrial' services, such as electricity, gas and water. While this change in the industry mix caused the demand for manual skills to decrease, it created a much greater demand for interactive skills and knowledge-based skills, which are skills that are sought after by the service sector (Kelly & Lewis 2010). Kelly and Lewis (2006) also suggest technological change taking place recently has caused a change in skills within all industries, such as manufacturing, increasing the demand for more knowledge-based and interactive skills. One would expect from this increase in demand for workers with university qualifications to observe an increase in the rate of return for degree holders.

While there is a considerable body of research on the returns to education, currently there is only a scant literature available on the business cycle effects upon the private rate of return to higher education. This is despite the expectation that the business cycle would not have neutral effects on participants in the labour market, but would have differential effects on workers according to their degree of skill. Daly and Lewis (2010) showed that during the recession and subsequent recovery up to 2001, there was an increase in the private rate of return for university degrees. However, this declined during the boom in 2006. They suggest that it may be due to strong growth in the economy over that period that raised the relative income of Year 12 completers. Corliss and Lewis (2011) suggested the business cycle had little effect on the relative income of tradespersons as a whole. However, it did effect trade occupations differently and created greater dispersion of income within the trade occupations as the market provided big rewards for the best paid tradespersons during high demand, causing income dispersions to increase. Other studies in the business cycles context have focused on skills wage differentials, such as Reder (1955), who examined the cyclicality of wage differentials. His findings suggested that the aggregate skill premium was countercyclical in the 1930s and 1940s. More recently, Keane and Prasad (1993), Castro and Coen-Pirani (2008) and Lindquist (2004) showed that the aggregate skill premium is acyclical. Therefore, it is of interest to investigate whether these same phenomena are observable for degree holders and qualified tradespersons. It is this relationship between the business cycle and its effect upon the private rate of return to higher education and trades training that is the subject of this chapter.

Demand for Skills

Australia has seen strong employment growth since the early 1990s, The overall growth in employment has been very different for different industries over the period from 1991 to 2006 (see Figure 2), and the changes have occurred at different stages for a range of industries, which suggests different drivers are affecting the structural changes taking place. For instance, the utilities sector (electricity, gas and water) experienced substantial restructuring and labour shedding throughout the 1990s as a result of the partial de-regulation and privatisation of the sector (Kelly & Lewis 2010). Manufacturing has experienced a steady decline over the entire period, mostly due to reduced protection and increased trade combined with increasing productivity and sophistication of manufacturing in Asia, particularly China (Kelly & Lewis 2010). This has enabled a wider range of consumer goods to be cost-effectively sourced from overseas. The growth in the service sector is largely due to changes in consumer demand, which has shown an increase in the demand for services (Kelly & Lewis 2010).

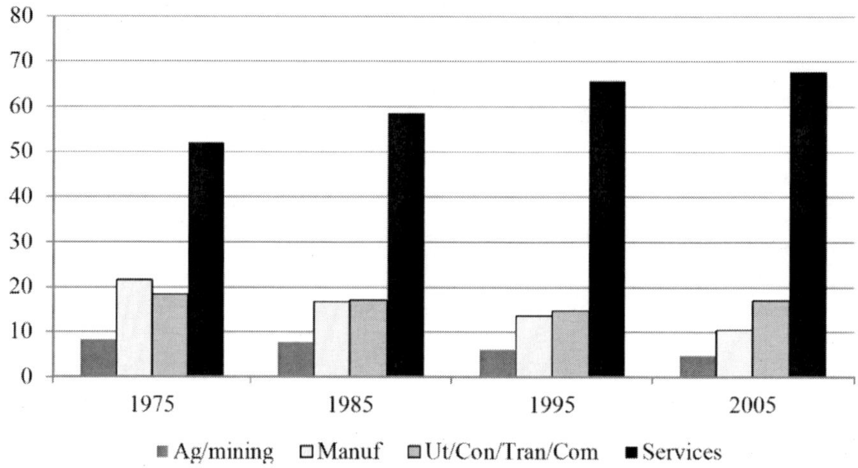

Source: Australian Bureau of Statistics 2007, *Labour force*, cat. No. 6202.0, Canberra.

Figure 2. Employment by Industry, 1975 to 2005, (%).

Changes in the industry mix have combined with technological change to systematically change the demand for skills (Kelly & Lewis 2003; 2006; 2010). This has also driven a restructuring of occupations within industries. Figure 3 shows the changes in employment for occupations.

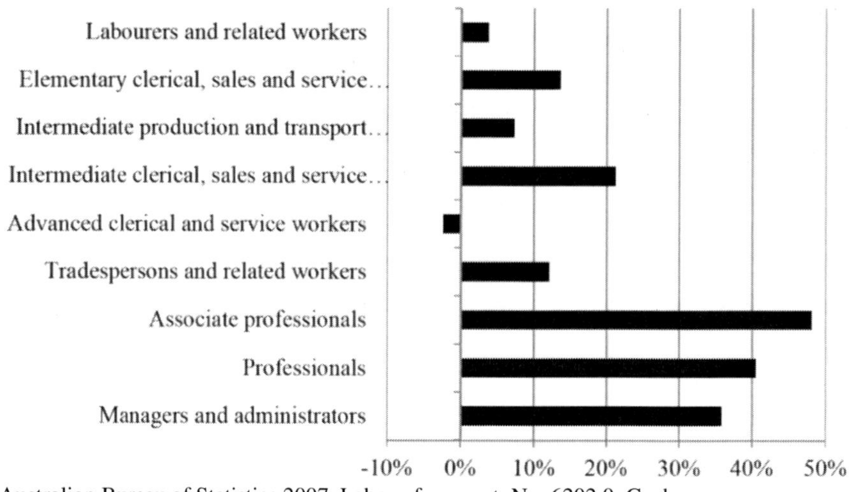

Source: Australian Bureau of Statistics 2007, Labour force, cat. No. 6202.0, Canberra.

Figure 3. Change in Employment by Occupation, 1996 to 2007.

As shown in Figure 3, the mix of occupations has changed quite dramatically over time. Higher skilled occupational groupings have grown considerably faster than the traditional blue and white collar low skilled and trade qualified occupations. The most remarkable growth in occupations has been for associate professionals and professionals, growing by 48 and 40 per cent, respectively. Advanced clerical and service workers were the only occupational grouping where total employment fell. Given the scale and duration of the economic expansion in Australia, this is quite remarkable.

Kelly and Lewis (2010) suggest recent decades have seen very important changes in the skill mix in the Australian economy. They found that while the economic recovery period of 1991 to 1996 was characteristic of skill changes resulting from structural change, for the recovery and boom periods technological change was the main influence on skills change. The change in skills due to technological change in the recovery and boom period was most apparent in the boom period 2001 to 2006. Technological change continues to be a key factor affecting the pattern of skill demand.

A driver for technological change is the rapid uptake of Information Communication Technologies ICT investment. This is observable in the 1990s and continued in the first half of the 2000s, and can be seen as an increasing share of ICT in the capital stock (Kelly 2007). The increasing importance of ICT in the capital stock is clearly affecting the type of skills demanded in the economy. Most likely, this is occurring due to direct demand for ICT related skills and indirectly through the enabling effects of ICT.

It is worth noting that it is not just the increasing emphasis of computers in the workplace and industry, but also the rapid increase in the uptake of software applications by industry. The rate of growth of the share of computer hardware in the capital stock actually accelerated during the economic boom, along with the uptake of software applications (Kelly 2007).

Kelly and Lewis (2010) suggest that ICT has allowed a considerable re-ordering of occupations within industries. That is, ICT is enabling a reorganisation of the workplace, towards one that places greater emphasis on skills, particularly interactive and cognitive skills. Kelly and Lewis (2010, p261) suggest interactive skills 'refer to the ability to relate between managers and employees, employees and employees and employees and customers' and cognitive skills 'relate to the possession of and ability to create knowledge'. Although it is highly likely that other influences, such as institutional change, have enabled firms to considerably change the employment mix of their workforces, it is unlikely that changes in 'soft' technologies (such as restructuring the banking industry workforce) would not have been made possible without the introduction of 'hard' technologies (such as automatic teller machines and the internet).

Figure 4 shows the change in skills demand from 1991 to 2006. The scale is from zero to 10, with zero taken to mean the least complex task (Kelly & Lewis 2010). Interestingly, interactive, cognitive and education skills have all increased over the period with interactive skills having the biggest increase from 1991 to 1996. These skills are generally acquired through higher education. This has important implications for future availability of tertiary places in Australia. It is also interesting to note the decline in motor skills, particularly from 1991 to 2001, which has implications for technical education and trades training.

The degree to which these skills are able to disperse through formal training and education require further exploration. Kelly and Lewis (2010) suggest that specific occupations, such as those characterised by performing routine cognitive or manual tasks, will likely continue to be at risk in the years ahead. They suggest that career guidance and allocation of training places should be mindful of these risks to employment in these occupations. This shift in the demand for skills influences the demand for post-secondary qualifications.

Overall given the strong growth in the Australian economy and that this growth has favoured those with skills typically developed at university you would expect to see increasing returns to higher education.

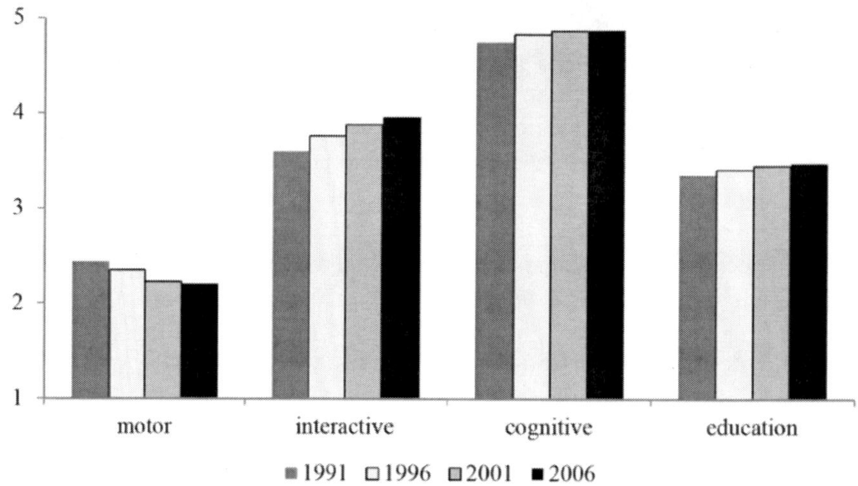

Source: Kelly & Lewis (2010).

Figure 4. Economy-Wide Mean Skill Levels, 1991 to 2006.

Supply of Skills

The education and training level of an individual has considerable influence over the kind of job opportunities and conditions of employment available to them. With considerable shifts in the demand for skills, corresponding shifts in the supply of labour with respect to education and training have occurred.

Additions to the stock of human capital in the domestic labour supply through education and training have increased considerably, although not enough to avoid the necessity for increased immigration. Figure 5 shows the increase in enrolments in trades, non-trades Technical and Further Education (TAFE) and university courses since 1999. The enrolments are indexed to 1999 equalling 100. The huge growth in non-trades TAFE training places taking place in the early 2000s was reversed in large part during the mid 2000s. Growth in university and TAFE enrolments continued throughout the period, with an overall increase of 41 per cent and 52 per cent, respectively. Thus, the supply of skilled labour has grown in response to an increase in demand.

Another source of skilled labour for the Australian economy has been the increasing use of migrant workers. In 2006, according to the Census (ABS 2006c), recently arrived migrant workers, that is those living over seas five years ago and now living and working in Australia, accounted for 4.8 per cent of the Australian labour force. Migration policy determines the supply of recent migrants in two ways. First, migration policy determines the level of migrant intake for any given year. Therefore, the supply of migrant labour is closely regulated and determined by the federal government. Second, migration policy determines the composition of migrants under the skills stream by ensuring all but refugees pass the scrutiny of the points test or coincide with one of the Migrants Occupations in Demand Lists (MODL). These check lists attempt to reflect structural changes in the domestic economy, which change the demand for skills (Department of Immigration and Citizenship [DIAC] 2012). Thus, for any given year, migration policy aims to adjust to best fit the changing needs of the domestic economy and is the main factor in allocating both the quantity and composition of supply of migrant labour on a national level.

Figure 6 shows net overseas migration from 1990/91 to 2006/07. Interestingly, the trend in net overseas migration contains features that coincide with the business cycle. While typically net overseas migration was around the 100,000 persons mark, from 1991 to 1993 it was considerably less, falling to just 30,000 persons in 1992/93 (during the economic recession), and from 2004 to 2006/07 the net intake was considerably more, rising to a peak in 2006/07 of approximately 232,800 persons (during the economic boom).

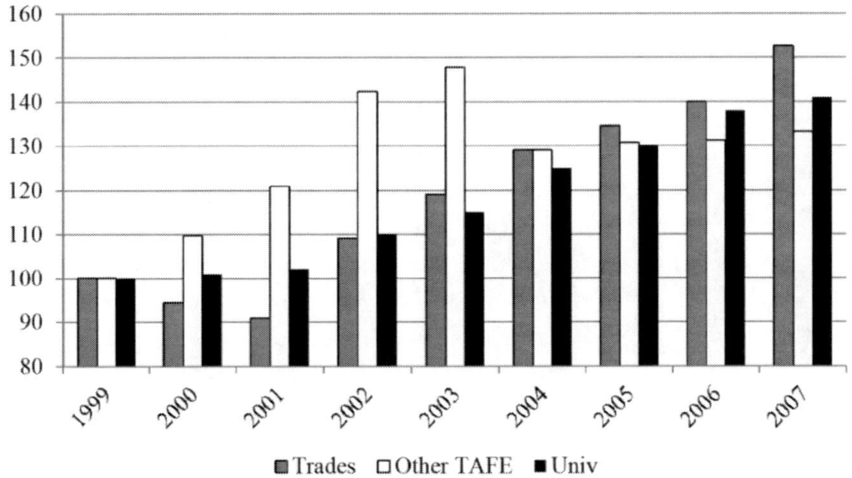

Sources: National Centre for Vocational & Educational Research 2010, Apprentices and trainees; Dept. Education Employment & Workplace Relations, various years, *Students: selected higher education statistics.*

Figure 5. Enrolment in Post-Compulsory Education, 1999 to 2007, Index 1999=100.

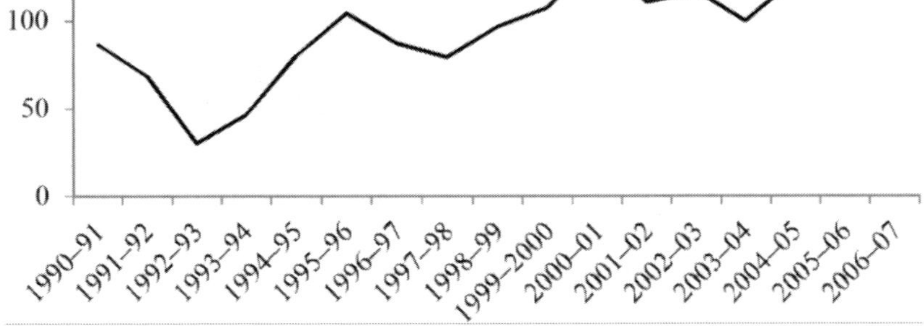

Source: Australian Bureau of Statistics 2006a, Australian economic indicators, cat. no. 1350.0, Canberra.

Figure 6. Net Overseas Migration (000s).

One source of migration that has attracted controversy is the greater orientation towards 457 work visas. The 457 visa enables businesses inside Australia to employ someone from outside Australia in a skilled job without them having to go through the usual procedures for permanent migration (DIAC 2012). Figure 7 shows the increase in 457 visa applications since their inception in 1996. While at the beginning of the scheme the numbers of applicant was a rather small, by 2003, seven years later, those numbers had almost doubled and by 2007 the number of 457 visas granted had doubled again, reaching 87,320.

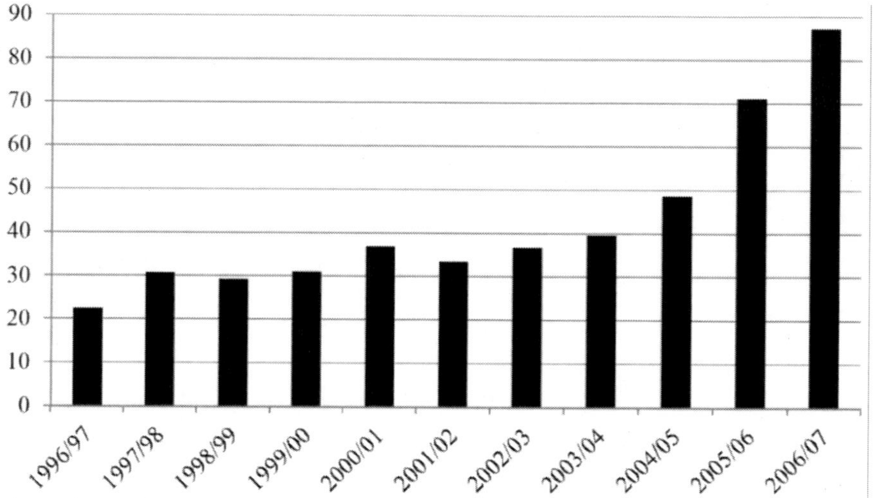

Source: Australian Parliamentary Library 2007, 457 visa applications, viewed www.aph.gov.au.

Figure 7. 457 Visa Applications Granted Since August 1996, (000s).

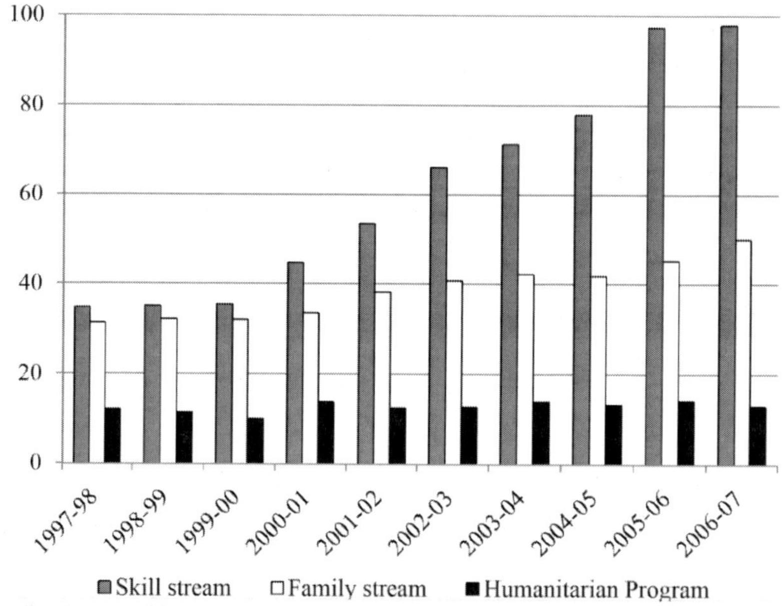

Source: Australian Bureau of Statistics 2006a, Australian economic indicators, cat. no. 1350.0, Canberra.

Figure 8. Permanent Visa Outcomes by Migration Programme, 1997 to 2006, (000s).

The market for tradespersons and university graduates have been some of the most affected by the introduction of the 457 visa category. A survey conducted by the then Department of Immigration and Multicultural and Indigenous Affairs (DIMIA), 'shows that 457 visa holders are generally highly skilled people, whether as managers, professionals or tradespeople' (Khoo, MacDonald & Hugo 2005, pviii).

Further evidence of the emphasis the current Australian migration system is placing on skilled migrants is indicated in Figure 8, which shows the increasing numbers of permanent migrants that are entering through the skilled migrant stream. In 1997, the number of migrants coming in under the skill stream was 34,670; this grew to 108,540 by 2007. While numbers in 1997 were not very different from the number of migrants coming in under different streams, by 2007 there were approximately 59,000 more migrants coming in under the skilled stream than the next largest family stream. It can also be seen that the number of migrants coming into Australia under the family stream has also risen considerably over the same period. In 1997, the number of migrants coming in under the family stream was 31,310; this grew to 49,870 by 2007. This is due to many of the skilled migrants that are coming into the country bringing their families with them. However, clearly a growing number of skilled migrants are not bringing their families and are possibly single.

With so many skilled migrants coming into Australia, it is interesting to note the jobs and the occupations in which they are finding employment. In 2006 the main occupation of employment was the professional occupation category in which 37 per cent of employed migrants are finding employment. Other common occupations are associate professionals, managers, tradespersons and some intermediate clerical jobs.

It appears that despite significant growth in the supply of new skilled labour through the expansion of TAFE and higher education in Australia, migration plays an important role in reducing the gap between the demand and supply of skilled labour. This is important for reducing inflationary pressure and allowing future economic growth.

Returns to Education and Training

This section examines the changes in earnings and earnings dispersion of tradespersons over the business cycle from 1991 to 2006, followed by the returns to investment into apprenticeship training and higher education over the business cycle.

Even with the economic boom, a number of trade occupations have seen little dramatic change in their relative median earnings between 1991 and 2006. Some trade occupations, for instance, mechanical, electrical and other trades, have all seen improvement in their relative median earnings over time. Food tradespersons, however, are paid well below the median earnings of all employed and their relative earnings have slipped substantially to just 71 per cent of the median in 2006, down 13 percentage points since 1991.

With respect to trades training, the data suggest the attractiveness of courses in the food trades is very low and has been worsening over time. Trade training has become more profitable for mechanical and electrical trades. Perhaps surprisingly, given the increased demand for construction tradespersons due to the mining boom and population growth (Lewis & Corliss 2010), relative earnings have not changed significantly over time, suggesting an increase in supply or substitution of less qualified labour by employers putting pressure off wages to rise. Lewis and Corliss (2010) found evidence of both these effects taking place—

that is, a considerable increase in the number of construction tradespersons coming from both foreign and domestic sources over the period and at the same time a deskilling with a reduction in the proportion of the construction tradespersons workforce that held formal qualifications.

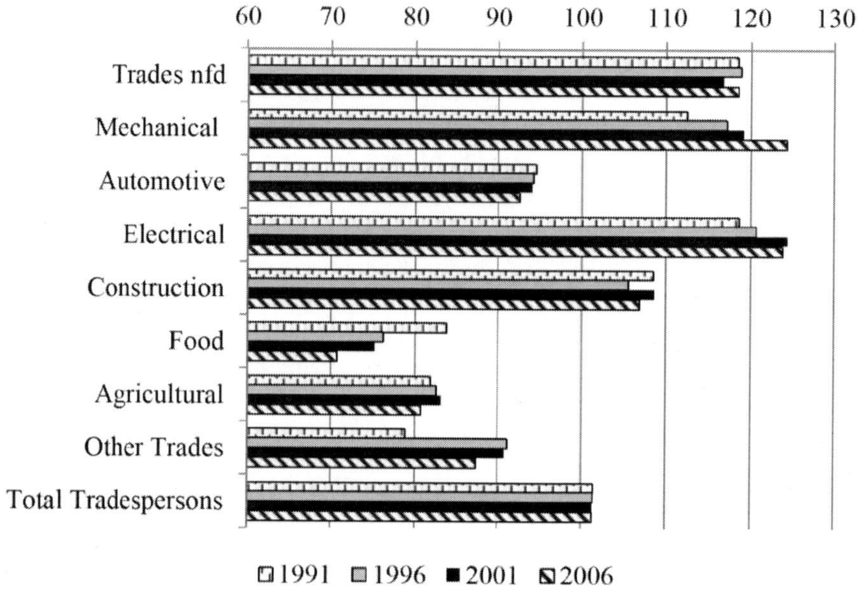

Source: Corliss and Lewis (2012).

Figure 9. Median Earnings of Tradespersons Relative to All Employed, (%).

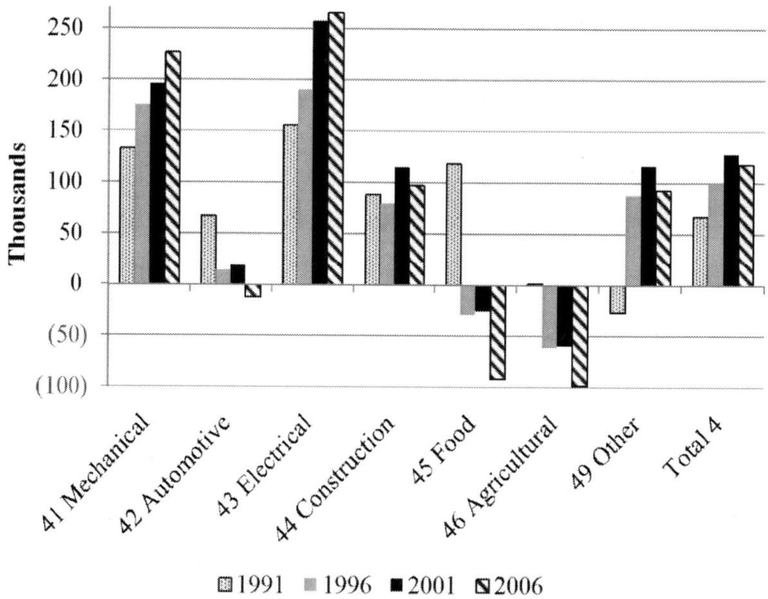

Source: Corliss and Lewis (2012).

Figure 10. Real Net Present Value Over Time, Males.

Another way of investigating the value of trades training is by looking at the Net Present Value NPV of lifetime earnings of the various trade occupations for qualified tradespersons compared to those with no post-school qualification—that is, those with only their Year 12 certificate. Those qualified as a tradesperson are defined to be those who have a level of skill commensurate with an Australian Qualification Framework AQF Certificate III or higher qualification (AQF 2009). Here the age/earnings profiles for those aged 18 to 65 were estimated by regressing earnings on age, taken at five-year intervals, to obtain smoothed earnings series. These earnings were adjusted for the relevant income tax payable to yield after tax earnings. No adjustment has been made for labour force status. A discount rate of 2 per cent is used, which is equal to the long-run average real bond rate. The results, in any case, are not too sensitive to the choice of real interest rate.

The results in Figure 10 suggest that for most trades the value of a trade qualification is high. However, for automotive trades the improvement has at best been modest and for food and agricultural trades the NPV was negative. Though not shown here, the results for women for most trades are negative, supporting the fact that they would be financially better off in another occupation only requiring Year 12 education. Figure 10 below shows the real NPV (calculated at 2 per cent) of different trades over time.

Interestingly, while the real NPV has increased significantly for mechanical and electrical trades, the real NPV for other trades has increased only modestly or even decreased. There is, therefore, quite a disparity in the returns to trade training over the business cycle depending on the trade. Again, the results for construction tradespersons show returns have not risen even in the face of growing demand in the construction industry. For the poorly paid trades, the incentive to invest in trade training has deteriorated further over time.

Turning now to higher education there also appear to be important business cycle effects on the rate of return to a university degree. Table 1 shows the number of graduates per 1000 population over 15 years of age increasing dramatically over the period 1991 to 2006, with nearly an 80 per cent increase in the proportion of graduates from 87 graduates per 1000 in 1991 to 156 graduates per 1000 in 2006. This increase in the number of graduates per 1000 population happened at the same time there was considerable population growth in the order of 22 per cent during the period 1991 to 2006. Both of these factor have significantly increased the number of graduates in Australia.

Holding everything else constant, such a large increase in the number of graduates in the Australian population over 15 years of age means it would be expected that the relative median incomes of graduates compared to those holding a Year 12 certificate would decrease. However, this is not the case, as shown in the table below. In fact, the earnings ratio of graduates to Year 12 certificate holders increased from 1991 to 2001 for males, and while females did see a fall from 1991 to 1996, the earnings differential became larger from 1996 to 2001.

It was previously discussed that at the bottom of the cycle, business cycle effects are concentrated on the unskilled, increasing unemployment and the competition for jobs at the top of the cycle. As the pool of unskilled labour has dried up, the business cycle effects put pressure on wages of the less skilled to rise. Table 1 shows a considerable fall in the earnings ratio for both male and female graduates, losing 49 per cent and 23 per cent, respectively, from the 2001 expansion to 2006 top of the cycle.

Table 1. Summary Statistics on the Graduate Labour Market in Australia

	1991	1996	2001	2006
Population 15+	13,085,092	14,040,303	14,856,774	15,918,082
Graduates/1000 pop'n	87	103	146	156
Males				
Median Income—Grads	$47,273	$53,159	$67,729	$62,921
Median Income—Year 12	$25,978	$28,598	$34,148	$42,356
Ratio Grad/Year 12	1.82	1.86	1.98	1.49
Females				
Median Income—Grads	$34,117	$37,632	$46,108	$42,259
Median Income—Year 12	$18,410	$21,894	$25,765	$27,164
Ratio Grad/Year 12	1.85	1.72	1.79	1.56

Source: Corliss, Lewis and Daly (2013).

However, as stated before, the graduate labour market is further complicated by structural and technological change taking place during the same period. Both structural and technological change have increased the demand for graduates in Australia. Structural change has increased the number of jobs in the service sector, which values skills that are developed in universities, such as knowledge, communication and cognitive skills (Kelly & Lewis 2006). Technological change driven by the rapid uptake of ICT investment affects the demand for skills directly by increasing demand for ICT-related skills and indirectly through the enabling effects of ICT (Kelly 2007).

There are a number of key assumptions that must be made in order to calculate the private rate of return. These include the following:

- The length of the degree and therefore the period for which earnings are foregone.
- Whether students earn any income while studying or not.
- The size of direct costs, including the purchase of books and equipment and fees.
- The size of any adjustment for ability or other unmeasured characteristics that are likely to affect the rate of return.

The following 11 fields of study were identified: humanities, science, allied health, mathematics and statistics, information technology, engineering, architecture, medicine, nursing, dentistry, education and visual and performing arts. In the base case for a bachelor degree, the length of the degree is assumed to be three years for humanities, science, mathematics and statistics, information technology, nursing and visual and performing arts, four years for allied health and engineering degrees and five years for degrees in architecture, medicine and dentistry.

To carry out the analysis over time, special tabulations of median income by qualification for each age between and including 18 to 64 years were prepared from the 1991, 1996, 2001 and 2006 Censuses. These incomes are the medians for all people with a given qualification in an age category and all labour market states are included: full and part-time employed, unemployed and not in the labour force. They, therefore, reflect the different employment outcomes for graduates compared with Year 12 completers and males compared with females, as well as any income differences that exist within a particular labour force status. A simple regression relating median income to age and age squared was estimated to provide a smooth series for median incomes at each age. Net incomes were then calculated using the 1990/91, 1995/96, 2000/01 and 2005/06 income taxation rates.

The results presented here are based on cross-sectional data from the censuses and, therefore, make the assumption that the future income stream of an 18 year old choosing between undertaking a degree or leaving the education system at the end of Year 12 is best represented by what people of differing ages with different levels of qualifications are currently earning in the respective Census year. The foregone earnings of undergraduates were assumed to be the average earnings of a high school graduate.

The base case is the simplest that can be modified to test the sensitivity of results to changes in assumptions. It assumes that university students do not earn income while studying and that there are explicit costs for students: undergraduates incur $1720 per year (in 2006 dollars) in direct study costs. These direct cost estimates were taken from the Australian Universities Student Finances Report 2006 (AVCC 2007). In addition, students are assumed to pay upfront the student fees applicable for each field of study and year at the relevant rate (i.e. 1991, 1996, 2001 or 2006) of the HECS charge and collect a 20 per cent discount for paying fees upfront. The base case results do not make any adjustment for ability or other unmeasured characteristics that may affect the private rate of return.

The Censuses provide unique data covering different stages of the business cycle from 1991, the middle of a recession; 1996, the recovery; 2001, the boom and 2006, labour shortages. Figures 11 and 12 show the private rates of return for males and females over the business cycle.

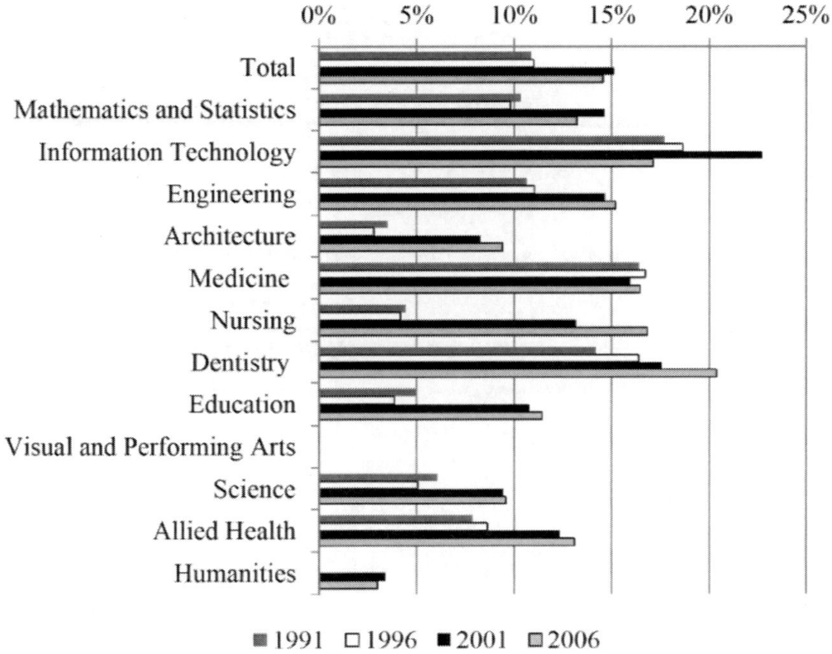

Source: Corliss, Lewis and Daly (2013).

Figure 11. Private Rates of Return for Males, 1991 to 2006.

The private rate of return for males, shown in Figure 11, experienced a dramatic increase between the 1996 recovery to 2001 expansion phase of the business cycle, for many of the fields of study under investigation. During this time, the rate of return increased from 11 per cent in 1996 to 15 per cent in 2001. This was most pronounced in nursing, education and mathematics. Other degrees recorded more modest increases in the private rate of return, with the exception of medicine observing a slight decrease. With the exception of information technology, where the rate of return fell sharply between 2001 to 2006, all the fields of study recorded an upward movement or remained relatively constant during the 2001 expansion to 2006 boom phase of the business cycle. While there is considerable variation in the private rate of return between the degrees shown here, the business cycle appears to affect them in a fairly consistent manner.

Figure 12 suggests a slightly different story for women than for their male counterparts over the business cycle. Consistent with males, female degree holders increased their private rate of return from 1996 to 2001, although it was not as pronounced as for males. The sample total rate of return increased from 12 per cent in 1996 to 14 per cent in 2001. The fields of study having the greatest increases in the private rate of return for females were visual and performing arts and engineering. A further difference was the downward adjustment in the female private rate of return occurring between 2001 and 2006 was more dramatic than for their male counterparts and affected more fields of study than just information technology, including mathematics and education, with minor reductions noted in some of the other fields of study.

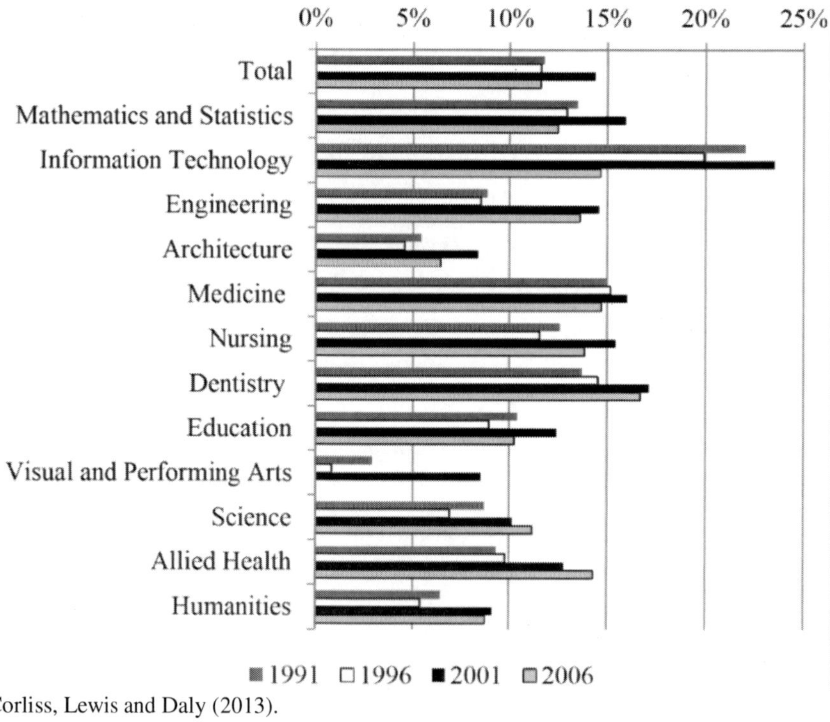

Source: Corliss, Lewis and Daly (2013).

Figure 12. Private Rates of Return for Females, 1991 to 2006.

Perhaps the most interesting results are the dramatic variation in the private rate of return for holders of information technology degrees. It is possible that the raised expectations of potential students in 2000 due to the very high private rate of return of information technology degrees compared with other fields of study created an oversupply of information technology graduates at a time when demand was coming off a high, putting downward pressure on wages and employment and dramatically reducing the private rate of return for information technology degree holders.

Overall, for the typical degree holder, the rate of return to higher education is quite high and has increased consideralby over the period for men in particular. This suggests that the demand for skilled labour in Australia has outpaced changes in the supply of skilled labour.

Returns to the Lowest Paid Graduates

Another important aspect of labour market adjustment is the dispersion of earnings for skilled labour, of the same type, between industries/occupations. Changes in the relative earnings for skilled labour between and within various industries/occupations send signals to the market, making them either more or less attractive to workers. This has important implications for improving the allocation of labour across the various industries/occupations. Additionally, whether or not everyone that has invested in obtaining certain qualifications has profited from the investment also sends signals to the labour market, which adjust the supply of skilled labour.

We know from earlier on in this chapter that structural change, technological change and the business cycle have had considerable influence in changing the demand for skills in Australia. It is not likely that these changes in the demand for skills will affect the Australian economy uniformly; instead, changes in the demand for skills will affect various industries/occupations differently by varying magnitude and direction. Additionally, increasing rates of return have been seen, generally, to higher education and to some trades training over time. One would expect to see, given the sizeable change in the demand for skills, considerable dispersion of earnings for skilled labour between and within the various industries/occupations.

The purpose here is to explore the relationship between the dispersion of earnings and investment in education and training. More specifically, the aim is to examine whether those lowest paid skilled workers have found their investment into trades training and higher education profitable.

When examining the dispersion of income, it is typical to examine both the lower and higher end of the income spectrum. However, this is not always possible, as in this case, those higher income bachelor degree holders often earn more than is possible to estimate given the limitation of the data source. Here, the main data source is the Census. The relevant question on income employs income bands, which become open ended at $104,000 per annum and, thus, it is not possible to estimate the income of the best paid degree holders as many high income earners fall into this open ended category.

This chapter is underpinned by the theoretical framework of human capital theory, which views further education and training as an investment for which the individual expects a return. Investigating the bottom 20 per cent is of interest since it throws lihgt on whether investment into trades training or university education are profitable for everyone. It may well be that not all tradespersons and university graduates that complete their study receive higher wages and would have been financially better off not undertaking the study. From society's point of view, examining the bottom 20 per cent of those investing in trades training and university education may help inform policy options, such as how much should the private individual contribute to the cost of their further education and how much should society contribute.

It is important to note that the current literature on the rate of return to trades training and university education in Australia has only a very limited analysis on the bottom 20 per cent (see for example Corliss, Lewis and Daly 2013). The analysis shown here provides new and interesting insights into the returns to education and training in Australia.

Here we first examine the lowest paid income tradespersons before moving on and investigating low income university graduates.

There are several ways in which earnings dispersion can be measured. Here, two simple but well-known measures are applied to earnings—namely, the ratio of earnings of the lowest 20 per cent (20th percentile) to the median (50th percentile) and the ratio of the earnings of the highest 20 per cent (80th percentile) to the median.

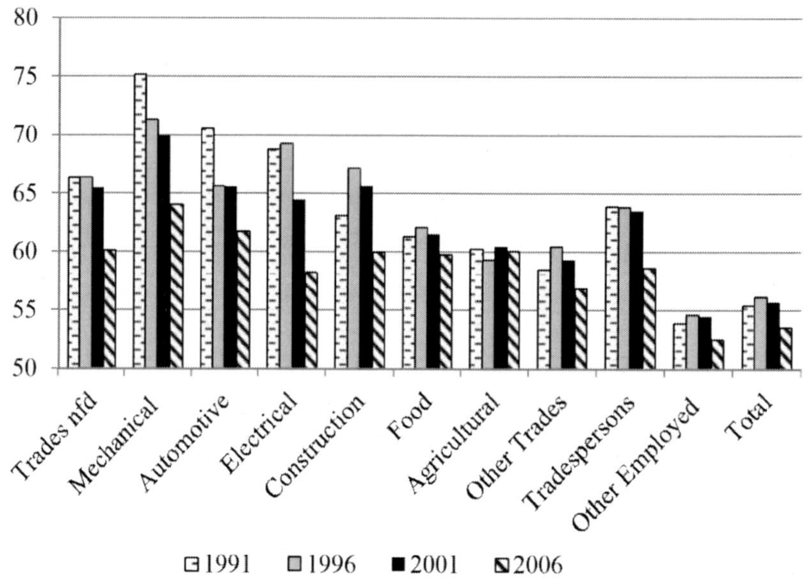

Source: Corliss and Lewis (2012).

Figure 13. Trade Occupations Ratio of 20th Percentile to Median Weekly Earnings, 1991 to 2006.

Figure 13 shows the ratio of the 20th percentile relative to the median's weekly earnings. It shows that there has been an observable downward trends in the 20th percentile relative to median weekly earnings for all tradespersons and for many of the individual trade occupations, over the period 1991 to 2006. This downward trend is very small for the years 1991 to 2001: it only fell by 1.2 percentage points from 63.9 per cent in 1991 to 62.7 in 2001. However, between 2001 and 2006, the 20th percentiles share of the median weekly earnings dropped by five percentage points from 62.7 in 2001 to 57.7 in 2006. The falls between 2001 and 2006 are consistent through all trade occupations and all other employed persons. The biggest falls were for the trade occupations of mechanical, electrical and building, by 6.2, 6.3

and 5.9 percentage points, respectively, over the period 2001 to 2006. The relative loss suffered by the 20th percentile is not due to reduced weekly earnings, since the 20th percentile weekly earnings for all tradespersons increased by $46 from $382 to $428 between 2001 and 2006. The relative loss occurred due to the median weekly earnings for all tradespersons rising much more over the same period by $133 from $608 in 2001 to $741 in 2006. Evidence presented here implies that for low income tradespersons, their relative position fell during the recent economic boom in Australia.

At the same time as the 20th percentile has fallen relative to the median, the 80th percentile of all tradespersons relative to the median has exhibited an upward trend, most notably between 2001 and 2006, in which it jumped from 142 per cent of the median to 160 per cent (Corliss and Lewis 2012). Of the trade occupations, the most significant change between 2001 and 2006 was observed in building, other trades and agriculture, which increased by 18 per cent, 18 per cent and 9 per cent, respectively. Some occupations observed notable change earlier than this however. For electrical tradespersons and for non-trade occupations the 80th percentile relative to the median increased significantly between 1996 and 2001 by 10 per cent and 11 per cent, respectively, and then observed little change between 2001 and 2006 (Corliss and Lewis 2012).

Clearly, the dispersion of earnings among trade occupations has been increasing over time. Thus, the highest earning tradespersons have been improving their position and were the major beneficiaries of changes in the Australian economy, including the economic boom. This implies that the labour market is increasingly providing better rewards for the best tradespersons or possibly for those willing to work in more difficult, unpleasant or dangerous jobs who receive a compensating differential.

Generally, for tradespersons, there has been considerable widening of the earnings distribution between the best and worst paid tradespersons. This suggests that there is considerable price (wage) adjustment in the labour market, which is not evident in considering aggregate measures such as medians.

Finally, here we examine the rates of return for low income university graduates holding a bachelor degree from 1991 to 2006.

As before the base case assumptions are adopted—namely, that university students do not earn income while studying and that there are explicit costs for students; undergraduates incur $1720 per year (in 2006 dollars) in direct study cost and students are assumed to pay upfront the student fees applicable for each field of study and year at the appropriate rate of the HECS charge and collect a 20 per cent discount for paying fees upfront. Here the results of the internal rate of return nearly all cannot be calculated or are negative and, therefore, have been omitted from the results. That is, the lowest paid university graduates would be better off not going to university. However, the NPV can be calculated and the estimates are presented in figures 14 and 15 in constant 2006 dollars. As explained earlier in the chapter, the NPV is calculated with a real rate of interest of 2 per cent, which is approximately the long-run real bond rate. The conclusions are not changed much by the choice of interest rate within reasonable bands.

Over time, the lack of incentive for low income degree holders remains fairly consistent. With some exceptions, namely those that obtained an Information Tecnology degree, for males had a small but positive NPV in 2001 and females observed a small but positive NPV in 1991 and 2001; however, the NPV does not remain positive for the entire period under question. Additionally, the only positive NPV for women studying education took place in 2006. Those that obtained a degree in dentistry for both males and females had positive NPV in 2001 and 2006, although the NPV of males was considerable higher, an extra $217,176 in 2006. However, these results suggest that for the lowest paid men and women graduates, only medicine consistently offers any incentive to undertake the training over the entire period.

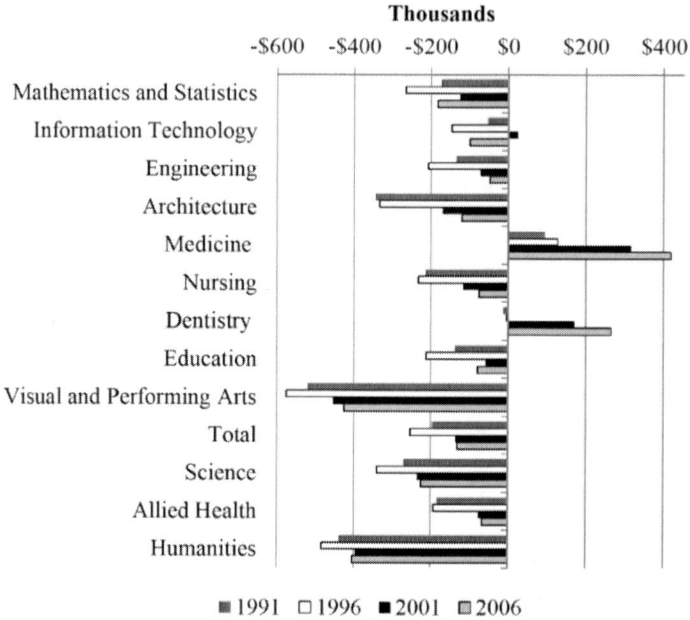

Source: Corliss, Lewis and Daly (2013).

Figure 14. Net Present Value of the 20th Percentile of Male University Graduates, 1991 to 2006.

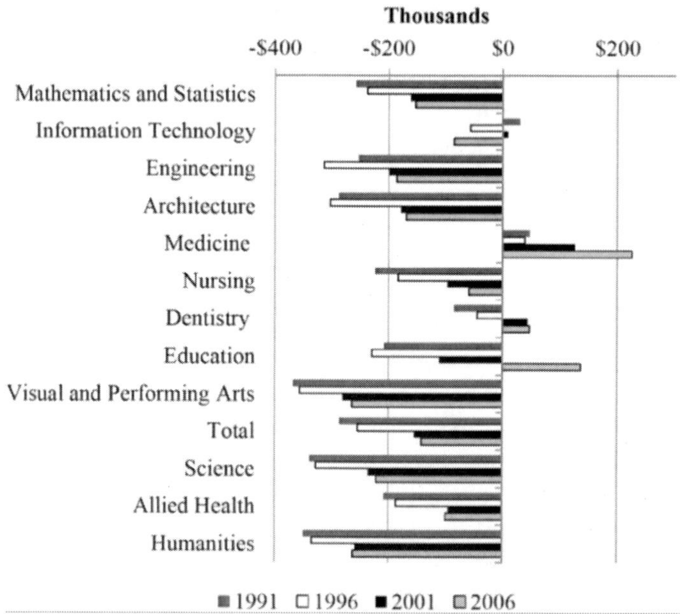

Source: Corliss, Lewis and Daly (2013).

Figure 15. Net Present Value of the 20th Percentile for Female University Graduates, 1991 to 2006.

These results demonstrate the risk students are taking by undertaking a university education. Along with the direct costs of study, there is a considerable sacrifice in potential earnings. Clearly, for the bottom 20 per cent of students, many would have been better off getting a full-time job than going to university.

The results also bring into question the efficacy of further expanding the number of university places in Australia. A further expansion of the number of university places offered may have a negative effect on the marginal entrants finding it increasingly difficult upon completion of study to find satisfactory employment.

Conclusion

This chapter examined the functioning of skilled labour markets in Australia, including adjustment in the domestic supply including skilled migration, the demand for skills, and the rate of return into higher education and trades training for the median in response to the forces of structural change, technological change and the business cycle covering the period 1991 to 2006.

The main findings were that the demand for skilled labour, higer education in particular, appears to be outpacing the change in supply. This is despite a considerable increase in the domestic supply of skills and significant skilled migration programs. For the median degree holder the rate of return to higher education is quite high for most degrees examined with the exception of visual and perfroming arts, although there was significant variation between the various disciplines. For tradespersons the results are more mixed with some trades such as electrical and mechanical tradespersons receiving high returns to trades training and other trade occupations such as automotive, food and agricutural tradespersons receiving a negative return to trades training.

The business cycle seems to have had a significant effect on the returns to both higher education and trades training. The returns to higher education appears to be procyclical, that is with increases in economic activity so to has the returns to higher education increased except at the top end of the cycle. At the top end of the cycle, labour shortages become the dominant factor causing wages of year 12 certificate holders to rise faster reducing the returns to higher education. While those trade occuptaions that already had high returns to trades training saw their returns increase with every subsequent stage of the business cycle, other trade occupation with low or even negative NPV saw returns worsen with every subsequent stage of the business cycle.

For low income degree holders and qualified tradespersons the investment in education and for all degrees with the exception of medicine, and trade occupations has been unprofitable and often has resulted in a considerable loss in life time earnings.

Generally, it appears that the market for skilled labour in Australia generally functions well. There appears to be no obvious great mismatch between the supply and demand for skilled labour other than short-term gaps, for which the use of skilled migration policies have been beneficial. The market for skilled labour appears to be emitting clear signals of changes to demand with corresponding changes to relative wages. The largely demand-driven system in higher educatiion would appear to be effective, with only a minor role for government intervention.

One of the most important implications of these findings is related to the strong growth in demand for skilled labour in the Australian economy. Without an adequate supply of skilled labour to the Australian economy, long-term growth may be stifled and pressure put on inflation. Therefore, the various government programmes currently in existence that aim to secure an adequate supply of skilled labour through education and training and migration are desirable. Importantly, the effects of structural/technological change on the demand for skills in the Australian economy show no signs of abating. Thus, various government policies intended to increase the supply of skilled labour should also be maintained into the future. However, there is always the danger in government controlling places, given their unfortunate history of 'picking winners' in the past.

Additionally, structural change leaves workers employed in industries that are in long-term relative decline with fewer employment opportunities and lower relative wages. It is important that government assists the transition of those workers from the industries in decline to industries growing as quickly and as easily as possible. The consequences for those workers otherwise will be periods of unemployment, causing loss of human capital, increased dependence on government benefits and, in some cases, causing them to become marginally attached to the labour force.

While the effects of structural/technological change have meant better pay and more employment opportunities for those with skills, it has also meant lower relative pay and fewer job opportunities for those without skills. This is an important source of inequality within the Australian economy. By offering greater access to some of the trades training and higher education places to those on lower incomes, these negative effects on inequality can be reduced. Currently, one of the aims of the federal governmentis to increase the proportion of enrolled university students that come from the lowest socio-economic quartile of the population by 2020. However, it must be borne in mind that the above caveat for the need to improve primary and secondary schooling to ensure the quality of university candidates does not diminish. Additionally it may be necessary to offer university students from the lowest socio-economic quartile of the population additional support while studying.

Another aim of the federal government is to lift the proportion of 25 to 35 year olds with a university education to 40 per cent by 2025. These findings raise questions about the level to which the higher education system in Australia can be expanded. If low income university graduates are finding their investment in higher education has not been profitable, then it is likely that further expansion in the sector will see a greater proportion of university graduates experiencing negative returns to the investment in higher education. If, under the current admission process, the best candidates for university selection have already been selected, this leaves a progressively less desirable pool of candidates to select from. This assumes that the current selection process for higher education in Australia works well and changing it will not result in a better pool of potential candidates to choose from.

Given the considerable change in the demand for skilled labour caused by structural and technological change which has caused increased demand for some skills and demand for other skills to decline, it would seem appropriate for government to play a limited role in informing propestive students of current and future changes to the returns to various types of education and training in australia. Government organisations could play a role in informing prospective students of the long-term trends in the demand for skills—in particular, those skills in which there is an acute shortage or severe oversupply. This will have the benefit of reducing skills shortages, such as the perceived skills shortages in 2006, allowing the economy to grow faster. It will also reduce the spells of unemployment for those that are trained in skills in long-term decline. However, there is little evidence that governments have a great deal of knowledge, experience or capacity in forecasting skills demand.

Given the increase in demand for higher education and the overall improvement in the rates of return to higher education, further expansion of the higher education system appears warranted. However, it is clear not all courses and subjects should be expanded. It is also important to bear in mind the caveat that a blanket expansion of the higher education system may not result in the expected benefits due to the current number of marginal students.

The skilled migration programme, and 457 in particular, visas have proven themselves to be valuable in filling short-term gaps between the supply and demand for skilled labour in Australia. It is important these programmes continue into the future to ensure adequate levels of skilled labour, particularly given that the business cycle, without these ameliorating policies, would cause periods of excess supply and shotrages of labour.

References

ABS. (2006a). *Australian economic indicators*, cat. no. 1350.0, Canberra.

ABS. (2006c). *Census of population and housing*, Canberra.

ABS. (2007). *Labour force Australia*, cat. no. 6202.0, ABS, Canberra.

Australian Parliamentary Library. (2007). 457 visa applications, viewed 24/2/2012, www.aph.gov.au

Australian Parliamentary Library. (2012).*The higher education contribution scheme*, viewed 20/9/2011, www.aph.gov.au

Australian Vice Chancellors Committee (AVCC).(2007). *Australian university student finances*, 2006, AVCC, Canberra.

Australian Qualifications Framework. (2009). *Qualifications*, viewed 20/3/2012 www.aqf.edu.au.

Bradbury, B. (2003).*Child poverty: areview, policy research paper* no. 20, Commonwealth Department of Family and Community Services, Canberra.

Bradshaw, J., Kemp, P., Baldwin, S. & Rowe, A. (2004). *The drivers of social exclusion.* Are view of the literature for the social exclusion unit in the breaking the cycle series, the Social Exclusion Unit, Office of the Deputy Prime Minister, UK, viewed 12/5/2009 www.socialexclusion.gov.uk.

Castro, R. &Coen-Pirani, D. (2008). 'Why have aggregates killed hours become so cyclical since the mid-1980s?', *International Economic Review*, vol. 49, no. 1, 135–185.

Corliss, M., Lewis, P. & Daly, A. (2013). The Rate of Return to Higher Education over the Business Cycle, *Australian Journal of Labour Economics*, vol. 16, no. 2, 219–236.

Corliss, M. & Lewis, P. (2012). The Earnings of Trades persons over the Business Cycle, *Economic Papers*, 30(3), 1-13.

Corliss, M. & Lewis, P.(2011). 'The economic boom, population and structural change and the market for trades persons', *Australian Journal of Labour Economics*, vol. 14, no. 3, 289–305.

Daly, A., Lewis, P., Corliss, M. &Heaslip, T. (2011). *The Private Rate of Return to a University Degree in Australia*, report to the Department of Education, Employment and Workplace Relations, DEEWR, Australian Capital Territory.

Daly, A. & Lewis, P.(2010). 'The private rate of return to an economics degree in Australia; an update', *EconomicPapers*, vol. 29, no. 3, 353–364.

Daly, A., McNamara, J., Tanton, R., Harding, A.& Yap, M.(2008). 'Indicators of risk of social exclusion for children in Australian households: an analysis by state and age group', *Australasian Journal of Regional Studies*, vol. 14, no. 2, 165–206.

Department of Education Employment &Workplace Relations (DEEWR). (2012). Various years, *Students: selected higher education statistics*, viewed 26/3/2010 www.deewr.gov.au

Department of Immigration and Citizenship (DIAC). (2012). Visas, immigration and refugees—employer sponsored workers, viewed 12/4/2012 at www.immi.gov.au

Keane, M & Prasad, E 1993, 'The relation between skill levels and the cyclical variability of employment', *Hours and Wages*, working paper no. 93/44, International Monetary Fund.

Kelly, R. & Lewis, P. (2003). 'The new economy and the demand for skills', *Australian Journal of Labour Economics*, vol. 6, no. 1, 135–152.

Kelly, R. & Lewis, P. (2006). 'Measurement of skill and skill change', in P Brown, S Liu & D Sharma, *Contributions to probability and statistics: applications and challenges*, World Scientific, Singapore.

Kelly, R. & Lewis, P.(2010). 'The change in labour skills in Australia over the business cycle', *Australian Bulletin of Labour*, vol. 36, no. 3, 260–277.

Kelly, R. (2007). 'Changing skill intensity in Australian industry', The Australian Economic Review, vol. 40, no. 1, 1–18.

Khoo, S., MacDonald, P.& Hugo, G.(2005).*Temporary skilled migrants in Australia: Employment circumstances and migration outcomes*, report to the Department of Immigration and Multicultural and Indigenous Affairs, Canberra.

Lewis, P. & Corliss, M.(2010). *Where tradies work: an analysis of the labour market for trades people*, National Centre for Vocational Education Research, Adelaide.

Lewis, P. (2006).*Minimum wages and employment*, Australian Fair Pay Commission research report no. 1/06 Australian Fair Pay Commission, Melbourne.

Lewis, P., Garnett, A., Hawtrey, K. &Treadgold, M.(2010).*The Australian economy: your guide, Pearson Education*, Sydney.

Lindquist, M. (2004) 'Capital-skill complementarily and inequality over the business cycle', *Review of Economic Dynamics*, vol. 7, 519–540.

National Centre for Vocational and Educational Research. (2010).*Apprentices and trainees*, 14/5/2010 viewed www.ncver.edu.au

Norton, A. (2012). 'Graduate winners: assessing the public and private benefits of higher education', Grattan Institute, Melbourne.

Reder, M. (1955). 'The theory of occupational wage differentials', *The American Economic Review*, vol. 45, no. 5, 833–852.

UNICEF. (2005).*Child Poverty in Rich Countries 2005*, report card no. 6, UNICEF, Innocenti Research Centre, Florence.

In: Business Cycles in Economics
Editor: Jason C. Hsu

ISBN: 978-1-63321-322-7

Chapter 11

UNCERTAINTY SHOCKS AND CONSUMPTION: EVIDENCE FROM THE U.S. DATA

Lilia Karnizova *

University of Ottawa, Ottawa, Canada

Abstract

Increased uncertainty is commonly believed to be an important factor in explaining weak growth of U.S. consumption during the Great Recession and the subsequent recovery. Yet, recent empirical research casts doubt on the importance of time-varying uncertainty in accounting for historical variability of U.S. consumption. This Chapter attempts to reconcile the two opposite views. Using several measures of uncertainty, this Chapter first evaluates comovement between aggregate consumption and uncertainty at different forecasting horizons. The comovement between consumption and all measures of uncertainty is negative in the short run. This negative comovement can extend beyond the five years, depending on a measure of uncertainty. However, the dynamic relation between aggregate consumption and uncertainty has not been stable over time for many measures of uncertainty. The results are particularly sensitive to the inclusion of the Great Recession and the subsequent periods into the data sample. When the latter periods are taken into account in the estimation, the comovement between aggregate consumption and uncertainty becomes more negative. Forecast error variance decompositions in recursive vector autoregression (VAR) models indicate that contributions of uncertainty shocks to explaining historical behavior of U.S. consumption have been rather modest. Despite this finding, uncertainty shocks can still play an important role during specific episodes. A historical decomposition of economic series in a multivariate VAR illustrates that uncertainty shocks have had a significant impact on the path of consumption during the period from 2008 to 2011.

Keywords: Uncertainty, consumption, U.S., uncertainty shocks, Great Recession, vector autoregression (VAR)

* E-mail address: lilia.karnizova@uottawa.ca; Tel.: 1-613-562-5800 x 2017; Fax: 1-613-562-5999; Address: Department of Economics, University of Ottawa, 120 University, Room 9053, Ottawa, Ontario, Canada, K1N 6N5.

Introduction

The slow pace of the U.S. economic recovery from the Great Recession of 2007-2009 has been commonly linked to weak consumer demand. During the recession, consumer purchases were severely affected. This decline in consumption was unusually large in comparison with other recessions (De Nardi et al., 2012). Furthermore, consumption was slow to recover after the peak of the recession.

What could hinder recent consumption growth? A possible reason is the environment of heightened economic uncertainty. Available indicators of economic uncertainty spiked in 2008-2009 and remained at historically high levels during the recovery. Surveys of firms have listed uncertainty as a critical detrimental factor to conducting business. Discussions of possible negative implications of heightened uncertainty have become prominent in the policy circles, media and academic world alike. Following empirical and theoretical results in (Bloom, 2009), shocks to uncertainty are now considered to be a plausible contender in explaining the origins of recessions.[1] This Chapter contributes to the literature on uncertainty shocks by studying a relation between aggregate consumption and measures of uncertainty.

A traditional mechanism through which increased uncertainty has a negative impact on economic activity is an option value of waiting. In the environment where there are adjustment costs and investment is irreversible, it is beneficial to wait until the uncertainty is resolved before committing to major outlays. Thus, heightened uncertainty can make firms and consumers feel more cautious and thereby delay investment and consumption expenditures. The option value theory was introduced into the analysis of investment decisions of firms in (Bernanke, 1983). This theory was further developed in (Dixit and Pindyck, 1994). In (Romer, 1990), the option value theory of investment was applied to analyze consumer decisions regarding purchases of durable goods. Recent theoretical models, surveyed in (Bloom et al., 2013), have proposed other channels through which time-varying uncertainty can influence investment decisions of firms. In the context of consumer behavior, however, the option value channel remains the main link between consumption and uncertainty.

The flip side of the unusual depth and duration of the consumption slump during the Great Recession is the increased private saving. Faced with more uncertain future, consumers have incentives to increase saving for precautionary reasons. It is estimated in (Mody et al., 2012, p. 117) that in the OECD countires "at least two-fifths of the increase in saving rates between 2007 and 2009 can be attributed to unemployment risk and the measure of GDP volatility."

Yet, empirical results reported in (Knotek and Khan, 2011) and (Beetsma and Giuliodori, 2012) cast doubt on the importance of time-varying uncertainty for understanding the behavior of U.S. consumers. Both studies use vector autoregression (VAR) models to identity surprise shocks to uncertainty and evaluate effects of uncertainty shocks on consumption. An overall conclusion from their analysis is that "variations in the amount of uncertainty - at least as they are commonly captured - do not appear to be a key factor driving household spending decisions and, in turn, economic weakness" (Knotek and Khan, 2011, p. 64).

The main focus in (Knotek and Khan, 2011) is on a relationship between different consumption categories and two measures of uncertainty. The first measure is based on references to the word "uncertainty" in newspaper articles. The second measure is the stock market volatility. Knotek and Khan find that a surprise increase in uncertainty has important

[1] The web-site of N. Bloom (http://www.policyuncertainty.com) contains an extensive list of references.

negative effects on all categories of consumer spending in bivariate models. However, these effects dissipate in larger systems. In (Beetsma and Giuliodori, 2012), economic uncertainty is measured only by the stock market volatility. Beetsma and Giuliodori uncover a structural change in responses of consumption to a surprise increase in the stock market volatility. The growth rates of aggregate consumption and its subcategories have become essentially insensitive to variations in the stock market volatility since the mid-1980s. Furthermore, uncertainty shocks explain only a small fraction of consumption expenditures historically in both (Knotek and Khan, 2011) and (Beetsma and Giuliodori, 2012).

This Chapter attempts to reconcile the above mentioned empirical findings on the effects of uncertainty shocks on consumption from VARs with the prevalent perception that heightened uncertainty mattered for consumption during the Great Recession and the following recovery. This is achieved through two strategies. First, this Chapter evaluates whether the conclusions in (Knotek and Khan, 2011) and (Beetsma and Giuliodori, 2012) are robust to different measures of uncertainty, data transformations and periods of estimation. Second, this Chapter computes a historical decomposition of economic series in a VAR to assess a contribution of uncertainty shocks to explaining aggregate consumption during the Great Recession and beyond.

Since measuring uncertainty is a difficult task, one possibility why previous empirical research fails to find significant effects of uncertainty shocks on consumption is the measurement issue. To investigate this possibility, this Chapter uses ten different measures of uncertainty proposed in the literature. Another possibility is that the relation between consumption and uncertainty measures may be sensitive to data transformations. Consumption series are expressed as deviations from the HP-filter in (Knotek and Khan, 2011) and in growth rates in (Beetsma and Giuliodori, 2012). Any data transformation of an economic time series emphasizes specific frequencies. A relation between two series may depend on the frequency of the analysis. From the theoretical literature, one would expect to have the strongest effect of uncertainty in the short run, and to find that these effects weaken over time.

This Chapter characterizes comovement between consumption and measures of uncertainty at different time horizons using a method proposed in (den Haan, 2000). The method is based on correlations of forecast errors from a VAR, computed at different time horizons. The method has an advantage of not imposing specific assumptions about stationarity of the data. It provides means to determine how consumption is related to uncertainty measures in the 'short run' and in the 'long run'.

The correlation coefficients between the VAR forecast errors reveal negative comovement between consumption and all uncertainty measures in the short run. For some measures of uncertainty, the correlations remain negative beyond the five years. Yet, consistent with the previous empirical results in (Beetsma and Giuliodori, 2012), the comovement between aggregate consumption expenditures and measures of uncertainty is sensitive to the periods of investigation. A particularly interesting finding is that for all measures considered, including the period of the Great Recession and beyond into the empirical sample substantially strengthens the negative relation between aggregate consumption and uncertainty. This finding provides support to the view emphasizing the role of uncertainty in explaining the recent U.S. economic experience.

This Chapter proceeds by estimating structural VAR models. The VAR analysis is designed to trace effects of uncertainty shocks on consumption over time and to compute a fraction of variation in consumption expenditures attributable to these shocks. The robustness of findings is checked by comparing the predictions from bivariate and multivariate systems.

Bivariate VAR models include aggregate consumption and a particular measure of uncertainty. For samples that include the Great Recession, a surprise increase in each measure of uncertainty has a significant negative effect of consumption. The sign and the magnitude of the impulse responses of consumption to uncertainty shocks are sensitive to the data sample and the measure of uncertainty used in the estimation. The most robust results occur with the measure of business uncertainty, recently constructed in (Bachmann et al., 2013). This measure is further used in a multivariate VAR model. The negative effects of uncertainty shocks on consumption remain present in a multivariate system. This result is robust to various identification assumptions on the ordering of the variables.

Consistent with the previous research, this Chapter finds modest contributions of uncertainty shocks to explaining historical variability of U.S. aggregate consumption. Despite this finding, uncertainty shocks can still play an important role during specific episodes.A historical decomposition of economic series in a multivariate VAR illustrates that uncertainty shocks have had a significant impact on the path of consumption during the period from 2008 to 2011. Two other episodes are worth mentioning. With the use of different econometric techniques, it has been argued in (Romer, 1990) that decisions of consumers to postpone purchases of durables goods in response to increased uncertainty were critical for the onset of the U.S. Great Depression. A consumption shock, possibly driven by the uncertainty surrounding the Gulf War I, has been emphasized as a likely origin of the 1990-1991 recession in (Blanchard, 1993).

Data Description

This section of the Chapter describes measures of uncertainty and consumption, used in the empirical analysis.

Measuring Consumption

Consumption is measured by the real private consumption expenditures, divided by the noninstitutional population aged 16 and over. The consumption series is from the Bureau of Economic Analysis (BEA), expressed in 2005 chained dollars. The population series is from the FRED data base of St. Louis Fed (label CNP16OV). The data are monthly, from 1962:07 to 2013:03.

Figure 1 plots the level of real personal consumption (per capita). The shaded areas in the figure represent the official dates of the U.S. recessions, as dated by the National Bureau of Economic Research (NBER). Over the sample period, the U.S. economy experienced seven recessions. Figure 1 illustrates that consumption usually declines during recessions. Yet, the period of the Great Recession, defined from 2007:12 until 2009:06 stands out. The magnitude of consumption decline is the most severe and its duration is the most persistent over a 50-year period. The pattern of consumption in the latest recession is in sharp contrast with other historical episodes. As documented in (De Nardi et al., 2012, p.3) "consumption either fell only modestly or increased following the peak" during all previous recessions.

Figure 2 demonstrates that consumers' behavior contributed significantly to the severity of the Great Recession and the subsequent slow recovery, at the very least from an accounting point of view. This figure plots the percentage change in real gross domestic product and consumption contribution to this percentage change.

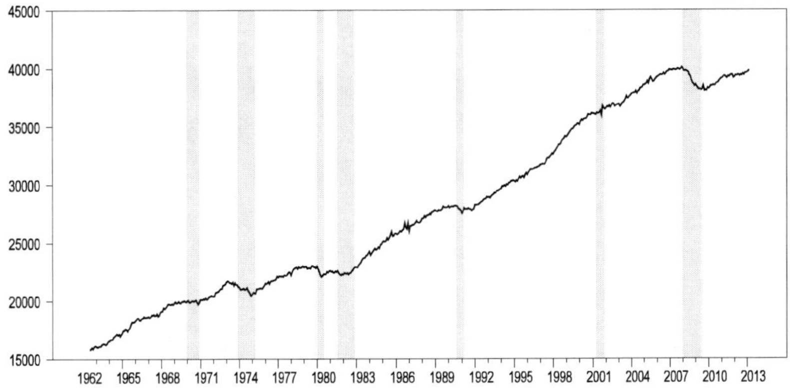

Notes: The shaded areas represent the NBER recessions.

Figure 1. Level of real personal consumption expenditures.

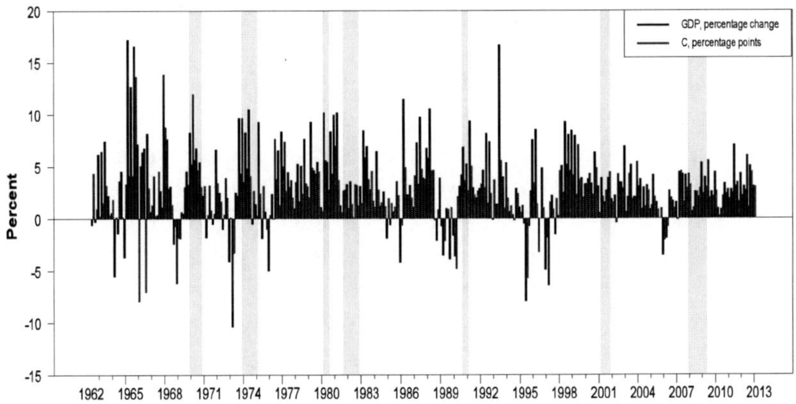

Notes: The black bars represent percentage change at annual rate of real GDP. The other bars are contributions of personal consumption expenditures to percentage change in real GDP (in percentage points at annual rate). The series are from Table 1.1.2 of Bureau of Economic Analysis. The shaded areas represent recessions as dated by the NBER.

Figure 2. Contribution of consumption to percentage change in real GDP.

The series in Figure 2 are quarterly, from table 1.1.2 of the BEA. One of the goals of this Chapter is to understand whether the unusual pattern of consumption during the Great Recession can be attributed to the increased economic uncertainty.

Measuring Uncertainty

Time-varying uncertainty can take different dimensions. From a perspective of consumers, it is the uncertainty about individual future income that should matter the most. "Greater uncertainty could simultaneously raise the likelihood that an individual may lose a job, resulting in lower near-term income prospects, or find a better job, resulting in higher income prospects" (Knotek and Khan, 2011, p. 65). Faced with the uncertain future income distribution, a consumer may prefer to wait until the uncertainty is resolved, to avoid purchases that are too luxurious or too frugal relative to the actual income. This Chapter focuses on the implications of the aggregate uncertainty on consumers' behavior. The underlying assumption is that the perceptions of income uncertainty of consumers are positively related to aggregate uncertainty.

Measuring unobserved uncertainty is an inherently difficult task. Several approaches have been proposed in the literature. The resulting proxies for uncertainty can be based on the realized volatility of economic series, the information from consumer or business surveys, interest rate spreads and reports in the media. The measures used in this Chapter can be grouped into three categories: (i) economy-wide measures of uncertainty, (ii) consumers' perceived uncertainty and (iii) business-related uncertainty. Each of these proxies has been found useful in explaining some aspects of aggregate behavior.

Economy-Wide Measures of Uncertainty

Stock market volatility (STVOL). The volatility of the stock market has been a traditional measure of uncertainty. The variable STVOL is the stock market volatility constructed in (Bloom, 2009) and updated to 2012:07. This measure is the actual volatility of the return on S&P500 index until 1990, and the implied volatility from VXO after. Prior to September 22, 2003, the index was known as "VIX." Many papers in the literature continue referring to this series by that name.[2] Extreme movements in stock prices can generate temporary uncertainty about future income for two reasons. First, fluctuations in stock prices make future incomes of stockholders to be more uncertain. Second, the stock market is an imperfect leading indicator of the real economy. Thus, unusual movement in stock prices can be associated with greater uncertainty about consumers' predictions of future income.

News based measure of uncertainty (GOOGLE). The Google News index of uncertainty is constructed in (Baker, Bloom and Davis, 2013). This measure is based on the count of "the articles in a given month mentioning "uncertainty" and phrases related to the economy" and divided "by a backward-looking moving average of the number of articles containing the word "today" to account for the overall increasing volume of news" (Bachmann et al., 2013, p. 229). The measure is taken from the replication data set provided for (Bachmann et al., 2013). As explained in (Bachmann et al., 2013), this measure is similar to the *New York Times* index of uncertainty in (Alexopoulos and Cohen, 2009).

Index of policy uncertainty (BBD). The index of policy uncertainty is from (Baker, Bloom and Davis, 2013). This index is based on three components: "(i) the frequency of references to economic uncertainty and policy in a set of 10 leading newspapers; (ii) the number of federal tax code provisions set to expire in future years; and (iii) the extent of

---

[2]See the information on http://www.cboe.com/micro/vxo/.

disagreement among economic forecasters over future federal government purchases and the future CPI price level."

Consumers' Perceived Uncertainty

In (Leduc and Liu, 2012a), measures of uncertainty are constructed from the survey of consumers conducted monthly by the University of Michigan.[3] The survey covers about 500 households in the U.S. since 1978. Consumers are asked to express their opinions about past, current and future economic conditions. There are three indices in the consumer survey that act as proxies for consumers' perceptions of uncertainty. The indices are equal to the fraction of respondents who choose "bad times ahead; uncertain future" in response to the following questions:

1. "About the big things people buy for their homes -- such as furniture, a refrigerator, stove, television, and things like that. Generally speaking, do you think now is a good time or a bad time for people to buy major household items? Why do you say so?" (Table 22)
2. "Generally speaking, do you think now is a good time or a bad time to buy a house?" "Why do you say so?" (Table 24)
3. "Speaking now of the automobile market -- do you think the next 12 months or so will be a good time or a bad time to buy a vehicle, such as a car, pickup, van, or sport utility vehicle? Why do you say so?" (Table 26)

The resulting measures are denoted by UDUR, UHOUSE and UAUTO in this Chapter. These measures represent consumers' perceptions of uncertainty in general, as the survey questions are not related to any specific form of uncertainty. Despite a relatively small number of respondents in the Michigan survey, the resulting series are weighted by age, income, region, and sex to be nationally representative.

Business-Related Uncertainty

The use of business-related measures uncertainty in examining consumers' behavior is useful if consumers and firms share their beliefs, if business opinions are an important input in forming consumers' views or if business forecasters reflect the perceptions of consumers' intentions.

Spreads. The variable SPREAD is the monthly spread of the 30-year Baa-rated corporate bond yield index over the 30-year treasury bond yield, taken from (Bachmann et al., 2013).GZSPR is the "GZ credit spread" defined as the average (cross-sectional) credit spread on senior unsecured corporate bonds issued by nonfinancial firms (in percentage points). The construction of this measure is described in (Gilchrist and Zakrajsek, 2012). The measure EBP is the excess bond premium (in percentage terms), taken from (Gilchrist and Zakrajsek, 2012).

Business forecast dispersion. The monthly series from the Federal Reserve Bank of Philadelphia's Business Outlook Survey are used in (Bachmann et al., 2013) to construct time-varying business-level uncertainty. The survey comprises the responses of 100 to 125 large manufacturing firms in the Third Fed district (Delaware, the southern half of New Jersey, and the eastern Pennsylvania). The survey is aimed at a relatively homogenous group

[3] http://www.sca.isr.umich.edu.

of firms, albeit the size of the respondents is small. The measure of uncertainty FDISP is constructed as cross sectional forecast dispersion, based on the answers to the questions about expected business conditions, and current shipments. The questions are as follows:

- Q3 "General Business Conditions: What is your evaluation of the level of general business activity six months from now versus [CURRENT MONTH]: decrease, no change, increase?"
- Q4 "Company Business Indicators: Shipments six months from now versus [CURRENT MONTH]: decrease, no change, increase?"

The sample is from 1969:05 to 2011:12. It is argued in (Bachmann et al., 2013) that the forecast dispersion provides a relatively good proxy for business-level uncertainty. Furthermore, surprise increases in uncertainty captured by the measure of forecast dispersion have significant and persistent effects on the U.S. economic activity. The analysis in (Bachmann et al., 2013, however, abstracts from possible effects of uncertainty shocks on consumption.

Time Series Properties of the Data

Figure 3 plots the time series of the ten measures of uncertainty used in this Chapter. The uncertainty measures are computed using different methodologies, and their measurement scales are rather different.

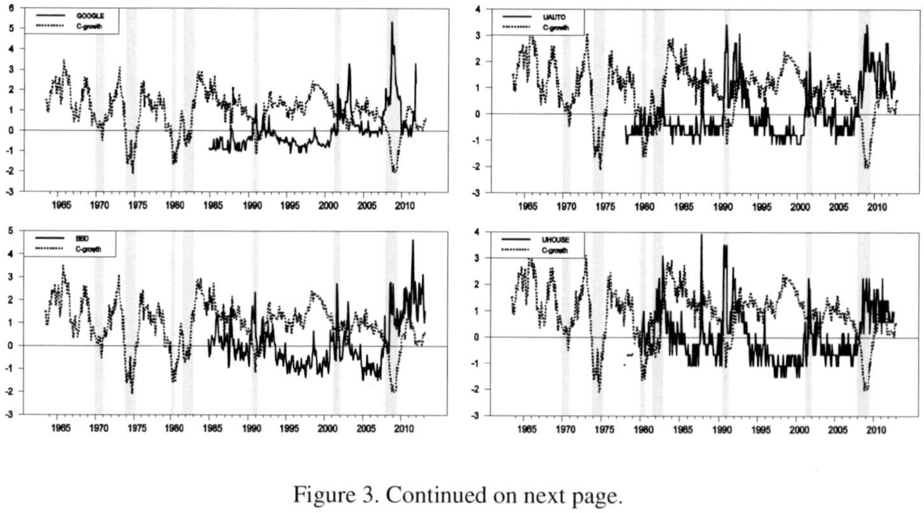

Figure 3. Continued on next page.

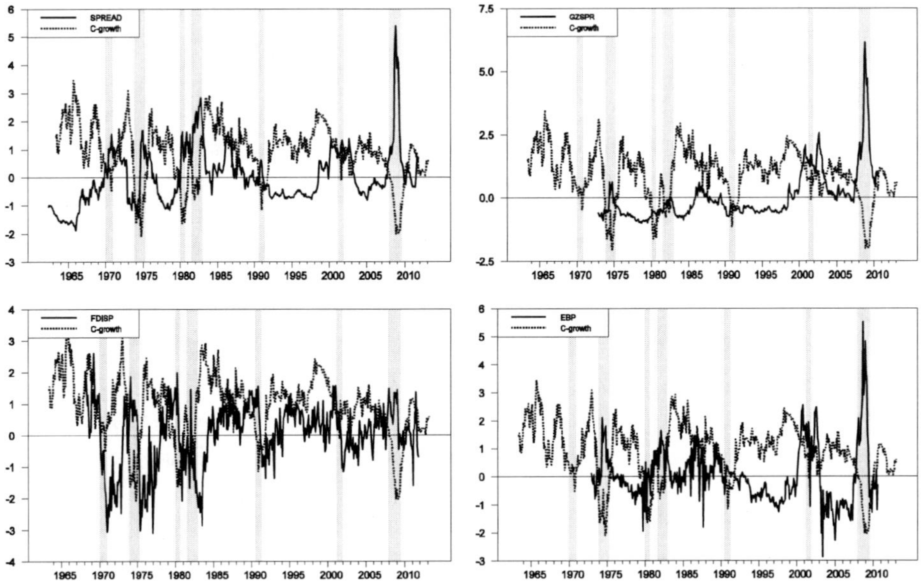

Notes: Measures of uncertainty are described in the text. Each measure of uncertainty has been demeaned and divided by its standard deviation. Consumption growth (C-growth) is computed from the previous year, as the log-difference between the real per capita consumption in the current month and its value 12 months ago. For comparability with the uncertainty measures, the resulting series is multiplied by 50. The shaded areas represent recessions as dated by the NBER.

Figure 3. Uncertainty measures and consumption growth.

Table 1. Descriptive data analysis

Uncertainty measure	Full data sample	Volatility	Auto-corr.	Correlation with C-growth over the following sample		
				Benchmark	Latest	Full
STVOL	1962:07-2012:07	0.37	0.85	-0.01	-0.34	-0.38
GOOGLE	1985:01-2011:12	0.64	0.91	-0.46	-0.72	-0.72
BBD	1985:01-2013:03	0.31	0.86	-0.24	-0.43	-0.43
UDUR	1978:01-2012:10	0.89	0.93	-0.49	-0.70	-0.57
UAUTO	1978:01-2012:10	0.85	0.85	-0.48	-0.62	-0.48
UHOUSE	1978:01-2012:10	0.64	0.74	-0.42	-0.51	-0.39
SPREAD	1962:07-2011:12	0.40	0.97	-0.01	-0.49	-0.45
GZSPR	1973:01-2010:09	0.65	0.98	-0.10	-0.58	-0.39
EBP	1973:01-2010:09	0.50	0.83	-0.09	-0.39	-0.35
FDISP	1968:05-2011:12	0.15	0.84	0.05	-0.03	-0.14

Notes: Uncertainty measures are described in the text. "Volatility" is the coefficient of variation, computed over the full sample. The only exception is the EBP measure, for which standard deviation is reported (since the series takes negative values). "Autocorr" reports the first order autocorrelation. Consumption growth (C-growth) is computed from the previous year, as the log-difference between the real per capita in the current month and its value 12 months ago. The "Benchmark" sample is 1985:01-2007:07. The "Latest" sample starts in 1985:01, and goes until the latest data observation available for the series.

To facilitate a graphical comparison, each measure of uncertainty is demeaned and normalized by its standard deviation over the full sample of available observations. Each panel of Figure 3 plots a separate measure of uncertainty (the solid lines).

It also superimposes the growth rate of consumption from the previous year, C-growth (the dashed lines). The latter series is computed as the log-difference between real per capita consumption in the current month and its value 12 months ago. For comparability with the uncertainty measures, the resulting consumption growth series is multiplied by 50. The shaded areas represent the NBER recessions. Table 1 complements the graphical representation of the time series. It reports volatility, autocorrelations and the coefficients of correlation with consumption growth, for different time periods.

Several observations can be made about the time series. First, all uncertainty measures tend to be countercyclical. That is, they tend to rise during economic recessions and fall during expansions. Second, the spikes in uncertainty measures during the 2007-2009 recession are high by historical standards. October and November 2008 are the two months when eight out of ten uncertainty measures reached their peaks. The remaining two measures, FDISP and UAUTO, took their second highest values during the Great Recession.[4]

Third, the uncertainty series generally exhibit similar properties: all measures are countercyclical, rather volatile and highly correlated over time. However, they do not always react to the same events. Interesting differences exist between consumers' and business perceptions of uncertainty. The case of the 1990-1991 recession deserves particular attention. During that episode, consumers' perceptions of uncertainty surged. Many more respondents named uncertain future as a reason that influenced consumption decisions with respect to buying large durables goods (UDUR), vehicles (UAUTO) and houses (UHOUSE). Consumers' perceptions of uncertainty were much stronger relative to the other measures of uncertainty. In fact, business-related measures and the stock market volatility were actually falling during the 1990-1991 recession. One of the likely reasons for changes in consumers' perceptions was the uncertainty surrounding the implications of the Gulf War I. Consumers' attitudes and a consumption-related shock have been identified as a possible cause of the 1990-1991 recession in (Blanchard, 1993). The differences between the FDISP, GOOGLE, BBD and SPREAD measures are discussed in detail in (Bachmann et al., 2013).

A casual observation from Figure 3 suggests that consumption growth and uncertainty measures are negatively related. This observation is confirmed by formal statistics in Table 1. In the full sample for each uncertainty measure (that is, over the total time periods of available observations), all uncertainty measures are negatively correlated with consumption growth. There is some sensitivity of unconditional correlations between uncertainty measures and consumption growth to the data sample. Correlations are generally weaker for the benchmark sample from 1985:01 to 2007:06, than for the full sample. The first period of the benchmark sample is chosen to be consistent with the break in the volatility of the most U.S. series. The last period is chosen to exclude the period of the Great Recession. According to the NBER, the business cycle peak was reached in 2007:12. The financial tribulations related to the 2007-2009 financial crisis started in 2007:09. Furthermore, empirical research has identified a structural change in the responses of consumption to a shock to the stock market volatility around 1984 (Beetsma and Giuliodori, 2012).

[4] During 2007-2009, the FDISP and UATO reached their peaks in 2008:02 and 2009:02.

The column “Latest” in Table 3 reports correlations coefficients between uncertainty measures and consumption growth for the period that extends the benchmark sample to the latest observations for each uncertainty measure. For example, the latest sample for the STVOL measure is from 1985:01 to 2012:07. Since all uncertainty measures spike during the Great Recession, comparing the correlations over the samples that include and exclude this period, provides some information on the interactions between uncertainty and economic activity historically and in the recent periods. For all the measures, the correlation with consumption growth becomes much stronger relative to the benchmark sample that ends in 2007:06.

Different measures of uncertainty may capture general economic uncertainty or different aspects of uncertainty to a various degree. One way to assess the comovement between these measures is to use correlation coefficients. Table 2 reports unconditional cross-correlations of the uncertainty measures, computed over the common sample period, from 1985:01 to 2010:09. All uncertainty measures are positively correlated, with an exception of the measure of business forecast dispersion FDISP with consumers’ perceptions of uncertainty and the news-based economic uncertainty index GOOGLE. FDISP is positively correlated with the stock market volatility STVOL, and with the other business-related uncertainty measures.

After analyzing several measures of uncertainty, (Bachmann et al., 2013, p. 231) conclude: “None of the uncertainty proxies are a perfect measure of a multidimensional and complex phenomenon, but it is apparent that all of them can potentially contribute to our understanding of the effects of uncertainty on economic activity.” Following their insight, this Chapter uses ten measures of uncertainty to establish a relation between uncertainty and consumption. From the discussion of the time series properties of the economic series, one can expect that the effects of uncertainty shocks may depend on the measure of uncertainty used, as well as on the time period studied.

Comovement between Uncertainty Measures and Consumption

This section establishes the comovement patterns between uncertainty measures and consumption following a method developed in (den Haan, 2000). The method is based on a VAR that includes aggregate consumption and a meausure of uncertainty. The comovement statistics corresponds to a correlation between forecast errors for consumption and the uncertainty measure at different forecast horizons.

The method has two main advantages. First, it does not require a transformation of the data to induce stationarity. The only requirement is the absence of a serial correlation in the VAR residuals. Second, the method provides means to analyze the comovement at different frequencies.

This Chapter relies on bivariate VARs to establish the comovement. The bivariate models provide parsimonious ways of modeling the joint dynamics of uncertainty and consumption. All bivariate VARs are estimated with 12 lags, a constant and a linear trend. Consumption series is included in levels. The benchmark estimation period is 1985:01-2007:07.

Table 2. Correlations between uncertainty measures, 1985:01-2010:09

	STVOL	GOOGLE	BBD	UDUR	UAUTO	UHOUSE	SPREAD	GZSPR	EBP	FDISP
STVOL	1.00	0.58	0.54	0.35	0.31	0.26	0.76	0.71	0.62	0.20
GOOGLE	0.58	1.00	0.60	0.76	0.67	0.49	0.63	0.80	0.47	-0.06
BBD	0.54	0.60	1.00	0.67	0.66	0.66	0.52	0.47	0.50	0.05
UDUR	0.35	0.76	0.67	1.00	0.93	0.78	0.42	0.53	0.38	-0.18
UAUTO	0.31	0.67	0.66	0.93	1.00	0.83	0.32	0.40	0.30	-0.13
UHOUSE	0.26	0.49	0.66	0.78	0.83	1.00	0.26	0.23	0.27	-0.11
SPREAD	0.76	0.63	0.52	0.42	0.32	0.26	1.00	0.87	0.79	0.23
GZSPR	0.71	0.80	0.47	0.53	0.40	0.23	0.87	1.00	0.71	0.08
EBP	0.62	0.47	0.50	0.38	0.30	0.27	0.79	0.71	1.00	0.26
FDISP	0.20	-0.06	0.05	-0.18	-0.13	-0.11	0.23	0.08	0.26	1.00

Notes: The table reports the cross-correlation of the various uncertainty measures, computed over the common sample period from 1985:01 to 2010:09.

Table 3. Consumption forecast variance due to uncertainty: bivariate models (in percent)

A. Sample: 1985:01-2011:12

Horizon	STVOL	GOOGLE	BBD	UDUR	UAUTO	UHOUSE	SPREAD	GZSPR*	EBP*	FDISP
$h = 1$	3.19	9.26	4.38	2.19	5.97	2.39	4.50	3.75	2.90	2.61
$h = 12$	7.33	15.63	8.69	5.97	5.61	2.93	14.01	15.87	18.78	12.19
$h = 36$	3.26	13.36	11.72	4.73	4.63	2.60	16.18	17.56	25.97	24.38
$h = 60$	1.91	12.57	15.00	3.94	4.22	2.63	13.27	14.61	28.43	28.94

B. Sample: 1985:01-2007:7

Horizon	STVOL	GOOGLE	BBD	UDUR	UAUTO	UHOUSE	SPREAD	GZSPR	EBP	FDISP
$h = 1$	1.59	8.43	4.72	1.92	6.91	3.36	0.39	1.15	0.38	1.53
$h = 12$	1.63	3.41	2.70	1.92	5.95	4.38	2.03	0.75	2.73	6.23
$h = 36$	13.76	3.55	1.16	2.59	9.57	9.38	7.09	4.30	1.79	12.27
$h = 60$	23.61	5.22	1.06	4.90	13.89	13.39	10.54	8.16	1.57	13.74

Notes: Each column corresponds to a bivariate VAR that includes a measure of uncertainty and the log real per capita consumption. The models are estimated with 12 lags, a constant and a linear trend. Consumption is included in levels. The star * indicates the sample 1985:01 – 2010:09. The table reports the percent of the total forecast error variance of consumption due to innovations in uncertainty. Uncertainty shocks are identified through a recursive ordering, with the uncertainty series listed first in the VAR.

Figure 4 reports the estimated correlations. The solid lines are point estimates of the correlations between the forecast errors for consumption and the uncertainty measure, which appears in the title of each panel of Figure 4. The correlations are reported for the time horizon from one to sixty months (five-years). The shaded ares are the bootstrap 95% confidence intervals, computed using 2500 iterations. The thick lines with dots plot the estimated correlations between the forecast errors over the latest sample. Recall that in this case the sample period includes the Great Recession. The estimation starts in 1985:1 and runs until the latest period of available data observations for the corresponding measure of uncertainty. For three measures, STVOL, SPREAD and FDISP, which go back to 1960s, Figure 4 also reports the estimated correlations for the full sample (the dashed lines). The dynamics for the GZSPR are very similar to the ones for the SPREAD measure. Thus, the GZSPR series is omitted from Figure 4 for the ease of the presentation of the results.

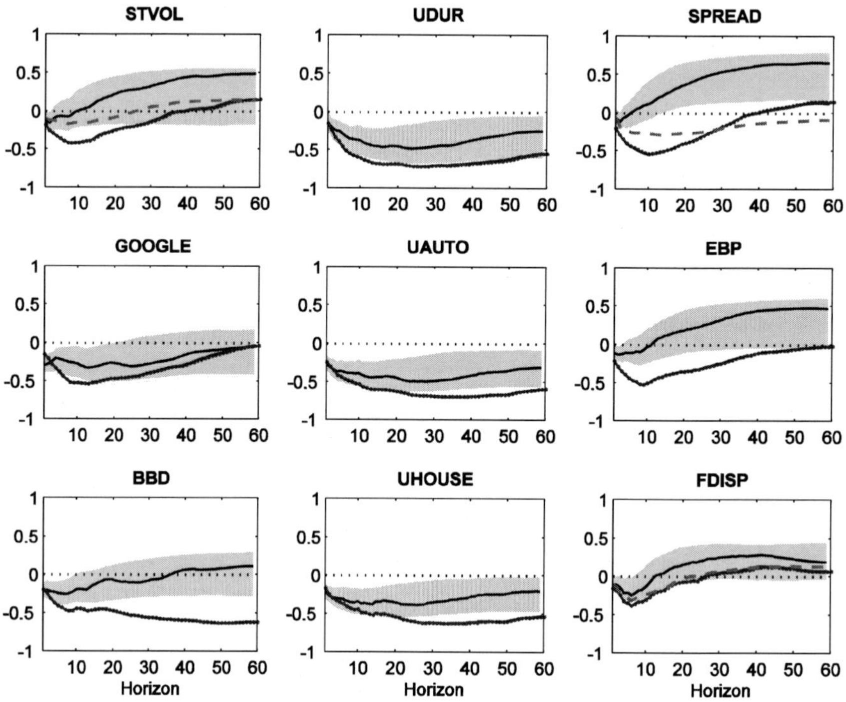

Notes: The solid lines are point estimates of the correlations between forecast errors for uncertainty measure and consumption for various forecast horizon, based on a bivariate VAR that include a measure of uncertainty (indicated in the title) and consumption. The shaded areas are the bootstrap 95% confidence intervals, computed using 2500 iterations. The thick lines with dots plot the estimated correlations between the forecast errors over the latest sample. The dashed lines represent estimates for the full sample.

Figure 4. Correlation between forecast errors of an uncertainty measure and consumption (bivariate VARs).

The results can be summarized as follows. First, there is a significant negative comovement between consumption and all uncertainty measures in the very short run (from one to two months) in the benchmark sample. That is, a surprise increase in uncertainty is associated with a decline in consumption. Second, in the benchmark case, the comovement at longer frequency depends on the measure of uncertainty. Consumers' perceptions of uncertainty (UDUR, UAUTO and UHOUHSE) comove negatively with consumption at all frequencies examined. The comovement is significant for the broad uncertainty measures GOOGLE and BBD up to one year, and significant with the STVOL measure only from one to two months. For the business-related uncertainty measures, the estimated correlations coefficients turn positive, at least after one year. They are statistically significant for the SPREAD measure. The comovement dynamics (negative in the short run, positive in the long run) may be consistent with the "wait-and-see" effects of the option value theory.

Third, the dynamic comovement between consumption and uncertainty measures is significantly affected by the inclusion of the Great Recession. Consistent with the results from the unconditional correlations reported in Table 1, the negative comovement between consumption and uncertainty measures becomes stronger. The estimated correlations become more negative and remain negative for longer forecasting horizons. For the STVOL, SPREAD, EBP and BBD measures, the pattern of dynamic comovement changes the shape, with the BBD measure of economic policy uncertainty being affected the most.

Fourth, the results for the longer samples, based on the stock market measure STVOL and on the measure of corporate spread SPREAD show large differences in the patterns of dynamic correlations. This finding is consistent with the results in (Beetsma and Giuliodori, 2012). Using a method of rolling regressions, Beetsma and Giuliodori have established a structural change in how various measures of consumption responded to an increase in the stock market volatility. Finally, the GOOGLE and the FDISP measures provide the most consistent patterns of dynamic comovement with consumption.

Evidence from Structural VARs

This section uses recursive VARs to estimate the effects of uncertainty shocks on consumption and to evaluate their quantitative importance. Previous research has shown that the effects of uncertainty shocks may be sensitive to the number of variables included into the VARs. For example, impulses responses of consumption to uncertainty shocks become statistically insignificant in multivariate specifications in (Knotek and Khan, 2011). This section reports the results from both the bivariate and multivariate VAR systems.

Results from Bivariate Models

Following the literature on uncertainty shocks, exemplified in (Bloom, 2009), an uncertainty shock is identified as an orthogonalized shock to a measure of uncertainty included in a VAR, using the Cholesky factorization of the variance-covariance matrix of VAR residuals. Since the identification results may depend on the ordering of the variables in the VAR, this section reports the results of two identification schemes. In the first scheme, the uncertainty measure is ordered first. Thus, uncertainty shocks are the only shocks that affect the uncertainty measure on impact. In the second identification scheme, the uncertainty is ordered last. Thus, it is assumed that consumption does not respond to uncertainty shocks in the initial period of the shock.

The bivariate VARs are estimated over the main sample from 1985:01 to 2011:12. The only exception is the GZSPR and EBP measures. The data for these two series end in 2010:09. To evaluate the impact of the Great Recession on the estimation results, the VARs are also estimated over the sample from 1985:01 to 2007:07. All specifications include the level of consumption, and are based on 12 lags and a constant.

Dynamic Effects of Uncertainty Shocks

Figure 5 reports the impulse responses of consumption, following one standard deviation increase in uncertainty. The solid lines are the point estimates for the VAR that orders the uncertainty measure first. The shaded areas represent the 95% confidence bands. The dotted lines are the impulse responses from the VAR estimated over the same period, when the uncertainty measure is included last. The dashed lines are the impulse responses from the VAR that lists the uncertainty measure first, but estimated over the sample that excludes the Great Recession.

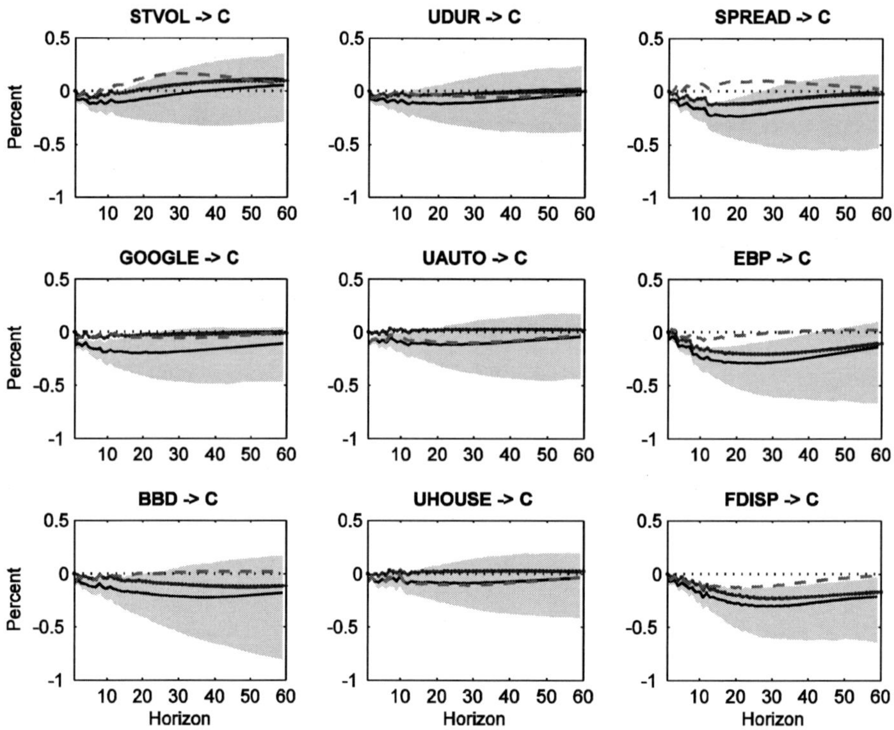

Notes: The impulse responses are based on bivariate VARs that include a measure of uncertainty and consumption (in levels). The sample is 1985:01-2010:09 for the EBP measure, and 1985:01-2011:12 for all other measures. The solid lines are the point estimates for the VAR that orders the uncertainty measure first. The shaded areas represent the 95% confidence bands. The dotted lines are the impulse responses from the VAR estimated over the same period, when the uncertainty measure is included last in the VAR. The dashed lines are the impulse response from the VAR that lists the uncertainty measure first, but estimated over the benchmark sample that excludes the Great Recession (1985:01-2007:07).

Figure 5. Impulse responses of consumption: bivariate models.

According to the option value theory of investment, a temporary increase in uncertainty can generate a bust-boom dynamics. An increase in uncertainty is expected to make consumers more cautious, as higher uncertainty increases probability of more extreme bad and good outcomes. Faced with the higher value of waiting, consumers are expected to postpone major purchases. When the uncertainty is resolved, the theory predicts a rebound of consumption and a possible overshooting of the original levels of consumption as consumers make up for the waiting period.

The results from the bivariate systems in Figure 5 indicate that consumption falls after an increase in uncertainty. The effects are protracted (typically last several months), but temporary (revert to zero and become insignificant over time). However, there is no evidence of consumption overshooting. Interestingly, the business-related measures of uncertainty have the largest and most significant impacts on consumption. The qualitative results are generally robust to changing the ordering of the variables in the VAR. As it was the case with the correlations between VAR forecast errors, the impulse responses of consumption to uncertainty shocks based on the SPREAD, EBP, BBD measures critically depend on whether the estimation period includes or excludes the Great Recession.

Historical Importance

It could be the case that even when the impulse responses of consumption to uncertainty shocks produce interesting and plausible dynamics, the importance of these shocks has been minimal historically. To judge the quantitative relevance of uncertainty shocks, Table 3 reports the percent variation in the forecast error variance of consumption due to these shocks. The statistics are reported for the samples that include and exclude the Great Recession. The results correspond to the VARs when the uncertainty measure is ordered first. Depending on the measure used and the time horizon, uncertainty shocks can account from 0.39 to 28.94 percent of the consumption forecast error variance. The largest contribution is made by the shocks to the FDISP-measure in the overall sample and to the STVOL-measure in the shorter sample.

Results from Multivariate Models

The bivariate VARs provide a parsimonious way to summarize dynamic relations between uncertainty measures and consumption. Yet, the structural analysis based on these systems restricts the number of unobserved shocks to only two. In reality, this is a very strong restriction on the number of structural disturbances. Consequently, the effects of uncertainty shocks from the bivariate models are likely be "contaminated" by the influences of other unobserved disturbances. Estimating larger VARs provides means to control for the effects of other possible shocks.

The results in this section are based on a VAR inspired by the specification used in (Bachmann et al., 2013). The system includes the log-level of the S&P 500 stock index, the logs of manufacturing production and manufacturing employment, the log of the aggregate consumer price index, the Federal Funds rate, the log of real per capita consumption, and a measure of uncertainty. All supplementary data for the VAR are from the replication file for (Bachmann et al., 2013), posted on the web-site of the "*American Economic Journal:*

Macroeconomics." The VARs are in levels, with 12 lags and a constant. The uncertainty shocks are identified by the recursive ordering, as in (Bachmann et al., 2013). In a base case scenario, the uncertainty measure is listed second, after the stock market prices. To check the robustness of the results, the impulse responses of consumption to uncertainty shocks are also estimated when the uncertainty measure is listed first and last in the VAR. Since this Chapter is interested in the effects of only uncertainty shocks, the ordering of the other variables in the VAR is not important.

The results in the previous sections have shown that the dispersion of business opinions, the FDISP measure of uncertainty, has the most robust relation with consumption. This section therefore reports the estimation results with the multivariate VAR for this measure. The VAR is estimated over the sample from 1968:05 to 2011:12. The robustness of the results is checked by reporting the estimates for the sample from 1968:05 to 2007:07.

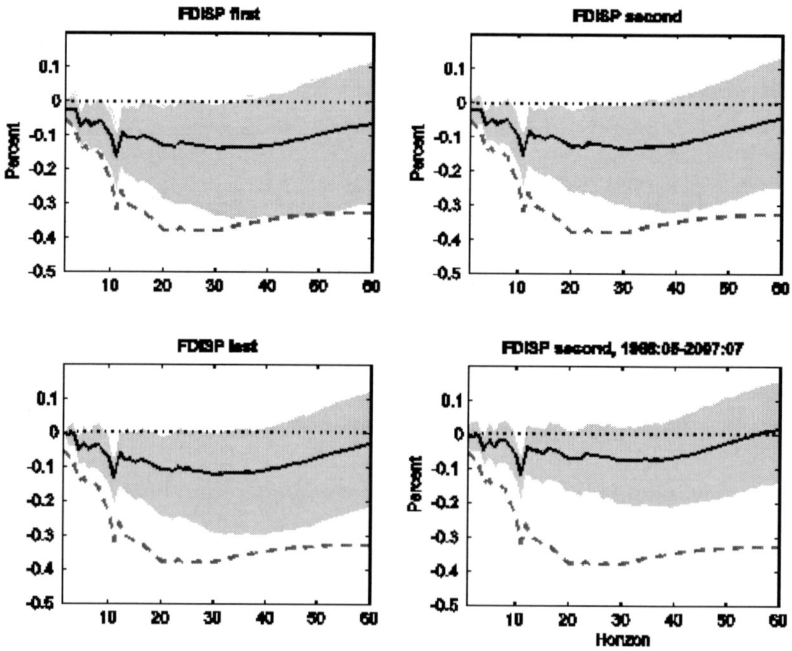

Notes: Unless indicated otherwise, the estimation sample is 1968:05-2011:12. The solid lines are the point estimates of the impulse responses. The shaded areas are the 95% confidence bootstrap bands. The dashed lines represent the impulse responses from the bivariate model for the full sample, with the uncertainty measure listed first. The title of each panel of the Figure indicates the position of the uncertainty measure FDISP in the seven-variable VAR. See the text for the description of the model.

Figure 6. Consumption impulse responses: multivariate models with FDISP.

Dynamic Effects of Uncertainty Shocks

Figure 6 reports the impulse responses of consumption to a one standard deviation uncertainty shock. The solid lines on the figure are the point estimates of the responses. The shaded areas are the 95% confidence bootstrap bands. The dashed lines represent the impulse responses from the bivariate model with consumption and the FDISP measure of uncertainty for the full sample, with the uncertainty measure listed first. The title of each panel of Figure6 indicates the position of the uncertainty measure FDISP in the seven-variable VAR. Figure 6 implies that the impulse responses of consumption are robust to the order of the uncertainty measure in the VAR. It should be noted that the estimated impulses responses of all other variables in the model are also robust across the specifications. Furthermore, the implied paths of the FDISP following an identified uncertainty are virtually identical across the specifications.

In multivariate VAR models, uncertainty shocks have negative effects on consumption. These effects accumulate over time and remain significant up to two or three years. The effects are temporary, as the impulses responses revert back to zero. Relative to the full sample, the results of the VAR model that ends in 2007:07 imply a faster reversion to the mean. Notably, the shape of the impulse responses in the bivariate models is rather different. In that specification, the uncertainty shock appears to have a long run effect on consumption. This difference suggests that in the bivariate models, uncertainty shocks are likely to pick up the effects of other structural disturbances.

Historical Importance

Table 4 reports the forecast error variance decomposition of consumption due to uncertainty shocks in the multivariate models with the FDISP measure of uncertainty. It is not a surprise that the contribution of the uncertainty shocks to explaining historical variation in consumption is diminished, relative to the statistics in Table 3 for the bivariate specifications. It is worth noting that the contributions of the uncertainty shocks are almost doubled at all horizons when the sample includes the 2007-2009 recession, as demonstrated by columns three and six of Table 4.

Uncertainty, Consumption and the Great Recession

The estimated impulse responses in Figure 7 imply that an increase in uncertainty has led to a fall in U.S. consumption, on average. The forecast variance decompositions in Table 4 indicate that uncertainty shocks have made a small contribution to explaining the consumption behavior. Still, it can be the case that a series of bad realizations of uncertainty shocks has been particularly important during a specific historical episode. Figure 7 illustrates that was indeed the case during the recovery after the Great Recession.

Table 4. Consumption forecast variance due to uncertainty: multivariate models with FDISP

Horizon	FDISP first	FDISP second	FDISP sixth	FDISP last	FDISP second 1968:01-2007:07
$h = 1$	0.40	0.25	0.00	0.00	0.04
$h = 12$	5.60	4.63	3.54	2.93	2.87
$h = 36$	7.97	7.23	5.95	5.19	3.88
$h = 60$	8.33	7.05	6.54	5.27	3.14

Notes: Unless specified otherwise, the estimation period is 1968:05-2011:12. Each column corresponds to a seven variable VAR, described in the text. The column's title indicates the place of the uncertainty measure in the model. The models are estimated with 12 lags and a constant. Consumption is included in levels. The star * indicates the sample 1985:01-2010:09. The table reports the percent of the total forecast error variance of consumption due to innovations in uncertainty.

Figure 7 is based on a historical decomposition of the variables included in the VAR, due to the uncertainty shocks. A historical decomposition breaks the historical values of a set of time series into a base projection and the accumulated effects of current and past innovations. It is a counterfactual experiment.

By construction, the observed U.S. series, such as consumption, is perfectly matched by the effects of the seven shocks in the seven-variable VAR. The baseline forecast shuts down all the shocks, starting in August 2008, and right before the collapse of Lehman Brothers in September 2008.

Figure 7 plots three lines for each series. The solid lines are the actual series. The long dashed lines are the base forecast. Starting in August 2008, the base forecast gives the paths of the variables in the absence of any shocks. The beginning of the forecast projection is chosen to precipitate the spikes in all measures of uncertainty in the fall 2008. The small dashed lines in Figure 7 indicate how the baseline forecast is modified by including the realized uncertainty shocks. The difference between the actual series and the base forecast is explained by the effects of the structural shocks in the model. The closer the modified forecast to the actual series, the more important the uncertainty shocks are.

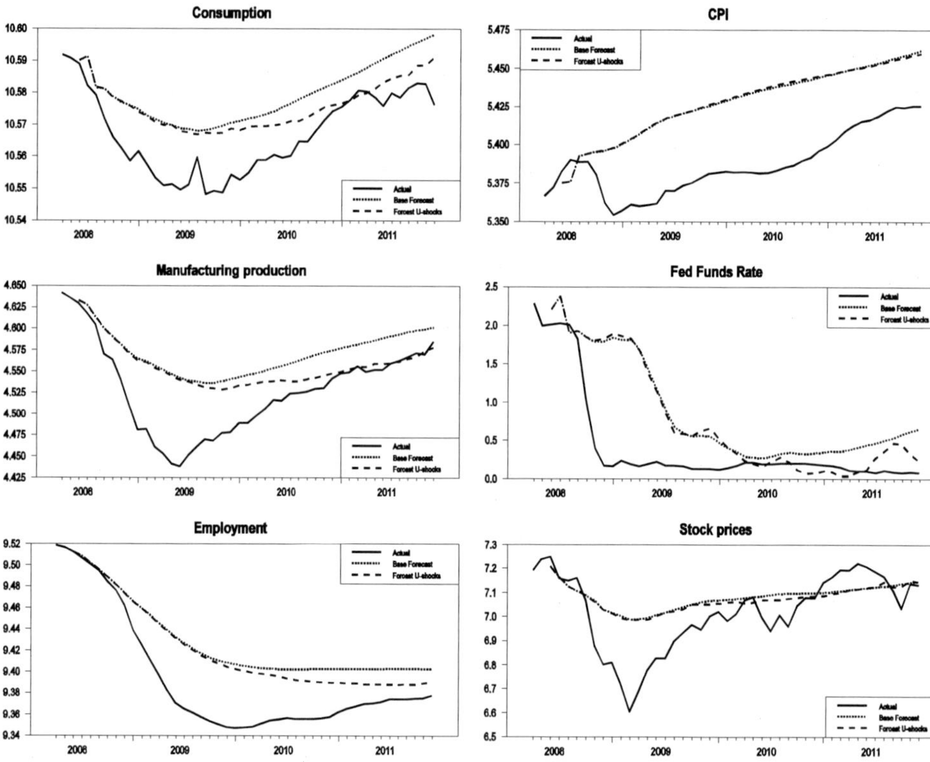

Notes: The solid lines are the actual series. The long dashed lines are base forecast. Starting in August 2008, the base forecast gives the paths of the variables in the absence of any shocks. The beginning of the forecast projection is chosen to precipitate the spikes in all measures of uncertainty in the fall 2008. The small dashed line indicates how the baseline forecast is modified by including the realized uncertainty shocks.

Figure 7. Effect of uncertainty shocks: a historical decomposition.

It is argued in (Romer, 1990) that the expectations of monetary policy and the actions of the newly created the Federal Reserve System were one reason contributing to uncertainty about future income at the onset of the Great Depression. In the case of the 2007-2009 recession, the Fed operated in the environment of unchartered waters. After a sharp decrease of the Federal Funds rate, the Fed effectively gave up its ability to stimulate the U.S. economy via a traditional interest rate channel. Unconventional policy measures, such as quantitative easing and conditional statements, were generally untested before. Thus, it is rather likely that the unconventional monetary policy was a part of the equation in increasing economic uncertainty.

The results of the historical decomposition in Figure 7 suggest that uncertainty shocks were important in explaining the slow pace of the recovery. The impulse response functions indicate that the effects of uncertainty shocks on consumption in the U.S. builds over time. Starting in mid-2009, the contribution of the uncertainty shocks to explaining the paths of the real economic variables increases. By mid-2012, about half of the distance between the actual values and the base forecast for consumption is explained by the effects of the uncertainty shocks.

These effects are especially strong for manufacturing production, and considerably strong for employment. The results echo the results in (Leduc and Liu, 2012a) regarding the effects of uncertainty shocks on unemployment. By contrast, the behavior of prices, both the consumer price index and the S&P500 stock market index, does not appear to be affected by the uncertainty shocks.

The historical decomposition in Figure 7 indicates that the uncertainty shocks may have been important in explaining why the Federal Reserve kept the interest rates at the low bound from mid-2010 to mid-2011. Concerns regarding economic uncertainty feature in the minutes of the Federal Reserve Committee (see citations in (Leduc and Liu, 2012b)). It is reassuring that the econometric results reflect these concerns as well. The results from the historical decomposition in Figure 7 are consistent with the findings in (Leduc and Liu, 2012a) and (Basu and Bundick, 2012). Using a VAR framework, Leduc and Liu have established that "uncertainty shocks accounted for at least one percentage point increases in unemployment in the Great Recession and recovery." Using a calibrated dynamic general equilibrium model, Basu and Bundick have found that the monetary policy amplified the effects of the uncertainty shocks on economic activity.

Conclusion

This Chapter examined the relation between aggregate consumption and several measures of uncertainty in the U.S. economy using different econometric techniques. Several broad lessons arise from the results.

First, U.S. consumption has a negative comovement with all measures of uncertainty in the short run. With some measures of uncertainty, consumption continue comove negatively even at the forecasting horizons over five years. Second, the dynamic relation between aggregate consumption and uncertainty has not been stable over time for many measures of uncertainty. The results are particularly sensitive to the inclusion of the Great Recession and the subsequent periods into the data sample. When the latter periods are taken into account in the estimation, the comovement between aggregate consumption and uncertainty becomes more negative. The instability of the relation between uncertainty measures and consumption creates challenges for policy-makers who need to forecast or influence consumption behavior, especially during the periods of heightened economic uncertainty. Fourth, there is very little evidence that a fall in consumption in response to an unexpected rise in uncertainty is followed by a subsequent rebound.

Finally, forecast error variance decompositions in VARs indicate that historical contributions of uncertainty shocks to explaining U.S. consumption have been modest. Despite this finding, uncertainty shocks can still play an important role during specific episodes. This Chapter found that increased uncertainty had a significant impact on aggregate consumption during the recent period of 2008-2011. The proposed historical decomposition of economic series in a multivariate VAR was consistent with a view that U.S. consumers, faced with the increased current and future uncertainty, held back their expenditures during the Great Recession and the recovery. The historical decomposition also suggested that uncertainty shocks gave one reason why the Federal Reserve kept the Federal Funds rate at low values for a prolonged period of time.

References

Alexopoulos, M., Cohen, J., (2009). Uncertain times, uncertain measures. *Working Papers*-352, University of Toronto, Department of Economics.

Bachmann, R., Elstner, S., Sims, E. R., (2013). Uncertainty and economic activity: Evidence from business survey data. *American Economic Journal: Macroeconomics* 5(2), 217–49.

Baker, S., Bloom, N., Davis, S., (2013).Measuring economic policy uncertainty. *Unpublished manuscript* 13-02, Chicago Booth Research Paper.

Basu, S., Bundick, B., (2012). Uncertainty shocks in a model of effective demand. *Working Paper* 18420, National Bureau of Economic Research.

Beetsma, R., Giuliodori, M., (2012). The changing macroeconomic response to stock market volatility shocks. *Journal of Macroeconomics* 34(2), 281–293.

Bernanke, B., (1983). Irreversibility, uncertainty, and cyclical investment. The *Quarterly Journal of Economics* 98(1), 85–106.

Blanchard, O., (1993). Consumption and the recession of 1990-1991.*American Economic Review* 83 (2), 270–74.

Bloom, N., (2009). The impact of uncertainty shocks. *Econometrica* 77(3), 623–685.

Bloom, N., Fernandez-Villaverde, J., Scheider, M., (2013). The macroeconomics of time varying volatility and uncertainty. *Journal of Economic Literature* forthcoming.

De Nardi, M., French, E., Benson, D., (2012). Consumption and the Great Recession. *Economic Perspectives* (Q I), 1–16.

denHaan, W., (2000). The comovement between output and prices. *Journal of Monetary Economics* 46(1), 3–30.

Dixit, A., Pindyck, R., (1994). *Investment under uncertainty*. Princeton, New Jersey: Princeton University Press.

Gilchrist, S., Zakrajsek, E., (2012).Credit spreads and business cycle fluctuations. *American Economic Review* 102(4), 1692–1720.

Knotek, E., Khan, S., (2011). How do households respond to uncertainty shocks? *Economic Review* (Q II).

Leduc, S., Liu, Z., (2012a). Uncertainty shocks are aggregate demand shocks. Federal Reserve Bank of San Francisco, *Working Paper series*, 2012-10.

Leduc, S, Liu, Z., (2012b). Uncertainty, unemployment, and inflation. *FRBSF Economic Letter* (September 17).

Mody, A., Ohnsorge, F., Sandri, D., (2012).Precautionary savings in the Great Recession. *IMF Economic Review* 60(1), 114–138.

Romer, C., (1990).The Great Crash and the onset of the Great Depression. *Quarterly Journal of Economics* 105(3), 597–624.

In: Business Cycles in Economics
Editor: Jason C. Hsu

ISBN: 978-1-63321-322-7

Chapter 12

ENDOGENOUS MONEY OR STICKY WAGES: A BAYESIAN APPROACH

Guangling Liu[*]
Department of Economics, University of Stellenbosch,
Stellenbosch, South Africa

Abstract

This paper attempts to answer question similar to that asked by Ireland (2003): What explains the correlations between nominal and real variables in the postwar US data? More precisely, this paper aims to investigate whether endogenous money, sticky wages, or some combination of the two, are necessary features in a dynamic New Keynesian model in explaining the correlations between nominal and real variables in the postwar US data. To do so, we develop a medium-scale dynamic stochastic general equilibrium model of endogenous money. The model is estimated using Bayesian maximum likelihood and compared with a restricted version of the structural model, in which wages are flexible. The empirical results suggest that the sticky-wage model with endogenous money well replicates the correlations between real balances and inflation, and real balances and the nominal interest rate; both sticky prices and sticky wages are necessary features to match the persistence of real wages; sticky prices play an important role in replicating the persistence of inflation and the additional of sticky wages improves the fit for the behavior of inflation persistence; the wage markup shock plays a prominent role in explaining the variation of both nominal and real variables. We conclude that both endogenous money and sticky wages are necessary features in a dynamic New Keynesian model in explaining the variation in the key macroeconomic variables, both nominal and real.

Keywords: Endogenous money, Sticky wages, New Keynesian model, Bayesian analysis

Subject Classification: E31, E32, E52

---

[*]E-mail address: davegliu@gmail.com

[†]I would like to thank Peter Ireland for helpful comments. Financial support from Economic Research Southern Africa (ERSA) is greatly acknowledged. The usual disclaimer applies.

1. Introduction

In a classical model economy, real variables are independent of monetary policy. However, monetary policy plays an important role in explaining the behavior of nominal variables, such as prices. As pointed out by Ireland (2003), under a Taylor-type interest rate rule, money supply and nominal interest rate become endogenous, at least most if not all, and the effects of changes in monetary policy can be interpreted plausibly as how nominal variables respond to real variables, not the other way around [1]. On the other hand, nominal rigidities provide a channel through which nominal variables drive movements in real variables. Ireland (2003) uses maximum likelihood to estimate a structural model of endogenous money with Rotemberg-type (quadratic costs) sticky prices (Rotemberg, 1982), and suggests that the nominal price rigidity, over and above endogenous money, plays a role in accounting for the key features of the postwar US data.

Recently, the New Keynesian model with both Calvo-type sticky prices and sticky wages (Erceg et al., 2000) has become the framework in the literature in monetary policy analysis (e.g., Giannoni & Woodford, 2003). The model has also been used in studying the persistence of effects of monetary policy shocks. For instance, both studies by Huang & Liu (2002) and Christiano et al. (2005) suggest that it is the sticky wages, not sticky prices, which play an important role in generating the observed inertia in inflation and persistent output movements in response to a monetary policy shock. Empirical results from Rabanal & Rubio-Ramirez (2005) show that models with both sticky wages and sticky prices dominate models with sticky prices only in explaining the US data. Matheron & Poilly (2009) also argue that the combination of sticky prices and sticky wages is central in order to obtain a good empirical fit of the model.

We view our paper as an extension to Ireland (2003) and a complement to Rabanal & Rubio-Ramirez (2005) and Matheron & Poilly (2009). We augment a medium-scale dynamic stochastic general equilibrium model with real balances, in which money becomes an argument in the utility function. In addition, we assume that the monetary authority follows an augmented Taylor-type interest rate rule, in which the short-term nominal interest rate is adjusted in response to the deviation of real money growth rate as well[2]. In doing so, the monetary policy rule provides a channel through which changes in real variables drive movements in nominal variables (Ireland, 2003). The paper is to investigate whether a dynamic New Keynesian model without nominal wage rigidities, but with an augmented Taylor-type interest rate rule, is capable of explaining the joint behavior of nominal and real variables and their connection to monetary policy. In other words, the paper aims to find out whether endogenous money, sticky wages, or some combination of the two, are necessary features in a dynamic New Keynesian model in explaining the correlations between nominal and real variables in the postwar US data. To do so, we employ the Bayesian technique to estimate the structural model of endogenous money, using the postwar US data from 1959:01 to 2008:02. We then compare the estimated structural models with and without

[1]Gali (2008) also argues that, with a Taylor-type monetary policy rule, the simple correlations of interest rates and real variables cannot be used as evidence of non-neutralities. The causal effects can, at least partially, run the other way around.

[2]The structural model is documented in detail in section 2. For a dynamic New Keynesian model with real balances, see Ireland (2003, 2004), Andres et al. (2005, 2009), and Gali (2008).

sticky wages.

In order to evaluate the structural model's ability of matching the correlations between nominal and real variables in the postwar US data, we conduct various tests and diagnoses, such as comparing the implied standard deviations and vector autocorrelation functions for the endogenous variables from the estimated variant versions of the model and the data. We also study each shock's contribution to the variance of the observable variables. These quantitative implications of the variant versions of the model will assist us in answering the question that we intend to answer in the paper. Finally, to accommodate the possible policy regime shift in 1979 and to check the robustness of the model estimates, we divide the full sample into two sub-samples, the first covering from 1959:01 to 1979:02 and the second covering from 1979:03 to 2008:02.

The main empirical results are as follows: the sticky-wage model with endogenous money well replicates the correlations between real balances and inflation, and real balances and the nominal interest rate; both sticky prices and sticky wages are necessary features in the model to match the persistence of real wages; sticky prices play an important role in replicating the persistence of inflation and the additional of sticky wages improves the fit for the behavior of inflation persistence; the wage markup shock plays a prominent role in explaining the variation of both nominal and real variables. We conclude that both endogenous money and sticky wages are necessary features in a dynamic New Keynesian model in explaining the variation in the key macroeconomic variables, both nominal and real.

2. A Structural Model with Money

The model presented here has many features typical of a standard dynamic New Keynesian model with nominal and real rigidities, particularly along the lines of Erceg et al. (2000), Christiano et al. (2005), and Smets & Wouters (2007). These common features such as Calvo-type sticky prices and wages, partial price and wage indexation, and capital utilization are documented below. Among them, in order to study the role for money in the model economy, we include real balances in the structural model. Since money becomes an argument of the utility function, the money demand function can be derived explicitly. Given that the effects arising with non-separable utility are negligible (McCallum & Nelson, 1999; Woodford, 2001; Andres et al., 2009), the utility function is assumed to be separable in consumption and real balances[3]. The model is closed by assuming that the monetary authority follows an augmented Taylor-type interest rate rule.

The Taylor rule, an empirical observation about the Federal Reserve's behavior [4], became a theory of inflation determinacy after it had been introduced into the New Keynesian framework. However, Cochrane (2007) points out that the Taylor coefficient required to stabilize inflation in the New Keynesian Taylor-rule setup is not identified in the data. Using the three-equation benchmark New Keynesian model, Cochrane (2007) argues that in a forward-looking New Keynesian model the Taylor principle is the condition for unstable

[3]For a detailed discussion on the separable and non-separable utility functions, see Walsh (2010) and Gali (2008).

[4]Clarida et al. (2000) use a single-equation regression to show that the Federal Reserve sufficiently controlled inflation by reacting more than one-for-one to inflation in the post-Volker era.

dynamics, which rules out multiple equilibria and forces forward-looking solutions. We leave to a future study the question of whether the Taylor principle holds in a medium-size New Keynesian DSGE model in which both backward-looking and forward-looking terms appear in the Phillips curve, as is the case in the current study. Nonetheless, we assume the monetary authority follows an augmented Taylor-type interest rate rule, in which the short-term nominal interest rate is adjusted in response to the deviation of the money growth rate as well. Bernanke (2006) argues that although monetary and credit aggregates have not played a central role in formulation of the US monetary policy since 1982, money growth may still contain important information about the state of the future economy. Therefore, attention to money growth is sensible as part of the eclectic modelling framework used by the Federal Reserve.

2.1. The Representative Household

The economy consists of a continuum of infinitely-lived households. In each period $t = 0, 1, 2, ...$, a representative household makes a sequence of decisions to maximize her expected utility over a composite consumption good C_t, real money balance M_t/P_t, and leisure $1 - N_t$:

$$E\sum_{t=0}^{\infty}\beta^t\Big[\frac{(C_t - hC_{t-1})^{1-\eta_c}}{1-\eta_c} + \xi_{m,t}\frac{(M_t/P_t)^{1-\eta_m}}{1-\eta_m} - \frac{(N_t)^{1+\eta_n}}{1+\eta_n}\Big] \tag{1}$$

where β is the subjective discount factor and η_n is the inverse of the elasticity of work effort with respect to the real wage. The habit formation parameter h measures the importance of the reference level relative to current consumption. As suggested by Fuhrer (2000), Amato & Thomas (2004), and Bouakez et al. (2005), including habit formation in household's utility function improves the short-run dynamic of the model in terms of replicating the hump-shaped response of consumption to monetary policy and other shocks. η_c is the coefficient for the relative risk aversion of the household, and η_m is the inverse of the interest elasticity of real money demand. The preference shock, $\xi_{m,t}$, acts as a shock to money demand, which follows a first-order autoregressive (AR(1)) process:

$$\xi_{m,t} = \rho_m\xi_{m,t-1} + \epsilon_{m,t}, \qquad 0 \leq \rho_m < 1, \qquad \epsilon_{m,t} \sim i.i.d.(0, \sigma_m^2) \tag{2}$$

In each time period, the representative household carries the government bond B_{t-1} and money M_{t-1} from the previous period into the current period t, and receives a lump-sum transfer T_t from the monetary authority and a nominal profit or dividend payment D_t from the intermediate-good firms. In addition, the household also receives its usual labor income W_tN_t, where W_t denotes the nominal wage. The model assumes that households own capital stock K_t and supply capital to the intermediate-good firms at a rental rate $R_{k,t}$. Following Christiano et al. (2005), the model further assumes that households can adjust the capital utilization at rate μ_t in each time period but face a cost $\psi(\mu_t)K_{t-1}$ [5]. Therefore, in each time period, the representative household maximizes her expected utility Eq. (1) subject to the following budget constraint:

$$C_t + X_t + \frac{B_t}{P_t} + \frac{M_t}{P_t} + \psi(\mu_t)K_{t-1} \leq \frac{W_t}{P_t}N_t + \frac{B_{t-1}(1+i_{t-1})}{P_t}$$

[5] The $\psi(\cdot)$ function is increasing and convex, whereas $\psi(1) = 0$.

$$+\frac{M_{t-1}}{P_t}+\frac{D_t}{P_t}+\frac{T_t}{P_t}+R_{k,t}(\mu_t)K_{t-1} \tag{3}$$

The first-order conditions result in the following linearized [6] equations:

$$c_t = \frac{h}{1+h}c_{t-1}+\frac{1}{1+h}E_t c_{t+1}-\frac{1-h}{(1+h)\eta_c}r_t \tag{4}$$

$$m_t = \frac{\eta_c}{\eta_m}(c_t-hc_{t-1})-\frac{1}{\eta_m}\frac{1}{i}i_t+\frac{1}{\eta_m}\xi_{m,t} \tag{5}$$

The consumption Euler equation Eq. (4) states that consumption for the current period depends on a weighted average of previous and expected future consumption. The habit persistence parameter captures the impact of the real rate on consumption given an intertemporal elasticity of substitution, i.e. the higher the habit persistence, the less the impact of the real rate on consumption is.

The money demand Eq. (5) states that the optimal condition of money holding requires that the marginal rate of substitution between money and consumption must equal the opportunity cost of holding money.

Besides the intertemporal budget constraint Eq. (3), the representative household is also subject to the following capital accumulation constraint as in Christiano et al. (2005):

$$K_t=(1-\delta)K_{t-1}+\xi_{x,t}\big[1-S\big(\frac{X_t}{X_{t-1}}\big)\big]X_t \tag{6}$$

where δ is the depreciation rate, X_t is the gross investment. The function S captures the presence of investment adjustment cost [7]. The investment shock $\xi_{x,t}$ is assumed to follow an AR(1) process:

$$\xi_{x,t}=\rho_x\xi_{x,t-1}+\epsilon_{x,t}, \qquad 0\le\rho_x<1, \qquad \epsilon_{x,t}\sim i.i.d.(0,\sigma_i^2) \tag{7}$$

The linearized first-order conditions are:

$$p_{k,t} = E_t\pi_{t+1}-r_t+[1-\beta(1-\delta)]E_t r_{k,t+1}+\beta(1-\delta)E_t p_{k,t+1} \tag{8}$$

$$x_t = \frac{1}{1+\beta}(x_{t-1}+\beta E_t x_{t+1}+\frac{1}{\nu}p_{k,t})+\xi_{x,t} \tag{9}$$

Eq. (8) is the Lucas asset price equation for capital. $P_{k,t}$ is the shadow value of the installed capital, which depends on both the expected future value of capital and its return $r_{k,t}$, taking into account the depreciation rate. The investment Eq. (9), which contains both backward-looking and forward-looking components, describes the dynamics of investment. ν is the investment adjustment cost parameter, $\nu=S''(\cdot)$.

2.2. Final Goods Production

In the final-good sector, firms are perfectly competitive. The representative firm produces the final good Y_t using a continuum of intermediate goods $Y_{j,t}$ indexed by j

[6] A lowercase letter represents its log deviation from steady state.

[7] In steady state, $S(\cdot)=0,\ S'(\cdot)=0,\ S''(\cdot)>0$.

($j \in [0,1]$), according to a constant elasticity of substitution (CES) production function of Dixit & Stiglitz (1977):

$$Y_t = \left(\int_0^1 Y_{j,t}^{\frac{\varphi_{p,t}-1}{\varphi_{p,t}}} dj \right)^{\frac{\varphi_{p,t}}{\varphi_{p,t}-1}} \tag{10}$$

where $\varphi_{p,t}$ measures the time-varying price elasticity of demand for each intermediate good $Y_{j,t}$. It acts as a price markup shock in the goods market. The price markup shock is assumed to be IID.

The representative firm maximizes its profit, and the first-order condition implies the demand for each intermediate good as the following:

$$Y_{j,t} = \left(\frac{P_{j,t}}{P_t}\right)^{-\varphi_{p,t}} Y_t \tag{11}$$

where $P_{j,t}$ is the price of the intermediate good j, and P_t is the price for the final good. Since the final-good firms operate in a perfectly competitive market, in equilibrium the representative firm's profit should equal zero. Hence, the equilibrium market price for the final good is given as the following:

$$P_t = \left(\int_0^1 P_{j,t}^{1-\varphi_{p,t}} dj \right)^{1/1-\varphi_{p,t}} \tag{12}$$

2.3. Intermediate Goods Production

In the intermediate-good sector, firms are monopolistically competitive. In each time period, the representative firm produces $Y_{j,t}$ units of intermediate good j according to the following constant-returns-to-scale production function:

$$Y_{j,t} = \xi_{z,t}(\mu_t K_{j,t-1})^{\alpha} N_{j,t}^{1-\alpha}, \qquad 0 < \alpha < 1 \tag{13}$$

where the aggregate technology shock $\xi_{z,t}$ follows an AR(1) process:

$$\xi_{z,t} = \rho_z \xi_{z,t-1} + \epsilon_{z,t}, \qquad 0 \le \rho_z < 1, \qquad \epsilon_{z,t} \sim i.i.d.(0, \sigma_z^2) \tag{14}$$

Households supply $N_{j,t}$ units of labor and $K_{j,t}$ units of utilized capital stock, where $K_{j,t} = \mu_t K_{j,t-1}$, to the representative firm j. The aggregate labor demand N_t is given by the following Dixit-Stiglitz form:

$$N_t = \left(\int_0^1 N_{j,t}^{\frac{\varphi_{w,t}-1}{\varphi_{w,t}}} dj \right)^{\frac{\varphi_{w,t}}{\varphi_{w,t}-1}} \tag{15}$$

where $\varphi_{w,t}$ measures the time-varying price elasticity of demand for different types of labor. It acts as a wage markup shock in the labor market. The wage markup shock is assumed to be IID.

Sticky wages are introduced in the manner as proposed by Erceg et al. (2000). Households are price setters in the labor market. In other words, wages are taken as a given by the intermediate-good firms. Given the nominal wage rate $W_{j,t}$, the representative intermediate-good firm j minimizes its cost and yields the demand for labor $N_{j,t}$:

$$N_{j,t} = (\frac{W_{j,t}}{W_t})^{-\varphi_{w,t}} N_t \tag{16}$$

where W_t is the aggregate wage index:

$$W_t = \left(\int_0^1 W_{j,t}^{1-\varphi_{w,t}} dj \right)^{1/1-\varphi_{w,t}} \tag{17}$$

Following Calvo (1983), in each time period only a random fraction $1 - \theta_w$ of households have the opportunity to reset their wages. This fraction is independent across households and time. In addition, the model assumes that households who cannot reset their wages simply index to the lagged inflation as in Christiano et al. (2005) and Smets & Wouters (2007). Therefore, the wage index $W_{j,t}$ is given by:

$$W_{j,t}^{1-\varphi_{w,t}} = \theta_w[(\frac{P_{t-1}}{P_{t-2}})^{\gamma_w} W_{j,t-1}]^{1-\varphi_{w,t}} + (1-\theta_w)(W_{j,t}^*)^{1-\varphi_{w,t}},$$

$$0 \leq \theta_w \leq 1, \quad 0 \leq \gamma_w \leq 1 \tag{18}$$

where γ_w is the degree of wage indexation, and $W_{j,t}^*$ represents the nominal wage level chosen by those households who can reset their wages at time period t.

The intermediate-good firms also face the same restriction in setting their prices. In each time period, the probability of being able to reset prices is $1 - \theta_p$, and firms who cannot reset their prices also index to the lagged inflation. Therefore the price index $P_{j,t}$ is given by:

$$P_{j,t}^{1-\varphi_{p,t}} = \theta_p[(\frac{P_{t-1}}{P_{t-2}})^{\gamma_p} P_{j,t-1}]^{1-\varphi_{p,t}} + (1-\theta_p)(P_{j,t}^*)^{1-\varphi_{p,t}},$$

$$0 \leq \theta_p \leq 1, \quad 0 \leq \gamma_p \leq 1 \tag{19}$$

The linearized first-order conditions are given by:

$$mc_t = \alpha r_{k,t} + (1-\alpha)w_t - \xi_{z,t} \tag{20}$$

$$\pi_t = \frac{1}{1+\beta\gamma_p}\left[\gamma_p \pi_{t-1} + \beta E_t \pi_{t+1} + \frac{(1-\beta\theta_p)(1-\theta_p)}{\theta_p} mc_t\right] + \epsilon_{p,t} \tag{21}$$

$$\begin{aligned} w_t = {} & \frac{1}{1+\beta}\{w_{t-1} + \beta E_t w_{t+1} + \gamma_w \pi_{t-1} - (1+\beta\gamma_w)\pi_t + \beta E_t \pi_{t+1} \\ & - \frac{(1-\beta\theta_w)(1-\theta_w)}{(1+\varphi_w \eta_n)\theta_w}[w_t - \eta_n n_t - \frac{\eta_c}{1-h}(c_t - hc_{t-1})]\} + \epsilon_{w,t} \end{aligned} \tag{22}$$

Eq. (20) implies that the real marginal cost is a function of the real rental rate of capital and the real wage, since capital and labor are used in producing the intermediate goods.

The New Keynesian Phillips curve Eq. (21) implies that inflation depends on past and expected future inflation. It also shows that the price indexation parameter γ_p governs the persistence in the response of inflation to a given shock. If $\gamma_p = 0$, Eq. (21) becomes a purely forward-looking Phillips curve. It is worth noting that inflation is a function of the current marginal cost, and that both γ_p and θp govern the contribution of marginal cost to the persistent response of inflation. Here, we follow Gali & Gertler (1999)'s argument that, as the theory suggests, real marginal cost is a significant and quantitatively important determinant of inflation, instead of an ad hoc output gap.

The real wage Eq. (22) states that, under staggered wage contracts, the usual intratemporal condition of real wage under fully flexible wages, that is that the real wage equals the marginal rate of substitution of consumption for labor, no longer holds. The representative household now takes into account not only past and expected future real wages, but also past, current, and expected future inflation rates. The representative household sets her real wage higher than the marginal rate of substitution, since she knows there is a possibility that she may not be able to reset her wage in the future. It is worth noting that the real wage equation here contains both backward-looking and forward-looking components of the wage rate and inflation rate, which induce the inertia into inflation through the marginal cost channel. This is because that, as shown in Eq. (20), real marginal cost is an increasing function of real wage, and real marginal cost is a quantitatively important determinant of inflation. Therefore, it is not surprising that it is the sticky wages, not sticky prices, which play an important role in generating the observed inertia in inflation in response to a monetary policy shock (Huang & Liu, 2002; Christiano et al., 2005).

2.4. The Monetary Authority

The model is closed by assuming that the monetary authority follows an augmented Taylor-type interest rate rule as in Ireland (2003) and Andres et al. (2009). That is, the monetary authority adjusts its instrument, the nominal short-term interest rate, in response not only to the deviations of output, inflation, and the lagged interest rate from their steady-state levels, but also to the deviation of money growth rate:

$$i_t = \kappa_i i_{t-1} + (1-\kappa_i)(\kappa_\varpi \varpi_t + \kappa_\pi \pi_t + \kappa_y y_t) + \xi_{i,t} \tag{23}$$

where ϖ_t represents the percentage deviation of money growth rate, $\varpi_t = m_t - m_{t-1} + \pi_t$. The monetary policy shock $\xi_{i,t}$ is assumed to follow an AR(1) process:

$$\xi_{i,t} = \rho_i \xi_{i,t-1} + \epsilon_{i,t}, \qquad 0 \leq \rho_i < 1, \qquad \epsilon_{i,t} \sim i.i.d.(0, \sigma_i^2) \tag{24}$$

3. Model Estimates

The model is estimated using Bayesian estimation techniques[8]. The mode of the posterior distribution is estimated by maximizing the log posterior function combining the prior information. Bayesian estimation and evaluation techniques have become the industrial standard for empirical work with DSGE models due to the following two main advantages. First, it allows one to formalize the use of a prior information based on previous studies either at a micro or macro level. Second, it provides a framework for evaluating fundamentally misspecified models on the basis of the marginal likelihood of the model or the Bayes' factor [9].

[8]Models are estimated using Dynare developed by Michel Juillard and his collaborators at CEPREMAP.

[9]For a detailed discussion on estimating DSGE models using Bayesian techniques, see Smets & Wouters (2003); An & Schorfheide (2007); Leeper & Zha (2001).

We compare the estimated results from the sticky-wage model (the structural model described in section 2) and the flexible-wage model. In the flexible-wage model, the only nominal rigidity is the Calvo-type sticky prices. In other words, wages are flexible and the indexation of price is dropped. Other features are the same as those in the sticky-wage model. The New Keynesian Phillips curve in the flexible-wage model is brought down to the one in the benchmark New Keynesian model in the literature. The idea here is to keep the nominal rigidities in the sticky-wage model variant, the flexible-wage model, as simple as possible, which allows us to investigate to what extent the role played by sticky wages in a New Keynesian model in explaining the correlations between nominal and real variables in the data.

Gavin & Kydland (1999) observe the changes in the cyclical behavior of nominal variables after 1979:03 when the Federal Reserve started implementing a policy to lower the inflation rate. It is believed that there was a regime shift in the Federal Reserve policy after Paul Volker's appointment as Chairman in August 1979 (Ireland, 2003). To accommodate the possible policy regime shift in 1979 and to check the robustness of the model estimates, we divide the full sample into two sub-samples, the first covering from 1959:01 to 1979:02 and the second covering from 1979:03 to 2008:02.

3.1. The Data

The model is estimated using quarterly data on real output (GDP), real money balances, real wage, inflation, and a short-term nominal interest rate over the period of 1959:1-2008:2. All data are obtained from the Federal Reserve Bank of St. Louis FRED database.

Real money balances is derived by dividing M2 money stock by the GDP deflator. Both real money balances and real output are in per-capita terms derived by dividing the civilian non-institutional population, aged 16 and over. Inflation is measured by the changes in GDP deflator. Real wage is calculated by dividing nominal wage by GDP deflator, whereas the measure of the nominal wage is the "hourly compensation for the non-farm business sector". The short-term nominal interest rate is measured by the 3-month Treasury bill rate. Finally, we detrend real output, real balances, and real wage. Therefore, the observable variables we refer to in the discussion of the empirical results are real output growth, real money growth, real wage growth (or wage inflation), inflation and nominal interest rate.

3.2. Prior Distributions

The prior distribution of the parameters are shown in columns 2-4 in Table 1. The Calvo parameters and friction coefficients of wage and price indexation are assumed to follow beta distribution, and the following prior means. The degree of wage stickiness θ_w is assumed to be 0.75, which implies that wages are fixed on average for a year. Prices are fixed on average for two quarters, i.e. $\theta_p = 0.5$. The degree of wage indexation is set at 0.5, whereas the degree of price indexation is set at 0.55.

In the utility function, the prior on habit formation parameter h is set at 0.7 with a standard deviation of 0.05, which is consistent with the literature (Boldrin et al., 2001; Rabanal, 2007). The coefficient of relative risk aversion η_c is assumed to follow gamma distribution with mean 2 and standard deviation 0.1. We adopt a normal distribution for the inverse of the interest rate elasticity of real money demand with mean 2.5, which is close to 2.56 in Walsh (2010), and standard deviation 0.1.

The inverse of the elasticity of capital utilization cost ψ and the investment adjustment cost parameter ν are assumed to follow gamma distribution. The mean is set at 98 for ψ with standard deviation 14.14, and 2 for ν with standard deviation 0.4.

We assume the real shock is more persistent than the nominal shocks. The persistence of the AR(1) processes is assumed to follow beta distribution with mean 0.75 and standard deviation 0.1 for ρ_x and ρ_m, mean 0.55 and standard deviation 0.05 for ρ_i, and mean 0.95 and standard deviation 0.02 for ρ_z. Whereas the standard deviations of the shocks are inverse-gamma distributed with a mean of 0.1.

The parameters of the monetary policy rule are assumed to follow normal distribution with standard deviation 0.05, and a mean of 0.65, 0.5, 1.38, 0.18, with respect to κ_i, κ_{ϖ}, κ_{π}, κ_y. These values are assigned based on a standard Taylor rule, close to the values reported in Andres et al. (2009).

Four parameters are fixed prior to estimation. As pointed out by Ireland (2003), the inverse of elasticity of labor supply η_n cannot be estimated directly without the data on employment, and the depreciation rate δ cannot be estimated if capital stock is not included in the data set. η_n is set equal to 1.5 and δ is set equal to 0.025. In addition, the discount factor β is calibrated to be 0.99, and the capital income share $\alpha = 0.24$. Values assigned on the above parameters are consistent with those in the literature (Smets & Wouters, 2007).

3.3. Parameter Estimates

The posterior mode of the parameters and the corresponding standard errors for both the sticky- and flexible-wage models are reported in Table 1[10]. The parameter estimates for the sticky-wage model are reported in columns 5 and 6 in Table 1. For the parameters that characterize the degree of price and wage stickiness, the results indicate a slightly higher degree of stickiness in wage than that in price. More Precisely, the estimated degree of wage stickiness of 0.66 implies an average three quarters duration of wage contracts, and a relatively high degree of wage indexation of 0.7. These findings are consistent with those in Christiano et al. (2005). However, a slightly lower degree of price stickiness of 0.62 is obtained from the estimated sticky-wage model, implying an average two-and-a-half quarters duration of price contracts. This value is lower than that in Gali & Gertler (1999), who report a degree of price stickiness of 0.83, obtained from the single-equation estimation.

The estimated productivity, money demand, and monetary policy shock processes are very persistent, whereas the investment shock is less persistent. The estimated standard deviations of the innovations to the investment shock and money demand shock are relatively large compared to those of the other shocks. Ireland (2003) also reports the same findings and points out that it helps the model explain the investment boom in the 1990s.

Finally, the parameter estimates of the monetary policy rule indicate that the Federal Reserve policy can be described as following an augmented Taylor rule. That is, the Federal Reserve adjusts the nominal interest rate in response not only to the deviations of output,

[10]As some parameter estimates are similar to those in the literature, only estimates of those key parameters are discussed here.

Table 1. Prior and posterior distributions (full-sample period)

	Prior distribution			Estimated posteprior mode			
				Sticky-wage model		Flexible-wage model	
Parameter	type	mean	std dev.	mean	std dev.	mean	std dev.
θ_p	Beta	0.5	0.1	0.6222	0.0203	0.4139	0.0202
θ_w	Beta	0.75	0.05	0.6543	0.068	—	—
γ_p	Beta	0.55	0.15	0.0791	0.0296	—	—
γ_w	Beta	0.5	0.2	0.7074	0.0622	—	—
η_m	Normal	2.5	0.1	2.6524	0.0995	2.7195	0.0972
h	Beta	0.7	0.05	0.8471	0.0256	0.8782	0.025
η_c	Gamma	2	0.1	2.0357	0.1003	2.0507	0.1008
ψ	Gamma	98	14.14	93.8545	13.8308	99.2903	14.4911
ν	Gamma	2	0.4	2.0024	0.3151	4.3591	0.5283
ρ_x	Beta	0.75	0.1	0.3128	0.0582	0.2842	0.06
ρ_m	Beta	0.75	0.1	0.8623	0.018	0.6306	0.0185
ρ_i	Beta	0.55	0.05	0.7228	0.0259	0.6305	0.0185
ρ_z	Beta	0.95	0.02	0.7306	0.0396	0.9979	0.0014
κ_i	Normal	0.65	0.05	0.3247	0.0306	0.1275	0.03
κ_ϖ	Normal	0.5	0.05	0.7373	0.0437	0.6979	0.0415
κ_π	Normal	1.38	0.05	1.167	0.0523	1.2492	0.0575
κ_y	Normal	0.18	0.02	0.1753	0.0204	0.158	0.0207
ϵ_i	Inv. Gamma	0.1	Inf	0.0145	0.001	0.0189	0.0013
ϵ_m	Inv. Gamma	0.1	Inf	0.1265	0.0064	0.1629	0.0093
ϵ_z	Inv. Gamma	0.1	Inf	0.0104	0.0009	0.0179	0.001
ϵ_x	Inv. Gamma	0.1	Inf	0.0792	0.0058	0.0795	0.0045
ϵ_p	Inv. Gamma	0.1	Inf	0.0076	0.0004	0.0135	0.0011
ϵ_w	Inv. Gamma	0.1	Inf	0.0116	0.0006	—	—

inflation, and lagged interest rate, but also to the deviation of money growth. The moderately significant estimate of κ_ω (0.73) proves the idea of augmenting the money growth into the standard Taylor rule in describing the Federal Reserve's policy. The estimated response of the nominal interest rate to inflation rate is 1.17. The response to output is 0.17, which is very close to the value (0.15) obtained using maximum likelihood estimation in Andres et al. (2009). The parameter estimates of monetary policy rule indicate the significance of endogenous money in explaining the correlations between money growth, interest rates and output.

The flexible-wage model is estimated using the same priors and standard deviations as those assigned in the sticky-wage model. The estimates are more or less consistent with those from the sticky-wage model[11]. However, compared to the sticky-wage model, two points are worth noting in the flexible-wage model estimates. First, price becomes slightly less sticky. The average duration of price contracts is about one-and-a-half quarters. This is a troublesome result as, ex ante, one would expect that price becomes more sticky once sticky wages and price indexation are dropped in the model. Second, among others, the productivity shock exhibits the most persistence with an AR(1) parameter of 0.99 (0.73 for sticky-wage model). These two significant changes in the flexible-wage model estimates imply that with the absence of sticky wages, the model requires a much more persistent

[11]Parameter estimates for the flexible-wage model are reported in the last two columns in Table 1.

Table 2. Posterior distributions (sticky-wage model)

	Estimated posteprior mode			
	Pre-1979		Post-1979	
Parameter	mean	std dev.	mean	std dev.
Parameter	mean	std dev.	mean	std dev.
θ_p	0.4412	0.0525	0.684	0.0287
θ_w	0.7833	0.0476	0.812	0.0366
γ_p	0.7643	0.0963	0.2097	0.0709
γ_w	0.8897	0.081	0.7675	0.0549
η_m	2.5951	0.0993	2.5844	0.0996
h	0.8294	0.0332	0.8443	0.027
η_c	2.0273	0.1001	2.0348	0.1003
ψ	95.584	13.9843	96.9642	13.9454
ν	2.9645	0.4095	2.7464	0.4246
ρ_x	0.558	0.0818	0.4698	0.0727
ρ_m	0.8124	0.0336	0.8047	0.0297
ρ_i	0.4674	0.0423	0.559	0.0424
ρ_z	0.9369	0.0372	0.8286	0.0357
κ_i	0.4886	0.0407	0.4149	0.0371
κ_ϖ	0.5828	0.0463	0.6355	0.0446
κ_π	1.2497	0.05	1.2189	0.05
κ_y	0.2035	0.0192	0.1889	0.0191
ϵ_i	0.0211	0.0019	0.0183	0.0014
ϵ_m	0.1293	0.0099	0.1749	0.0115
ϵ_z	0.0156	0.0023	0.0149	0.0017
ϵ_x	0.0735	0.0116	0.1485	0.013
ϵ_p	0.0132	0.0011	0.0099	0.0007
ϵ_w	0.013	0.001	0.0134	0.0009

productivity shock process to account the movements in the observable variables.

We report the parameter estimates for the two sub-samples of both the sticky- and flexible-wage models in Tables 2 and 3. Overall, parameter estimates are consistent across the models and sub-sample periods, indicating our results are robust. It is worth noting that in both the sticky- and flexible-wage models, the estimated ϵ_x and ϵ_m for the post-1979 sub-sample period are much larger than those for the pre-1979 sub-sample period, which confirms the observation of the investment boom in the 1990s.

One interesting finding here is the degree of price indexation estimated for the sticky-wage model falls sharply moving from the pre-1979 (0.76) to the post-1979 (0.21) sub-sample period. Fig. 1 shows the implied vector autocorrelation for inflation from the estimated variant versions of the model and the data. It shows that there is no significant decline in the inflation persistence across the two sub-sample periods in the data and, indeed the sticky-wage model does a better job in replicating the persistence of inflation for the post-1979 than for the pre-1979 sub-sample period, indicating that the price indexation does

Table 3. Posterior distributions (flexible-wage model)

	Estimated posteprior mode			
	Pre-1979		Post-1979	
Parameter	mean	std dev.	mean	std dev.
θ_p	0.5194	0.0357	0.4927	0.03
θ_w	—	—	—	—
γ_p	—	—	—	—
γ_w	—	—	—	—
η_m	2.6295	0.0976	2.6422	0.098
h	0.7758	0.0433	0.8377	0.0489
η_c	2.0517	0.0999	2.064	0.1005
ψ	103.5271	13.4129	106.7247	13.4854
ν	3.381	0.422	3.7052	0.4752
ρ_x	0.4179	0.0736	0.394	0.0549
ρ_m	0.6741	0.0358	0.5897	0.033
ρ_i	0.5569	0.0335	0.5959	0.0337
ρ_z	0.9964	0.001	0.9979	0.0014
κ_i	0.2981	0.0365	0.1726	0.0342
κ_ϖ	0.6242	0.0453	0.6807	0.0433
κ_π	1.3742	0.0518	1.3282	0.0561
κ_y	0.16	0.0201	0.146	0.0205
ϵ_i	0.0262	0.0023	0.0244	0.0019
ϵ_m	0.1302	0.0115	0.2009	0.0151
ϵ_z	0.0398	0.0037	0.0302	0.0026
ϵ_x	0.1172	0.0109	0.1522	0.0125
ϵ_p	0.0219	0.0024	0.0178	0.0017

not contribute that much in reproducing the persistence of inflation. In contrast, the sticky prices might play a crucial role in reproducing the persistence of inflation as the estimated degree of price stickiness increases from 0.44 for the pre-1979 to 0.68 for the post-1979 sub-sample period.

4. Tests and Diagnoses

This section presents sets of diagnostic statistics, which help us to evaluate the empirical performance of the variant versions of the model. First, we compare the standard deviations of the observable variables from the estimated variant versions of the model and those of the data. As shown in Table 4, for both pre-1979 sub-sample period and post-1979 sub-sample period, the sticky-wage model does better in matching standard deviations from the US data, except for output. Compared to the flexible-wage model, the sticky-wage model overstates the volatility of output for both sub-sample periods. Ellison & Scott (2000) and Ireland (2003) find similar weakness of their sticky-price models.

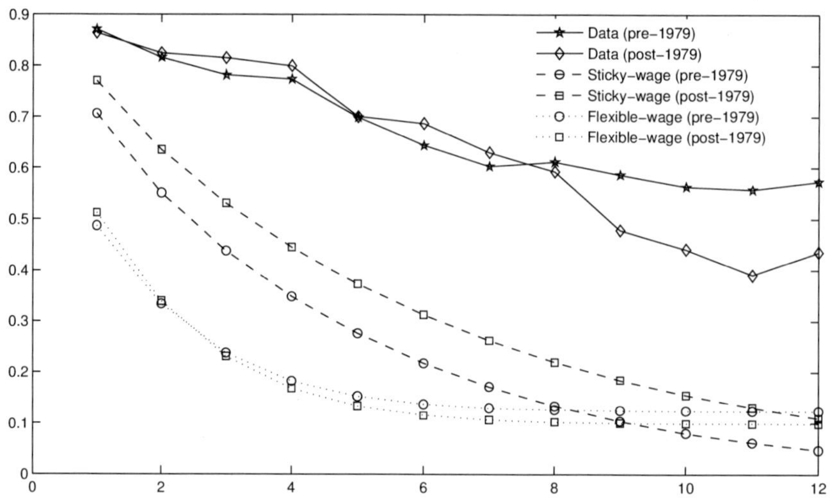

Figure 1. Inflation persistence: data vs models.

Second, to investigate the capability of the sticky- and flexible-wage models of explaining the joint behavior of real output, real balances, real wages, inflation, and nominal interest rate, we compare the implied vector autocorrelation functions for the endogenous variables from the estimated variant versions of the model and the data. Overall, the sticky-wage model outperforms the flexible-wage model in explaining the joint behavior of the endogenous variables for both sub-sample periods.

Table 4. Standard deviations (data vs. models)

	Pre-1979			Post-1979		
Variable	Data	Sticky-wage	Flexible-wage	Data	Sticky-wage	Flexible-wage
y	0.0444	0.0927	0.0455	0.0314	0.0859	0.0454
m	0.0078	0.0147	0.0191	0.0079	0.0119	0.0133
w	0.0299	0.0356	0.6115	0.0216	0.0330	0.6093
π	0.0078	0.0105	0.0288	0.0032	0.0036	0.0053
i	0.0049	0.013	0.0191	0.0056	0.0051	0.0045

As shown in Figs. 2 and 3, compared to the flexible-wage model, the sticky-wage model does a much better job of replicating the autocorrelation functions of the endogenous variables especially for real output, real wages, and nominal interest rate. It is worth noting that both sticky prices and sticky wages are necessary features in the model to match the persistence of real wages, which is consistent with the findings of Rabanal & Rubio-Ramirez (2005) and Matheron & Poilly (2009). In our case, the feature of sticky wages is even more crucial in generating the persistence of real wages. In contrast to Rabanal & Rubio-Ramirez (2005), both the sticky- and flexible-wage models are able to match the persistence of the nominal interest rate, whereas neither sticky-wage model nor sticky-price model can generate the observed nominal interest rate autocorrelation function in their study. Moreover, the sticky-wage model matches the observed nominal interest rate autocorrelation function better than the flexible-wage model, for the pre-1979 sub-sample period in particular. It is less satisfying in terms of replicating the autocorrelation function of real balances, even though the sticky-wage model still does a better job than the flexible-wage model. Finally, the additional of sticky wages improves the fit for the behavior of inflation persistence[12]. This is due to that, as pointed out in section 2.3, real marginal cost is a significant and quantitatively important determinant of inflation and real marginal cost depends partially on the real wage, as indicated by the New Keynesian Phillips curve Eq. (21).

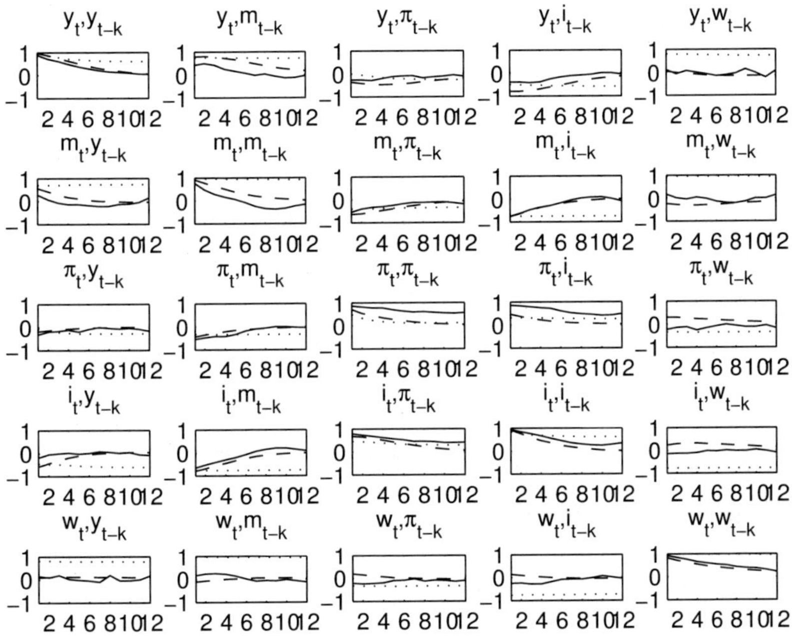

Figure 2. Vector autocorrelation functions (pre-1979): flexible-wage model (dotted line), sticky-wage model (dashed line) and data (solid line).

The sticky-wage model also performs reasonably well in reproducing the correlations between nominal and real variables at various leads and lags. A few points are worth noting here. First, the model performs extremely well in reproducing the correlation between output and real wages, whereas the flexible-wage model does a very bad job. It indicates that sticky wages play a crucial role in explaining the correlation between the two variables. Second, the sticky-wage model well replicates the "inverted leading indicator" property of the nominal interest rate as reported by Ireland (2003) and Matheron & Poilly (2009) and the

[12]Also see Fig. 1.

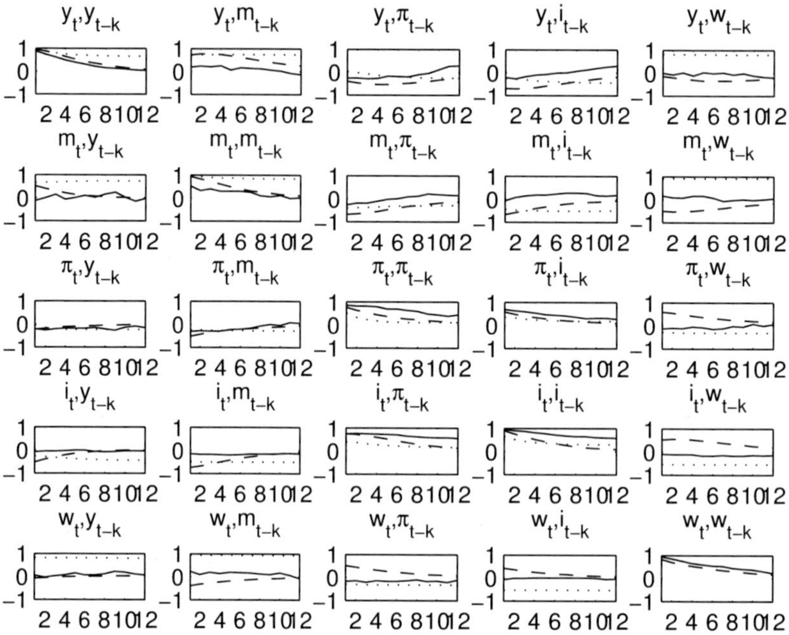

Figure 3. Vector autocorrelation functions (post-1979): flexible-wage model (dotted line), sticky-wage model (dashed line) and data (solid line).

positive correlations between output and lagged real balances in the data found by Ireland (2003). As far as inflation is concerned, both the sticky- and flexible-wage models do well in reproducing the correlation between output and inflation. However, it appears that the sticky-wage model does a slightly better job than the flexible-wage model for the post-1979 sub-sample period. Finally, it is important to point out that the sticky-wage model with endogenous money well replicates the correlations between real balances and inflation, and real balances and the nominal interest rate.

To sum up, the above tests and diagnoses suggest that both endogenous money and sticky wages are necessary features in a dynamic New Keynesian model in explaining the correlations between nominal and real variables. In addition, sticky prices play an important role in replicating the persistence of inflation and the additional of sticky wages improves the fit for the behavior of inflation persistence.

5. Endogenous Money or Sticky Wages?

To complement the tests and diagnoses conducted in previous section, in this section, we study each shock's contribution to the variance of the observable variables. These quantitative implications of the variant versions of the model will assist us in answering the question whether endogenous money, sticky wages, or some combination of the two, are necessary features in a dynamic New Keynesian model with endogenous money in explaining the correlations between nominal and real variables in the postwar US data.

The estimated sticky-wage model contains six shocks in total. In addition to the investment shock, the monetary policy shock, and the real technology shock as the one in the RBC literature, the stochastic dynamics of the model are also driven by the money demand shock, the price markup shock and wage markup shock. It is standard to include both price and wage markup shocks in the New Keynesian framework. Both the price and wage markup shocks are empirically important to capture price and wage dynamics. However, the price and wage markup shocks generate a trade-off problem as long as the monetary authority aims at stabilizing both inflation and the output gap (Smets & Wouters, 2007).

Introducing six shocks in the sticky-wage model allows us to estimate the sticky-wage model and the flexible-wage model using the same data set of five observable variables as documented in section 3.1. Since the estimation uses five variables, both models must include at least five shocks [13]. Kydland & Prescott (1982) argue that in the basic RBC framework, the U.S. business cycle fluctuations are purely driven by real technology shocks. This one-shock assumption makes the real business cycle model stochastically singular. Using a version of the King et al. (1988) model, Ingram et al. (1994) point out that it is impossible to derive the realizations of the productivity shocks using a singular model if the variance-covariance matrix of the observable variables is actually nonsingular. In order to overcome this singularity problem, one needs to elaborate the model by including at least as many shocks as there are endogenous variables in the model. This approach, in addition, can be served to identify sources of output variation.

Table 5 reports the independent contribution of each shock to the variance of the endogenous variables for both the sticky-wage and flexible-wage models for the full-sample period.

Looking first at the estimated results from the sticky-wage model, one important finding is that, except for the real wage, the contribution of the technology shock in explaining the variation of both nominal and real variables is negligible. In other words, the additional of sticky wages reduces the contribution of neutral technology shocks to explaining output fluctuations substantially.

The variation in real variables is explained mainly by nominal shocks: the monetary policy shock, the money demand shock, and the wage markup shock in particular. The policy shock together with the wage markup shock account for the most variation in output, 63 percent and 26 percent respectively. The money demand shock and wage markup shock are equally important in explaining the variation in real balances, whereas a 15 percent contribution of the policy shock is also non-negligible. Not surprisingly, the wage markup shock together with the productivity shock are dominant factors in explaining the variation in the real wage.

[13] There are five shocks in the flexible-wage model. The wage markup shock is shut down.

Table 5. Variance Decompositions (full-sample period)

Variable	Sticky-wage model						Flexible-wage model				
	ϵ_z	ϵ_x	ϵ_m	ϵ_i	ϵ_p	ϵ_w	ϵ_z	ϵ_x	ϵ_m	ϵ_i	ϵ_p
y	3.02	3.01	4.35	62.96	0.6	26.07	58.26	8.74	6.12	24.91	1.97
m	3.6	0.46	39.7	14.56	1.83	39.86	70.61	1.21	17.77	8.11	2.3
w	12.9	0.03	0.38	3.08	8.46	75.15	99.78	0	0.05	0.12	0.05
π	9.33	0	1.14	8.77	12.98	67.78	5.88	0.75	7.52	76.26	9.58
i	4.69	0.53	24.11	17.86	2.36	50.45	20.03	1.86	60.99	13.44	3.68

Note: numbers are in percentage.

Table 6. Variance Decompositions (sticky-wage model)

Variable	Pre-1979						Post-1979					
	ϵ_z	ϵ_x	ϵ_m	ϵ_i	ϵ_p	ϵ_w	ϵ_z	ϵ_x	ϵ_m	ϵ_i	ϵ_p	ϵ_w
y	13.33	5.56	1.84	51.55	2.34	25.38	8.52	10.86	5.1	41.29	2.26	31.98
m	11.63	0.73	15.18	26.23	3.28	42.94	4.52	0.98	23.71	14.18	2.06	54.54
w	40.28	0.03	0.04	0.46	11.06	48.14	18.16	0.05	0.09	0.28	9.18	72.24
π	21.64	0	0.09	0.64	19.5	58.14	10.58	0	0.1	0.18	13.77	75.36
i	13.56	0.74	5.97	29.14	3.78	46.81	5.65	1.08	11.25	16.8	2.52	62.7

Note: numbers are in percentage.

Table 7. Variance Decompositions (flexible-wage model)

	Pre-1979					Post-1979				
Variable	ϵ_z	ϵ_x	ϵ_m	ϵ_i	ϵ_p	ϵ_z	ϵ_x	ϵ_m	ϵ_i	ϵ_p
y	66.79	10.93	1.02	18.26	3	68.14	16.48	1.66	12.19	1.54
m	94.32	0.68	2.83	0.53	1.65	85.7	2.33	8.21	1.78	1.98
w	99.69	0	0.01	0.21	0.08	99.81	0.01	0.03	0.11	0.04
π	14.22	0.69	1.54	64.46	19.08	11.13	1.95	5.06	66.86	15
i	62.64	3.66	20.66	3.35	9.7	31.29	6.04	52.13	5.13	5.42

Note: numbers are in percentage.

The variation in nominal variables is explained mainly by nominal shocks as well. The wage markup shock explains a big part of the variation in inflation (68 percent); the price markup shock, the policy shock, and the productivity shock also explain a proportion of the variation in inflation, namely 13 percent, 9 percent, and 9 percent respectively. Similarly, the wage markup shock accounts for half of the variation in nominal interest rate, whereas the rest is explained mainly by the money demand shock (24 percent) and the policy shock (18 percent).

Turning to the flexible-wage model, the conclusion diverges. The productivity shock accounts for most of the variation in real variables, whereas the variation in nominal variables is explained mainly by nominal shocks. In the flexible-wage model, the productivity shock explains half of the variation in output, and the rest is explained mainly by the policy shock (25 percent) and the investment shock (9 percent). Besides the productivity shock, the contribution of money demand shock to the variation of real balances is non-negligible (18 percent). Not surprisingly, with flexible wages, the variation in real wage is solely explained by the productivity shock.

As far as nominal variables are concerned, the policy shock contributes the most (76 percent) in explaining the variation in inflation. Intuitively, in the sticky-wage model, both the estimated degree of wage stickiness θ_w and the degree of wage indexation γ_w are relatively high. Since inflation depends partially on marginal cost and marginal cost depends partially on the real wage, the variation in inflation is explained mainly by the wage markup shock. However, in the flexible-wage model, the assumption of flexible wages together with the absence of a wage markup shock weakens the contribution of marginal cost to the response of inflation.

The variance decompositions for the two sub-sample periods are reported in Tables 6 and 7. The results are consistent with those from the full-sample period estimation. It is worth noting that the contribution of the investment shock to the variation in output is increased in the post-1979 sub-sample period across models, which confirms the finding in section 3.3 that there is an investment boom in the 1990s.

In short, both the estimated sticky- and flexible-wage models suggest that variation in nominal variables in the postwar US business cycle is explained mainly by nominal shocks. As far as real variables are concerned, the conclusion diverges. The estimated sticky-wage model shows that nominal shocks dominate in explaining the variation in real variables. However, the fluctuations in real variables are mainly driven by the productivity shock in the flexible-wage model.

Finally, it is worth noting, as McCallum (2001) pointed out, in this type of theoretical models, the systematic component of monetary policy (coefficients) also plays an important role in explaining the variation in key macroeconomic variables[14]. As one can see from section 3.3 that the estimated monetary policy coefficients are consistent across the models and sub-sample periods, which implies that the postwar US monetary policy can be described as the augmented Taylor rule suggested here. Thus, both endogenous money and sticky wages account for the fluctuations in the postwar US business cycle.

[14] See Ireland (2003).

6. Conclusion

The comparison study of the implied vector autocorrelation functions for the endogenous variables from the estimated variant versions of the model and the data suggests that the sticky-wage model with endogenous money well replicates the correlations between real balances and inflation, and real balances and the nominal interest rate; both sticky prices and sticky wages are necessary features in the model to match the persistence of real wages; sticky prices play an important role in replicating the persistence of inflation and the additional of sticky wages improves the fit for the behavior of inflation persistence.

The results of the variance decomposition suggest that the wage markup shock plays a prominent role in explaining the variation of both nominal and real variables in the stick-wage model. The wage markup shock accounts for 26 percent of the variation in output. Among other shocks, the wage markup shock dominates in explaining the variation in inflation. On the other hand, real variables cannot be determined independently of monetary policy. The policy shock accounts for 63 percent of the variation in output in the sticky-wage model, and 25 percent in the flexible-wage model , indicating that monetary policy is non-neutral.

In summary, our findings suggest that both endogenous money and sticky wages are necessary features in a dynamic New Keynesian model in explaining the joint behavior of the key macroeconomic variables, both nominal and real.

References

Amato, J. D., & Thomas, L. (2004). Implications of habit formation for optimal monetary policy. *Journal of Monetary Economics*, 51, 303–325.

An, S., & Schorfheide, F. (2007). Bayesian analysis of dsge models. *Econometric Reviews*, 26, 113–172.

Andres, J., Lopez-Salido, J. D., & Nelson, E. (2005). Sticky-price models and the natural rate hypothesis. *Journal of Monetary Economics*, 52, 1025–1053.

Andres, J., Lopez-Salido, J. D., & Nelson, E. (2009). Money and the natural rate of interest: structural estimates for the united states and the euro area. *Journal of Economic Dynamic and Control*, 33, 758–776.

Bernanke, B. S. (2006). Monetary aggregates and monetary policy at the federal reserve: a historical perspective. Frankfurt, Germany. Speech at the Fourth ECB Central Banking Conference.

Boldrin, M., L., C., & Fischer, J. (2001). Habit persistence, asset returns and the business cycle. *American Economic Review*, 77, 647–666.

Bouakez, H., Cardia, E., & Ruge-Murcia, F. J. (2005). Habit formation and persistence of monetary policy. *Journal of Monetary Economics*, 52, 1073–1088.

Calvo, G. (1983). Staggered prices in a utility-maximizing framework. *Journal of Monetary Economy*, 12, 383–398.

Christiano, L. J., Eichenbaum, M., & Evans, C. L. (2005). Nominal rigidities and the dynamic effects of a shock to monetary policy. *Journal of Political Economy*, 113, 1–45.

Clarida, R., Gali, J., & Gertler, M. (2000). Monetary policy rules and macroeconomic stability: evidence and some theory. *Quarterly Journal of Economics*, 115, 147–180.

Cochrane, J. H. (2007). Identification with taylor rule: a critical review. *Working Paper, No. 13410. National Bureau of Economic Research* .

Dixit, A., & Stiglitz, J. (1977). Monopolistic competition and optimum product diversity. *American Economic Review*, 67, 297–308.

Ellison, M., & Scott, A. (2000). Sticky price and volatile output. *Journal of Monetary Economics*, 46, 621–632.

Erceg, C. J., Henderson, D. W., & Levin, A. T. (2000). Optimal monetary policy with staggered wage and price contracts. *Journal of Monetary Economy*, 46, 281–313.

Fuhrer, J. C. (2000). Habit formation in consumption and its implications for monetary-policy models. *American Economic Review*, 90, 367–390.

Gali, J. (2008). *Monetary policy, inflation, and the business cycle: an introduction to the New Keynesian framework.*. Princeton University Press. Princetion.

Gali, J., & Gertler, M. (1999). Inflation dynamics: a structural econometric analysis. *Journal of Monetary Economics*, 44, 195–222.

Gavin, W. T., & Kydland, F. E. (1999). Endogenous money supply and the business cycle. *Review of Economic Dynamics*, 2, 347–369.

Giannoni, M. P., & Woodford, M. (2003). Optimal inflation targeting rules. *Working Paper, No. 9939. National Bureau of Economic Research*, .

Huang, X. D., & Liu, Z. (2002). Staggered price-setting, staggered wage-setting, and business cycle persistence. *Journal of Monetary Economics*, 49, 405–433.

Ingram, B. F., Kocherlakota, N. R., & Savin, N. E. (1994). Explaining business cycle: a multiple-shock approach. *Journal of Monetary Economics*, 34, 415–428.

Ireland, P. N. (2003). Endogenous money or sticky prices? *Journal of Monetary Economics*, 50, 1623–1648.

Ireland, P. N. (2004). Money's role in the monetary business cycle. *Journal of Money, Credit, and Banking*, 36, 969–984.

King, R. G., Plosser, C. I., & Rebelo, S. T. (1988). Production, growth and business cycles: I. the basic neoclassical model. *Journal of Monetary Economics*, 21, 195–232.

Kydland, F. E., & Prescott, E. C. (1982). Time to build and aggregate fluctuations. *Econometrica*, 50, 1345–1370.

Leeper, E. M., & Zha, T. (2001). Assessing simple policy rules: a view from a complete macroeconomic model. *Economic Review*, 4, 35–58.

Matheron, J., & Poilly, C. (2009). How well does a small structural model with sticky prices and wages fit postwar us data? *Economic Modelling*, 26, 266–284.

McCallum, B. T. (2001). Analysis of the monetary transmission mechanism: methodological issues. In D. Bundesbank (Ed.), *The Monetary Transmission Process: Recent Developments and Lessons for Europe* (pp. 11–43). New York: Palgrave.

McCallum, B. T., & Nelson, E. (1999). An optimizing is-lm specification for monetary policy and business cycle analysis. *Journal of Money, Credit, and Banking*, 31, 296–316.

Rabanal, P. (2007). Does inflation increase after a monetary policy tightening? answers based on an estimated dsge model. *Journal of Economic Dynamic and Control*, 31, 906–937.

Rabanal, P., & Rubio-Ramirez, J. F. (2005). Comparing new keynesian models of the business cycle: a bayesian approach. *Journal of Monetary Economics*, 52, 1151–1166.

Rotemberg, J. (1982). Sticky prices in the unites states. *Journal of Political Economy*, 90, 1187–1211.

Smets, F., & Wouters, R. (2003). An estimated dynamic stochastic general equilibrium model of the euro area. *Journal of the European Economic Association*, 1, 1123–1175.

Smets, F., & Wouters, R. (2007). Shocks and frictions in us business cycles: a bayesian approach. *American Economic Review*, 97, 586–606.

Walsh, C. E. (2010). *Monetary theory and policy, 3rd edition*. Cambridge: The MIT Press.

Woodford, M. (2001). Inflation stabilization and welfare. *Working Paper, No. 8071. National Bureau of Economic Research*.

In: Business Cycles in Economics
Editor: Jason C. Hsu

ISBN: 978-1-63321-322-7

Chapter 13

FINANCIAL INTERMEDIATION AND MONETARY POLICY: A CLOSER LOOK AT DEALER BALANCE SHEETS AND MONEY MARKETS

Elizabeth Klee * ***and Win Monroe***
Federal Reserve Board, Washington, D. C., US

Abstract

Historically, the Federal Reserve has interacted with 20 to 40 "primary dealers" –banks and securities broker-dealers that transact directly with the Federal Reserve -- in its open market operations. This chapter uses the example of the primary dealers to answer questions about financial intermediation more generally. Our results suggest that changes in available collateral, either through Treasury auctions or Federal Reserve operations, can cause a temporary primary dealer portfolio reallocation, which can help the market more easily absorb the collateral, and as a consequence, can boost or dampen financing rates. Importantly, most of these frictions are short-lived, and conditions revert back to "normal" within a week or so of the initial impact of the shock.

Introduction

How do financial intermediaries affect market prices? This is a classic question in economics and finance, ranging from how banks determine loan rates to how securities dealers affect stock prices. In theoretical, fricitionless markets, the existence of intermediaries should have no effect on market prices or quantities. In practice, intermediaries do have real effects on markets because financial intermediation is an imperfect market with barriers to entry, economies of scale, and natural monopolies, which result in non-atomistic intermediaries and other frictions.[1] Understanding these effects is critical to gain insight into price formation and market equilibrium.

---

* E-mail address: elizabeth.c.klee@frb.gov

[1] See Kohn (2008) chapter 3 for discussion of market imperfections in financial intermediation and Adrian, et al. (2010) for empirical examples of asset price effects.

This question is interesting for a broad set of institutions and markets, and also for the specific case of the intermediaries connected to monetary policy implementation. Historically, the Federal Reserve has interacted with 20 to 40 "primary dealers" -- bank or securities brokers that transact directly with the Federal Reserve -- in its open market operations. Primary dealers are required to participate meaningfully in the Federal Reserve's operations, bidding to buy or sell securities to the Federal Reserve, as well as in Treasury security auctions.[2] They too, however, are intermediaries, and have to manage their own balance sheet and capital position, in addition to these exogenous changes in their assets. Previous research has found that these exogenous changes in their assets are partially persistent and potentially have implications for intermediation.[3]

This chapter uses the example of the primary dealers to answer questions about financial intermediation more generally. Specifically, if there are limited effects of dealer intermediation, then dealer activities should not have a material effect on market prices. However, if markets are imperfect, there is the potential for dealer inventories to affect financing rates.

In order to explore the possibility that dealer inventories affect market prices, this chapter investigates the correlation between dealers' securities holdings, rates in the Treasury General Collateral (GC) repo market – where dealers finance these holdings – and Federal Reserve and Treasury purchases and sales of Treasury securities. The results suggest that the level of dealers' securities holdings are significantly correlated with rates in the overnight Treasury GC repo market. Overall, these effects are relatively modest. We show that some of the temporary rise in dealer positions can be attributed to immediate effects of Federal Reserve purchases and sales in its various quantitative easing programs, although levels and rates revert to normal levels soon after the initial shock. In addition, like many parts of the financial system, the primary dealers have operated under different financial conditions pre- and post-crisis. Given the level and behavior of the rates before and after the crisis, we compare our results for the full sample with results for the subsamples before and after the crisis.

Our results suggest that Fed securities purchases can cause a temporary primary dealer portfolio reallocation putting limited upward pressure on GC repo rates. Importantly, most of these frictions are short-lived, and conditions revert back to "normal" within a week or so of the initial impact of the shock. For example, we find that Federal Reserve sales of short-dated securities in the maturity extension program (MEP), otherwise known as "operation twist," tended to push up dealer positions in concert. We also find that some of the rise in dealer positions is attributable to participation in Treasury auctions.

While these results are interesting in their own right as they illustrate important supply effects in the market for fixed-income securities, more generally they point to the importance of the intermediary structure in the monetary policy transmission mechanism.[4] Textbook examinations of monetary policy transmission usually posit that the first few implementation steps work seamlessly.[5] By demonstrating that there are frictions, we can better judge the effectiveness of changes in the composition of securities held by the public on interest rates,

---

[2] The Background section below offers more detail on this subject.
[3] Fleming and Rosenberg (2008).
[4] D'Amico, et al. 2012 find similar supply effects and market segmentation when examining stock and flow effects of the Federal Reserve's large scale asset purchases, but did not focus on the role of financial intermediation.
[5] See Chapter 16 in Mishkin 2001 for a representative example.

and therefore gain greater insight into some of the temporary impacts of the Federal Reserve's asset programs.[6]

The remainder of this chapter gives some background on dealers' balance sheets before and after the financial crisis, discusses our empirical results, and highlights a few questions for further research.

Background

The Federal Reserve has historically transacted with between 20 and 40 primary dealers in securities purchases and sales whether on the behalf of the FOMC or the U.S. Treasury. The number of primary dealers has declined over the last several decades mostly due to consolidation in the banking and dealer-broker industries.[7] Primary dealers trade approximately $600 billion in US Treasury securities daily and must participate in all Federal Reserve operations and Treasury auctions, making primary dealers an integral nexus in the market for Treasury securities.[8,9]

Generally, dealers finance their purchases of Treasury securities by lending the securities out in the repo market. Dealers are large participants in the repo market, and thus potentially non-atomistic participants. This implies that when their inventories change significantly, it can lead to changes in the price for financing in the repo market. Because dealers must meaningfully participate in all Federal Reserve and U.S. Treasury auctions, dealers took on large amounts of Treasury securities as deficits increased and had to build up inventories to deliver to the Federal Reserve during its large scale asset purchase programs.

This chapter's analysis covers the period from fall 2005 to the end of 2013 when all of the relevant data was available. Figure I shows repo rates over the full sample. The DTCC GCF repo rate ranged from around 5.25 percent in 2006 to below 25 basis points, when overnight interest rates reached their effective lower bound after 2008. Figure II shows the same rate but only for the post-crisis sample on a smaller scale; this figure shows some variability in the rate. Clearly the two periods before and after the crisis constitute dramatically different financial environments, so our analysis will also look at each subsample before and after the peak of the crisis.

---

[6] D'Amico, et al. 2013 also suggest that the existence of supply and scarcity frictions

[7] Chapter 14 in Stigum, 2007 provides a good overview and recent history of primary dealers.

[8] Estimate from the New York Federal Reserve's Primary Dealer statistics: http://www.newyorkfed.org/markets/gsds/search.html

[9] The Federal Reserve Bank of New York defines the requirements for primary dealer participation as follows:

"The New York Fed will expect a primary dealer to bid in every auction, for, at a minimum, an amount of securities representing its pro rata share, based on the number of primary dealers at the time of the auction, of the offered amount. Its bid prices should be reasonable when compared to the range of rates trading in the when-issued market, taking into account market volatility and other risk factors.

Primary dealers that do little business with the New York Fed over a period of time, that repeatedly provide bids and offers in the New York Fed operations or Treasury auctions that are not reasonably competitive, or that fail to provide useful market information and commentary, are not meeting the New York Fed's expectations of a primary dealer. In those situations, the New York Fed may limit a primary dealer's access to any or all of the primary dealer facilities or operations, and may suspend or terminate a primary dealer if it continues to fail to meet these business standards. "

Details, as well as a historic list of primary dealers, can be found on the New York Federal Reserve's website: http://www.newyorkfed.org/markets/pridealers_policies.html

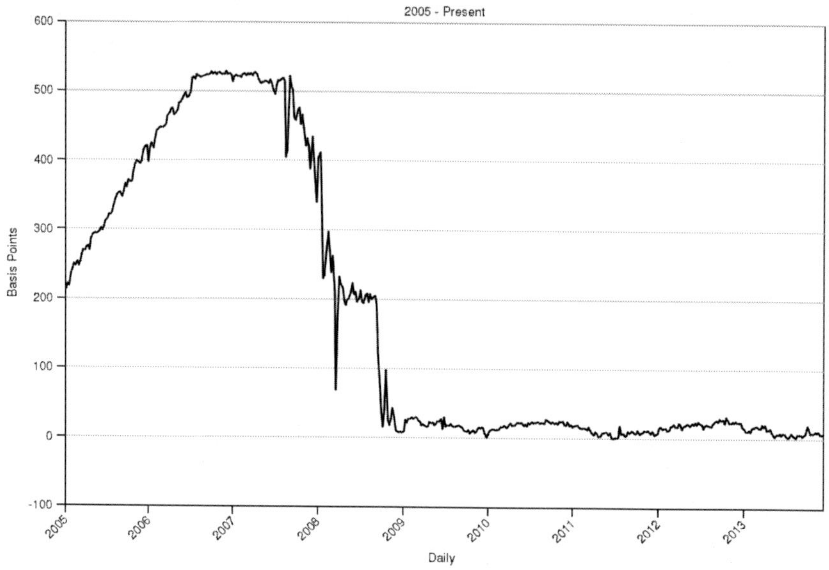

Figure 1. DTCC Treasury GCF Repo Rate.

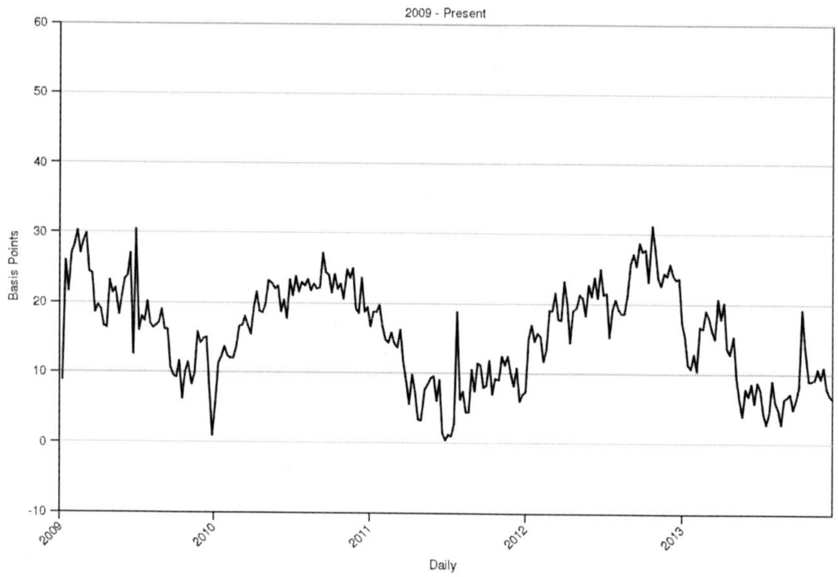

Figure 2. DTCC Treasury GCF Repo Rate.

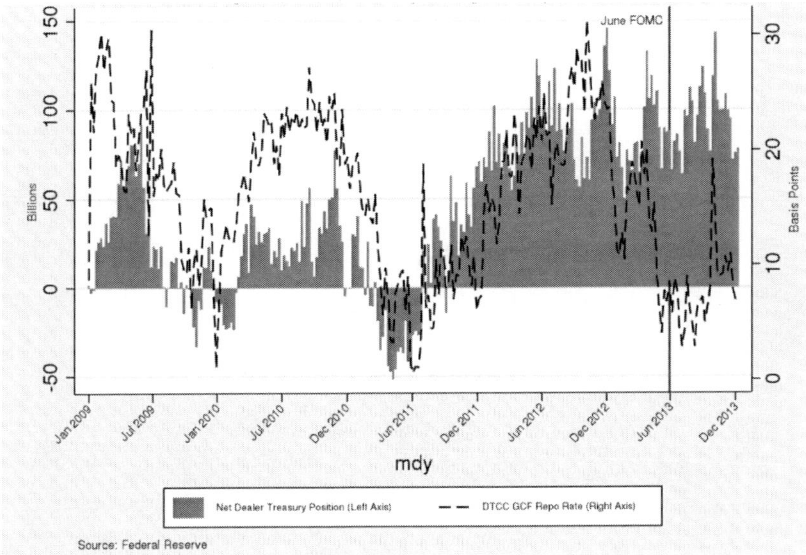

Source: Federal Reserve.

Figure 3. Dealers Treasury Holdings and Repo Rates.

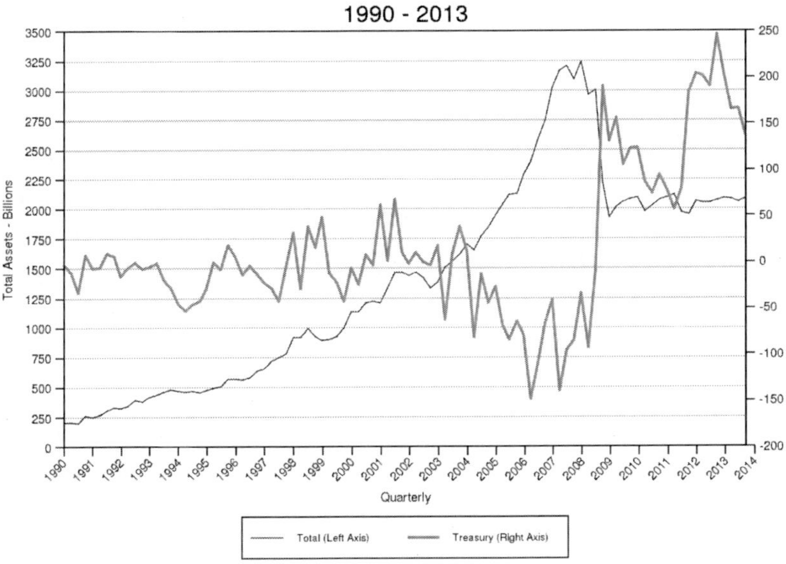

Figure 4. Dealer and Broker Total Assets vs. Net Treasury Position.

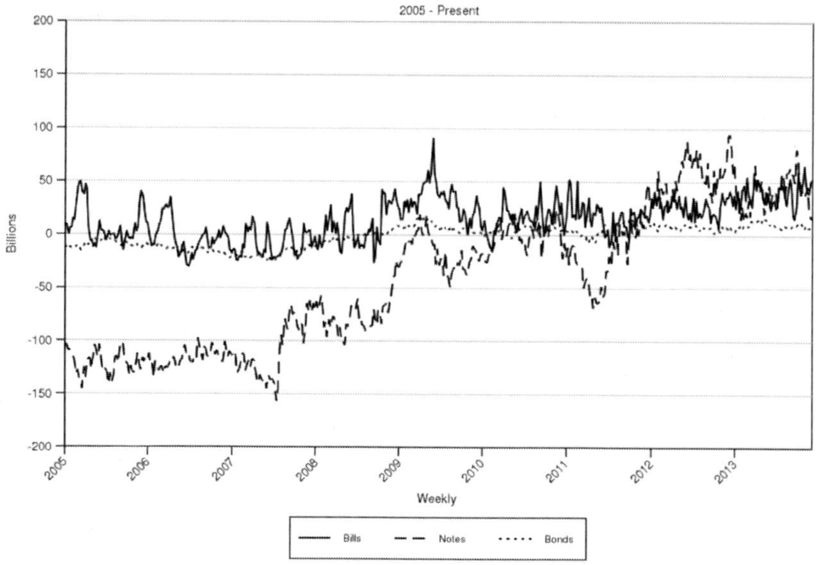

Figure 5. Dealer Positions in Treasuries.

Figure III plots net dealer positions in Treasury securities against the DTCC GCF Repo rate. The net dealer position in Treasury securities represents the amount of the inventory they need to finance. The movements in the two series suggest that as the need for financing increases, the rate for financing increases as well. The relationship becomes a little more tenuous after mid-June 2013, when dynamics for rates and collateral diverged.

Also noteworthy is the fact that dealer positions have moved up considerably since the start of the financial crisis. As shown in Figure IV, while dealers were generally short Treasury securities before the crisis, their positions rapidly switched to long during the crisis and remain around roughly \$150 billion at the end of 2013. Figure V shows dealers' net position on a weekly frequency for bills, notes and bonds.[10] Visual inspection suggests that dealers traditionally keep a roughly balanced position in bills and bonds, and a net short position in notes. This relationship changed during the period of acute financial stress from late 2008 to early 2009 when dealers jumped to a net long position in all three security tenors. Specifically, there has been a gradual climb in positions starting in late 2011 up to the present for bills and since 2009 for bonds. In contrast, dealers' net positions in notes have changed significantly over the period, beginning with a consistent short position from mid-2005 to late 2008 with some increase as the US economy deteriorated in 2007, to a net long position since the financial crisis. With this overall significant rise in dealer positions comes a need to finance these positions. Our results suggest that increases in dealer positions tend to push up the Treasury GC repo rate. These estimates are robust to possible endogeneity of dealer positions to financing rates, as we conduct a battery of tests to ensure that our estimates are unbiased.

By using data on U.S. Treasury debt issuance and Federal Reserve purchases in conjunction with Federal Reserve data on primary dealers' positions in these securities we can

[10] Strictly speaking the tenor ranges are less than 1 year remaining maturity, more than one year and less than 11, and more than 11, but we refer to them as bills, notes and bonds for convenience. These categories correspond to the data available in the dealer position data from the FR2004 primary dealer survey.

clearly illustrate dealers' unique role as financial intermediaries for monetary policy and measure the effect of these programs on repo markets. We use a data set that includes weekly dealer positions, Federal Reserve open market operations, net Treasury securities issuance, and Treasury auction allocations from September 2005 to December 2013 to evaluate the impact of net dealer positions on repurchase agreement rates. All estimates are on a weekly frequency, as the dealer position data are available only at this frequency. Our data come from three sources: First, data on primary dealers' net positions result from a weekly survey conducted by the New York Federal Reserve Bank and represent dealers' positions as of closing each Wednesday. Second, the Treasury auction and net issuance data comes from the U.S. Treasury and is daily data aggregated to weekly on a Wednesday-to-Wednesday basis to accord with the primary dealer data. Finally, the data for Federal Reserve purchases and sales are published on the New York Federal Reserve website and are transaction level data, which we again aggregate weekly on a Wednesday-to-Wednesday basis.

Empirical Exercises

Dealer Positions

In our preliminary analysis, we perform a simple check for correlation of dealer positions, Federal Reserve actions, Treasury issuance, and financing costs. To this end, we evaluate the following specification:

$$(position_{it} - position_{it-1}) = \alpha_i + \sum_{i \in J} \beta_i Fed_{it} + \xi_b bills_t + \xi_c coupons_t$$
$$+\gamma[(yield_{it} - dtcc_t) - (yield_{it-1} - dtcc_{t-1})] + \epsilon_{it}, i \in J, i = 1, ..., m. \quad (1.1)$$

where $position_{it}$, is the aggregate dealer position in tenor i of J tenors at time t, Fed_{it} are Federal Reserve purchases or sales in that tenor, $bills_t$ and $coupons_t$ represent net Treasury issuance in bills and coupons, respectively, and ($yield_{it}$ - $dtcc_t$) is the spread between the average yield in that tenor and the cost of financing these positions in the repo market. We divide the tenor ranges into bills, notes, and bonds due to the differences in dealer behavior for these ranges as seen previously in Figure 5.

Table 1 shows the regression of changes in dealer positions in these tenor ranges on Federal Reserve operations, Treasury net issuance, and the spread between the average yield and financing rates for different tenor ranges. Given the substantial changes in Federal Reserve operations and the change in pace of Treasury issuance before and after the crisis, we also run the same regressions over the pre-crisis subsample and the post-crisis subsamples.

The first three columns show regressions on dealer balance sheets in the full sample, the next six columns show the same regressions for the pre-crisis and post-crisis samples. Overall, the results suggest some effects of both price and quantity on dealers' positions, although differences corresponding to tenor exist due to active dealer balance sheet management dynamics.

For the full sample, dealers' positions in Treasury bills were influenced Treasury's issuance of bills and the spread between the average yield in those securities and financing rates in repo markets. The Treasury bills net issuance coefficient implies that for every $1 billion in net Treasury bills issuance, dealers' net position in bills rose by roughly $100 million or about 10 percent of purchases. Financing costs also affect dealer holdings of securities: When the spread between the earning rate and the financing rate is high, investors were more willing to buy the securities from dealers and if the spread fell, dealers held more as the residual holders of these securities. This suggests that dealers may have been less able to unwind positions in short-dated securities if they were comparatively more expensive to finance, pushing these costs to dealers.

Moving further out the maturity spectrum reveals that dealer behavior depends importantly on the tenor of the securities. Dealer positions in notes were influenced by Federal Reserve purchases and sales as well Treasury net issuance, but not the yield-to-financing spread. Federal Reserve purchases in this tenor range created downward pressure on dealer positions in these securities: for every $1 billion in Federal Reserve purchases, dealer balance sheets declined $200 million and sales pushed up dealer balance sheets by about the same margin. Treasury net issuance of coupons also intuitively increases dealers' net positions in these securities and by a comparable magnitude as net bill issuance did for dealers' holdings of bills. The spread between the average yield on notes and financing rates is not significant, suggesting that factors other than this spread influenced dealer positions. Dealers' net positions in longer dated securities are not statistically associated with any of these factors over the full sample.

While it is instructive to consider the sample as a whole, it is important to note that there are key differences in the results pre-and post-crisis in some tenors. For the pre-crisis subsample we see that changes in dealer positions in bills are similar to the full sample. Every billion increase in Treasury net bill issuance is associated with an increase in dealer positions for bills of about 10 percent of net issuance. In addition, a 1 basis point increase in the difference of the spread between the average yield and repo rates implies a $100 million decrease in dealers' bills holdings. For intermediate tenor securities in the pre-crisis period we find that only Treasury net issuance of coupons is statistically significant, where a $1 billion dollar increase in net issuance results in about $100 million increase in dealers' net position; financing costs and Fed actions are no longer significant. A $1 billion dollar Federal Reserve purchase is associated with a decrease of about 50 percent of the purchase in dealers' net position in these securities. Because dealer positions in this tenor were particularly lean, the results suggest that dealers sourced the securities in order to meet Federal Reserve demand. This demand was generally driven by the need to offset growth in the autonomous factors on the Federal Reserve's balance sheet, such as currency or the pool of reverse repurchase agreements held for foreign and international accounts.

In the post-crisis subsample, dealers' positions in bills are no longer influenced by the average yield and repo spread, except in bonds. For bonds, increases in the spread resulted in decreases in dealers' net position. Federal Reserve sales are also significant, but decrease dealer balance sheets in this tenor. While the direct effect of Fed sales would be to increase dealer positions at least on impact, the results are consistent with some portfolio rebalancing of dealers in response to Fed actions. Treasury net issuance of bills is the primary sole factor associated with changes in dealers' positions in bills and every billion in new net issuance is associated with a $91 million increase in dealers' net positions in bills.

Table 1.

	Change in Dealer Positions, Bills	Change in Dealer Positions, Notes	Change in Dealer Positions, Bonds	Change in Dealer Positions, Bills	Change in Dealer Positions, Notes	Change in Dealer Positions, Bonds	Change in Dealer Positions, Bills	Change in Dealer Positions, Notes	Change in Dealer Positions, Bonds
	Full Sample			Pre-Programs			Post-Programs		
Fed Purchases, Notes	0.0249	-0.186***	-0.00573	-0.128	0.918	-0.483**	0.0108	-0.143*	-0.00881
	(0.549)	(-2.747)	(-0.537)	(-0.0699)	(0.733)	(-2.048)	(0.230)	(-1.649)	(-0.686)
Fed Purchases, Bonds	-0.000202	-0.156	-0.0475	4.225	-2.897	-0.283	0.107	-0.0294	-0.0656
	(-0.000723)	(-0.531)	(-0.857)	(0.343)	(-0.363)	(-0.342)	(0.351)	(-0.0753)	(-0.887)
Fed Sales, Bills	-0.191	0.0188	0.0114	0.189	0.0600	0.0529	-0.753	0.250	-0.0528
	(-1.626)	(0.0727)	(0.407)	(0.933)	(0.269)	(1.146)	(-1.609)	(0.689)	(-0.661)
Fed Sales, Notes	0.156	0.196*	0.0125	-0.338	-0.0824	-0.0755	0.199	0.194	0.0154
	(1.092)	(1.646)	(0.525)	(-0.785)	(-0.173)	(-0.665)	(1.310)	(1.395)	(0.549)
Treasury Net Issuance, Bills	0.0949***	0.00769	-0.000824	0.0969***	-0.00342	-0.000174	0.0896***	0.0259	-0.00223
	(9.524)	(0.479)	(-0.242)	(7.197)	(-0.195)	(-0.0421)	(3.642)	(0.837)	(-0.440)
Treasury Net Issuance, Coupons	-0.00278	0.0833***	-0.00399	-0.0566	0.104**	-0.000415	0.00683	0.100***	-0.00940*
	(-0.156)	(3.862)	(-1.137)	(-0.789)	(2.043)	(-0.0409)	(0.258)	(2.837)	(-1.730)
Yield in Tenor - Repo	-0.0425**	0.0112	-0.00386	-0.105***	0.0248	-0.00399	-0.0167	0.00809	-0.0153*
	(-2.419)	(0.410)	(-0.834)	(-3.211)	(0.740)	(-0.820)	(-0.678)	(0.188)	(-1.952)
AR(1)	-0.266***	-0.333***	-0.235***	-0.159**	-0.195***	-0.230***	-0.343***	-0.392***	-0.271***
	(-6.252)	(-7.634)	(-5.228)	(-2.203)	(-2.890)	(-2.817)	(-5.905)	(-6.322)	(-4.649)
AR(2)	-0.264***	-0.0405	-0.255***	-0.199**	-0.0723	-0.168**	-0.347***	-0.0503	-0.332***
	(-5.404)	(-0.841)	(-5.542)	(-2.537)	(-1.009)	(-2.421)	(-5.796)	(-0.709)	(-5.076)
AR(3)	-0.155***	-0.102**	-0.170***	-0.0104	0.0462	-0.158**	-0.268***	-0.154**	-0.202***
	(-3.907)	(-2.519)	(-3.503)	(-0.174)	(0.783)	(-2.104)	(-5.040)	(-2.411)	(-3.072)
Constant	-0.194	-0.347	0.156*	-0.0871	-0.208	0.206**	-0.279	-1.618	0.396
	(-0.409)	(-0.625)	(1.673)	(-0.131)	(-0.311)	(2.040)	(-0.253)	(-1.093)	(1.622)
Sigma	10.26***	10.23***	2.032***	9.680***	8.826***	1.790***	10.25***	10.99***	2.160***
	(35.35)	(33.33)	(28.76)	(24.56)	(21.89)	(17.69)	(22.09)	(22.58)	(21.01)
Observations	467	467	467	208	208	208	259	259	259

z-statistics in parentheses. *** $p<0.01$, ** $p<0.05$, * $p<0.1$.

Table 2.

	Change in Dealer Positions, Notes	Change in Dealer Positions, Bonds	Change in Dealer Positions, Notes	Change in Dealer Positions, Bonds	Change in Dealer Positions, Notes	Change in Dealer Positions, Bonds
	Full Sample	Full Sample	Pre-Crisis	Pre-Crisis	Post-Crisis	Post-Crisis
Change in Dealer Positions, Notes, L1	-0.324***	0.0256***	-0.227***	0.00897	-0.375***	0.0327***
	(-7.017)	(2.772)	(-3.341)	(0.628)	(-5.971)	(2.622)
Change in Dealer Positions, Notes, L2	0.0304	-0.0107	-0.0810	-0.0177	0.0845	-0.00939
	(0.662)	(-1.165)	(-1.193)	(-1.243)	(1.345)	(-0.754)
Change in Dealer Positions, Bonds, L1	0.325	-0.160***	1.152***	-0.195***	-0.208	-0.131**
	(1.425)	(-3.507)	(3.532)	(-2.841)	(-0.671)	(-2.135)
Change in Dealer Positions, Bonds L2	0.479**	-0.236***	0.485	-0.123*	0.535*	-0.290***
	(2.106)	(-5.174)	(1.453)	(-1.749)	(1.737)	(-4.746)
Treasury Net Issuance, Bills	-0.000700	-0.000709	-0.0107	0.00156	0.0196	-0.00467
	(-0.0383)	(-0.194)	(-0.560)	(0.388)	(0.576)	(-0.694)
Treasury Net Issuance, Coupons	0.0891***	-0.00281	0.0987**	-0.000929	0.0955***	-0.00324
	(4.752)	(-0.747)	(2.086)	(-0.0934)	(4.076)	(-0.697)
Federal Reserve Purchases	-0.188***	-0.0104	0.844	-0.291	-0.147	-0.00825
	(-2.747)	(-0.760)	(0.760)	(-1.248)	(-1.599)	(-0.452)
Federal Reserve Sales	0.173*	0.0142	0.0152	0.0211	0.272*	0.00622
	(1.676)	(0.687)	(0.105)	(0.694)	(1.906)	(0.219)
Constant	-0.377	0.126	-0.232	0.170	-1.400	0.128
	(-0.588)	(0.981)	(-0.328)	(1.144)	(-1.090)	(0.504)
Observations	465	465	206	206	259	259

z-statistics in parentheses.

*** p<0.01, ** p<0.05, * p<0.1.

Dealers' net position in intermediate tenors are pushed up $98 million for each billion in Treasury's net issuance of coupons and down $155 million by Federal Reserve purchases. In longer dated securities, dealers' net positions are actually decreased by treasury net issuance of coupons and when the spread between the yield and repo rate increases.

There are two potential countervailing effects of an increase in this spread. Dealers may find holding the securities more attractive, as they are able to finance them relatively more cheaply. On the other hand, investors also face similar incentives, and would be more likely to demand to hold the securities themselves in order to derive this benefit. Apparently, this latter effect dominates and the coefficient on this term is negative, suggesting that overall, demand from customers dominates the dealers' decisions.

As noted in the last few lines of the table, the autoregressive terms are generally negative and statistically significant. As might be expected from behavior of a dealer intermediary, there is strong mean reversion in dealer positions, suggesting that any of these effects are likely somewhat transitory, and that dealers generally permit smooth transmission of Treasury and Federal Reserve operations to the private sector. In particular, roughly 30 percent of the previous period's change is unwound in the next period, with another third or so in the weeks following any of these changes in positions.

Dealer Balance Sheet Management

Taking a closer look at the portfolio rebalancing aspects of dealer positions, table 2 displays information on the interaction between dealer allocations at the longer end of the curve using a VAR version of equation (1.1). Specifically, our equation of interest is

$$\begin{pmatrix} medium_t \\ long_t \end{pmatrix} = \begin{pmatrix} c_1 \\ c_2 \end{pmatrix} + \begin{pmatrix} A_{1,1} & A_{1,2} \\ A_{2,1} & A_{2,2} \end{pmatrix} \begin{pmatrix} medium_{t-1} \\ long_{t-1} \end{pmatrix} + \begin{pmatrix} D_{1,1} & D_{1,2} \\ D_{2,1} & D_{2,2} \end{pmatrix} \begin{pmatrix} Treasury_t \\ Fed_t \end{pmatrix} + \begin{pmatrix} \varepsilon_{1t} \\ \varepsilon_{2t} \end{pmatrix}$$

The advantage of running these positions in a system is that it allows us to investigate more specifically how dealer balance sheets adjust in light of changes in costs or flows.

Over the whole sample, as shown in the first column, in the middle of the curve, increases in the net position at the middle of the curve tend to be offset the next period. In addition, dealer positions in the middle part of the curve are associated with previous increases at the long end of the curve, potentially suggesting that even if dealer portfolios grow, there could be some attention paid to balancing the maturity structure. Interestingly, the cross effect on notes from bonds appears to be mostly driven by the pre-crisis sample, as the effect is no longer significant in the post-crisis sample. For bonds, the effect is the opposite, with a significant boost from notes to bond holdings, but not causality the other way. Even though these run in different directions, both subsample results point to balance sheet management by dealers in the face of new supply.

That said, there is a general trend of increasing positions in line with rises in longer-dated securities. There does appear to be at least some inventory effect of additional coupon issuance that dealers do not offset completely; while most of the issuance appears to be dissipated, about 10 percent remains in dealer's holdings. Fed sales also tend to boost intermediate maturity securities holdings to some degree. Fed purchases, however, do mitigate this effect somewhat, as these operations are associated with holdings declining about 15 percent of the level of the purchase.

Table 3.

	DTCC Repo Rate Full Sample	DTCC Repo Rate Pre-Crisis	DTCC Repo Rate Post-Crisis
Dealer Positions, Bills	0.243***	0.408**	0.0841***
	(3.324)	(2.331)	(3.929)
Dealer Positions, Notes	-0.132	-0.525***	0.0534**
	(-1.540)	(-3.111)	(2.341)
Dealer Positions, Bonds	0.291	0.307	0.00108
	(0.728)	(0.358)	(0.0103)
Fed Purchases, Notes	0.0603	1.123	0.0263
	(0.158)	(0.220)	(0.480)
Fed Purchases, Bonds	-0.610	-0.875	-0.153
	(-0.396)	(-0.0416)	(-0.871)
Fed Sales, Bills	-0.678***	-1.593***	0.0744
	(-3.430)	(-2.963)	(0.541)
Fed Sales, Notes	-0.503	-3.477***	-0.155*
	(-1.499)	(-3.014)	(-1.811)
Treasury Net Issuance, Bills	-0.0406*	-0.0607	-0.000460
	(-1.718)	(-1.043)	(-0.0417)
Treasury Net Issuance, Coupons	0.0304	0.120*	0.0111*
	(1.075)	(1.679)	(1.808)
Early Sales Dummy	-17.37***	1.473	
	(-2.895)	(0.106)	
AR(1)	1.022***	1.014***	0.552***
	(47.41)	(21.78)	(10.18)
AR(2)	-0.423***	-0.457***	0.346***
	(-12.40)	(-6.545)	(6.546)
AR(3)	0.399***	0.438***	0.0190
	(17.77)	(9.797)	(0.292)
Constant	121.9	130.0	12.41***
	(0.511)	(0.310)	(4.549)
Sigma	14.83***	20.61***	3.227***
	(57.71)	(27.47)	(27.64)
Observations	468	209	259

z-statistics in parentheses.
*** $p<0.01$, ** $p<0.05$, * $p<0.1$.

The Treasury GC Repo Rate

Part of the reason why dealers may have found it more profitable to hold inventories of Treasury securities in the current environment relative to previously may have something to do with the cost of financing these positions. It may also be that the dealer positions themselves have contemporaneous effects on the costs of financing these positions. Untangling the causal effects of this relationship is difficult, but we attempt to do so in this section. In order to explore this hypothesis more carefully, we now turn to how dealer positions, Fed actions, and Treasury issuance affect the Treasury GC repo rate. Our preliminary equation of interest is

$$r_t = \gamma + \sum_{i \in J} \delta_i position_{it} + + \sum_{i \in J} \beta_i Fed_{it} + \xi_b bills_{it} + \xi_c coupons_{it} + EarlySalesDummy + \mu_t$$

where r_t is the overnight Treasury GC repo rate and all other variables are as defined above. We also include a dummy for early Federal Reserve sales. These sales occurred when the run up in the credit and liquidity facilities occurred, making it difficult to isolate the impact of Federal Reserve actions versus market conditions more generally. We performed a battery of unit root and autocorrelation tests. We find that over the entire sample, the repo rate exhibits a unit root, although some of that may be because of a broader trend in interest rates. In addition, we use autocorrelation tests to suggest the appropriate lag length to use when estimating an autoregressive process to describe our data adequately.

Table 3 reports the results. In the full sample, repo rates tend to fall with Federal Reserve sales of short-dated Treasury securities. Still, changes in dealer positions apparently had a significant effect on the repo rate, although with opposite signs on the change in bills and notes positions. Additionally, in the full sample as well as both subsamples increases in dealer positions in bills always result in significant upward pressure on rates and in the post-crisis sample dealer positions in notes does the same in the post-crisis sample. The coefficients are much smaller in the post-crisis period, though this may reflect the generally lower level of rates.

With the exception of Federal Reserve sales of shorter maturity securities in the pre-crisis period, Treasury and Federal Reserve transactions do not seem to have a direct effect on repo rates over any part of the sample once we control for dealer positions in those securities.

Controlling for Endogeneity

As eluded to earlier, there is a classic simultaneity problem with evaluating the effect of dealer positions on repo rates. In general, dealers use the repo market to finance holdings of securities; as a result, repo rates can be viewed as a “financing rate” from the perspective of the dealer. However, as dealers are potentially nonatomistic entities in securities markets, it is possible that both the supply of securities on their balance sheets and their demand for more securities affect the level of financing rates. In order to control for this possibility, we need to use a two-stage specification with an instrumental variable that is correlated with the supply of securities on dealer balance sheets, but is predetermined and not correlated with current levels of rates. We use the foreign investors’ participation in Treasury auctions in this role.

A little background is helpful to understand this instrumental variable. Dealers are required to "participate meaningfully" in Treasury auctions. In this role, the dealers are expected to take up the portfolio of the auction not demanded by other entities. Another group that participates broadly in auctions is foreign institutions. Next to the dealers, foreign institutions take down the largest share of Treasury auctions. In addition, the level of dealer participation in an auction and the level of foreign participation are positively correlated, in that larger auction sizes potentially lead to increases in both. That said, factors that influence foreign participation are plausibly exogenous to dealer participation. For example, a large share of foreign purchases is directed to delivering Treasury securities to foreign official institutions for foreign-exchange reserve management.[1] Factors such as financing positions in the repo market are likely less relevant to these foreign institutions, as these are buy-and-hold investors. As such, foreign takedown in Treasury auctions can be used as an instrument for dealer positions.

With all this in mind, we instrument the dealer takeup in tenor range i of J tenor ranges with foreign auction purchases in all tenors as

$$takeup_{it} = \alpha_i + \sum_{i \in J} \beta_i Foreign_{it} + \varepsilon_{it}, i \in J$$

Using these take-ups in the first stage, we can evaluate our main equation of interest in the second stage,

$$r_t = \gamma + \sum_{i \in J} \delta_i takeup_{it} + \sum_{i \in J} \xi_i Treasuryissue_{it} + \mu_t$$

In practice, we evaluate these equations not sequentially, but simultaneously using a generalized method of moments procedure. In order to control for serial correlation in the error terms, we use Newey-West autocorrelation-adjusted standard errors, with the number of lags determined automatically by the Bartlett algorithm.

We present both the first stage and the second stage results for our preliminary specification, as both are important for understanding dealer dynamics. As with the previous regressions, we run them for the entire sample and then again, broken in to subsamples for the pre-crisis and post-crisis periods. For the first-stage regressions, each tenor bucket for foreign investor auction take up has a strong positive coefficient with the corresponding to the dealer net position, e.g. foreign auction take up of treasury securities under one year and dealer positions in these same securities. This result could simply represent supply effects in these tenors: total takeup for both groups increases, as might be expected. The one exception is intermediate tenors after the crisis; the coefficient is positive, but not statistically significant.

There are also interesting cross-portfolio effects in the first-stage regressions. For the sample as a whole, dealer takeup in short-dated auctions is also positively correlated with foreign takeup of longer-dated securities, and negatively correlated with foreign investor takeup in medium tenors. These patterns suggest some portfolio substitution effects that the dealers may be absorbing from foreign investors, although the causal evidence is not clear.

For the second stage regressions, we find that over the full sample, while Treasury bill auction amounts place upward pressure on rates, dealers help absorb some of the effect, as their takedown at auctions dampens this effect. Behavior at the longer-end of the maturity spectrum is different, as interestingly, dealer positions in longer dated securities are positively associated with repo rates. This could be in part explained by the relatively higher coupon on these longer-dated securities, making them more profitable to hold, despite the financing costs.

[1] See Bertaut et all 2009

Table 4.

	Dealer Auction Take-up, Bills	Dealer Auction Take-up, Notes	Dealer Auction Take-up, Bonds	Dealer Auction Take-up, Bills	Dealer Auction Take-up, Notes	Dealer Auction Take-up, Bonds	Dealer Auction Take-up, Bills	Dealer Auction Take-up, Notes	Dealer Auction Take-up, Bonds
	Full Sample			Pre-Programs			Post-Programs		
Fed Purchases, Bills	-6.066***	-0.847	-0.043	-5.707***	0.075	-0.007	-807.087***	92.694***	1.901
	(-5.07)	(-1.08)	(-1.007)	(-5.58)	(0.18)	(-0.438)	(-11.94)	(2.73)	(0.365)
Fed Purchases, Notes	0.154	0.067	-0.028*	-0.605	-0.373	0.070	0.132	0.098*	-0.031*
	(0.77)	(1.24)	(-1.907)	(-0.37)	(-1.42)	(1.050)	(0.73)	(1.92)	(-1.928)
Fed Purchases, Bonds	4.2***	0.728**	0.061	5.754	2.437***	-0.0458	1.889***	0.532	-0.013
	(4)	(1.98)	(0.794)	(0.93)	(2.78)	(-1.384)	(2.77)	(1.26)	(-0.164)
Fed Sales, Bills	-0.383*	-0.17*	-0.008	0.278*	0.086**	0.004	-1.203***	-0.214	-0.039
	(-1.78)	(-1.71)	(-0.841)	(1.93)	(2.29)	(1.403)	(-3.39)	(-0.8)	(-1.042)
Fed Sales, Notes	0.139	0.226	0.050	-2.814***	0.033	-0.004	-0.344	0.178	0.031
	(0.47)	(1.49)	(1.598)	(-5.43)	(0.54)	(-0.667)	(-1.37)	(1.08)	(0.952)
Treasury Net Issuance, Bills	0.504***	0.069***	0	0.525***	0.010	-0.001	0.369***	0.064***	0.002
	(8)	(3.74)	(0.0172)	(7.76)	(0.72)	(-0.884)	(6.76)	(2.65)	(0.374)
Treasury Net Issuance, Coupons	0.089	0.402***	-0.002	0.045	0.114***	0	0.022	0.597***	-0.007
	(1.4)	(3.79)	(-0.362)	(0.38)	(3.94)	(0.194)	(0.32)	(5.87)	(-0.655)
Early Bill Sales	3.268	3.112*	-0.485**	14.174**	0.4	-0.093*	ommitted	ommitted	ommitted
	(0.94)	(1.88)	(-2.099)	(2.52)	(0.41)	(-1.679)			
Foreign Take-up, Bills	0.921***	-0.299***	-0.017	2.652***	-0.025	0.007	0.667***	-0.217**	-0.039*
	(2.95)	(-3.2)	(-0.989)	(3.05)	(-0.15)	(0.240)	(2.8)	(-2.16)	(-1.837)

Table 4. Continued

	Dealer Auction Take-up, Bills	Dealer Auction Take-up, Notes	Dealer Auction Take-up, Bonds	Dealer Auction Take-up, Bills	Dealer Auction Take-up, Notes	Dealer Auction Take-up, Bonds	Dealer Auction Take-up, Bills	Dealer Auction Take-up, Notes	Dealer Auction Take-up, Bonds
	Full Sample			Pre-Programs			Post-Programs		
Foreign Take-up, Notes	-0.329***	0.991**	0.027	-0.154	2.761***	0.014*	-0.153	0.417	0.036
	(-2.29)	(2.21)	(1.310)	(-0.4)	(19.12)	(1.780)	(-0.88)	(1)	(-1.246)
Foreign Take-up, Bonds	3.36***	-0.401	3.278***	-17.062***	3.742	5.633***	2.50***	-0.894	3.268***
	(3.69)	(-0.34)	(8.736)	(-3.25)	(1.42)	(4.920)	(2.65)	(-0.61)	(11.29)
Yield in Bills - Repo	-0.026	0.007	-0.001	-0.064	-0.005	-0.001	-0.031	0.016	-0.003
	(-1.19)	(0.51)	(-0.443)	(-1.3)	(-0.54)	(-1.615)	(-1.13)	(0.97)	(-1.050)
Yield in Notes - Repo	-0.018	-0.009	0	0.053	0.01	0	-0.039	-0.02	0.004
	(-0.49)	(-0.98)	(-0.0413)	(0.99)	(0.78)	(0.480)	(-0.95)	(-1.33)	(0.926)
Yield in Bonds - Repo	0.061***	-0.003	0.001	0.01	-0.006	0	-0.016	-0.019	-0.003
	(4.09)	(-0.69)	(1.330)	(0.36)	(-0.91)	(0.113)	(-0.53)	(-1.45)	(-1.037)
Constant	34.233***	6.544***	0.069	25.726***	1.644	-0.094	74.774***	12.703***	1.751
	(11.28)	(6.38)	(0.524)	(5.68)	(1.51)	(-0.542)	(9.68)	(3.12)	(1.611)
Observations	468	468	468	209	209	209	259	259	259

z-statistics in parentheses.

*** $p<0.01$, ** $p<0.05$, * $p<0.1$.

Table 5.

	DTCC Repo Rate	DTCC Repo Rate	DTCC Repo Rate
	Full Sample	**Pre-Crisis**	**Post-Crisis**
Dealer Auction	-13.78***	-12.59***	0.895***
Takeup, Bills	(-7.740)	(-9.867)	(3.443)
Dealer Auction	-2.583	1.013	0.0754
Takeup, Notes	(-1.080)	(0.971)	(0.227)
Dealer Auction	10.46***	-44.16***	-0.837***
Takeup, Bonds	(2.749)	(-4.006)	(-2.806)
Fed Purchases, Bills	-68.56***	-66.64***	-1.837
	(-3.452)	(-5.072)	(-0.565)
Fed Purchases, Notes	1.544	11.73	-0.0561
	(0.552)	(0.630)	(-0.500)
Fed Purchases,	21.64	79.67	-3.374***
Bonds	(1.509)	(0.837)	(-3.233)
Fed Sales, Bills	-8.503**	0.225	1.252***
	(-2.017)	(0.166)	(2.976)
Fed Sales, Notes	-6.621	-31.91***	0.765***
	(-1.409)	(-5.274)	(2.844)
Treasury Net	7.350***	6.958***	-0.305***
Issuance, Bills	(5.524)	(9.603)	(-2.706)
Treasury Net	1.273	-0.905	-0.0190
Issuance, Coupons	(0.701)	(-0.974)	(-0.0808)
Early Sales Dummy	51.29	98.83*	
	(0.951)	(1.769)	
Constant	1,049***	962.6***	-47.87**
	(11.60)	(16.56)	(-2.445)
Observations	468	209	259

z-statistics in parentheses.
*** $p<0.01$, ** $p<0.05$, * $p<0.1$.

In the pre-crisis sample, dealer takedown at auctions in short and longer tenor securities are negatively associated with repo rates, suggesting that dealers help to smooth through some of the effects of increased supply from auctions. Net Treasury issuance of bills also continues to support rates by increasing the supply of collateral and we also see Federal Reserve purchases and sales putting upward and downward pressure on rates, respectively. The post-crisis sample illustrates some different behavior. Our instruments are weak at shorter tenors, suggesting somewhat changed relationships between dealer demand and foreign demand at auctions and dealer positions. The instruments are still strong for longer-dated securities. For these auction tenors, we see larger dealer takedown putting downward pressure on repo rates, consistent with dealers' inventories used to smooth pressures in the market and absorb temporary bulges in collateral.

Conclusion

The ability of dealer positions to influence financing rates highlights the importance of institutions and the institutional framework when measuring the impact of the supply of securities on interest rates. The financial crisis highlighted the importance of quantity as well as rate factors in determining financial conditions, and using dealer inventory management to explore this phenomenon more closely is instructive. Overall, our results suggest that even when controlling for endogeneity, that there is potentially some co-determination of dealer positions and financing rates. It is also important to recognize that most of these effects are generally short-lived, and tend to dissipate quickly, consistent with the overall condition of the dealer markets as very safe, liquid, and able to transact in any size at any time.

References

Adrian, Tobias, Brian Begalle, Adam Copeland, and Antoine Martin. "Repo and Securities Lending." Federal Reserve Bank of New York Staff Reports Number 529, December 2011.

Adrian, Tobias, Moench, Emanuel, and Shin, Hyun Song."Financial Intermediation, Asset Prices, and Macroeconomic Dynamics," Federal Reserve Bank of New York Staff Reports Number 422, January 2010.

Adrian, Tobias and Michael Fleming. "What Financing Data Reveal about Dealer Leverage," *Federal Reserve Bank of New York Current Issues in Economics and Finance* 11(3), March 2005.

Bartolini, Leonardo, Spence Hilton, Suresh Sundaresan, and Chistopher Tonetti. "Collateral Values by Asset Class: Evidence from Primary Securities Dealers." *Review of Financial Studies*, January 2011, vol. 24, issue 1, pp. 248-78.

Bertaut, Carol C., William L. Griever, and Ralph W. Tryon. "Understanding U.S. Cross-Border Securities Data." *Federal Reserve Bulletin*, February 2009.

Bertaut, Carol C. "Assessing the Potential for Further Foreign Demand for the U.S. Assets: Has Financing U.S. Current Account Deficits Made Foreign Investors Overweight in U.S. Securities?" *Federal Reserve Board, International Finance Discussion Papers,* Number 950, October 2008.

D'Amico, Stefania and Thomas B. King. "Flow and Stock Effects of Large-Scale Treasury Purchases: Evdience on the Importance of Local Supply." *Federal Reserve Board, Finance and Economics Discussion Series*: 2012-44, February 2012.

D'Amico, Stefania, Roger Fan, and Yuriy Kitsul. "The Scarcity Value of Treasury Collateral: Repo Market Effects of Security-Specific Supply and Demand Factors," *Federal Reserve Bank of Chicago Working Paper Series* –2013-22.

Fleming, M. J. and Rosenberg, J. V. "How do Treasury dealers manage their positions?" *Federal Reserve Bank of New York Staff Report* 299 March, 2008.

Kohn, Meir. "Financial Institutions and Markets," 2nd ed. Oxford University Press, 2004.

Mann, Catherine L with Oren Klachkin. "“U.S. Treasury Auction Yields During Boom, Bust, and Quantitative Easing: Surprise! Role for Fed and Foreign Purchasers,”." first version Sept 2011 updated March 2012.

Mishkin, Frederic S. “The Economics of Money, Banking, and Financial Markets,” 6th ed. Addison Wesley Longman, 2001.

Stigum, Marcia and Anthony Crescenzi. “Stigum’s Money Market,” 4th ed. McGraw-Hill, 2007.

In: Business Cycles in Economics
Editor: Jason C. Hsu

ISBN: 978-1-63321-322-7

Chapter 14

MODELING INTRA AND INTER CORRELATIONS IN CREDIT DEFAULT LOSSES

M. Syrkin and A. Shirazi
Federal Reserve Bank of New York, New York, NY, US

Abstract

Comparing alternatives for a simultaneous incorporation of intra and inter correlations into the credit portfolio loss distribution within the asymptotic single risk factor (ASRF) model and showing that the resulting distribution depends on the type of a dominant correlation: whether it is of intra d-d/lgd-lgd or inter d-lgd type. Showing that the classic Vasicek distribution (derived originally for intra d-d correlations only), modified to embrace both intra and inter correlation types by properly constructing composite mean and correlation parameters, offers an analytic solution which covers an entire range of correlations and is easy to use as opposed to a more formal approach of a bivariate joint default probability density which requires numerical averaging over the underlying latent factors and applies only when intra correlations dominate.[1]

1. Introduction

Modeling credit default losses in large portfolios is materially complicated by correlations of loss variables – defaults and recoveries. While modeling intra correlated defaults (d-d correlation) is more or less well developed- at least, in terms of the asymptotic single risk factor (ASRF) approach, the situation is much less elaborated for intra correlated loss-given-defaults (lgd-lgd correlation), and even less so for inter d-lgd correlations. At the same time, a pressing need does exist – and especially for large and diversified portfolios – for practically efficient and computationally less demanding models incorporating simultaneous correlations of generic default parameters, even at the expense of using heavily stylized approaches. In this context the role of analytically tractable models rises substantially

[1] This paper is identical to the article originally published on 03/28/2013 at SSRN under the same title and under the permission of FRBNY.

as they allow to focus on capturing leading analytic trends and thus significantly reduce the computing time, while furnishing an accuracy quite comparable with the one resulting from much more sophisticated alternatives.

The authors benefited from a number of prior empirical and theoretical studies (acknowledged here without pretending for any particular order and completeness) which facilitated a recent evolution of ideas, and which help better understand the motivation behind this work. On the empirical side there is a considerable variety of works demonstrating a positive correlation between default and loss-given-default rates (e.g. Gupton et al (2000), Frye (2003), Altman et al(2004) and others). On the modeling side the first and foremost is the path-breaking classic solution for a correlated default distribution by Vasicek (1987, 2002) (within ASRF) in infinitely grained uniform portfolios. Further, in the last decade there was a number of models utilizing a single systematic factor, but differing in number of idiosyncratic factors and the way they were incorporated into the resulting loss rate model (e.g. Frye (2000), Pykhtin (2003), Tasche (2004), among others, and for the review see as well Witzany(2009)).Witzany (2011) also discusses a model with two systematic factors aiming at better capturing the effect of correlations between defaults and recoveries. On the alternative venue, Sanchez et al (2008) model the impact of d-lgd correlations on the loss distribution variance by using the conditional variance with conditioning of the lgd expectation analogous to the one from the ASRF approach. We will return to this conditioning aspect in more detail later in the text. Also, Frye and Jacobs (2012) argue that the model where the conditional lgd rate is a deterministic function of the default rate – as opposed to traditional models without that functional dependency- quite often offers a better fit to the empirical data than more traditional results from the statistical regression of lgd rates on default rates.

With that prior work in mind, we aim here at showing how correlations in the default prone portfolio can be classified and systematically accounted for within a similarly stylized default and loss-given-default models. At the same time, all aspects related to empirical data suitable as inputs to the model are intentionally left aside as this should be a subject of a separate study. In Sec. 2 we review a standard technique of ASRF models for intra d-d correlations and the Vasicek distribution for default rates. Sec. 3 does the same for lgd-lgd correlations and lgd rates. In Sec. 4 we introduce and compare two different approaches to inter d-lgd correlations: individual and collective modes. Sec. 5 presents some comparison of results for loss rates stemming from both models. Brief conclusions are summarized in Sec. 6. For the ease of reading and in the interest of the broader readership, most of calculations are moved to Appendices and the main text only refers to the corresponding results as needed.

2. Brief Review of ASRF Correlated Defaults Model

An individual obligor default is driven by a Bernoulli (binary) random variable (rv) d taking only values 0 and 1 and unconditional mean equal pd = E(d). The fractional number of uncorrelated defaults in a uniform portfolio of N identical assets is given then by a Binomial random variable x: a normalized sum of uncorrelated Bernoulli variables $x = \Sigma\, d_i/N$. In the limit of $N \rightarrow \infty$x follows a delta –function distribution peaked at E(x) =pd.

Further, in the Merton picture, the default onsets as the hidden/latent idiosyncratic variable (say, normally distributed) crosses some threshold level K, and therefore pd = E(d) =

$\Phi(K)$, where Φ is a normal cumulative distribution function (cdf).In ASRF, default correlations are modeled parametrically, i.e. defaults are governed by a function (say, an indicator function) of a latent rvW^d_i ,incorporating a common for all assets market latent factor "u" which mixes with the idiosyncratic obligor specific latent rv "e_i" via a one-factor copula model as in $W^d_i = \alpha^{1/2}u+(1-\alpha)^{1/2}e_i$, with $Var(W_i) = 1$,where $\alpha^{1/2}$ is a factor loading and α is the latent correlation coefficient. Although the latent factor distribution is arbitrary, meeting only some general convergence requirements, we would assume it being normal.

Accordingly, the probability of default is no longer fixed pd= $\Phi(K)$, but rather a conditional expectation $E(d|u)$ as follows

$$pd(u) = E(d \mid u) = \Phi[(\Phi^{-1}(pd) - \sqrt{\alpha u}) / \sqrt{1-\alpha}] \tag{2.1}$$

which is a function of the latent factor "u" and recovers initial pd for $\alpha = 0$. There are two important facts about pd(u) worth mentioning here. First, the underlying unperturbed value pd serves as an expected value of pd(u) over the latent factor distribution, i.e. E[pd(u)] = pd. Traditionally this is viewed as the result of a one-factor copula construction which holds true for any latent factor distribution (with the only necessary requirements of convergence of all integrals). It is instructive though to see how this result materializes via a direct but more technical derivation for, say, a normal distribution, which is given in Appendix 1. Second, the backbone advantage of introducing the correlation parametrically via a one-factor copula is that for every given latent factor value u the default events of individual obligors in the portfolio remain independent. That means that the total fractional portfolio loss still follows a binomial distribution for finite N and becomes delta-function around E(x|u)= pd(u) for $N\to\infty$. After averaging over a u-distribution the portfolio fractional loss pdf becomes:

$$\text{pdf: } f(n) = \binom{N}{n} \int [pd(u)]^n [1 - pd(u)]^{N-n} \varphi(u) du \tag{2.2}$$

Where $\varphi(u)$ is the normal density. The important consequence of (2.2) is that for any non-vanishing correlation parameter α, the loss distribution for $N\to\infty$is no longer delta-peaked, but is spread proportionally to the correlation value α. This is the essence of the classic result of Vasicek (1987, 2002):

$$\begin{aligned} &\text{cdf: } F_V(pd, \alpha; z) = \Phi\{\frac{1}{\sqrt{\alpha}}[\sqrt{1-\alpha}\Phi^{-1}(z) - \Phi^{-1}(pd)]\} \\ &\text{pdf: } f_V(pd, \alpha; z) = \sqrt{\frac{1-\alpha}{\alpha}} \exp\left\{0.5\, [\Phi^{-1}(z)]^2 - \frac{0.5}{\alpha}[\sqrt{1-\alpha}\Phi^{-1}(z) - \Phi^{-1}(pd)]^2\right\} \end{aligned} \tag{2.3}$$

which derivation is briefly reviewed in Appendix 1.Rewriting probability density function in (2.3) as

$$f_V(z) = \sqrt{\frac{1-\alpha}{\alpha}} \exp\left\{\frac{1}{\alpha}(\alpha - \frac{1}{2})\, [\Phi^{-1}(z)]^2 - \frac{1}{\alpha}\sqrt{1-\alpha}\Phi^{-1}(z)\Phi^{-1}(pd) - \frac{1}{2\alpha}[\Phi^{-1}(pd)]^2\right\} \tag{2.4}$$

produces the exponent containing three terms: the first component is symmetric in z and ensuring that the density vanishes at end points 0 and 1, the second adds asymmetry to the density, and the last one is just a normalization constant. Generic pdf profile features are especially pronounced if pd = 0.5: last two terms disappear and the density becomes symmetric with $\cap$ or $\cup$ shapes for α < 0.5 and α > 0.5 respectively. At α = 0.5 the density undergoes a "phase transition" and is unity for any z. Ifpd≠ 0.5 the second term only adds some asymmetry to the above features and makes the pdf for α = 0.5non-constant but still monotonous (Vasicek, 2002).

We will also need an explicit expression for default correlations: as is well known, they are different from latent (asset) correlations but induced by the latter. In a one-factor framework, the covariance and correlation between two default rvs are

$$\begin{aligned} Cov(d_i, d_j; \alpha) &= \Phi_2(\Phi^{-1}(pd_i), \Phi^{-1}(pd_j), \alpha) - pd_i pd_j \\ Corr(d_i, d_j; \alpha) &= Cov(d_i, d_j; \alpha) / \sqrt{Var(d_i) Var(d_j)} \end{aligned} \tag{2.5}$$

where Φ_2 is a bivariate normal cdf. Therefore, for a uniform portfolio the coefficient of d-d correlation A = P(α) can be written as

$$\mathrm{A} = P(\alpha) = \frac{Var(pd(u))}{Var(d)} = \frac{1}{pd(1-pd)}[\Phi_2(\Phi^{-1}(pd), \Phi^{-1}(pd), \alpha) - pd^2] \tag{2.6}$$

where P(α) is some universal mapping function. For further calculations we will need both direct P(α) and inversed $P^{-1}(\alpha)$. As P(α) is generally non-linear, some exact cases and limits are of interest. First, for pd=0.5(representing some generic estimator), we have

$$\mathrm{A} = P(a) = \frac{2}{\pi}\arcsin(\alpha) \tag{2.7}$$

Further, in the limit of small α we have a linear asymptotic dependence

$$Cov(d_i, d_j)_{\alpha \to 0} \to \alpha \cdot \varphi^2[\Phi^{-1}(pd)], \; P(\alpha)_{\alpha \to 0} \to k\alpha, \; k = \frac{\varphi^2[\Phi^{-1}(pd)]}{pd(1-pd)} \tag{2.8}$$

which is quite acceptable for small α, say, α< 5%. In the opposite limit of $\alpha \to 1 \;\; P(\alpha) \to 1$. These extreme cases, for the benefit of quick practical estimations of P(α) and inversed $P^{-1}(\alpha)$ as well, can be combined in some workable approximations. Below is a simplest second order interpolation

$$\tilde{P}(\alpha) = \alpha[k + \alpha(1-k)] \tag{2.9}$$

which covers the whole range [0,1] and is easily invertible when obtaining α for a given A. More refined versions are suggested in Appendix 2.

3. Modeling Correlated Recoveries or Loss Given Defaults

For loss given defaults the situation is more complex because loss-given-default lgd is no longer binary, and there exists a substantial wealth of empirical studies on particular distribution profiles (see, for instance, Schuermann [2004]). For instance, one of the popular approaches fits the empirical data with the two-parametric Beta (a,b)-function. For our purposes the specific distribution type is not as important, and therefore we will use a heavily stylized approximation for lgdrv (see, for instance, Witzany (2009)): a binary(0,1) model– in a full analogy to the default case -with a number of loss-given-defaults as a random variable y $=\Sigma\ lgd_i/N$ following a binomial distribution. In the limit of $N\rightarrow\infty$ the latter becomes a delta – function distribution peaked at E(y)=plgd (we use plgd for an expected lgd instead of elgd for more immediate analogy with defaults). Thus, analogously to the one factor copula default model from Sec. 2, we introduce a latent process $W^{lgd}_i = \beta^{1/2}\ v+(1-\beta)^{1/2}e_i$, which is different from W^d_i and where "v" is a new latent common factor and β is the correlation for different obligor latent factors. Hence, $plgd(v) = \Phi[(\Phi^{-1}(lgd) - \sqrt{\beta}v) / \sqrt{1-\beta}]$ gives a conditional mean E(lgd|v) = plgd(v) and the unconditional mean over all possible vis E[plgd(v)] = lgd as in Sec. 2. Obviously, formulas (2.3 -2.6) apply with lgd_i replacing d_i,plgd replacing pd, β replacing α, B = P(β) replacing A = P(α) and so on.

Sanchez et al. (2008) argue in favor of keeping convenient ASRF expressions for conditional means plgd(v) in conjunction with distributions for lgd other than binary, and therefore less restrictive and more realistic than binary. For instance, in terms of the Beta-function distribution that would essentially mean calibrating one of the Beta lgd distribution parameters according to $plgd(v) = \int_0^1 lgd\ Beta(a(v),b;lgd)\ d(lgd)$, while leaving the other parameter free for further adjustments.

4. Correlated D-LGD Models

The way the portfolio loss rate formation takes place depends on correlation – or better say coupling – between constituent loss variables: defaults and loss-given-defaults. Conceptually, we may first obtain random variables of a portfolio level fractional default rate x and fractional loss-given-default rate y as defined above in Sec.2 and 3, and then multiply them $x\times y$ to arrive at a portfolio level loss rate variable. With that, the correlation between defaults and loss-given-defaults enters at the portfolio/collective level. Alternatively, we multiply individual asset default and loss-given-default variables into individual loss variables $d_i\times lgd_i$ and combine them into the portfolio loss rate variable. This way the d-lgd correlation enters at the individual level. The choice between these two options, which will be referred to as an individual mode (with notation [(d*lgd) - (d*lgd)]) and a collective mode (with notation [(d-d) * (lgd-lgd)]) respectively, can be formalized as follows.

Consider a two-argument coupling function C(1,2) signifying the strength of the correlation/covariance between defaults d_i and d_j (d-d correlations), between loss-given-defaults lgd_i and lgd_j (lgd-lgd correlations), and between defaults d_i and loss given defaults lgd_j (d-lgd correlations). The individual mode then corresponds to the condition

$C(d_i,d_j)$~$C(lgd_i, lgdj)$<<$C(d_i,lgd_i)$, meaning the dominance of inter correlations, while the opposite case $C(d_i, lgd_i)$~$C(d_i, lgd_j)$>>$C(d_i,lgd_i)$ points out to the collective mode and dominance if intra correlations, where "~" stands for the same order of magnitude and"<<"/">> " for much smaller/bigger, respectively.

Generally speaking, individual and collective modes produce expectedly different portfolio loss distributions. Question arises, what these distributions are and how material is the divergence between them. We begin here with some conceptual reasoning. First of all, in the absence of any correlation, intra or inter, individual and collective modes immediately produce the same portfolio loss distribution of a binomial type - simply because any binomial variable can be represented as a sum of binary variables and the product of binary variables is again a binary variable. Obviously, this result holds in the limit of $N\rightarrow\infty$ where a binomial distribution becomes a delta-function. The incorporation then of intra-correlations impacts both modes but in a different way: the individual mode leads to the Vasicek distribution with the composite mean, variance and correlation parameter constructed from intra and inter covariances, while in the collective mode the result differs from Vasicek because the multiplicative convolution does not preserve the Vasicek type of distributions being convoluted. Naturally, this difference extends further in the presence of inter correlations. We will now consider both scenarios in more detail.

Individual Mode, (d*lgd)-(d*lgd)

In the individual mode we obtain the loss rate rv of the individual obligor $d\times lgd$ (obligor indices are dropped in the spirit of uniform portfolio) which is again binary rv according to Sec. 2 and 3. The rest, in essence, is a standard ASRF one-factor parameterization of a uniform correlation between individual loss rvs resulting in the distribution type (2.2) with composite mean, variance and correlation parameter.

More specifically, modeling losses in an individual mode includes following simple steps.

First, set desirable latent *intra* correlation coefficients α and β as in Sec. 2 and 3, as well as latent *inter* correlations for diagonal$\gamma_0(d_i,lgd_i)$, and non-diagonal $\gamma_1(d_i,lgd_j)$ coefficients, respectively (i.e the d-lgd correlation for the same and different obligors, respectively).

Second, following (2.6-2.9), map latent correlations into default correlations: i.e. convert latent correlations α andβ to default correlations, A, B, and latent γ_0 and γ_1 into default correlations Γ_0, Γ_1.

Third, use simple algebra of covariances in Appendix 2, to obtain the resulting composite default loss rvs correlation $\Lambda(\lambda)$, where λ is a correlation for an underlying latent factor.

Fourth, by inverting an equation of the (2.6) type, i.e. using$\Lambda^{-1}(\lambda)$,recover λ and use it in the Vasicek type distribution for portfolio losses.

The details of the derivation are given in Appendix 2,with the final expression for the loss distribution given below

$$\text{cdf: } F_V(pl,\lambda;z) = \Phi(\frac{1}{\sqrt{\lambda}}[\sqrt{1-\lambda}\Phi^{-1}(z) - \Phi^{-1}(pl)])$$
$$\text{pdf: } f_V(pl,\lambda;z) = \sqrt{\frac{1-\lambda}{\lambda}}\exp\left\{0.5\,[\Phi^{-1}(z)]^2 - \frac{0.5}{\lambda}[\sqrt{1-\lambda}\Phi^{-1}(z) - \Phi^{-1}(pl)]^2\right\} \quad (4.1)$$

and the first two moments $\bar{z}$ and $\overline{z^2}$ (mean loss and mean square loss) are

$$\begin{aligned}
&\bar{z} = pl = \bar{l} = \overline{d \times lgd} = \bar{d}_i \times \overline{lgd_i} + C_0 \\
&C_0 = Cov(d_i, lgd_i; \gamma_0) = \Gamma_0 \sqrt{Var(d_i)Var(lgd_i)} = \Phi_2(\Phi^{-1}(pd_i), \Phi^{-1}(plgd_i), \gamma_0) - pd_i pgld_i \\
&\overline{z^2} = \Phi_2[\Phi^{-1}(pl), \Phi^{-1}(pl), \lambda]
\end{aligned} \tag{4.2}$$

Here *pl* (probability of loss, $\bar{l}$) is a composite mean, λ is a composite latent correlation for losses in the Vasicek type distribution as described above, γ_0 and Γ_0 are diagonal (i.e. the correlation for the same obligor) latent factor and loss correlations, respectively, and Φ_2 is a bivariate normal cdf.

Formulas (4.1-4.2, A 2.6-2.9) demonstrate the following essential trends. While the mean of the portfolio loss is affected only by the diagonal inter correlation Γ_0, the variance and composite correlation parameter are impacted by both intra (d-d/lgd-lgd) and inter d-lgd inter correlations. Specifically, intra-correlations increase the correlation Λ (and λ) and hence make the distribution wider, increasing tail losses in the process. The role of inter correlations is different: non-diagonal inter correlations Γ_1 directly increase the loss correlation Λ, while the diagonal inter correlations Γ_0 do not contribute on their own, but only enhance or reduce (depending on the relative values of default parameters indicated in Appendix 2) the contribution of all other correlation types.

Collective Mode, (d-d)*(lgd-lgd)

In a collective mode the portfolio loss rate rv is a product of correlated (via inter correlations) portfolio d and lgd rates, and, therefore, we can not merely take a multiplicative convolutions of d and lgd Vasicek distributions. However, we can do that for delta-distributions for each pair of latent factors (u,v) and then average the result over the distribution of correlated pairs of (u,v). Details are given in Appendix 3and the resulting cdf and pdf according to (A 3.3) are

$$\begin{aligned}
&cdf: \quad F(z) = \iint \frac{dudv}{2\pi\sqrt{1-\gamma^2}} \exp\{-\frac{u^2 + v^2 - 2\gamma uv}{2(1-\gamma^2)}\} \mathbf{1}[z - pd(u)plgd(v)] \\
&pdf: \quad f(z) = \iint \frac{dudv}{2\pi\sqrt{1-\gamma^2}} \exp\{-\frac{u^2 + v^2 - 2\gamma uv}{2(1-\gamma^2)}\} \boldsymbol{\delta}[z - pd(u)plgd(v)]
\end{aligned} \tag{4.3}$$

where$\mathbf{1}$(s) is an indicator function equal 0 for negative s and equal 1 for non-negative s and $\boldsymbol{\delta}$ (s) is a delta-function. It follows, that (4.3) delivers a generalized bivariate cdf off the curve $pd(u)plgd(v) - z = 0$. According to (4.3), the first two moments $\bar{z}$ and $\overline{z^2}$ are given by

$$\bar{z} = \iint \frac{dudv}{2\pi\sqrt{1-\gamma^2}} pd(u)plgd(v)\exp\{-\frac{u^2+v^2-2\gamma uv}{2(1-\gamma^2)}\}$$
$$\overline{z^2} = \iint \frac{dudv}{2\pi\sqrt{1-\gamma^2}} [pd(u)plgd(v)]^2 \exp\{-\frac{u^2+v^2-2\gamma uv}{2(1-\gamma^2)}\} \tag{4.4}$$

which are bi- and quadra-variate normals (see Sanchez et al, 2008).

Equations (4.3) allow for some verifiable exact limits in their respective domains of applicability. For example, setting in (4.3) $\gamma = 0$ for no inter correlations immediately reduces the loss rate pdf to

$$f(z) = \int_z^1 \frac{ds}{s} f_V(pd, \alpha; z) f_V(plgd, \beta; \frac{z}{s}) \tag{4.5}$$

where f_V are Vasicek pdfs from (2.3). Formula (4.5) is but a multiplicative convolution of uncorrelated default and loss-given-default distributions, which must be the case in the absence of inter correlations. Taking (4.5) further by setting pd = plgd = 0.5 and $\alpha = \beta = 0.5$, results in a particular simple density f(z) = ln(1/z).

On the general note, the major deficiency of the collective formalism (4.3 - 4.4) is that it is valid only when $\gamma \ll \alpha, \beta$, i.e. when intra correlations dominate, and does not apply otherwise. The reason is that the inter correlation parameter γ enters (4.3 - 4.4) only via the weighting exponents but is absent from conditional averages pd(u) and plgd(v). As a result, when both α, $\beta \to 0$ then, regardless of γ, the loss distribution spread vanishes so that the distribution tends to a δ-function. This problem reflects the limitations of the one-factor setting and can be overcome only by adding more latent factors.

The other weakness is that because of a relatively non-trivial structure of conditional expectations pd(u) and plgd(v),the collective formalism (4.3-4.4) possesses considerably less analytical tractability than its individual mode counterparty. Therefore, even though the distribution and moments come out in a closed integral form, their practical value for, say, extracting analytic trends and losses calculations is quite limited by the need for a direct numerical implementation. In that respect an individual mode offers a clear advantage. Certain conclusions from comparing a collective mode with an individual mode will be drawn in the next section.

5. Some Comparisons between Individual and Collective Modes

From the general standpoint it is intuitively clear and expected, except for a trivial case of no any correlation at all, that individual and collective modes produce different distributions, at least in principle. While it can be rigorously shown that densities (4.3) in general do not render Vasicek densities (4.1), the proof is quite technical and is not heuristically critical, and therefore we do not give it here, but rather provide a direct constructive illustrations. For example, consider second moments and assume for simplicity no inter correlations $\gamma = 0$.

Then the second moment from (4.4) factorizes into the product $\Phi_2[\Phi^{-1}(pd),\Phi^{-1}(pd),\alpha]\cdot\Phi_2[\Phi^{-1}(lgd),\Phi^{-1}(lgd),\beta]$ while in the individual mode it is different and equal to $\Phi_2[\Phi^{-1}(pd\times plgd),\Phi^{-1}(pd\times plgd),\lambda]$ with λ given by (A 2.8) from Appendix 2. Clearly, these two expressions do not coincide in general (except, may be, for a special choice of λ) which illustrates the point. And further, when inter correlations are present, there are even more reasons to expect differences. The numerical results given below confirm these conclusions, however, they also show that there exists a certain range where both modes agree quite close, which is very beneficial from the practical standpoint.

Below we exemplify some numerical results (where for simplicity and ease of the analysis restricting ourselves within pd = plgd = 0.5, leaving more results for later).

Figures 1-7 illustrate densities and corresponding cumulative functions for three major domains: the area 1, of intra correlation dominance $\gamma \ll \alpha, \beta$; area 2, the opposite extreme of $\gamma \gg \alpha, \beta$ where inter correlations dominate; and intermediate range $\gamma \sim \alpha, \beta$ – area 3. The major differences are observed in area 2 (Figure 5-7), which is of no surprise since a collective mode is invalid here as was explained above in Sec. 4.Therefore, the correct distribution in this area is given by an individual mode from the Vasicek formula(4.1- 4.2). Intuitively, we could have expected the opposite conclusion in the area 1, where the collective mode applies. However, in the area 1(Figure1-4)the individual mode proves very close to a collective mode which is the result of a proper construction of a composite mean and correlation parameter. Therefore, as an individual mode gives a correct result in both extreme areas 1 and 2, it is quite natural to expect that this is also the case in the intermediate range 3 (Figures 8-9) and that i) the individual mode gives a good coverage in the entire range of relationships between γ and α, β and ii) the differences in the intermediate range 3 also stem exclusively from the limitations of the collective mode. This is a main advantage of the individual mode formulas (4.1) and is of a particular significance for applications because it allows for use of Vasicek formulas regardless of the relationship between γ and α, β.

Another important aspect of the comparison is that in the one-factor setting the collective mode treats d-lgd correlations in an "averaged" way and does not discriminate between diagonal and non- diagonal inter correlations i.e. d_i-lgd_i vs. d_i-lgd_j.

This is quite counterintuitive (and unrealistic even within a limited context of a stylized modeling framework) and clearly is a defect of the collective mode compared to an individual mode which is free from that problem.

Conclusion

The main conclusions are as follows.

The profile of the loss rate distribution is determined by the relative strength of intra vs inter correlations and as such this strength impacts the choice of a suitable formalism to describe the distribution.

At the same time, the one-factor based Vasicek type distribution with properly constructed composite mean and correlation parameters demonstrates a stable performance regardless of the relationship between intra and inter correlations. Taken together with an analytical character of the model, this makes the individual mode an effective and flexible tool for loss estimations from the practical standpoint in particular.

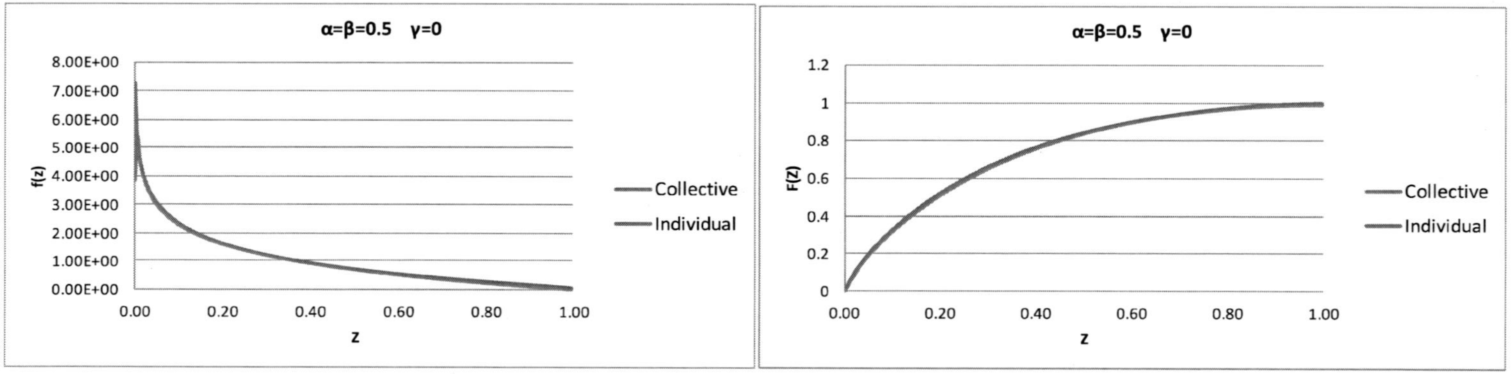

Figure 1.

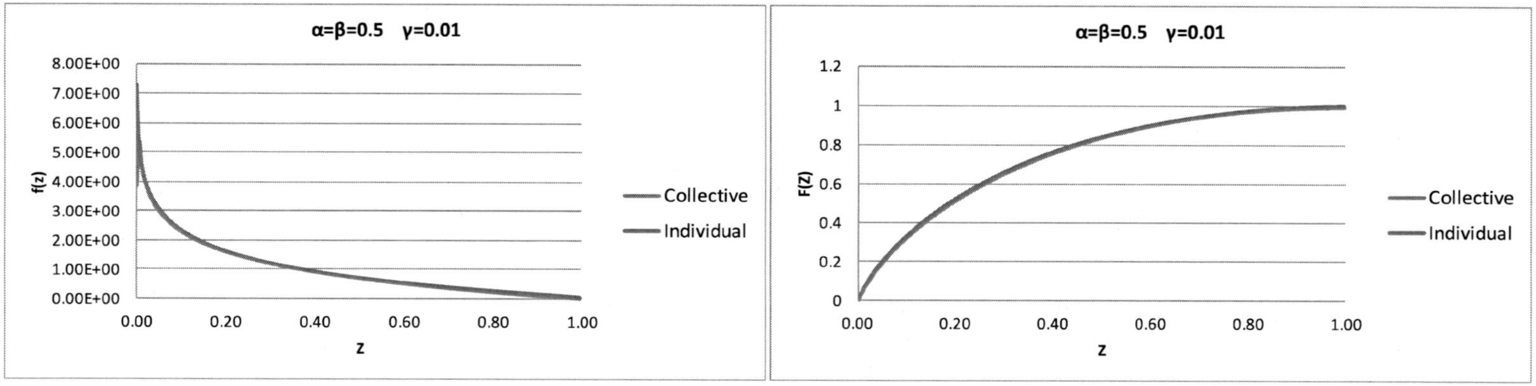

Figure 2.

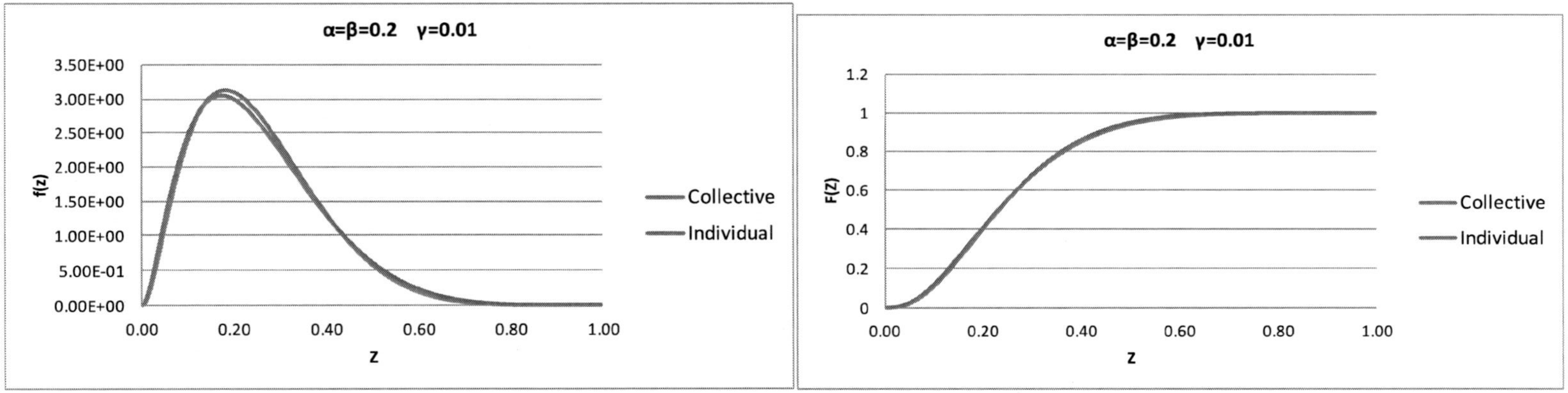

Figure 3.

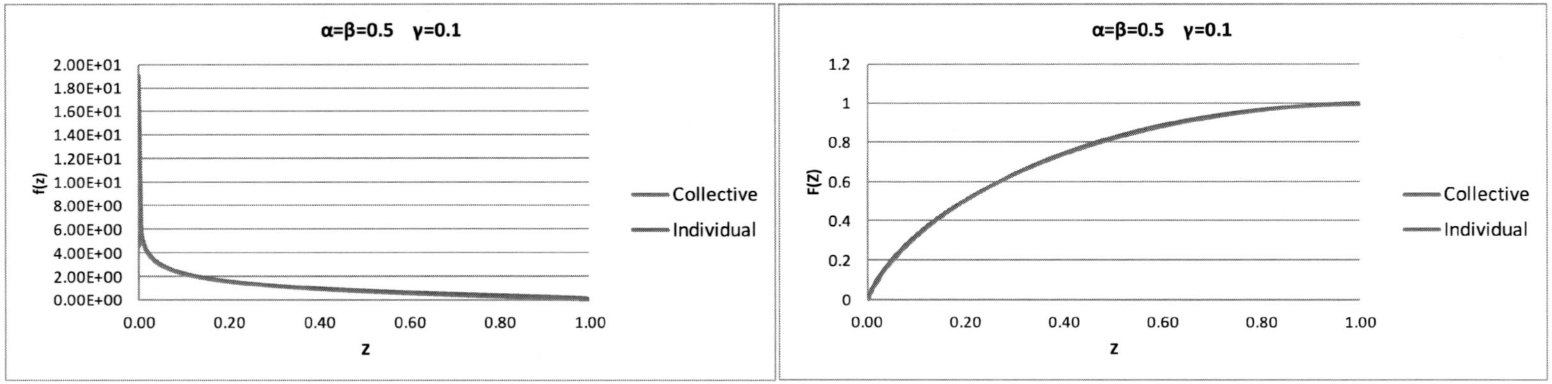

Figure 4.

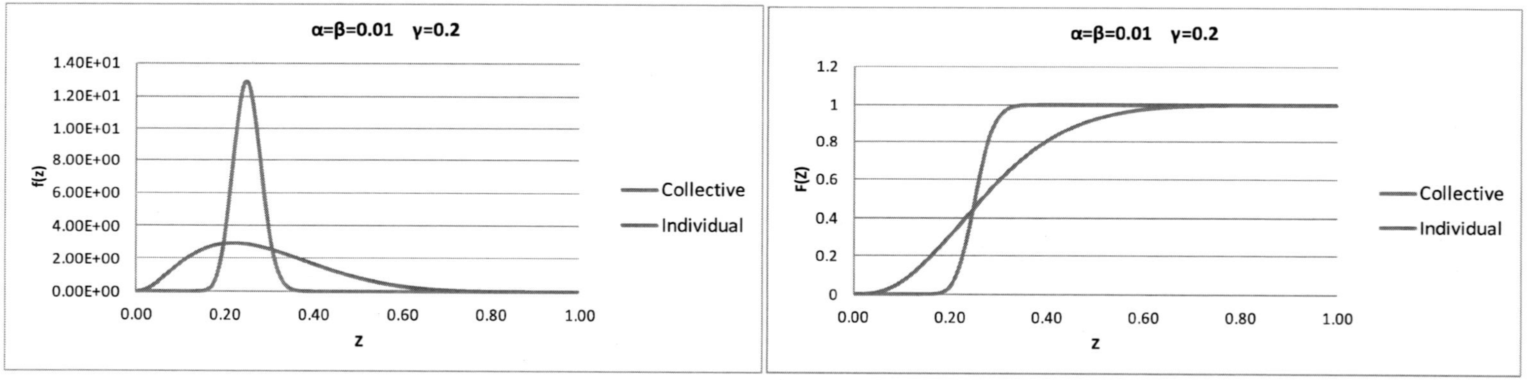

Figure 5.

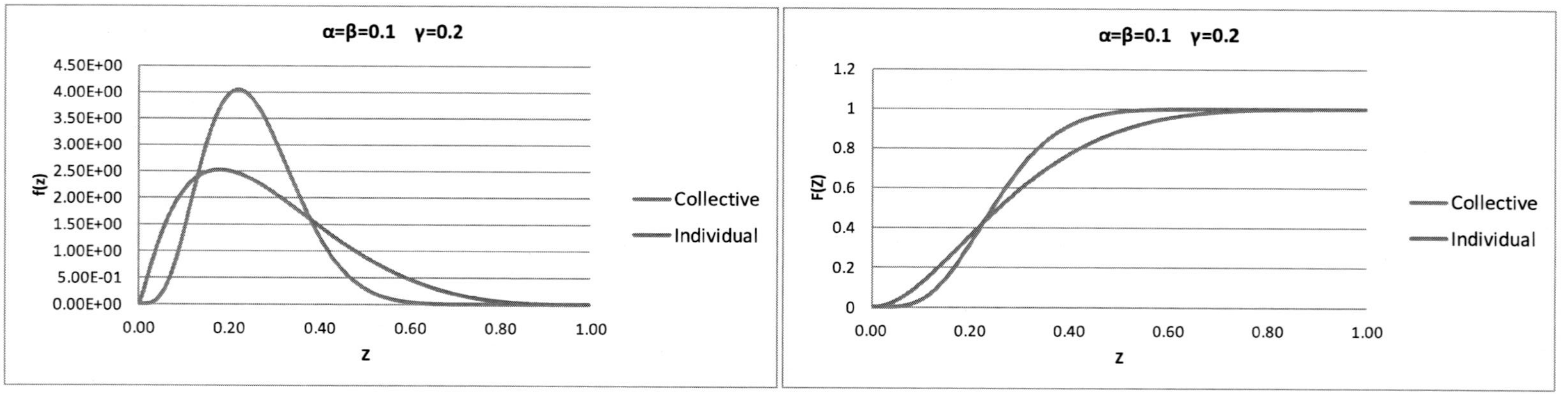

Figure 6.

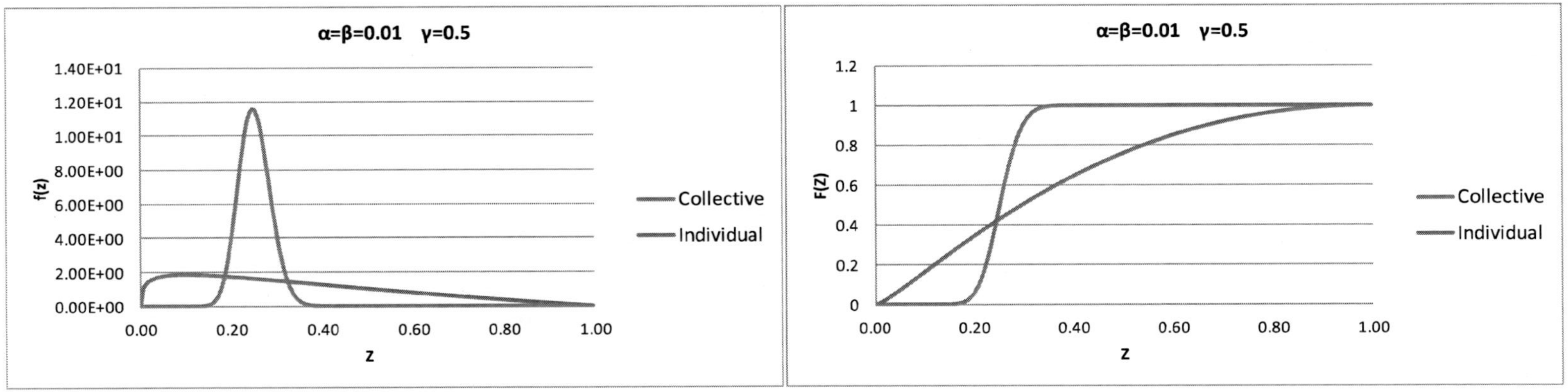

Figure 7.

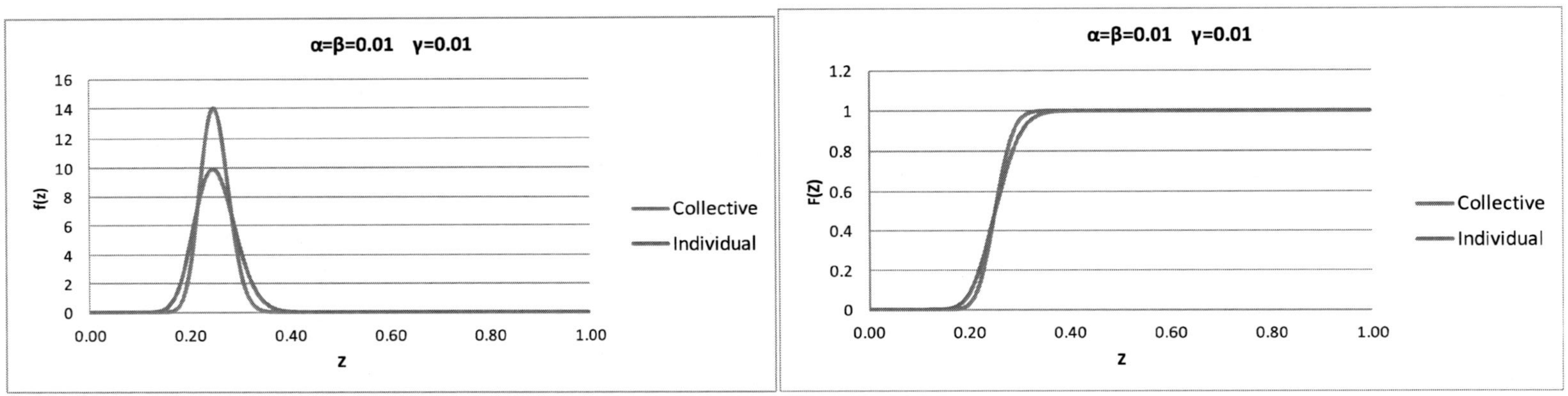

Figure 8.

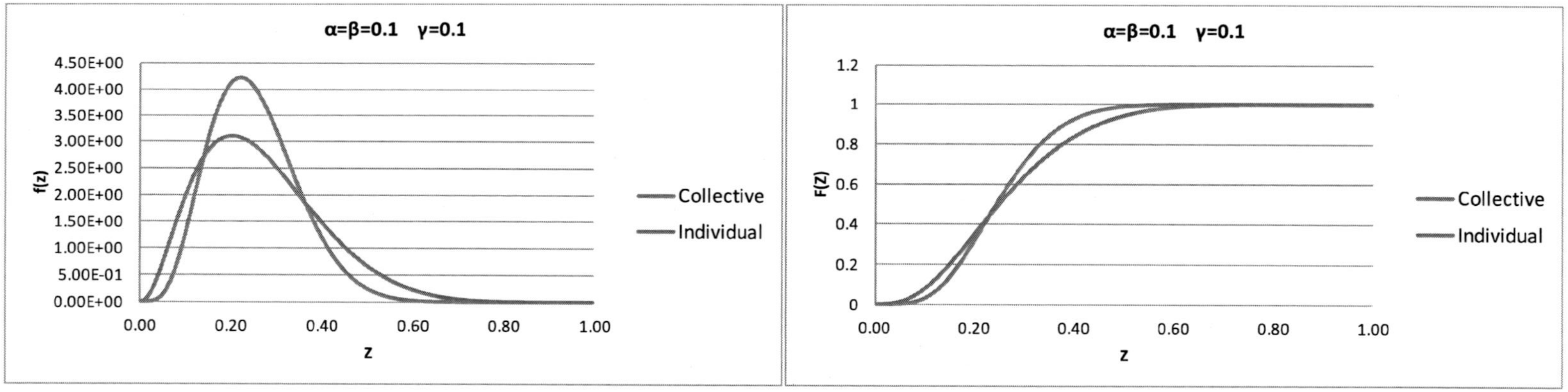
α=β=0.1 γ=0.1
f(z)
4.50E+00
4.00E+00
3.50E+00
3.00E+00
2.50E+00
2.00E+00
1.50E+00
1.00E+00
5.00E-01
0.00E+00
0.00
0.20
0.40
0.60
0.80
1.00
z
Collective
Individual
α=β=0.1 γ=0.1
F(Z)
1.2
1
0.8
0.6
0.4
0.2
0
0.00
0.20
0.40
0.60
0.80
1.00
z
Collective
Individual

Figure 9.

Also, an additional flexibility of the individual mode is that it allows to discriminate between diagonal and non-diagonal inter correlations, and, more broadly, permits modeling by choosing correlations optionally either between underlying latent risk factors or directly between default related rvs.

On the other hand, it is of a considerable interest to explore further the potential of the collective mode formalism as a general framework in the two-factor settings.

Finally, as indicated in the introduction, the next step should be a study of how to relate inputs into both individual and collective modes to an existing empirical data.

Acknowledgments

We are grateful to John Kambhu and Karen Schnek for the interest to work and support and to John Frye for the presentation on the substance of the recent work (Frye and Jacobs (2012)).

Appendix 1

Review of the Vasicek distribution

In a uniform infinite $N \to \infty$ portfolio for any latent variable u the conditional default rate probability density z is a delta-function $\delta[z - pd(u)]$ peaked around the conditional default probability $pd(u) = \Phi[(K - \sqrt{\alpha}u)/\sqrt{1-\alpha}]$, where $K = \Phi^{-1}(pd)$ and Φ stands for a normal distribution. The unconditional default rate cdf $F(z)$ (i.e. probability of all default fractions being smaller than z) obtains from weighting with a normal density as follows

$$F(z) = \int \mathbf{1}[z - pd(u)]\varphi(u)du = \int_{-\infty}^{u_0} \varphi(u)du = \Phi(u_0),\ u_0 = [\Phi^{-1}(z)\sqrt{1-\alpha} - K]/\sqrt{\alpha} \quad \text{(A 1.1)}$$

and where $\mathbf{1}[z - pd(u)]$ is an indicator function and therefore

$$F_V(z) = \Phi(\frac{1}{\sqrt{\alpha}}[\sqrt{1-\alpha}\Phi^{-1}(z) - \Phi^{-1}(pd)]) \quad \text{(A 1.2)}$$

Respectively the unconditional default rate pdf is

$$f(z) = \int \delta[z - pd(u)]\varphi(u)du = \int_{-\infty}^{\infty} du\ \varphi(u)\delta[u - u_0(z)]/pd'(u) = \varphi(u_0)/pd'(u_0) \quad \text{(A 1.3)}$$

with the final expression

$$f_V(z) = \sqrt{\frac{1-\alpha}{\alpha}} \exp\left\{0.5\,[\Phi^{-1}(z)]^2 - \frac{0.5}{\alpha}[\sqrt{1-\alpha}\Phi^{-1}(z) - \Phi^{-1}(pd)]^2\right\} \quad \text{(A 1.4)}$$

The calculations above can be viewed as obtaining the pdf of $g = pd(u)$ given the pdf of u according to $\varphi(u)du = \varphi_1(g)dg$ and then having $\varphi_1(g) = \varphi(u)\, dg / du$ transformed back with $u = pd^{-1}(g)$.

In conclusion of this Appendix we illustrate how to prove that E[pd(u)] = pd. A technically simple way would be by taking the derivative dE[pd(u)] /dK over the Merton threshold level K. Because φ(u) is normal, the differentiation w.r.t. K and the integration over u leads to φ(K). Taking then an integration over K results in $\Phi(K) = \Phi[\Phi^{-1}(pd)] = pd$.

Appendix 2

Correlations of individual loss rates in individual **[(d*lgd)-(d*lgd)]***mode*

In this Appendix we calculate the covariance and correlation between loss rate rvsd×lgd. For further potential applications and ease of appreciating the formula symmetry, we will not incorporate the fact that for any binary random variables we have $s^2 = s$ and Var(s) = ps(1-ps). This can be easily substituted in the final results.

Now, assume a uniform intra correlation (coefficient A) among default rvs d_i and a uniform intra correlation (coefficient B) among loss-given-default rvs lgd_i, but for now ignore aninter-correlation between defaults and loss-given defaults. Saying differently, we look for the correlation between individual loss rates induced by intra d-d and lgd-lgd correlations *only*. Set $Z_i = d_i \times lgd_i$ and consider a covariance $Cov(Z_i, Z_j)$ (below we use $\overline{x}$ for the mean value of x). The correlation between loss rvs Z_i and Z_j is $\Lambda_{ij} = Cov(Z_i, Z_j) / \sqrt{Var(Z_i)Var(Z_j)}$. Because of $Cov(a,b) = \overline{ab} - \overline{a}\overline{b}$ we obtain

$$\Lambda_{ij} = \frac{\overline{lgd_i} \cdot \overline{lgd_j} Cov(d_i, d_j) + \overline{d_i} \cdot \overline{d_j} Cov(lgd_i, lgd_j) + Cov(d_i, d_j) Cov(lgd_i, lgd_j)}{\sqrt{Var(Z_i)Var(Z_j)}} \quad \text{(A 2.1)}$$

For a uniform portfolio (identical assets and correlations among all of them) $Cov(d_i, d_j) = \mathrm{A} \cdot Var(d)$, $Cov(lgd_i, lgd_j) = \mathrm{B} \cdot Var(lgd)$ and so

$$Cov(Z_i, Z_j) = \mathrm{A} \cdot \overline{lgd}^2 Var(d) + \mathrm{B} \cdot \overline{d}^2 Var(lgd) + \mathrm{A} \cdot \mathrm{B} \cdot Var(d) Var(lgd) \quad \text{(A 2.2)}$$

where for a notational convenience $\overline{d}$ and $\overline{lgd}$ stand for pd and plgd, respectively.

Analogously,

$$\sqrt{Var(Z_i)Var(Z_j)} = \overline{lgd}^2 Var(d) + \overline{d}^2 Var(lgd) + Var(d) Var(lgd) \quad \text{(A 2.3)}$$

and, therefore, the loss rate correlation coefficient is

$$\Lambda_{intra} = \Lambda_{ij} = \frac{\text{A} \cdot \overline{lgd}^2 Var(d) \; + \; \text{B} \cdot \overline{d}^2 Var(lgd) + \; \text{AB} \cdot Var(d)Var(lgd)}{\overline{lgd}^2 Var(d) \; + \; \overline{d}^2 Var(lgd) + \; Var(d)Var(lgd)} \qquad \text{(A 2.4)}$$

or, introducing relative variables $R_d = \overline{d}^2 \; / \; Var(d), \;\; R_{lgd} = \overline{lgd}^2 \; / \; Var(lgd)$

$$\Lambda_{intra} = \frac{\text{B} \cdot \dfrac{\overline{d}^2}{Var(d)} + \text{A} \cdot \dfrac{\overline{lgd}^2}{Var(lgd)} + \text{AB}}{\dfrac{\overline{d}^2}{Var(d)} + \dfrac{\overline{lgd}^2}{Var(lgd)} + 1} = \text{AB} \frac{\dfrac{\overline{d}^2}{Cov(d_i, d_j)} + \dfrac{\overline{lgd}^2}{Cov(lgd_i, lgd_j)} + 1}{\dfrac{\overline{d}^2}{Var(d)} + \dfrac{\overline{lgd}^2}{Var(lgd)} + 1} \qquad \text{(A 2.5)}$$

Therefore, the correlation and covariance are

$$\Lambda_{intra} = \text{AB} \frac{R_d \; / \; \text{A} + \; R_{lgd} \; / \; \text{B} + \; 1}{R_d \; + \; R_{lgd} \; + \; 1}, \qquad \text{(A 2.6)}$$
$$Cov_{intra} = Cov(Z_i, Z_j) = \text{AB} \cdot Var(d)Var(lgd) \cdot [R_d \; / \; \text{A} + \; R_{lgd} \; / \; \text{B} + \; 1]$$

where index “intra” points out to intra correlations. In other words, the covariance/correlation between individual loss rates is a function of intra d-d and lgd-lgd covariances/correlations, respectively. The final step now is to add here an inter correlation between defaults and loss-given defaults d-lgd. To that end we introduce matrices $C_{ij} = Cov(d_i, lgd_j)$ of a linear and bi-linear $CC_{ij} = Cov(d_i d_j, lgd_i lgd_j)$ covariances, respectively. For a uniform portfolio denote C_0 the diagonal covariance i = j for the same obligor and C_1 the non-diagonal covariance i ≠ j between different obligors. Also, set $CC_0 = Cov(d_i^2, lgd_i^2)$ and $CC_1 = Cov(d_i d_j, lgd_i lgd_j)$ for diagonal and non-diagonal bi-linear covariances, respectively. With that, formula (A2.6) modifies as follows

$$\Lambda = \Delta_1 + \Delta_2, \;\; \Delta_1 = \text{AB} \frac{R_d \; / \; \text{A} + \; R_{lgd} \; / \; \text{B} + \; 1}{R_d \; + \; R_{lgd} \; + \; 1 + S_0}, \;\; \Delta_2 = \frac{S_1}{R_d \; + \; R_{lgd} \; + \; 1 + S_0} \qquad \text{(A 2.7)}$$
$$S_0 = (CC_0 - 2C_0 \overline{dlgd} - C_0^2) / [Var(d)Var(lgd)]$$
$$S_1 = (CC_1 - 2C_0 \overline{dlgd} - C_0^2) / [Var(d)Var(lgd)] \approx (C_1^2 + 2C_1 \overline{dlgd}) / [Var(d)Var(lgd)]$$

where combinations S_0 and S_1 account for diagonal and non-diagonal inter correlations. Note that S_0 can be both positive or negative depending on relative values of CC_0, C_0, $\overline{d}$ and $\overline{lgd}$. Also, interestingly enough, because S_0 is located in the denominator, it does not contribute on its own to the composite correlation Λ: depending on its sign, S_0 only enhances or reduces the impact of d-d, lgd- lgd and non-diagonal d-lgd correlations. Also note, that in the last line of(A2.7)S_1 accounts only for d_i-lgd_j inter non-diagonal correlations (intra d-d, lgd-lgd and diagonal d_i-lgd_i inter correlations are accounted for by other components of (A2.7))and therefore S_1 can be transformed to incorporate this fact explicitly. Finally, the latent correlation λ for the mixing copula underlying the loss variables $l_i = d_i \times lgd_i$ recovers analogously to (2.8-2.9) of the main text via

$$\Lambda_{\lambda\to 0} = P(\lambda)_{\lambda\to 0} \approx \lambda \cdot \frac{\varphi^2[\Phi^{-1}(pl)]}{pl(1-pl)} = k\lambda, \quad k = \frac{\varphi^2[\Phi^{-1}(pl)]}{pl(1-pl)} \qquad \text{(A 2.8)}$$

$$\tilde{P}(\lambda) = \lambda[k + \lambda(1-k)]$$

with help of a mean value

$$pl = \bar{l} = \overline{d \times lgd} = \bar{d}_i \times \overline{lgd_i} + C_0 = pd \times plgd + C_0$$

$$C_0 = Cov(d_i, lgd_i; \gamma) = \Phi_2(\Phi^{-1}(pd_i), \Phi^{-1}(plgd_i), \gamma) - pd_i pgld_i \qquad \text{(A 2.9)}$$

We conclude this Appendix with a possible refinement of the interpolation (2.9), Sec. 2 and (A 2.8). By adding a nonlinear term of λ(1-λ) into (2.9) we have

$$\tilde{P}(\lambda) = \lambda[k + \lambda(1-k) \; + m\lambda(1-\lambda)] \qquad (0.1)$$

where m is an adjustable parameter. The choice of m≈-0.6 for pd = plgd = 0.5 keeps the relative error within ≤2%.

Appendix 3

Correlation between loss rates in a collective **[(d-d)*(lgd-lgd)]***mode.*

In a collective mode the d-d and lgd-lgd correlated distributions are governed by corresponding latent processes /copulas, and to obtain the final loss distribution we, generally speaking, need to perform a multiplicative convolution of two Vasicek distributions. However, in the presence of the inter d-lgd correlations this is not as straightforward. Therefore, we render each distribution with an integral representation over latent variables and then, after making a convolution for each pair of random latent factors (u,v), perform an averaging over both latent factor distributions. The details are as follows.

The portfolio loss rate follows as the composition of d and lgd rate. Specifically, for any given pair of latent variables u, v corresponding to conditional probabilities $pd(u)$ and $plgd(v)$ the loss rate conditional pdf is a multiplicative convolution of $\delta[z - pd(u)]$ and $\delta[z - plgd(u)]$

$$\int \frac{dz'}{z'} \delta[z' - pd(u)] \delta[\frac{z}{z'} - plgd(v)] = \delta[z - pd(u) plgd(v)] \qquad \text{(A 3.1)}$$

And then the unconditional default rate cdf and pdf follow after weighting over the bivariate normal density $\psi(u,v)$ as in

$$F(z) = \int \mathbf{1}[z - pd(u)plgd(v)]\psi(u,v)dudv, \quad f(z) = \int \delta[z - pd(u)plgd(v)]\psi(u,v)dudv \quad \text{(A 3.2)}$$

F(z) in (A3.2) gives a generalized bivariate normal cdf off the curve pd(u) ×plgd (v) = z and *f(z)* is a corresponding pdf. We note in passing, that as for one-dimensional case, obtaining pdf can be viewed as obtaining the pdf of $z(u,v) = pd(u)plgd(v)$ given the bivariate normal density $\psi(u,v)$ according to $\psi(u,v)dudv = \varphi_1[pd(u)plgd(v)]d[pd(u)plgd(v)]$.

In particular, for a correlated bivariate normal distribution we have

$$\begin{aligned} cdf: \quad F(z) &= \iint \frac{dudv}{2\pi\sqrt{1-\gamma^2}} \exp\{-\frac{u^2+v^2-2\gamma uv}{2(1-\gamma^2)}\}\mathbf{1}[z - pd(u)plgd(v)] \\ pdf: \quad f(z) &= \iint \frac{dudv}{2\pi\sqrt{1-\gamma^2}} \exp\{-\frac{u^2+v^2-2\gamma uv}{2(1-\gamma^2)}\}\delta[z - pd(u)plgd(v)] \end{aligned} \quad \text{(A 3.3)}$$

where γ is the correlation between underlying latent factors u and v.

Disclaimer

The views expressed in the communication are solely of the authors and do not necessarily coincide with those of Federal Reserve Bank of New York or Federal Reserve System.

References

Altman, E., Resti A., Sironi, A. (2004), Default recovery rates in Credit risk modeling, *Economic notes* by Bancadei Paschi, v. 33, (2-2004), pp. 183-208.

Frye, J. (2000), Depressing recoveries, *Risk*, v. 13(11), pp. 106-111.

Frye, J. (2003), A false sense of security, *Risk*, v.16(8), pp. 63-67.

Frye, J., Jacobs, M. (2012), Credit loss and systematic loss given default, *Journal of Credit Risk*, v. 8(1), pp. 1-32.

Gupton, G., Gates, D., Carty, L., (2000), Moody's Global Credit Research, Special Comment.

Pykhtin, M. (2003), Unexpected recovery risk, *Risk*, v. 16(8), pp. 74-78.

Sanchez, F., Ordovas, R., Martinez, E., Vega, M. (2008) Uncovering PD/LGD liaisons, *Risk*, v. 21 (1), pp. 110-114.

Schuermann, T. (2004), What do we know about loss given default, Wharton Financial Institutions Center, 04-01.

Tasche, D. (2004), The single risk factor approach to capital charges in case of correlated loss given default rates, Working paper, Deutsche Bundesbank, Feb. 2004.

Vasicek, O. (1987), Probability of loss on a loan portfolio, KMV Working Paper.
Vasicek, O. (2002), Loan portfolio value, *Risk*, v. 15(12), pp. 16-162.
Witzany, J. (2009), Loss, Default, and Loss Given Default, IES Working Paper, N 21/2009.
Witzany, J. (2011), A Two Factor Model for PD and LGD correlation, *Bulletin of the Czech Econometric Society*, v. 18(28).

INDEX

A

B

C

D

E

F

G

H

I

K

L

M

N

O

P

R

S

T

U

W